Frédéric Louis Godet

Commentary on the Gospel of St. John:

With a critical introduction - Vol. 3

Frédéric Louis Godet

Commentary on the Gospel of St. John:
With a critical introduction - Vol. 3

ISBN/EAN: 9783337714123

Printed in Europe, USA, Canada, Australia, Japan

Cover: Foto ©Thomas Meinert / pixelio.de

More available books at **www.hansebooks.com**

CLARK'S

FOREIGN

THEOLOGICAL LIBRARY.

FOURTH SERIES.
VOL. LVI.

Godet on the Gospel of St. John.
VOL. III.

EDINBURGH:
T. & T. CLARK, 38 GEORGE STREET.

PRINTED BY MORRISON AND GIBB,

FOR

T. & T. CLARK, EDINBURGH.

LONDON, ... HAMILTON, ADAMS, AND CO.
DUBLIN, ... GEORGE HERBERT.
NEW YORK, ... SCRIBNER AND WELFORD.

COMMENTARY

ON THE

GOSPEL OF ST. JOHN.

With a Critical Introduction.

TRANSLATED FROM THE SECOND FRENCH EDITION OF

F. GODET, D.D.,
PROFESSOR OF THEOLOGY, NEUCHATEL,

BY S. TAYLOR AND M. D. CUSIN.

VOLUME THIRD.

EDINBURGH:
T. & T. CLARK, 38 GEORGE STREET.

PREFATORY NOTE.

THE first part of this Volume, embracing pp. 1-235, has been translated by Miss SOPHIA TAYLOR, the translator of Luthardt's Apologetic Works, etc. The remainder of the Volume has been translated by Mrs. CUSIN, a translator of the earlier part of this Commentary and of the "Commentary on St. Luke;" and revised by the Rev. ALEX. CUSIN, M.A.

CONTENTS OF VOLUME III.

SECOND PART.

THIRD CYCLE (XI. AND XII.)

FIRST SECTION.

	PAGE
The Resurrection of Lazarus (xi. 1-57),	2
Of the Resurrection of Lazarus,	2

SECOND SECTION.

The Last Days of the Ministry of Jesus (xii. 1-36), . . . 45

THIRD SECTION.

Retrospective Glance at the Mysterious Fact of Jewish Unbelief (xii. 37-50), ... 82

THIRD PART.

(XIII.-XVII.)

THE DEVELOPMENT OF FAITH IN THE DISCIPLES, . . . 94

FIRST SECTION.

The Facts (xiii. 1-30), ... 95

SECOND SECTION.

The Discourses (xiii. 31-xvi. 33), ... 119

THIRD SECTION.

The Prayer (xvii. 1-26), ... 191

FOURTH PART.

(XVIII. AND XIX.)

	PAGE
THE PASSION,	221

FIRST SECTION.

The Arrest of Jesus (xviii. 1-11),	222

SECOND SECTION.

The Trial of Jesus (xviii. 12-xix. 16),	228

THIRD SECTION.

The Crucifixion of Jesus (xix. 17-42),	262
Of the Day of Jesus' Death,	283

FIFTH PART.

(XX. 1-29.)

THE RESURRECTION,	304
Of the Resurrection of Jesus,	322

CONCLUSION (xx. 30, 31),	332
APPENDIX (xxi. 1-25),	337

COMMENTARY ON THE GOSPEL OF ST. JOHN.

THIRD CYCLE.

CHAPTERS XI. AND XII.

ALL was now ripe for the catastrophe; the development begun at ch. v. was accomplished. The national unbelief, now consummated, had only to produce its fruit: the condemnation of Jesus. And this final crisis was entailed by a third *good work* (x. 32), the resurrection of Lazarus.

So true is it that this point of view, viz. the development of Jewish incredulity, is the governing principle to which the exposition of facts is in this whole section subordinated, that the triumphal entry (xii. 12–19), the event which forms, in the synoptic Gospels, the opening of the narrative of the Passion, is here only brought forward as one of the factors of this development.

This cycle is divided into three sections:—

I. Ch. xi.: The resurrection of Lazarus, with its direct result: the condemnation of Jesus.

II. Ch. xii. 1–36: Three facts forming the transition from the active ministry of Jesus to His Passion.

III. Ch. xii. 37–50: A retrospective glance by the evangelist at that great fact of Jewish unbelief, which has occupied him since ch. v.

FIRST SECTION.

XI. 1–57.—THE RESURRECTION OF LAZARUS.

I. THE PREPARATION—vv. 1–16; II. THE FACT—vv. 17–44
III. ITS CONSEQUENCE—vv. 45–57.

I. *The Preparation.*—Vv. 1–16.

St. John first describes the general situation (vv. 1, 2); then the behaviour of Jesus towards the sisters (vv. 3–6); and lastly, His conversations with His disciples before departing (vv. 7–16).

Vv. 1, 2. "*Now a certain man was sick, Lazarus of Bethany, the town of Mary and her sister Martha. It was Mary who anointed the Lord with ointment, and wiped His feet with her hair, whose brother Lazarus was sick.*"—The stay of Jesus at Perea (x. 40–42) was interrupted by the news of a friend's sickness, which summoned Him to Judea. Lazarus being introduced in his condition of a sick man, ἀσθενῶν, *sick*, stands first. The particle δέ, *now* or *but*, brings out the change which this circumstance brought about with respect to Jesus. St. John immediately adds the name of the place where Lazarus dwelt, because it was the situation of this town (in Judea) which occasioned the conversation between Jesus and His disciples which then took place. But why should the author designate Bethany as the town of *Mary and her sister Martha*, two individuals whose names have not as yet occurred in this Gospel? He evidently takes it for granted that these two sisters were already known to his readers by evangelical tradition, and especially by the fact recorded by St. Luke (x. 38–42). *Bethany*, now El-Azirieh (from El-Azir, the Arabic name of Lazarus), is a small village situate on the eastern slope of the Mount of Olives, three-quarters of a league from Jerusalem. The supposed house of Lazarus and his sepulchre have both been pointed out since the 4th century.—The two prepositions ἀπό and ἐκ, here similarly employed, are regarded by Meyer as synonymous (comp. i. 45); it would nevertheless be possible in these passages to refer the first to the more external fact, that of dwelling, and the second to the more inward relation, that of origin: Lazarus dwelt *at* Bethany, *whence* he was.—The name of Mary is mentioned before that of Martha, and the latter is designated as *her sister*, and Lazarus as *her brother* (ver. 2), not because she was the eldest, for vv. 5 and 19, and Luke x. 38 sqq., seem to prove that Martha had the chief care in the house. The precedence here given to Mary arises, no doubt, from the fact, about to be mentioned (ver. 2), in which she played the chief part. Hence the important place accorded to her by tradition. Comp. the saying of Jesus, Matt. xxvi. 13. Besides, tradition had not preserved the name of Mary in the narrative of the anointing of Jesus; comp. Matt. xxvi. 6 sqq., Mark xiv. 3 sqq., where we read merely: *a woman*. This omission or reticence in the tradition explains the form of St. John's narrative at ver. 2: "This Mary, of whom I am now speaking, is the very woman of whom it is related that she anointed . . . and wiped . . ." At the close of the verse, St. John returns from this episode to the fact which forms the subject of his narrative: *It is she whose brother Lazarus was sick.*

Hengstenberg devotes twenty-six pages to prove that Mary, the sister of Lazarus, was, according to the idea which generally prevailed before the Reformation, the same person as Mary Magdalene (Luke viii. 2), and as the woman which was a sinner who anointed the feet of Jesus (Luke vii. 36 sqq.). On this theme he composes quite a little romance, according to which Galilee was the scene of Mary's dissolute life. Martha, her sister, is said to have become acquainted, during a visit to the feast, with Simon, a rich Pharisee residing at Bethany, and after marrying him to have received into her house both her sister Mary, who had renounced her transgressions, and her brother Lazarus, who had fallen into poverty. This is to account for the entrance of Mary into the feast-chamber (Luke vii.), for she was at home in the house of Simon, while the murmuring of the latter is regarded as a brother-in-law's malicious mischief. There is nothing, even to the parable of Dives and Lazarus, which may not in this way be explained, etc. etc. This dissertation, however, proves only one thing, and that is the facility with which an intelligent and learned man can prove anything which he *wishes* to prove. The only argument of any value is the similarity of the expressions in John xi. 2 and Luke vii. 37, 38. But then, how different is the scene! On the one side, Galilee; on the other, Judea: there, the early days of Christ's ministry; here, one of the days preceding His passion: there, a discussion on the forgiveness of sin; here, a conversation on the sum expended: while the repetition of such homage is, according to Eastern customs, so natural, that we cannot grant the least probability to the double identity of individuals which Hengstenberg seeks to establish.

Vv. 3, 4. *" The sisters then sent to Jesus, saying: Lord, behold, he whom Thou lovest is sick. When Jesus heard, He said: This sickness is not to death, but it is for the glory of God, that*[1] *the Son of God might be glorified thereby."*—The message of the sisters was full of delicacy, hence the evangelist reports it in their own words (λέγουσαι, *saying*). The address, *Lord*, alludes to the miraculous power of Jesus; the term ἴδε, *behold*, to the impression which this unexpected intelligence would not fail to make upon Him; lastly, the expression ὅν φιλεῖς, *he whom Thou lovest*, to the tender affection by which Jesus was bound to Lazarus, and which made it their duty not to leave Him uninformed of the danger to which His friend was exposed. On the other hand, they by no means urge Him to come; as, indeed, how could they, knowing, as they did, the perils which awaited Him in Judea? They merely state the case, leaving it to Himself to decide how He would act.

The saying of Jesus (ver. 4) is not given as an answer to the message; we are told, not that *He answered*, but that *He said*. It was a statement made as much to the present disciples as to the absent sisters. It shows but very slight acquaintance with the always original and frequently paradoxical character of our Lord's sayings, to be able to imagine that He really meant to say that Lazarus would not die of this illness, and that He was only subsequently convinced of His mistake on the reception of a second message, which is assumed in the narrative (ver. 14). Undoubtedly, Lücke observes with perfect justice, that the

[1] ℵ repeats αλλα before ινα.

glory of Jesus did not imply omniscience. But His moral purity did exclude the assertion of anything which He did not know, and it is very evident that the evangelist himself did not attribute such a meaning to this saying. The expression made use of by Jesus was amphibological; and whether it involved an announcement of recovery or a promise of resurrection, it meant at any rate that the *definitive* result of this sickness would not be death, οὐ πρὸς θάνατον.—The glory of God is the renown diffused in men's hearts by His power, working for the sake of His holiness or His love. And what would be more likely to produce such an effect than a victory over death?—At ver. 40, Jesus recalls this saying to Martha in the words: "*Said I not unto thee, that if thou wouldest believe, thou shouldest see the glory of God?*" When, then, He spoke these words, He already knew what He would do; He had asked all of His Father, and had obtained all from Him at the very moment when He uttered this promise, and that even before the messenger had departed to carry his answer to Bethany (ver. 42). But this manifestation of divine power was also to reflect its splendour on Him who was its agent. In fact, God is only glorified on earth in the person of His Son, in whom He reveals Himself, so that the first end, the glory of God, involves the second, the honour of the Son. "Ἵνα, *so that*, does not, then, indicate another end in juxtaposition with the first (ὑπέρ), but explains the manner in which the first is to be attained. This passage shows how far the name *Son of God*, in the mouth of our Lord, surpasses the title *Messiah*.—The pronoun δι' αὐτῆς, *by it*, may be referred to the glory, but it is more natural to refer it to the sickness.—This saying recalls that of ix. 3, but excels it in greatness, in proportion as the resurrection of Lazarus surpasses in power the cure of the man born blind.

Vv. 5–7. "*Now Jesus loved Martha, and her sister, and Lazarus. When, then, He had heard that he was sick, He remained yet two days in the place where He was; then, after that, He saith to His disciples:*[1] *Let us go again*[2] *into Judea.*"—To understand the relation of these three verses, and the intention of ver. 5 in particular, we must remember that the μέν of

[1] A D K Γ Δ Λ Π, 20 Mnn. add αυτου after μαθηταις.
[2] ℵ omits παλιν, A reads πολιν (*to the Jewish city*).

ver. 6 supposes an understood δέ in ver. 7 : "Jesus loved Martha . . .; when, then, He had heard . . . He remained, *it is true* (μέν); *but* then (δέ) He saith: Let us go . . ." We then feel that the remark of ver. 5 : *He loved*, bears not upon the fact of ver. 6 : *He remained*, but upon that of ver. 7, the order to *set out*. This very simple explanation overthrows several forced suppositions; that, for example, that St. John meant to say : " *Though* Jesus loved . . .," or the still more forced : " *Because* He loved, He remained, that He might still longer try the faith of the sisters." St. John here uses the more dignified term ἀγαπᾶν, instead of the affectionate one, φιλεῖν (ver. 3); not, as exegetes say, because he was speaking of the affection of Jesus for women,—for the disciple of the Lord is above such prepossessions,—but because the nobler term better suits the pen of the evangelist, while the expression of tenderness is more suitable in the mouth of the sisters.—Martha here occupies, as also in ver. 19, the first place; she had precedence in the home by reason of her age, and perhaps, too, of her social position as a widow and the mistress of the house.

Baur explains the delay mentioned, ver. 6, by the desire of Jesus to let Lazarus die for the sake of raising him, and finds in this circumstance evidence of the non-authenticity of the narrative. But nothing in the text hints at any such intention on the part of Jesus; and even ver. 15 : " *I am glad for your sakes that I was not there*," decidedly excludes it; for Jesus might, indeed, rejoice at a divine dispensation, but not at a circumstance which He had willingly and purposely occasioned. Besides, the sequel shows that when Jesus received the message, Lazarus had already breathed his last. For if we reckon the four days which, according to vv. 17 and 39, elapsed between the burial of Lazarus and the arrival of Jesus at Bethany, these days can only be distributed as follows. The fourth was that on which Jesus travelled from Perea to Bethany (a distance of from eight to ten leagues), the third and second were the two days' stay at Perea, and the first that on which the messenger brought Jesus the intelligence. Hence it was at the beginning of this first day, shortly after the departure of the messenger, that Lazarus died, and in the course of this day that he was, according to Jewish custom, buried. Thus towards evening, when Jesus first received the news of his sickness, Lazarus was already resting in the sepulchre. The distance between Jerusalem and the Jordan being seven leagues, it must have been a good day's journey from Bethany to the actual abode of Jesus on the other side of that river.—We see how incorrect is the calculation of Keim (i. p. 495), that "it would take Jesus three days to go from this country of Perea to Bethany," while nothing of the kind results from St. John's narrative. Nor is Meyer less mistaken in taking for the first of the *four* days which elapsed after the burial of Lazarus (ver. 17), that which *followed* the two days of waiting in Perea. For why should Jesus have taken three whole days in going from the Jordan to Bethany? As to the cause which hindered His immediate departure, we may undoubtedly conjecture, with Lücke and Neander, that it was the work of His ministry in Perea. But would it not be better to say, with Meyer, that He waited for the signal of the Father, by which He always regulated His proceedings? God might act in such wise as the *man* Christ Jesus would not of Himself have done, and might prolong this time of waiting for the purpose of rendering the miracle more manifest and more striking, with a view to His own glory and that of His Son.

The expression: ἔπειτα μετὰ τοῦτο, literally, *then after that*, is not a pleonasm, but tells how long this waiting at first seemed to the sisters, and perhaps also to Jesus Himself.— It should be noticed that Jesus did not say: Let us go to Bethany, but: Let us go *into Judea*. It was an allusion to the perils which threatened them in that country, and elicited from the disciples an expression of that feeling of alarm which He knew to be in their hearts, and desired to overcome before setting out. With the same purpose He added the word πάλιν, *again*, which recalled the danger He had incurred during his last stay at Jerusalem. It is in vain that Meyer protests against this purpose.

Vv. 8–10. " *The disciples say unto Him: Master, the Jews of late sought to stone Thee, and goest Thou thither again? Jesus answered: Are there not twelve hours in the day? If any man walk in the day, he stumbleth not, because he seeth the light of this world; but if a man walk in the night, he stumbleth, because there is no light in him.*"—At the word Judea, the disciples, as their Master expected, expostulated. He profited by their objection to give them sublime instruction with respect to their future ministry. The answer of Jesus (vv. 9, 10) has naturally a double meaning. Lücke and de Wette apply the image of *day* to the purely moral idea of the *task* to be accomplished: to quit the path of duty laid down, is to plunge into spiritual darkness, and perish. But the expression *twelve hours* cannot, from this point of view, be well explained. Bengel, Meyer, and Hengstenberg go to the opposite extreme. In their view, the image *day* has a purely *temporal* sense, and refers to the season of *earthly life:* " The time granted me has not yet elapsed, and so long as it lasts no one can hurt me; when it has elapsed, I shall fall into the hands of my enemies." But the expression *to stumble* is too active a one to designate a purely passive result; and what can we do with the expression, *there is no light in him*, as applied to Jesus? Meyer says it is a feature belonging to the image, and of no importance; but such an expedient is only resorted to to save an untenable explanation. The image *day* here designates both the *life-task* and the *life-time*, the day of work, like ix. 4. The whole imagery is taken from the situation in which Jesus found Himself and His disciples. It was morning, the sun was rising; they had before them a good day's journey, twelve full hours. During all this time we may travel without danger; it is only when walking by night, and when daylight is past, that there is danger of stumbling. But this was unnecessary, as they might before night reach Bethany, the end of their journey. Taken in its moral sense, the similitude signifies: " I may fearlessly go wherever duty calls me. I know that my twelve hours of work are not yet over. The duration of my earthly life is meted out and secured to me by a higher will. So long as it lasts, I may walk without fear on the road prescribed by my mission. It is daylight to me, for a greater sun than *that of this world* enlightens my path, even that of the Divine will, which discloses our task step by step. The danger of stumbling will not begin until, by basely eluding a foreseen danger, we arbitrarily prolong the time of our life, and add, so to speak, a thirteenth hour's journey to the twelve which are lawfully ours. From that time we cannot fail to stumble. For the sun of the Divine will would no longer shine within us; an hour of life not given us by God would be an hour without duty, and without a mission." The application of this answer to the state of things at the time is very obvious: "The Jews will not be able to shorten by a single moment the time granted me for accomplishing my work on earth; real danger, that of walking without God, can only reach me if, as you seem to propose, I should arbitrarily endeavour to prolong my life, by refusing to go whither duty calls me." This saying applies to the believer who, in a time of persecution, should prolong his life by denying the faith, to the physician who should flee at the approach of a contagious disease, etc. A life thus lengthened would no longer be illumed by the light of the Divine will. A man in such a situation would in vain seek the direction of his own by a higher will. He could no longer do aught but sin and morally perish ($\pi\rho o\sigma\kappa\acute{o}\pi\tau\epsilon\iota\nu$, stumble). Meyer objects that this idea does not suit the context, because the disciples merely desired that Jesus should not shorten His life, not that He should prolong it. As though a desertion of duty did not, by refusing to shorten, really seek to prolong it! This meaning is confirmed by the parallel passage, 1 John ii. 10, 11, in which the analogy of the ideas and expressions is remarkable. St. John there applies to him who loves or does not love his brother, what Jesus here says of His own yielding or not yielding to the appeal of the sisters of Lazarus.

This saying is, both in form and matter, the pendant of that which Jesus advanced (ix. 4) as a reason for the cure of the man born blind. The only difference is, that then it was evening; and seeing the sun descending towards the horizon, I cannot, He said, *lose* a moment of the short time which is left me for giving light to the world. Now it was morning. The time which is given me, said Jesus, is quite sufficient; I must not by cowardice try to *add* a single hour to the day of my life as meted out to me by the Divine appointment. In these two words: to add nothing, to lose nothing, is summed up the whole duty of man with respect to the task and time of his earthly life.

Vv. 11–13. "*These things said He, and after that He saith: Our friend Lazarus sleepeth, but I go to awake him. Then they* said[1] to *Him: Lord, if he sleep, he shall do well. But Jesus spake of his death, and they thought that He had spoken of taking rest in sleep.*"—The words ταῦτα εἶπε, *he said these things, and* . . ., are by no means superfluous. They signify: having uttered this truth, He immediately applied it to the actual circumstances.—The epithet: *our friend*, appealed to their affection for Lazarus, just as the expression: *he whom thou lovest* (ver. 3), had done to His own friendship for him.—Some expositors have supposed that it was not till now that Jesus knew, by means of a second message, of the death of Lazarus. But ver. 4, rightly understood, shows that He had knowledge of this event, in a supernatural manner, from the time when His attention was drawn to the state of His friend by the message of the sisters, and at which He pronounced that promise.— Jesus delights to present death under the image of sleep, and thus to transform it into a phase of life.

Strauss finds the misunderstanding of the disciples (at ver. 12) inconceivable, and Reuss is of the same opinion. But they do not take into consideration how extremely desirous the disciples were to find some excuse for dissuading Jesus from going to Judea. After the promise of ver. 4, they no longer thought it possible for the sickness to terminate in death, and they represented this mysterious sleep, from which Jesus desired to go and awaken Lazarus, as a favourable crisis, which would *of itself* end in convalescence. What improbability, then, is there in the circumstance stated?—The general term κοίμησις (ver. 13) is derived from κεκοίμηται (ver. 11).

Vv. 14–16. " *Then said Jesus unto them plainly: Lazarus is dead, and I am glad for your sakes that I was not there, to the intent ye may believe; nevertheless let us go unto him. Then said Thomas, which is called Didymus, unto his fellow-disciples: Let us also go, that we may die with Him.*"—Jesus had (vv. 9, 10) dismissed the motive alleged against this journey, and afterwards stated (vv. 11, 12) the positive reasons which induced Him to undertake it; He now explained Himself, and gave the order to depart.—Παῤῥησίᾳ, as at xvi. 25: *without figure.*—There would have been, as we have already

---

[1] T. R., with 10 Mjj. the Mnn. It[plerique] Vg., reads ιπον ουν οι μαθ. αυτου.—ℵ B C D K X read αυτω, either before or after οι μαθ., and omit αυτου.—A and 1 Mn., which Tischendorf follows, omit οι μαθ. αυτου, and read αυτω.

remarked, manifest dissimulation in our Lord's mode of expression (ver. 15), if this death had been the consequence of His own way of acting.—The words: *to the intent ye may believe*, are a comment upon the regimen: *for your sakes*. Undoubtedly the disciples were already believers, but, as Hengstenberg says, by growing, faith *originates;* and at each new stage which it reaches, the preceding stage seems to it nothing but unbelief. The increase of faith which they would obtain at that grave would soon be greatly needed, when they would be called upon to behold that of their Master.—There is something abrupt in the last words: *nevertheless let us go to him*, which seem meant to constrain them, and to overcome the last remains of opposition. They yielded, but not without the unbelief, still lurking in the heart of some, becoming manifest.

In fact, the saying of Thomas to his fellow-disciples shows more love to the person of Jesus than faith in the wisdom of the step He was about to take. The meaning of it is: Well, if He is resolved to perish, let us perish too! The Thomas who speaks thus is indeed the same Thomas whom we meet with in xiv. 5 and xx. 25—a man of great candour and resolution, but one little inclined to subordinate the visible to the invisible. This undesigned consistency in the part played by the secondary characters is, as Luthardt has shown, one of the most striking features in St. John's narrative, and one of the best proofs of the historical truth of his Gospel.—The name *Thomas* (from the Aramaic תאומא, Hebrew תאם) signifies *twin*. The name *Didymus*, which has the same meaning in Greek, was undoubtedly that by which this apostle was most generally called by the Greek Christians among whom St. John wrote. This explains the repetition of this translation at xx. 24 and xxi. 2. Hengstenberg sees in this name *twin* an allusion to the fact that there were in Thomas two men, a believer and an unbeliever, a Jacob and an Esau!

What wisdom and what love are manifested in the manner in which Jesus prepared His disciples for a journey so repugnant to them! How sublime are the thoughts which on this occasion He instilled into their hearts! What beauty and what fitness in the images by which He endeavoured to make them intelligible!

II. *The Miracle.*—Vv. 17–44.

1st. Vv. 17–27. Jesus and Martha.

Vv. 17–19. "*When Jesus came, He found that he had been in the grave four days already. Now Bethany was nigh unto Jerusalem, about fifteen stadia off; and*[1] *many of the Jews came to*[2] *Martha and Mary, to comfort them concerning their brother.*"[3] —On the four days, see remarks on ver. 6. The expression: *He found,* refers to the intelligence given Him on His arrival. —It is well known that the Jews were accustomed to bury the dead before sunset on the very day of their decease.—St. John mentions the nearness of Bethany to Jerusalem for the sake of explaining the presence of so large a number of Jews (ver. 19); 15 stadia are a walking distance of about 45 minutes. This distance is reckoned from Jerusalem (ἐγγὺς τῶν Ἱεροσολύμων), which explains the use of the preposition ἀπό.—The in^{ep.}, *f*·t *was* refers to the part played by Bethany in this na_a, l,ive, which was no longer recent when St. John wrote; it is unnecessary to suppose that he used the past tense because of the destruction of this town in the Roman war.—The turn of expression, *αἱ περὶ Μάρθαν* (ver. 19), so usual with the Greeks, is got rid of by the Alex. reading, but erroneously, as even Meyer and Tischendorf admit. This form represents Martha and Mary as surrounded by the members of their household, and seems dictated by the notion of the etiquette which prevails in mourning ceremonies. It certainly implies that the two sisters were in comfortable circumstances. These visits of condolence generally lasted seven days (1 Sam. xxxi. 13; 1 Chron. x. 12).—The sequel shows that the term *Jews,* here used, preserves the tinge which it bears throughout this Gospel. The connection of Martha and Mary with these people did not hinder them from belonging, for the most part, to the party hostile to Jesus (vv. 28, 37, 46).

Vv. 20–24. "*When Martha heard that Jesus was coming, she went and met Him, but Mary sat in the house. Then said Martha unto Jesus: Lord,*[4] *if Thou hadst been here, my brother*

---

[1] א A B C D L X: πολλοι δε instead of και πολλοι.
[2] T. R. reads προς τας περι Μαριαν κ. M. with 12 Mjj. (A Γ, etc.) and nearly all the Mnn., while א B C D L X and 4 Mnn. read προς (or προς την) Μαριαν κ. M.
[3] א B D L omit αυτων.   [4] B omits κυρι.

had not died;[1] *but*[2] *I know that even now, whatsoever Thou wilt ask of God, God will give it Thee. Jesus said unto her: Thy brother shall rise again. Martha said unto Him: I know that he shall rise again in the resurrection at the last day."*
—Martha, who was undoubtedly occupied in domestic affairs, was the first to receive the news of our Lord's arrival, and in her eagerness ran to meet Him without thinking of her sister, whom her grief was keeping in the inner apartment. Such as the two sisters are represented in Luke x. 38 sq., such exactly do we here find them. The narrative of St. John seems to allude to that of his predecessor, while on the opposite supposition, the manner in which they harmonize is only the more striking.—The saying of Martha (ver. 21) is not a reproach. For how could she be ignorant of the fact that her brother was dead before Jesus had received the news of his illness? And how, especially, would she have allowed herself to complain of His mode of acting, at the time when she was about to make the very greatest of requests? She merely expressed her regret that Jesus had not been there at the time of his illness, and this regret only helped to prepare for the petition she was about to make.—'Ἀλλὰ καὶ νῦν: *But even now,* although so late! She knew that there must be no such thing as despair with a Being such as He. "Thou couldest not come to cure my brother, but even in death he may experience the virtue of Thy prayer." The ἀλλά, *but,* must then be maintained in the text.—The indefinite expression, *whatsoever,* leaves that which is too great to express to be understood. The reticence of this indirect request is admirable. The repetition of the word Θεός, *God,* at the close of both the propositions of ver. 22, was undoubtedly prompted by the greatness of the expected work: "Thou art the wellbeloved of God; God will give Thee the life of my brother." Martha was inspired with this confidence not only by the resurrections effected in Galilee, but more especially by the promise of Jesus, which her messenger would not have failed to report, and above all by His sudden arrival.

Martha's faith was more lively than enlightened. She

---

[1] א B C D K L X Π read απιθανιν instead of ιτιθνηκιι, which is the reading of A E F G H M S U Γ Δ Λ and almost all the Mnn.
[2] א B C X omit the αλλα of T. R. before και νυν.

believed in a prodigy to be effected by power, but was not yet initiated into that spiritual sphere from which it was to emanate. Before granting her desire, Jesus endeavours to put her into a condition in which she may be capable of both understanding and receiving. With this view He proceeds, as in chs. v. vi., by first giving to His promise the most general form: "*Thy brother shall rise again.*" Hengstenberg even thinks that in these words He did not allude to the approaching raising of Lazarus, which, in His opinion, did not deserve to be called a resurrection, because a return to this sad state of existence is unworthy of such a name. But is it not doing violence to the text, to refuse to recognise in this saying a promise of the event which was about to take place?—A belief in the resurrection of pious Israelites, as an inauguration of the Messianic reign, already taught, Dan. xii. 2, and 2 Macc. vii. 9, 14, etc., was very general in Israel, especially in those circles in which Pharisaic teaching prevailed.[1]

Martha certainly felt what Jesus meant to say, but, with a view of making quite sure of it, she applied His saying to the *final* resurrection, which she regarded as certain. This gave Jesus occasion to explain Himself, and to declare expressly what she hardly dared to hope. Hence there is neither a mournful resignation (Meyer), nor a relapse after a flight of faith (Luthardt), in this answer of Martha, but the language of this active and energetic woman constantly breathes a masculine faith. But this faith was not as spiritual as it was strong, nor was it as yet sufficiently fixed upon the person of our Lord, whose answer was intended to develop it in both these respects.

Vv. 25, 26. "*Jesus said unto her: I am the resurrection and the life: he that believeth in me, though he were dead, yet shall he live, and whosoever liveth and believeth in me shall never die: believest thou this?*"—To this great future *event* of the resurrection, of which Martha spoke, Jesus opposed His own person (ἐγώ, *I*), and His person as present (εἰμί, *I am*). Victory over death is not a purely physical fact, but a personal work,—an act of which Jesus, then present, is the author, and which He could, if He chose, as easily accomplish at that very moment

---

[1] Schürer, *Neutest. Zeitgesch.* p. 395 sq. The differences of opinion, existing in this general expectation of the resurrection, are fully shown by this writer.

us after the lapse of ages. He thus concentrated the thoughts of Martha upon Himself, and gave her faith its proper object. He sought to exchange adherence to a doctrinal truth for confidence in Himself. He acted in just the same manner in chs. iv. vi., when, after some moments of conversation, He substituted Himself for the abstract notions of living water and bread from heaven.—After declaring Himself to be the Resurrection, Jesus proclaimed Himself *the Life*. It might have been thought (see our 1st edit.) that He spoke thus from the view-point of His relations with us; for death is our natural element, from which we must be rescued by Christ, in the way of resurrection, before possessing life in Him. But it is better to admit, with Luthardt, that our Lord here passes from the physical resurrection to that deeper fact which is its *condition*; if He is the Resurrection, it is because He is first of all *the Life*. Jesus was striving to spiritualize Martha's faith. He revealed to her that the impartation of life, of which He is the source, is the principle of that physical resurrection which He will effect in His people. Hence they who are united to Him by faith possess, notwithstanding the temporary accident of death, a life which nothing can interrupt, and in this life the pledge of the resurrection of the body. This applied to Lazarus, who, though dead, might in virtue of this life of faith be at any moment recalled to earthly existence by Jesus. Besides, and this applied to the living by whom Jesus was surrounded, every believer is in reality and for ever shielded from death (ver. 26). To die with full light, in the clear certainty of the life which is in Jesus, to die only to continue to live to Him (ver. 25), is no longer that fact which human language designates by the name of death (see rem. on vi. 50, viii. 54). It is as though Jesus had said: In me, death is certain to live, and the living is certain never to die. The epithet ὁ ζῶν, *he who liveth* (ver. 26), is the antithesis to κἂν ἀποθάνῃ, *though he were dead* (ver. 25); and both expressions should be taken in their proper meaning.

This saying, by leading Martha's thoughts from the isolated act of resurrection which was about to be effected, to its spiritual and permanent principle, gave the miracle its true value with respect to her own religious life, made that act a ray of the glory of Jesus, and was a means of uniting the soul of Martha to Himself, the source of life. Before proceeding to act, then, He asks her: "*Believest thou this?*"

Ver. 27. "*She said unto Him: Yea, Lord, I believe that Thou art the Christ, the Son of God, which should come into the world.*" —To see, as some do, in this confession of Martha, only an acknowledgment that she had not understood the words just uttered by Jesus, and to make it mean: I do not comprehend these deep matters, but my theology, in a few words, is, I believe Thee to be the Messiah, is strangely to undervalue it. Such a meaning would give to this solemn scene a puerile and almost ridiculous character. By her answer: *Yea, Lord*, Martha certainly appropriated all that Jesus had affirmed concerning His person. But being unable to find terms in which to express her faith in things so new to her, she made use of words with which she was familiar, to declare that Jesus was to her all that was greatest, and that whatever He might say concerning His person, He would never say too much for the faith of her to whom He was speaking. *The Christ:* the end of the theocratic revelations and dispensations; *the Son of God:* the individual in whom God is manifested as in no other, and who is in intimate and mysterious relation with God.

The expression: *which should come into the world*, is not a third title, but an apposition, explanatory of the other two. The present part., ἐρχόμενος, *he that cometh*, is the present of the idea: He who, according to the divine promise, necessarily comes. *The world* is the foreseen theatre of His Messianic agency. There is a great psychologic truth in this answer of Martha's; by it she implicitly acknowledged that He was all that He said: *the resurrection and the life*. 'Εγώ, *I*, whom thou art questioning; πεπίστευκα (perfect): that is the conviction *I possess*.

2d. Vv. 28–37. Jesus and Mary.

Vv. 28–30. "*And when she had said this,*[1] *she went away, and called Mary her sister secretly, saying: The Master is come, and calleth for thee. As soon as she heard, she riseth*[2] *quickly*

---

[1] ℵ B C L X Cop.: τουτο instead of ταυτα, which is the reading of the 14 other Mjj., almost all the Mnn. It. Vg. and Syr.

[2] ℵ B C D L X It. Sah.: ηγιρθη instead of ιγιιρεται.

*and cometh*¹ *to meet Him. Now Jesus was not yet come into the town, but was*² *in the place where Martha met Him."*—The words: *He calleth for thee,* are enough to prove that Jesus had indeed given Martha this commission. He would certainly desire to prepare Mary, as well as her sister, for the miracle, which could only be really beneficial to either on this condition. Perhaps the caution with which Martha delivered this message (λάθρα, *secretly*) had been advised by Jesus Himself; He had heard by whom she was surrounded, and though He would not flee from danger, neither would He seek it.

Mary's lively emotion at the reception of the message is depicted by the pres. ἐγείρεται, *riseth*, which is certainly the true reading, and by the adverb which accompanies it.—That Jesus had not entered Bethany was not merely because the grave was outside the town (Luthardt); some important motive must have detained Him, or He would have gone at once to the house of mourning, to which His heart called Him. He certainly desired to avoid anything which might attract notice; and the purpose of the following verse is to show how this desire was frustrated by a will higher than His, which had resolved to give this miracle the greatest publicity. Jesus acted as He ought; God acted as He pleased. That which now happened is somewhat similar to what is related in Matt. ix. 31; Mark vii. 24, 36.

Vv. 31, 32. "*The Jews then which were with her in the house, and comforted her, when they saw her rise up hastily and go out, followed her, saying:*³ *She*⁴ *goeth to the grave, to weep there. When, then, Mary was come to the place where Jesus was, she fell down at*⁵ *His feet, saying: Lord, if Thou hadst been here, my brother*⁶ *had not died."*—One and the same thought had occupied the mind of the two sisters, and perhaps that of the dying man during his last hours: If Jesus were but here! But upon this common background of grief and regret are depicted some significant differences between

---

¹ The same (minus D): ηρχιτο instead of ερχεται.
² אּ B C X It. Vg. and Cop. : ην ετι (*was still*) instead of ην (*was*).
³ אּ B C D L X, 7 Mnn. Syr^sch and Cop. read δοξαντες instead of λεγοντες.
⁴ אּ: οτι Ιησους υπαγει (*Jesus goeth!*).
⁵ אּ B C D L X : προς instead of εις.
⁶ אּ B C L Δ place μου before απεθανεν.

the two sisters. We have remarked upon the masculine character of Martha's faith. Mary seems, on the contrary, entirely absorbed in grief; hers is a nature wholly feminine. And like all persons of sensitive disposition, she makes no energetic effort to conquer the depression which overwhelmed her, but lets herself fall, as Martha had not done, at Jesus' feet —the place, moreover, in which she delighted (Luke x. 39; John xii. 3). Nor does she add, as her sister had done, a word of faith and hope to the expression of her grief. Lastly, there are, in the exclamation which was common to both, two shades of difference which are not accidental. Instead of ἐτεθνήκει, *he is dead* (the actual state), she says: ἀπέθανε, he has performed *the act* of dying (the Aorist), as if it were still the terrible moment when the separation took place. Thus the pronoun μου, *of me*, is in her mouth placed before ὁ ἀδελφός, *the brother*, and even, according to the Alex. reading, before ἀπέθανε; it is as though a part of herself were gone.—Then there is in Martha a practical character and an elastic nature capable of energetic reaction against an overwhelming sentiment; in Mary, a sensibility surrendered to without a trace of reaction against the feeling which absorbs her. How true is every feature of this picture!

Jesus knew the human heart too well to attempt to treat Mary in the same manner which He had just employed with Martha. A grief like hers needed sympathy and action, not instruction and conversation.

Vv. 33, 34. "*When Jesus, therefore, saw Mary weeping, and the Jews also weeping which came with her, He shuddered in His spirit, and troubled Himself,*[1] *and said: Where have ye laid him? They said unto Him: Lord, come and see.*"— The particle *therefore* establishes a relation of causality between the grief of Mary and those who accompanied her and the unusual emotion by which Jesus was at that time overcome. This relation is confirmed by the words: *when He saw*, and by the repetition of the participle *weeping*, with which both propositions end, like a refrain. It is now generally acknowledged that the term ἐμβριμᾶσθαι (from βριμάζειν, *to neigh*, *to roar*) can only designate a shudder of indignation. See the thorough demonstration in the article

---

[1] D, some Mnn. and Sah.: εταραχθη τω πνευματι ως εμβριμωμενος.

of Gumlich, *Studien und Kritiken*, 1862, pp. 260-269. This sense is even applicable in such passages as Matt. ix. 30 and Mark i. 43, though with a special tinge. We must first of all, then, reject the meaning: *to be seized with grief* (Lücke), and: *to sigh deeply* (Ewald). But what could have been the object of this indignation? According to Chrysostom, Cyril, and other Greek expositors, the very emotion which He felt at the sight of the sorrow of those around Him, with this difference, that, according to Chrysostom, τῷ πνεύματι, *His spirit*, designates the *object* of His indignation (He was indignant *at* His own spirit, that is to say, at the emotion which mastered Him); while Cyril sees in the Spirit the *agent* of this indignation, and makes it the divine nature of Jesus, *by means of which* He sought to overcome this movement of entirely human sympathy. The explanation of Chrysostom is reproduced by Hilgenfeld: "His divinity was irritated at the emotion of His humanity, and violently repressed it." But this non-natural meaning would require, in any case, the use of ψυχή, *soul*, instead of πνεῦμα, *spirit*. For the soul is the seat of the *natural* emotions—comp. xii. 27; πνεῦμα, *spirit*, designating the region of those higher feelings which pertain to the relation of the soul with the divine. Besides, if Jesus had really struggled against an emotion of sympathy, how came He to resign Himself to it the very next moment with such perfect simplicity (ver. 35)? Meyer thinks that His indignation was excited by the hypocritical tears of the Jews, as contrasted with the sincere grief of Mary. But the two participles, *weeping*, stand in a relation, not of contrast, but of agreement. Others (Keim, Strauss) refer this indignation to the want of faith which He discerned both in Mary and the Jews. But the word *weeping*, which is twice repeated to explain the emotion of Jesus, contains, indeed, the notion of grief, but not that of unbelief. Besides, He wept also the next moment. Several exegetes (Calv., Olsh., Luthardt) are of opinion that the Saviour's indignation was directed against the power of death, and against Satan, who wields this murderous weapon against men (viii. 44). In fact, in the sight of Jesus, death is no more an event than resurrection: these two facts are *actions*, the results of a personal will. If this explanation is adopted, we must admit that, while the indignation felt by our Lord (ver. 33) concerned the murderer, the tears which He shed (ver. 35) express His compassion for the victims. From this point of view, however, it is very difficult to account for the words which follow: *He troubled Himself.* The emotion of Jesus seems, according to this remarkable expression, to have been of a more personal kind than this explanation supposes. An emotion of an entirely similar kind is mentioned xiii. 21, when Jesus saw the treason of Judas about to be perpetrated: *He was troubled in spirit.* The *spirit* is the seat of the religious emotions, as the *soul* is that of the natural affections. Thus Jesus says (xii. 27): *My soul is troubled*, because the anticipation of His sufferings made His nature shudder; while in the other passage (xiii. 21) it was in His *spirit* that He was moved, because He found Himself in immediate contact with evil in its most hateful form, and felt horror at the proximity of the invisible being who had taken possession of the heart of Judas. This parallel passage throws light upon the shuddering of Jesus (ver. 33). The sobs which He heard around Him urged Him to effect the resurrection of His friend; but, on the other hand, He well knew that to yield to this impulse was to give His enemies, and him who inspired their action, the signal for His own death. They would make the most glorious of His miracles the excuse for His condemnation, nay, some even of those whose sobs were urging Him to perform it, would themselves turn informers against Him. He was filled with horror at the thought that He would have to pay with His life for the crime of having vanquished death, and His holy soul was stirred to its inmost depths at such diabolical perversity.— The words: *He troubled Himself*, indicate a physical commotion, a bodily trembling, which might be perceived by the witnesses of this scene. The expression chosen by the evangelist is such as to obviate any notion of an either unreasonable or merely passive agitation. Hence it does not denote, as Meyer and others think, the natural reaction of the moral upon the physical feelings. On the contrary, immediately after the emotion which had just seized Him, He spontaneously formed a strong resolve, and overcame the horror with which His prevision had filled His soul.

The physical agitation indicated by the words: *He troubled Himself*, is an indication of the inward determination with which He shook off the impression, and which was expressed in the short and abrupt question, *Where have you laid him?* The repetition of καί, *and*, brings out the close connection of these different emotions, which followed each other in such rapid succession.

Vv. 35–37. "*Jesus wept.*[1] *Then said the Jews: Behold, how He loved him! But some of them said: Could not this man, who opened the eyes of the blind, have caused that even this man should not have died?*"—The storm had passed, and Jesus, in approaching the sepulchre, no longer felt anything but tender sympathy for the grief which had possessed the heart of His friend at the moment of separation, and that which the two sisters were at that very moment feeling. The word δακρύειν, *to weep*, does not, like κλαίειν, indicate sobs (ver. 33), but tears; it is the expression for a calm and gentle sorrow. Baur does not admit that it is possible to weep for a friend so soon to be restored, and regards this feature as a proof of the non-authenticity of the narrative. Assuredly, if this Gospel were, as he believes, the production of speculative thought, it would not have contained this 35th verse. Jesus would, as the true Logos, with nothing human except the outward appearance, have raised His friend with triumphant looks and unmoistened eyes. But the evangelist, from the first, lays down the principle: The Word was made *flesh*. "It is not with a heart of stone that the dead are raised," says Hengstenberg; and Heb. ii. 17 teaches us that he who would help the unhappy, must first of all surrender his heart to feeling that very suffering from which he desires to deliver them. It is a remarkable thing, that the very Gospel in which the deity of Jesus is most clearly asserted, is also that which makes us best acquainted with the profoundly human side of His life. The very criticism of the German scholar proves how little such a Jesus is the offspring of speculation.—The solemn brevity of the sentences in these 34th and 35th verses is worthy of remark.

Even on the borders of the grave we encounter the inevitable division produced by the person of Jesus whenever He mani-

[1] ℵ D and some Mnn. read καὶ before ιδακρυειν.

fested Himself, whether by word or deed. Among the Jews themselves, there were some whose hearts were touched at the sight of these tears. Sympathy with misfortune is neutral ground—a purely human region, in which all hearts, not utterly hardened, may meet. But some of them found in these tears of Jesus a reason for suspicion. One of two things must, they thought, be the case; either He had not that friendship for Lazarus which He was affecting to feel, or He did not really possess that miraculous power of which He had pretended to give a proof in the cure of the man born blind. In either case there was something doubtful about His behaviour. Many exegetes (Lücke, de Wette, Tholuck, Gumlich) give a favourable meaning to the question of these Jews, ver. 37. But the evangelist, by the very turn of the expression (*some among them*), identifies the Jews of ver. 37 with those of ver. 46. Besides, it would be impossible, with such a meaning, to understand the relation between this question of the Jews and the fresh emotion manifested by our Lord (ver. 38).—Strauss finds it strange that these Jews should not here refer to the resurrections of dead persons effected by Jesus in Galilee, rather than to the healing of the blind man. And certainly no evangelist of the second century would have failed to put into the mouths of these Jews allusions to these resurrections, then so well known in the church through the Synoptic Gospels; while, on the other hand, so natural a circumstance as that inhabitants of Jerusalem should rather refer to the last striking miracle performed by Jesus in that city, and under their own eyes, does but manifest the historical truthfulness of St. John. A cure which had given rise to so much discussion, and had been the subject of such opposite judgments, was naturally the first to present itself to their minds.

3d. Vv. 38–44. Jesus and Lazarus.

Vv. 38, 39. "*Jesus therefore, again shuddering in Himself, cometh to the grave. It was a cave, and a stone lay upon it. Jesus said: Take ye away the stone. Martha, the sister of him that was dead,*[1] *saith unto Him: Lord, (by this time) already he stinketh, for he hath been there four days.*"—This repeated feeling of indignation on the part of Jesus was evidently called forth

[1] The Mss. are divided between τιθνηκοτος (T. R. and the Byzantines) and τιτελευκοτος (א A B C D K L Π).

by the malicious remark of the Jews (ver. 37), as St. John gives us to understand by *therefore* (ver. 38). And in the explanation which we have offered of the cause of this indignation (ver. 33), the relation between the two facts is easy to understand. The emotion, however, seems to have been less profound than on the former occasion, and more easily overcome. This very natural detail is a fresh proof of the faithfulness of the narrative.

The sepulchre was a cave hollowed out in the rock, either horizontally or vertically. The verb ἐπέκειτο would signify in the first case that the stone *was placed at the entrance* of the cave, in the second, *upon* its opening. If the tomb now shown as that of Lazarus is really such, it was of the latter of these forms. It is a cave cut in the rock, and descended into by a ladder of twenty-six steps. Robinson has, however, in this as in so many other instances, proved that tradition is not authentic. —The stones by which such caves were closed, being merely intended to keep off wild beasts, might be easily removed.— There is between this second feeling of indignation on the part of Jesus, and His peremptory command: *Take ye away the stone*, a relation analogous to that which we have already remarked between His first emotion of the kind and the question: *Where have ye laid him?* The state of expectation into which this command would throw the crowd may be easily imagined.

Did the remark of Martha proceed, as many expositors think, from a feeling of incredulity? The expression: *the sister of him that was dead*, which adds nothing to what the reader already knows, leads us rather to think that Martha was preoccupied with the painful sensation about to be experienced by our Lord and His companions by means of one so dear to her. As a sister, she would feel a certain amount of perplexity and difficulty on this account; besides, it must be remembered how closely the notion of pollution was, among the Jews, connected with that of death and corruption. We have here, then, an exclamation dictated by a feeling of respect for Him to whom she was speaking: *Lord;* and a kind of delicacy with respect to the person, so sacred to her, of him of whom she speaks: *the sister of him that was dead*. It is possible that the assertion of Martha: *he stinketh already,* might have been a mere supposition on her part, which she justified by adding: *for he has already been there four days.* But it is more natural to regard these words as the expression of a fact of which she had already had experience. The explanation: *for he has been there . . .,* while pointing out the cause of this fact, contains a slight allusion to the delay of Jesus. But, it is asked, had not Lazarus been embalmed? Undoubtedly he had, but after the manner of the Jews, who limited themselves to wrapping the body in perfumes, a process which could not prevent corruption. It has been supposed that, the arrival of Jesus being expected, the body had been placed in the tomb without the performance of this ceremony. Ver. 44, however, which shows that the limbs of Lazarus were, like those of any other corpse, enveloped in bandages (comp. xix. 40), does not favour this opinion. If Martha's remark did not arise from unbelief, it might nevertheless, by recalling this fact, occasion some failure of faith at this decisive moment.

Vv. 40-42. "*Jesus saith unto her: Said I not unto thee, that if thou believest thou shalt see*[1] *the glory of God? Then they took away the stone.*[2] *And Jesus lifted up His eyes and said: Father, I thank Thee that Thou hast heard me. As for myself, I know well that Thou hearest me always, but I said it because of the people who surround me, that they may believe that Thou hast sent me.*"—Several exegetes refer the words: *Said I not unto thee . . . ?* to the conversation of vv. 23-27. And, indeed, the words of Jesus: *If thou believest . . .,* do remind us of the expression: *He that believeth in me* (vv. 25, 26), and the question: *Believest thou this?* (ver. 27). But the characteristic expression of the present verse: *the glory of God,* is absent from these declarations, while it forms the salient feature of the promise of ver. 4. It was, then, this latter promise of which Jesus especially reminded Martha. He well knew that it had been reported to the two sisters by their messenger, and it had, indeed, formed the starting-point of the conversation, vv. 23-27, which confirmed and developed it. Hence, *Said I not unto thee,* stands for: Did

---

[1] 15 Mjj. read οψη instead of οψει, which is the reading of T. R. with K U Γ Π.
[2] T. R., with 9 Byz. Mjj. (E G H, etc.), here adds the words : ου κυ ο τιθνηκως κειμενος. A K Π have quite shortly : ου ην.

I not send thee word?—*The glory of God* is here, precisely as at Rom. vi. 4, the glorious triumph over death and corruption (ver. 39) of God's omnipotence exerted for the sake of His love. This is the sight Jesus promises to Martha, and opposes to the painful sensations which she dreads for the spectators and herself so soon as the stone is removed.—It is not necessary to see a reproach in the words: *Said I not unto thee, that if thou wouldest believe . . .?* as though Martha had shown a want of faith in speaking as she had done at ver. 39, in presence of the manifest signs of decomposition which had already begun. He exhorts her to a supreme act of faith, giving her as a foundation His former promise. She had already scaled the arduous steeps of the mountain; one last peak had to be gained, and the spectacle of the glory of God, of life triumphing over death, would be displayed before her eyes. Man always desires to see in order to believing. Martha is called upon to give an example of the contrary process: of believing in order to see. In expressing Himself as He did, Jesus by no means made the fulfilment of His promise depend, as Meyer supposes, upon the faith of Martha. What He makes contingent upon this last act of confidence which He demands from her, is not the miracle, but her own enjoyment of it (to *see* the glory). The bodily eye alone is not sufficient for the enjoyment of such a light. The received reading: *the stone from the place where the dead lay,* seems to be a paraphrase. The Alex. reading, which is simply: *the stone,* does not explain the other two. May not the third, that of A K Π, *the stone from where it was,* be the original text? Its brevity (οὗ ἦν) accounts on the one hand for the Byzantine gloss, and on the other for the entire omission of the sentence by the Alexandrines.—Jesus *lifted up His eyes.* To man, the visible heaven is the most eloquent witness of the invisible power of God. And so truly was Jesus man, the Word made flesh (comp. xvii. 1), that it was by gazing upon that infinite expanse that He sought His Father's face and prepared Himself for inward communion with Him.—The miracle was in the eyes of Jesus already effected, hence He gave thanks for it as for a thing accomplished: *Thou hast heard me.* He thus confirmed the view of His miracles announced by Martha (ver. 22): they were just so many answered prayers. The difference, however, between His position and that of others sent by God, who performed similar works, was the perfect assurance of being heard with which He addressed God. As the Son, He drew freely upon the divine treasury, and Besser well remarks: "Undoubtedly He performed all His miracles by faith, but by a faith peculiar to Himself, that of being the Son of God manifested in the flesh."

If Jesus, as in the present instance, expressed His gratitude aloud, it was not, as He Himself added, because there was anything extraordinary in the conduct of the Father towards Him on this occasion. This act of thanksgiving is anything but an exclamation extorted by surprise at being exceptionally heard; constantly heard by the Father, He is continually giving Him thanks. That which urged Him at this solemn moment to do so aloud was the sight of the people by whom He was surrounded. He had in private conversation prepared His disciples and the two sisters to behold and understand the work He was about to perform. He now desired to dispose the people also, whom His Father had unexpectedly assembled around this tomb, to behold *the glory of God*—that is, to see in this miracle not merely a prodigy, but a sign. Otherwise the astonishment they might feel would be unfruitful, and would not terminate in faith. It was for this reason that our Lord uttered in an audible voice that sentiment of filial gratitude which at all times filled His heart. By addressing His Father, He had just put God into the position of either granting or withholding His co-operation. If Lazarus remained in the tomb, let Jesus be acknowledged an impostor, and all His other miracles attributed to Beelzebub! If God, who was thus solemnly invoked, should manifest His arm, let Jesus be acknowledged as sent by Him! Thus this act of thanksgiving before the still occupied sepulchre made this moment one of solemn ordeal, like that of Elijah on Carmel, and imparted to this miracle a supreme and unique character in the life of Jesus.—Criticism has called this prayer "a prayer of pomp" (Strauss, Weisse, Baur), and found in this circumstance a reason for suspecting the authenticity of the narrative; but it has failed to grasp the whole bearing of the act. The Jews had regarded the cure of the man born blind as startling and inexplicable, but, viewing it as a breach of the Sabbath, had denied its divine character. By giving thanks to God on the present occasion, before all the people, previously to performing the miracle, Jesus positively makes God participate in the work about to be effected. Jehovah, the God of Israel, will be henceforth either the authenticator of His mission, or the accomplice of His imposture.—It is interesting to compare this expression: *Thou hast heard me*, with the assertion of M. Réville, when, speaking after the manner of Scholten, he says: " The fourth Gospel knows nothing of Jesus praying as a man" (*Rev. de Théol.*, 1865, vol. iii. p. 316).

Vv. 43, 44. "*And when He had thus spoken, He cried with a loud voice: Lazarus, come forth. And*[1] *he that was dead came forth, his feet and hands bound with bandages, and his face wrapped in a napkin. Jesus saith unto them: Loose him, and let him*[2] *go.*"—Jesus, having thus impressed its true character on the miracle, proceeded to accomplish it. The loud voice with which He spoke was the expression of a decided will, sure of being obeyed. As a man is called by name to awaken him from sleep, so did Jesus rouse Lazarus from death, which is but a sounder sleep (vv. 11, 12), by calling him loudly. Undoubtedly these external signs were only, as Hengstenberg says, for the individuals present, the power of raising the dead dwelling, not in the voice, but in the will of Jesus expressed thereby.—When speaking to the daughter of Jairus, and to the young man of Nain, He had said only: *Arise*, or: *Awake*, because they lay in a bed or on a bier. In the present instance He said: *Come forth*, because Lazarus was within the sepulchre. The simplicity and brevity of these two words: δεῦρο ἔξω (literally: *here, out!*), are in glorious contrast with their efficacy.

The expression: *he came forth*, ver. 44, does not necessarily indicate that he walked, especially if the sepulchre were dug vertically, but simply that he arose, which he could easily do notwithstanding the linen cloths in which he was enveloped; nor need we, on this account, suppose that each limb was

---

[1] Καὶ is omitted in B C L Sah., but found in all the other Mjj. (including ℵ) and Vss.
[2] B C L read αυτον after αφετε.

separately swathed, according to the custom of the Egyptians.—
The detail: *his face was bound about with a napkin*, is the
touch of an eye-witness, and recalls the impression—an impression never to be obliterated—made upon the spectators
by the sight. While they remained motionless with astonishment, Jesus, with perfect calmness, and as though nothing
extraordinary had occurred, invited them to take their part in
the work: Every one to his office; I have raised, it is for you
to loose him. The words: *Let him go*, mean quite simply:
Restore to him that power of motion of which, by this binding, you have deprived him.—The term ὑπάγειν, *to go away*,
has in it a touch of triumph, like the command of Jesus to
the impotent man: *Take up thy bed, and walk!*

The resurrection of Lazarus is the miracle of friendship, as
the prodigy at Cana was the miracle of filial piety, and that
not merely because the affection of Jesus for the family at
Bethany was its cause, but especially because Jesus performed
it with the distinct consciousness that by restoring his friend
to life He was signing His own death-warrant (comp. vv. 8–16
and vv. 33–38). The self-sacrifice of friendship here rises to
the height of heroism, a fact well understood by St. John,
of whose narrative this thought, which is clearly brought out
by the passage next following, is the very soul.

III. *The Effect produced by this Miracle.*—Vv. 45–57.

1st. And first, its immediate effect upon the spectators.

Vv. 45, 46. "*Then*[1] *many of the Jews, those who had come*[2]
to Mary, and had seen the things[3] *which He did, believed in Him.
But some of them went their ways to the Pharisees, and told them
what*[3] *Jesus had done.*"—Again a division among the spectators, and a more far-reaching one than on preceding occasions.
It is indeed natural to oppose the words: *many of the Jews*,
to those of the next verse: *but some of them*. The antithesis,
moreover, of the two verbs: *believed* (ver. 45) and *went their
ways* (ver. 46), corresponds with that of the subjects. There
is, however, a difficulty in this explanation, viz. that the participles: *who had come*, and *who had seen*, do not in Greek agree

---

[1] ℵ: δε instead of ουν.   [2] D: των ελθοντων instead of οι ελθοντες.
[3] B C D read ο instead of α at ver. 45, as do also C D M at ver. 46.

with the word *Jews*, but with the word πολλοί, *many* (not: many of the Jews . . ., but: *many, those who* . . .), so that this turn of the phrase seems to imply that *all* those *who had come* believed without exception. But in this case what are we to do with τινές, *some*, which seems, on the other hand, to constitute a part of the πολλοί, of those *many* who came to Mary? Meyer accepts the consequence of this construction, and maintains (as Origen has done before him) that, as they already believed, they took this step of going to the Pharisees *with a good purpose*. But this opinion is incompatible with the evident and double antithesis between vv. 45 and 46, already pointed out. Hence I rather hold that the *some*, τινές, must not be included in the category of those numerous visitors to Mary and Martha who now believed, ver. 45, but that the pronoun αὐτῶν, *of them*, ver. 46, refers to *the Jews* in general ('Ιουδαίων, ver. 45). There were certainly other Jews present besides those who came to visit the sisters—Jews not predisposed in favour of Jesus by sympathy for the mourners. It was these who, faithful to their part of *Jews*, hastened to carry the great news to the Pharisees, the most vehement enemies of Jesus. This explanation is perhaps confirmed by the expression: those who came *to Mary* (ver. 45), which seems to make what is there said refer only to those who were in the house with her (ver. 31).

2d. Vv. 47–53. The more remote effect of the resurrection of Lazarus.

Vv. 47–50. " *Then gathered the chief priests and the Pharisees a council, and said: What do we? for this man doeth many miracles. If we let Him thus alone, all will believe on Him, and the Romans will come and destroy both*[1] *our place and nation. But one among them, Caiaphas, being high priest that same year, said unto them: Ye know nothing at all, and do not reflect*[2] *that it is expedient for us*[3] *that one man should die for the people, and that the whole nation perish not.*"—The resurrection of Lazarus did not occasion the death of Jesus, but it did give rise to the resolution to condemn Him. The vessel was full,

---

[1] D K ɪɪ, 10 Mnn. and some Vss. omit καὶ before τὸν τόπον.
[2] ℵ A B D L, some Mnn. and Or. read λογίζεσθε instead of διαλογίζεσθε.
[3] The Mss. are divided between ἡμῖν (T. R. with A E G, etc.) and ὑμῖν (B D L M X Γ). ℵ omits both.

and this was the drop which made it overflow.—The *Pharisees* are specially mentioned as the instigators of this hostile meeting (ver. 46, ix. 15).—The absence of the article before συνέδριον may be explained by admitting that St. John here treats this word as a proper name (the Sanhedrin). It is, however, more natural to take this term here in the general sense of *assembly, council*, which it has also in classical Greek.—The present ποιοῦμεν, *what do we?* instead of the future, is inspired by the imminence of the danger, and the certainty that something must be done: " Why do we not act ? He is acting (ποιεῖ)." "Οτι : *because.* The fear expressed, ver. 48, was not without foundation. The slightest rising might have furnished the Romans with an excuse for depriving the nation of those last remnants of independence which it still enjoyed, and for blotting out its name from the map of the world. And then what would become of the power of the Sanhedrin? Οὕτως : without opposing His *action* by our own. The minds of the rulers, while recurring to the destruction of the nation, dwell chiefly on that of their own power. This is emphatically expressed by the position of the pronoun ἡμῶν before the two substantives. Jesus reproduced this expression in the words of the husbandmen, Matt. xxi. 38. Jerusalem and Israel were their affair. *Our place* naturally means the capital, as the seat of their government, rather than the temple, or the whole of Judea. Taken in this sense, the term is more easily connected with that which follows : *our nation*, that which we govern from this place. Speaking from a political point of view, and opposing one nation to another, they use the term ἔθνος, instead of the more honourable one λαός, for the people of Israel.

The expression : *one of them*, does not allow us to suppose that Caiaphas was presiding; for even though it now seems proved that the high priest was, in virtue of his office, also president of the Sanhedrin (Schürer, *Lehrb. der N. T. Zeitgesch.* p. 411), it must be remembered that the present was not a regular meeting (ver. 47).—Amidst a host of irresolute spirits, hesitating between conscience and interest, a man of energetic character, who boldly denies the rights of conscience and decidedly brings forward the claims of the state, always has a chance of carrying his point.—If this circumstance had taken place in the palmy days of the theocracy, the expression :

being the high priest that same year, would be incomprehensible; for, according to the Mosaic law, the high-priesthood was held for life. But since the Roman supremacy, the rulers of the land, dreading the power derived from a permanent office, had adopted the custom of frequently exchanging one high priest for another. According to Josephus (*Ant.* xviii. 2. 2), the Roman governor, Valerius Gratus, "deprived Ananus of the high-priesthood and conferred it on Ishmael, and afterwards deposing him, made Eleazar, son of Ishmael, high priest. A year after he also was deposed, and Simon nominated in his stead, who, retaining the dignity for a year only, was succeeded by Joseph, surnamed Caiaphas." The latter continued in office from the year 25 till 36 of our era, and consequently throughout the ministry of Jesus. These frequent changes justify the expression of the evangelist, and deprive criticism of any excuse for saying that the author of this Gospel did not know that the Jewish pontificate lasted for life. But since Caiaphas was high priest for eleven consecutive years, why did St. John three times over (vv. 49, 51, xviii. 13) use the expression: high priest *that year?* Certainly because he desired to recall the importance of that unique and decisive year, in which the perfect sacrifice terminated the typical sacrifices and the Levitical priesthood as exercised by Caiaphas. It devolved upon the high priest to offer every year the great atoning sacrifice for the sins of the people, and this was the office now performed by Caiaphas, as the last representative of the ancient priesthood. By his vote he, in some degree, appointed and sacrificed the victim, who in that ever memorable year "*was to bring in everlasting righteousness, and to cause the sacrifice and the oblation to cease*" (Dan. ix. 24, 27). This vote was rendered more remarkable by the contrast between the divine truth of its matter and the diabolical intention of him who uttered it. The apostrophe of Caiaphas to his colleagues exhibits a certain amount of rudeness. This feature, as Hengstenberg observes, agrees with the conduct of that Sadducean sect to which Caiaphas probably belonged (comp. Acts iv. 6 and v. 17, and Joseph. *Ant.* xx. 9. 1). Josephus says (*Bell. Jud.* ii. 8. 14): "The Pharisees are friendly to each other, and cultivate mutual harmony, with a view to their common interests; but the manners of the Sadducees are far rougher, both to each other and to their equals, whom they treat as strangers." Hengstenberg takes διαλογίζεσθε in an intransitive sense, and the ὅτι following in the sense of *because*. After reproaching them for their general want of knowing how to act: *Ye know nothing at all*, he brings forward the special difficulty which they were unable to solve. The compound διαλογίζεσθε : you are incapable of clearing up by your present discussion, is preferable to the simple λογίζεσθε, which is the result of either negligence or a mistaken correction. — The reading ἡμῖν, *for us*, has, in reality, the same meaning as the variation: ὑμῖν, *for you;* but it better disguises the selfish nature of the deliberation (comp. the ἡμῶν of ver. 48).—The choice of the terms λαός and ἔθνος, which correspond with עם and גוי, is not arbitrary. The first designates the multitude of individuals composing the theocratic nation, in opposition to the single individual who was to perish, while the second signifies Israel as a body politic, in opposition to the foreign nation of the Romans.

Vv. 51, 52. "*Now this he spake not of himself, but being high priest that year, he prophesied that Jesus should die for that nation, and not for that nation only, but also that He should gather together in one body the children of God that were scattered.*"—Several expositors (Luthardt, Brückner) deny that St. John here attributes the gift of prophecy to the high priest as such; it was not, they think, as high priest, but as high priest *that year*, that Caiaphas gave utterance to this prophetic statement. But this explanation gives the impression of being a mere expedient. The relation between the participle ὤν, *being*, and the Aorist προεφήτευσεν, *he prophesied*, naturally leads to the notion that the evangelist refers the prophetic character of the words of Caiaphas to his office, even if we regard this notion as only a Jewish superstition. In the O. T. the normal centre of the theocratic nation was not the king, but the priest. In all the great crises of the nation's fate, it was the high priest who received, in virtue of a prophetic gift communicated for the occasion, the decision of the Most High for the welfare of His people (Num. xxvii. 21 ; 1 Sam. xxx. 7 sq.). St. John by no means asserts that the high priest was generally endowed with this prophetic power; He merely regards Caiaphas as playing at this decisive moment the part assigned him in such cases as God's accredited organ to His people, and that notwithstanding the contrast existing between his individual character and the spirit of his office. In fact, when the heart of the high priest was in harmony with his office, that heart became the normal instrument of the divine decision. But if, as in the present case, the heart of the individual was in opposition to his office, it might be expected that the Divine oracle would, as in the present instance, be uttered by that consecrated mouth in the form of a most diabolical maxim. And what could be more worthy of the Divine Spirit than, while respecting his office, to make His degenerate instrument thus condemn himself with his own mouth? St. John has already, more than once, called our attention to the fact that the adversaries of Jesus, when deriding Him, were prophesying in spite of themselves: *No man knoweth whence he is* (vii. 27); *Will he go and teach the Greeks?* (vii. 35). If the devil often travesties the words of God, God sometimes chooses to parody those of the devil, by bestowing upon them unintended truth. It was such a "divine irony" that was, in the highest degree, manifested in the present instance. For this was the central point of human history, the moment at which the most Divine of mysteries was to be accomplished in the form of the greatest of crimes.

According to several expositors, ὅτι is not the direct complement of the verb which precedes it. Meyer: "he prophesied *as to* the fact that Jesus . . ." Luthardt: "he prophesied *for truly* Jesus was to . . ." They have been led to these forced explanations by ver. 52, the words of which go beyond the tenor of the saying of Caiaphas. But it is the close of ver. 51 which alone is the object of *he prophesied*, while ver. 52 is added by the evangelist to impress upon his readers the unexpected extension acquired in its realization, by the principle, *one for all*, laid down by Caiaphas. St. John never forgets that he is writing with a view to Greek readers, and never omits an opportunity of pointing out their share in the fulfilment of the divine promises. If the parallelism between the thought of this 52d verse and the saying x. 16 is considered, there can be no hesitation in applying the term *children of God* to heathens predisposed to believe, in the same sense in which St. John uses the expressions: *to be of God*

(viii. 47), *to be of the truth* (xix. 37). The term *children of God* naturally involves an anticipation based upon the actual moral condition of these future believers, and not, as Meyer thinks, upon divine predestination.

Ver. 53. " *Then from that day forth they took counsel*[1] *to put Him to death.*"—The *then* gives us to understand that the advice of Caiaphas was adopted (Luthardt). St. John brings out the decided importance of this meeting, and hence, indirectly, that of the resurrection of Lazarus, which occasioned it. Indeed, from that time a permanent conspiracy against the life of Jesus was organized. The daily conferences of His enemies became, to use Lange's expression, "meetings of Messianic murder." There was no longer any hesitation as to the end, indecision from this time forth being felt only with regard to the means.

3d. The stay at Ephraim: vv. 54–57.

Jesus was forced to retire to a lonely place. The rulers, on their part, took a fresh step on the road on which they had already advanced so far.

Vv. 54–57. " *Jesus therefore walked no more openly among the Jews; but went thence into a country near to the wilderness, into a city called Ephraim,*[2] *and there continued*[3] *with His*[4] *disciples. Now the Jews' Passover was nigh at hand: and many went out of the country up to Jerusalem before the Passover, to purify themselves. Then sought they for Jesus, and said among themselves, as they stood in the temple: What think ye, that He will not come to the feast? Now the chief priests and the Pharisees had also*[5] *given commandment*[6] *that if any man heard where He was, he should show it, that they might take Him.*"—Ephraim is sometimes spoken of in conjunction with Bethel (2 Chron. xiii. 19; Joseph. *Bell. Jud.* iv. 9. 9). It lay some distance north of Jerusalem—eight miles according to Eusebius, twenty to the north-east according to Jerome. The place was, on account of its retired situation, and its proximity to the desert,

---

[1] ℵ B D, 4 Mnn. and Or. (once) read εβουλευσαντο instead of συνεβουλευσαντο.
[2] ℵ L It. Vg. Ir. read Εφριμ instead of Εφραιμ.
[3] ℵ B L and Or. read εμεινεν instead of διετριβεν.
[4] ℵ B D I L Γ Δ omit αυτου.
[5] 11 Mjj. (ℵ A B, etc.) 35 Mnn. It. Vg. Syr. Cop. and Or. omit και, which is the reading of T. R. with D E G H I S Γ. Mnn.
[6] ℵ B I M, 3 Mnn. and Or. read εντολας instead of εντολ.κι.

favourable to the design of our Lord. He might there prepare His disciples in solitude for His approaching end, and, if pursued, retire to the desert. This desert is, as Lange remarks, the northern extremity of that barren strip by which the table-land of Judah and Benjamin is separated in its whole length from the valley of the Jordan and the Dead Sea. From this locality Jesus might, at the time of the Passover, either join the pilgrims from Galilee, who were going to Jerusalem by the direct route through Samaria, or go down to Jericho, in the plain of the Jordan, and put Himself in front of the caravan from Perea. We know from the Synoptists that He took the latter step.—Μετά (ver. 54) is not synonymous with σύν; the meaning is: He there confined Himself to the society of His disciples; and not merely: He was there with them.

Ἐκ τῆς χώρας (ver. 55) does not relate to the *country* of Ephraim in particular (Grotius, Olshausen), but to the *country* in general, as opposed to the capital (ver. 54): "They went up from different parts of the country."—The law did not prescribe any special purifications before the Passover, but the people were commanded, in several passages of the O. T., to purify themselves before any important event (Gen. xxxv. 2 ; Ex. xix. 10, 11, etc.), and this principle had naturally been applied to the Feast of the Passover (2 Chron. xxx. 16–20).

Ver. 56 graphically depicts the restless curiosity of these country-people, who were collected in groups in the temple and discussing the approaching arrival of Jesus ; comp. vii. 12.— Ἑστηκότες, *standing*, in an attitude of expectation.—Ὅτι does not depend on δοκεῖ ; it is more natural to separate the two propositions and make them two distinct questions.—The Aorist ἔλθῃ may quite well refer to an act about to be accomplished in the immediate future.

Ver. 57 adds a new and more special motive to those which rendered the coming of Jesus improbable ; for thus is its connection by the particles δὲ καί, *now . . . also*, explained. It would not have been very difficult for the authorities to discover His place of retreat. Hence the motive for this order must rather have been a desire to intimidate our Lord and His disciples, and to accustom the people to regard Him as a guilty and dangerous man. It was another link in the series of hostile measures so well detailed by St. John since the beginning of ch. v. Comp. v. 16, 18, vii. 32, ix. 22, xi. 53.—The *chief priests* were the authorities from whom the command officially emanated; the evangelist adds the *Pharisees* because they were its actual authors. Comp. vii. 45.—In the Babylonian Gemara (edited from ancient traditions about 550) is found the following passage: "Tradition reports that Jesus was crucified (hanged) on the evening of the Passover, an officer having during the preceding forty days publicly proclaimed that this man, who by his imposture had seduced the people, ought to be stoned, and that any one who could say aught in his defence was to come forward and speak. But no one doing so, he was hanged on the evening of the Passover" (Lightfoot, *Hor. Hebr. et Talm.* p. 460).—It would be difficult to avoid comparing this passage with that of St. John. In both there is a public proclamation on the part of the Sanhedrin relating to the approaching condemnation of Jesus, and at the same time too marked a difference between them to allow it to be supposed that either gave rise to the other.

The history of the raising of Lazarus, says Deutinger, is distinguished above all the narratives of the fourth Gospel by its particularly vivid and dramatic style. The characters are drawn by a hand at once firm and delicate. Nowhere are the relations between Christ and His disciples so strikingly shown; we are, as it were, initiated, by this history, into the confidential intimacy, the affectionate interchange of thought and feeling, which existed between the Master and His followers. The disciples are portrayed in the most attractive manner; their simple frankness and noble devotedness are made manifest. The Jews themselves, whose obstinate resistance to the efforts of Jesus is what we chiefly hear concerning them in this Gospel, appear in a more favourable light, as friends of the sorrowing sisters, the man appearing even in the Jew. Especially, how sharp and delicate is the sketch of the characters of the two women; with what refinement, and with what deep psychological feeling, is the difference in their respective behaviour detailed![1] In these characteristics of the narrative, so well

[1] *Das Reich Gottes, nach dem Apostel Johannes,* 1862, vol. ii. pp. 67 and 68.

summed up by the German author, we find the first evidence of its intrinsic truth: "it is not thus that fiction is written," and especially it was not thus that fiction was written in the second century; witness the apocryphal gospels.

The reality of the fact here narrated is also brought out by its relation to the whole preceding and subsequent history of Jesus. The evangelist is fully conscious of the *consequences* of the fact which he is recalling, he is continually pointing them out during the course of the narrative: vv. 47 (*therefore*) and 53 (*from that day forth*). Comp. xii. 9–11, 17–19. How should the author have assigned to a purely fictitious occurrence so decisive a part in the organism of Christ's life?

Moreover, not one of the explanations intended to eliminate this fact from the circle of authentic narratives in the life of Jesus is tenable.

(1) The so-called *natural* explanation of Paulus, Gabler, and A. Schweizer: In consequence of the message of ver. 3, Jesus did not from the first think the malady dangerous; subsequently, on receiving fresh information (Paulus reckons four messages), and making more exact inquiries, He found out that it was but a lethargy. Arriving at the sepulchre, He perceived some signs of life in the supposed corpse, for which He gave thanks (vv. 41 and 42), and called upon Lazarus to come forth. The latter, revived by the coolness of the sepulchre, the odour of the perfumes, and, at the moment of the opening of the grave, by the warmth of the external air, arose in full vigour. So Paulus and Gabler. According to A. Schweizer, the confidence of Jesus in the recovery of His friend was based upon His faith in the Divine assistance promised to His cause; and the pretended miracle was only the fortunate coincidence of this religious confidence with the circumstance that Lazarus was not really dead.—This explanation has been condemned by no one more severely than by Strauss[1] and Baur.[2] The former shows, against Paulus and Gabler, that the terms in which Jesus announces the resurrection of Lazarus are too positive to be anticipations founded on uncertain symptoms, and that the meaning of the entire narrative is, and can be, according to the intention of the narrator, nothing else than that

---

[1] *Vie de Jésus*, vol. ii. part i. pp. 154-165.
[2] *Theol. Jahrb.* vol. iii. 1844.

which every reader finds in it, viz. the raising of Lazarus from the dead by the miraculous power of Jesus. The opinion of Baur as to the manner in which the fourth Gospel in general, and this passage in particular, is treated by Schweizer, is as follows:—" Devoid of all feeling for the unity of the work, he tears this Gospel to rags for the purpose of eliminating therefrom, as superstitious interpolations, all which he is unable to explain in a tame and rationalistic manner, and of leaving to the marvellous action of chance all that he allows to remain." These last words, indeed, define the opinion of Schweizer concerning this miracle.

But let us now consider the explanations brought forth by these two critics in place of those of their predecessors.

(2) The *mythical* explanation of Strauss is as follows :—The O. T. having related that resurrections of dead persons had been effected by mere prophets, the Christian legend could do no less than attribute similar miracles to the Messiah. But can it really be supposed possible that a legend should attain to the height of a narrative, with such wonderful shades of colouring, and with characters so sharply and accurately drawn? It cannot be understood, as Renan justly observes, how a creation of the popular mind should get itself framed in such personal remembrances as those which refer to the relations of Jesus with the family of Bethany. Besides, legends idealize, and would never have invented a Christ moved to the very depths of His soul and shedding tears at the grave of the friend whom He was about to raise from the dead ! And is not Baur right, when, arguing against Strauss, he says : " If a mythic tradition of this kind had really been propagated in the church, it would not have failed to have been included, with so many similar narratives, in the Synoptic history. It is against all probability that so important a miracle, and one to which a decisive influence on the final catastrophe is attributed, should have remained a local legend, restricted to a very narrow circle." Notwithstanding these difficulties, M. Réville, " for his part, feels no embarrassment " in explaining the history of Lazarus by the mythic process. The legend meant to represent by Lazarus the pariahs of Jewish society (comp. Luke xvi. 20), whom Jesus rescued from their spiritual death by loving and weeping over them. " He bent over this

tomb (of Israelite pauperism), crying to Lazarus: Come forth, and come to me; and Lazarus came forth, pale, . . . tottering."[1] Such fancies are unworthy of discussion, and are judged as severely by M. Renan as by ourselves; he calls them expedients of theologians at their last gasp, saving themselves by allegory, myth, and symbol (p. 503). One circumstance especially ought to prevent any serious critic from attributing a legendary origin to this history. Myths of this kind are fictions isolated from each other, but we have seen how integral a part of the organism of St. John's Gospel the history of the raising of Lazarus forms. The work of St. John is evidently of one casting. With regard to such an evangelist, criticism is irresistibly driven to the dilemna: historian or inventor? Baur's merit consists in having appreciated this situation, and, since by reason of his doctrinal premises he could not admit the first alternative, in having boldly pronounced in favour of the second.

(3) The *speculative* explanation of Baur, according to which this history is a fiction, intended to give a body to the metaphysical thesis laid down, ver. 25: *I am the resurrection and the life.* This explanation suits the notion entertained by Baur of this Gospel, which, in his opinion, is a composition of an entirely ideal character. But is this, we ask, compatible with the simplicity, the candour, the prosaic character, and, if we may be allowed the expression, the hither and thither of the whole work? From beginning to end, situations are described for their own sake, and without the least tendency to idealizing (comp. *e.g.* the close of this chapter, the stay at Ephraim, the proclamation of the Sanhedrin, the conversations with the pilgrims to Jerusalem). Far rather does the narrative present features which are entirely non-intellectual and antispeculative. The Jesus who shudders and weeps is certainly not the creation of a theorist. The very offence which Baur takes at these circumstances of the narrative proves it. The productions of intellect are quite transparent to intellect. The more mysterious and unexpected the circumstances, the more manifest is it that they are taken from reality. Besides, if this narrative were the product of the idea, it ought to be completed by a discourse in which the fact would be spiri-

[1] *Revue Germanique*, 1st Dec. 1863, p. 613.

tualized and the idea itself brought forward. Every reader is impressed with the fact that the writer himself believes in all earnestness in the reality of the fact which he is relating, and that he has no notion of creating. When Plato clothes his deep doctrines with a veil of myths, his own self-projection in his creations, and his spontaneous choice and use of this form of instruction, are easily discerned. Here, on the contrary, the author is himself under the power of the fact he is relating; his heart is penetrated and his whole self possessed thereby. If, then, he created, he was himself the first dupe of his own fiction. Lastly, we must remember that, according to Baur's school, the author of the fourth Gospel does not believe in a true incarnation, but regards the Logos as having only assumed the appearance of humanity. And yet he is said to have here invented a scene in which the human nature of Jesus is in full force. Such a picture would be diametrically opposed to the thought which is said to have inspired the work. How is it possible to impute such clumsiness to so skilful a person as Baur's pseudo-John?

(4) Hence we see modern critics turning more and more to a somewhat different kind of explanation. Weisse had already suggested the notion that this history was nothing else than a parable transformed into a fact by tradition, and this notion is now reproduced by Keim, Schenkel, etc. The parable which gave rise to this history is said to be that of Dives and Lazarus (Luke xvi.), which the author of the fourth Gospel worked up into this picture. Renan himself, to a certain degree, adopts this mode of explanation. He at first regarded the raising of Lazarus as a pious fraud, to which Jesus was not entirely a stranger. "His friends," he says, "desired a great miracle, for the conviction of the unbelieving inhabitants of Jerusalem. . . . Lazarus, still pallid from his recent illness, had himself swathed in bandages, like a corpse, and placed in the family grave. . . . Jesus desired to see once more the friend whom He loved . . ." The rest may be understood. M. Renan makes every excuse for Jesus. "Amidst the impurity of Jerusalem, he was no longer himself. . . . Desperate, driven to extremities, . . . He yielded to the torrent. He rather submitted to than performed the miracles exacted by public

opinion." Now, however, M. Renan yields to the general feeling, which revolts against this explanation, and loudly proclaims its *moral* impossibility. The friends of Jesus, he now says, desired a great prodigy: they wanted a resurrection. Mary and Martha undoubtedly confided this feeling to Jesus. If, said these pious sisters, a dead man were to rise, the living would perhaps repent. "No," answered Jesus; "if Lazarus himself were to return to life, they would not believe." This saying subsequently became the subject of singular mistakes. . . . The supposition was changed into a fact . . .; tradition attributed to Martha and Mary a sick brother, whom Jesus raised from the grave. In a word, the misunderstanding in which this history originated is just like one of those cock-and-bull stories so common in small Oriental towns (13th edit. pp. 372-374).—Our only refutation shall be that this history tells us just the opposite of the saying which is said to have originated it. The Jews do *believe* after witnessing the fact, and the saying of Jesus, Luke xvi., which the narrative is said to illustrate, is: They would not be persuaded though one rose from the dead. It is not so easy a matter to get rid of a narrative of this kind by means of criticism.

But if this is a real fact, why is it not related in the Synoptic Gospels?

And first let it be remarked, that the manner in which the oral tradition, of which these books are the compilation, was formed, is still in many respects an insoluble problem. Hence it would be irrational to sacrifice reasons so positive as those which speak for the reality of the fact, for a difficulty, to solve which the most necessary elements are absent. M. Renan himself says: "The silence of the Synoptists with respect to the episode of Bethany does not seem to me of much account (p. 507). . . . If we reject this narrative as imaginary, the whole edifice of the last weeks of the life of Jesus is shattered by the same blow" (p. 514).

According to Lücke, the authors of the Synoptic Gospels were ignorant of this miracle, the remembrance of which was lost among so many similar occurrences. It may, however, be asked, whether such a miracle was not marked by special features which would prevent its being forgotten. Meyer says that the Synoptists meant only to relate events which transpired in Galilee. But how is so singular a selection to be explained? And do not their narratives include all the last sojourn at Jerusalem? Grotius, Herder, and Olshausen suppose that they desired to spare the family of Lazarus, which dwelt near Jerusalem, and might, by the open mention of this miracle, have been exposed to the vengeance of the still powerful Sanhedrin. Comp. xii. 10 : *The chief priests consulted that they might put Lazarus also to death.* This ingenious hypothesis might, indeed, apply to St. Matthew's Gospel, which was written in Palestine, but it is difficult to explain by it the silence of Mark and Luke, who wrote in countries at a distance from the Holy Land. Hengstenberg adopts the opinion that the raising of Lazarus belonged to a series of more profound transactions which did not form part of tradition, and were instinctively reserved for St. John. This opinion approximates to that of Heidenreich, who thought that no writer till John felt himself capable of depicting such a scene. Few will, however, find this explanation satisfactory.

I do not deny that there is an amount of truth in some of these suppositions, perhaps even in all. But if they are really to contribute to the solution of the problem, they must be placed in another light.

And first of all, we must start from the fact that in the apostolic mind no one special fact in the ministry of Jesus, not even the most striking of all, was of that supreme importance which we are now inclined to attribute to it. The point of view taken up by the apostles in their preaching was utterly different from that which we occupy when we make their teaching the subject of critical study. They were labouring to found a church and to save the world; we are endeavouring to reconstruct a history. No wonder, then, if narratives, composed from the former point of view, should contain much that is enigmatical to us. The death and resurrection of Jesus—events more decisive, and, in a religious aspect, incomparably more important, than the raising of Lazarus—had succeeded this miracle, and must for a time have eclipsed both this and every other single miracle of our Lord's ministry. Apostolic preaching, in its first phase, confined itself to the announcement and demonstration of the supreme fact: The Lord is risen. This was the foundation on which the church was built by the apostles. The time was not yet come for the relation of anecdotes. Undoubtedly the general miraculous agency of our Lord was referred to, as we see from the discourses of the apostles in the Book of the Acts (ii. 22, x. 37), but particular narratives were still kept in the background. If the details of Christ's ministry played any part during this first phase of Christian teaching, it was in private conversations. The great official proclamation of the gospel found nothing to place side by side with the death and resurrection of the Messiah, those great facts by which the world's salvation was effected. It was on this point also that the instructions of Jesus were concentrated after His resurrection (Luke xxiv. 26, 45–47).

It was subsequently, and when the first gale had begun to spend itself, that old memories were first disinterred. Under the influence of that apostolic preaching which founded churches, the ministry of catechists, whose office it was to edify them by detailing the different facts of our Lord's life, arose and was developed. Some of these narratives were put in circulation by the apostles themselves—probably those which constituted the permanent and universal stock of oral evangelization, and which passed in a tolerably uniform manner into the written tradition, into our Synoptic Gospels. Others were first started by those members of the church who had either been subjects or witnesses of the facts. These remained a part of the oral tradition in, as far as possible, the form given them by their first narrators, and, coming more or less accidentally to the knowledge of the writers of the Gospels, they formed the special treasure of each of our Synoptists. A third kind, finally, were purposely and at first withdrawn from public narration, or were only included in it with a certain reserve of names or things. Such reserve was, in different respects, required for the sake of those who had played a part in these facts. Thus, in recounting the blow with the sword given by St. Peter at Gethsemane, which was really a criminal act, and might have compromised the cause of Christ, it was usually said in oral tradition: *one of those who were with Jesus* (Matthew); or, *one of those who were present* (Mark); or again, *one among them* (Luke); while

St. John, relating the same fact, long after the death of St. Peter and the fall of the Sanhedrin, gives without hesitation the name of *Peter* from his own remembrance.

It is possible that there might also be some special reason for reserve with respect to the narrative concerning the family at Bethany. St. Luke (x. 38 sqq.) speaks, indeed, of two sisters, and designates them by their names; but he omits that of the town in which they dwelt, and says: "Jesus entered into a certain village." Undoubtedly, because he was himself ignorant of its name. And why, but because tradition, having from the first omitted it, had not furnished him with this information? St. Matthew (xxvi. 6 sqq.) and St. Mark (xiv. 3 sqq.) certainly name Bethany, but are silent as to the names of the sisters: "*A woman came*," is the manner in which they commence the account of the anointing by Mary. Simon the leper, the only individual named by them, seems to be brought forward to cast the rest into the shade. Is it asked: What reason was there for such reserve on the part of tradition? Perhaps fear of the vengeance of the Sanhedrin, which, as long as that tribunal possessed authority, might so easily reach the dwellers at Bethany. Perhaps, also, the very close and personal character of our Lord's relations with Lazarus and His family. There was a feeling that the home at Bethany, that sanctuary still inhabited by the family into whose intimacy the Lord had been received, should be respected in public teaching, and in the preaching of the gospel within the churches; that if, notwithstanding, general edification should occasion the bringing forward of these individuals, this should only be done, as by St. Luke, by leaving the name of their abode unmentioned. As to the raising of Lazarus, it was here necessary to tell everything or nothing; so the last alternative was chosen, and this fact was excluded from the series of narratives commonly recorded. Meyer objects that, at the time of the compilation of the Synoptic Gospels, there was no longer any object in such reserve, because the parties interested were no longer living. This reason is, however, of no value, since the point in question is the *formation* of tradition immediately after the day of Pentecost, and not its *compilation* thirty or forty years afterwards. It was not till towards the close of the apostolic age, when St. John wrote from a single source, and independently of traditional accounts, certain facts of the history of Jesus, that he could lift the veil from this long-hidden sanctuary, and bring forward before the eyes of the whole church the revered beings by whom Jesus had then been surrounded.

In any case, the mention or the omission of any single miracle performed by the Lord, is too accidental a circumstance to mislead a criticism under wise self-restraint, to give more weight to the silence of one, two, or even three of our documents, than to the plain, positive, and circumstantial testimony of the fourth. No part of the gospel history is better attested than the appearance of Jesus to five hundred brethren, spoken of by St. Paul (1 Cor. xi.); and yet there is no express mention of this appearance in our four Gospels. Spinoza, according to the testimony of Bayle, declared to his friends, that if he could have persuaded himself of the raising of Lazarus, he would destroy his whole system, and embrace, without reserve, the common faith of Christians. And this is just what explains the fact of its being at present as violently attacked as that of our Lord Himself. But let the reader take up St. John's narrative, and read it again without any previously formed opinion, . . . and the conviction to which the pantheistic philosopher was unable to attain will spontaneously and irresistibly arise within him, and he will, on the testimony of this account, every particular of which bears the stamp of truth, simply accept the fact with all its consequences, rather than let himself be carried hither and thither by a criticism, each new attempt of which gives the lie to that which preceded it.

SECOND SECTION.

XII. 1–36.—THE LAST DAYS OF CHRIST'S MINISTRY.

This section contains three divisions :—I. The supper at Bethany, vv. 1–11; II. Christ's entry into Jerusalem, vv. 12–19; III. The last scene of His ministry in the temple, vv. 20–36.

These three facts are selected by the evangelist as marking the transition from our Lord's public ministry to His Passion. This tendency in the narrative comes out in the first portion, in the discontent of Judas, which was the prelude to his treason, and in the answer of Jesus containing the announcement of His own approaching death; in the second, in ver. 19, which shows that, in consequence of the triumphal entry, the rulers were reduced to the necessity of either doing homage to Jesus or getting rid of Him; and lastly, in the third, in the whole discourse of Jesus in answer to the step taken by the Greeks, and in His final adieu to the Jewish nation, ver. 36.—In the two first portions, the evangelist, at the same time, shows the influence exercised on the course of the events which he recounts by the resurrection of Lazarus: vv. 2, 9–11, 17–19. Thus there is an underlying connection between the different parts of this apparently fragmentary account. And this chapter is, as Luthardt justly observes, at once a conclusion and an introduction.

I. *The Supper at Bethany.*—Vv. 1–11.

In presence of the great conflict now anticipated by all, the devotion of our Lord's friends increases; while as a counterpoise, the national enmity, which has an instrument among the twelve, breaks out within this inner circle, Jesus with perfect gentleness announcing to the traitor the approaching result of his hostility.

Ver. 1. "*Therefore Jesus, six days before the Passover, came to Bethany, where Lazarus was which had been dead,[1] whom He raised from the dead.*"—We learn from the Synoptists, unless their accounts are at variance with that of St. John, that Jesus went from Ephraim to Jericho, to go up to Jerusalem with the companies of pilgrims who were arriving from Perea. He thus took the same road subsequently traversed in an inverse order by Epiphanes, who tells us that he went up from Jericho to the plateau with a man who accompanied him across the desert of Bethel and Ephraim. I cannot understand why this simple hypothesis should scare the im-

[1] Ο τιθνηκως is omitted by א B L X It^aliq, Syr. Tisch. (8th edit.). These words are found in the 14 other Mjj., all the Mnn. It^plerique, Vg. Cop. Tisch. (7th edit.).

partiality of Meyer. He brings forward in objection the information in xi. 54; but the time of silence was now over with Jesus.—We know from St. Luke, that even before entering Jericho He was surrounded by a considerable crowd (xviii. 36), that He passed the night at the house of Zaccheus (xix. 1 sq.), and that general expectation was excited to the highest degree (xix. 11, and Matt. xx. 20 sq.). The distance from Jericho to Bethany might be accomplished in six or seven hours. The body of the caravan continued its journey to Jerusalem the same day, while Jesus and His disciples stopped at Bethany. This halt is not mentioned by the Synoptists, but this is no reason for calling it in question. One or more of the Synoptists often leave gaps which can only be filled up by the help of the third. Two cases of the kind occur in the account of the following days: Mark xi. 11–15 tells us that a night elapsed between the triumphal entry and the expulsion of the sellers in the temple, an interval which would not be supposed from reading the other accounts. Again, according to Mark xi. 12 and 20, there was an interval of a day and night between the cursing of the fruitless fig-tree and the conversation respecting it between Jesus and His disciples, while in St. Matthew the conversation seems to have immediately followed the miracle. These seeming contradictions arise from the fact, that in the traditional teaching the moral and religious importance of events greatly outweighed the chronological interest. If such, notwithstanding their general parallelism, are the mutual relations of the Synoptic narratives, we need not be surprised if this phenomenon is reproduced upon a still greater scale in the relation between the Synoptic and the fourth Gospels.

The οὖν, *therefore*, refers to xi. 55 : *The Jews' Passover was at hand.* The turn of expression: πρὸ ἐξ ἡμ. τ. π., *six days before* . . ., may be explained by a Latinism (*ante diem sextum calendas*), in which the preposition is transposed (Bäumlein); or perhaps the most natural explanation of this phrase in Greek is as follows:—To the definition of time: *before* (the space of) *six days*, is added, under a genitive form, the point from which the computation is made: *the Passover* (Winer, sec. 61, 5). Jesus knew that He should want all that time to strike a last and great blow in the capital. On what day, then, must we, according to this expression, place the arrival of Jesus at Bethany? Opinions differ on this point, according as the day of arrival or the first day of the Passover is included or not included in the six days; as the Passover is considered to begin on the 15th, the first great Sabbatic day of the Paschal week, or on the 14th, the day of preparation on which the lamb was slain; and finally, as the Friday on which Jesus suffered is, in the sense usually attributed to the Synoptists, regarded as the 15th Nisan, or, in the sense mostly—and, as I think, justly—given to St. John, as the 14th, the day of the preparation. It is impossible for us to follow out in detail all the different ramifications to which these different issues give rise. The summary of their results is as follows:—Some (Tholuck, Lange, Wieseler, Hengstenberg, Luthardt, Lichtenstein, etc.) place the arrival of Jesus at Bethany on Friday the 7th or 8th Nisan; others (Meyer, Ewald), on Saturday the 8th or 9th; others (de Wette, Andreæ, etc.), on Sunday the 9th or 10th; while Hilgenfeld, Baur, Scholten, and Bäumlein make it Monday the 10th or 11th. Among these possible suppositions, that which now seems the most probable is that stated by Andreæ in the excellent paper entitled, "der Todestag Jesu" (in the *Beweis des Glaubens*, Nos. July to Sept. 1870). The sixth day would be the 14th Nisan—that is, according to the very lucid chronology of St. John, the Friday on which Christ was crucified (see at the close of ch. xix. the detailed discussion of the whole question). This would make the day of the arrival at Bethany to be Sunday the 9th Nisan. Jesus, after passing the Sabbath at Jericho with Zaccheus, would, early next morning, travel with the caravan from Jericho to Bethany, where He remained while the other travellers proceeded to Jerusalem. It was on the evening of this day that the banquet, about to be related, was given Him, and on the next day, Monday, that He made His solemn entry into Jerusalem. In this manner everything is clear and simple.

In my first edition, I left the 14th Nisan, the Friday on which Jesus died, outside the six days, as one of the days of the feast. In fact, this day does play a prominent part in the institution of the Passover (Ex. xii.); and Josephus (*Antiq.* xii. 15. 1) counts *eight* feast days, which shows that he includes the 14th. But, on the other hand, it must be admitted that, if *the feast of Unleavened Bread* began on the 14th, *the Passover*, properly so called, did not begin till the 15th and ended on the 21st. These two great Sabbatic days formed the beginning and end of the Paschal week. Another objection to this mode of computation is, that by starting from Thursday the 13th, and counting backwards six days, we get Saturday the 8th as the day of the arrival at Bethany. Now it cannot possibly be admitted that Jesus would make so long a journey, as that from Jericho to Bethany, on the Sabbath. Meyer, to escape this objection, which applies to his calculation also, supposes that Jesus on the preceding evening reached a point sufficiently near to Bethany to leave only the distance which it was lawful to travel on the Sabbath (20 minutes). But, in that case, why did He not come on that evening to Bethany? I had proposed a somewhat different solution of this difficulty, —viz., that Jesus arrived on the Friday evening near enough to Bethany to allow him to reach it that same evening during the first hour of the Sabbath, which began at about six o'clock in the evening, this Saturday being the *first* of the six days before the feast. The banquet would be given Him the next evening, about the close of this Sabbath, and on the next morning (Sunday) He would make His entry into Jerusalem. But this combination seems to me less simple than that proposed by Andreæ.

Expositors who desire to impose upon the text of St. John, the chronology generally supposed to be that of the synoptic account, regard the 14th (according to their view, the *Thursday* of the Paschal week) as one of the days of the feast. Hence they reckon the six days backwards from Wednesday the 13th, which brings them to the 8th Nisan (the Wednesday, according to them, before the feast) as the day of the arrival at Bethany. If the premises of this computation are admitted, there is nothing to object to the result.

According to Hilgenfeld, Baur, etc., who make the 15th the starting-point of their computation, and include this day in the six, the arrival at Bethany took place on Monday the 10th Nisan; and most of these expositors think that the evangelist was by this date seeking to establish a typical relation between the arrival of Jesus and the Jewish custom of setting apart the Paschal lamb on the 10th Nisan, an intention which would evidently compromise the historical character of the narrative. But this pretended relation between the arrival of Jesus and the setting apart of the Paschal lamb is a mere imagination, of which the narrative does not afford the slightest indication. And how should this coincidence have ever come into he minds of the Greek Christians, for whom St. John was writing, without such indication?

Vv. 2, 3. "*Therefore they made Him a supper there, and Martha served; and Lazarus was one of those*[1] *who sat at table with Him.*[2] *Then took Mary a pound of ointment of pure nard, very costly, and anointed the feet of Jesus, and wiped His feet with her hair; and the house was filled with the odour of the ointment.*"—When did this repast take place? Naturally, according to our hypothesis, on the Sunday evening, the expression next day (ver. 12) designating Monday.—The subject of ἐποίησαν, *they made*, is indefinite, and hence cannot have been the members of the family of Lazarus,—a fact also brought out by the express mention of the presence of Lazarus and the serving of Martha, both circumstances which would have been self-understood, if the supper had taken place in their house. Hence the unexpressed subject of the verb is more probably certain inhabitants of the locality, who might feel impelled to testify their gratitude to one who had honoured their obscure town by so glorious a miracle. This connection of ideas seems expressed by the *therefore* (ver. 2) placed immediately after the striking detail: *the dead man whom He had raised*. The circumstance by which they were especially urged at this time to pay this public respect to Jesus, was the hatred on the part of the rulers to which they saw Him exposed. This banquet was a courageous answer to the edict of the Sanhedrim (xi. 57), an honour done to the man whom it had proscribed.

The text does not tell us in whose house the repast took place. But Lazarus being there as a guest, and not as host, it must have been in another than his. This confirms quite naturally the accounts of St. Matthew and St. Mark, who say pointedly that the supper took place in the house of Simon the leper,

---

[1] א B L, It. Vg. read ἐκ before τῶν ἀνακειμένων.
[2] T. R. with only a few Mnn.: συνανακειμένων αὐτῷ. All the Mjj.: ἀνακειμένων σὺν αὐτῷ.

undoubtedly one healed by Jesus, who claimed the privilege of entertaining Him in the name of the rest. It is inconceivable how so simple a combination can seem to Meyer a process of spurious harmonizing. Not every one could receive Jesus, but every one desired to contribute, to the best of his ability, to the homage now paid Him. The inhabitants of Bethany, by the banquet given in their name; Martha, by her personal service, even in the house of another; Lazarus, by his presence, which glorified the Lord more than all that others could offer —as is expressed by the epithet ὁ τεθνηκώς, wrongly omitted by some Alex.; and lastly, Mary, by such royal prodigality as could alone express the feeling which animated her.

The general custom among ancient nations was to anoint the heads of guests on festal occasions. "*Thou preparest a table before me; Thou anointest my head with oil; my cup runneth over,*" said David to the Lord, when describing, under the image of a banquet given him by God, the delights of communion with Him (Ps. xxiii. 5). The omission of this ceremony was brought forth by Jesus as a lack of courtesy (Luke vii. 46). Such an error was not committed at Bethany, where Mary took upon her this office, reserving to herself the right of performing it after her own fashion.—Μύρον is the generic name for all kinds of liquid perfume, and νάρδος, *nard*, that of the most costly among them. This word, of Sanscrit origin, designates a plant which grows in India, and of which some less esteemed varieties are found in Syria. Its juice was enclosed in special flasks (*nardi ampullæ*), and it was used not merely to anoint the body, but also to perfume wine. We have translated πιστικός by *pure*. This word, which is alien to classical Greek, only occurs in the N. T. in the parallel passage of Mark. Among the later Greeks it was used to designate a person *worthy of confidence*, hence one to whom was confided the care of a vessel or a flock. It would therefore mean nard, which might be depended on as genuine. This sense is the more applicable, because nard was liable to all kinds of adulteration. Pliny enumerates nine plants by which it might be imitated, and Tibullus uses the expression *nardus pura*, which gives almost the character of a technical expression to this πιστικῆς in Mark and John. The meaning *drinkable* (from πίνω, πιπίσκω) is much less probable, not only because the natural form would be πιστός or πότιμος, but especially because the notion of its being drinkable has no reference to the context. An attempt has also been made to derive the word from the name of a Persian town Pisteira, said to be sometimes shortened into Pista (comp. Meyer on Mark xiv. 2), but this is an expedient of no value (comp. Meyer, Hengstenberg, and especially Lücke and Wichelhaus). The epithet πολυτίμου, *very costly*, can only refer to the former of the two substantives, though Luthardt thinks otherwise; for it was not the plant (νάρδου), but the perfume (μύρου), that had been purchased. Λίτρα, *a pound*, answers to the Latin *libra*, and means a pound of twelve ounces, an enormous quantity for so expensive a perfume. But neither quantity nor quality were to be lacking in Mary's homage.

These hermetically sealed bottles of nard were probably brought from the East; to make use of their contents the neck had to be broken, which was accordingly done by Mary, as we are told in Mark xiv. 3. As there was something striking and solemn in this action, she must have performed it in the sight of the other guests, and consequently over the head of Jesus, as already seated at the table. Thus His head received the first-fruits of the perfume (comp. Matt. and Mark: she poured it *upon His head*). But afterwards, as no ordinary guest was in question, and Mary desired to give the Lord not merely a mark of esteem and affection, but also of adoration, she united to the customary anointing of the head, a homage altogether unusual. As if the costly liquid had been only common water, she poured it on His feet in such quantities as to bathe them; and, being therefore obliged to wipe them, she used for that purpose her own hair. This last particular brought the homage to a climax. She might have heard of what the woman that was a sinner had done in Galilee (Luke vii.), and have desired that the friends of Jesus should not do less for Him than a stranger had. It was regarded among the Jews, says Lightfoot (vol. ii. p. 633), as a disgrace for a woman to loosen the bandeaux which bound up her tresses and to appear with dishevelled hair.[1] Hence Mary by this act testified, that as no sacrifice was too costly for her purse, so no service was

---

[1] *Sotah*, fol. 5, 1: "The priest unbinds the hair of a suspected woman ... as a sign of reproach." *Vajicra Rabba*, fol. 188, 2: "Kamith, who had had

too mean for her person. The reason for the certainly not accidental repetition of the words τοὺς πόδας, *his feet*, is easily perceived. It was to this, the least noble part of His person, that she paid such unusual homage. There is not in the whole account a single detail which does not breathe with the adoration which inspired this act.

The identity of this fact with that related in Matt. xxvi. 6–13 and Mark xiv. 3–9 is undeniable. The trifling discrepancy, that in the Synoptics the perfume is poured upon *the head* and not upon *the feet* of Jesus, may, as we have just seen, be easily explained. After the anointing in the customary form, this bathing of the feet with perfume, of which John has preserved the memory, and which gives this scene its unique character, took place, would it not be absurd to suppose that she poured a whole pound of liquid on His head? As to the place occupied by the circumstance in the synoptic narrative, this was evidently determined by its *moral* relation with the fact related immediately afterwards, viz. the treachery of Judas (Matt. v. 14–16; Mark v. 10, 11). This association of ideas had fixed the conjunction of these two facts in the oral tradition, whence it had passed into the written compilation. The relation of the anointing of Jesus at Bethany with the fact narrated in Luke vii. is altogether different. We have already mentioned (p. 3) the particulars which do not permit us to identify the two narratives. Keim lays down the law, that an act of homage of this kind could not have taken place twice. But anointing, as well as bathing the feet, necessarily took place at every repast to which an invitation had been given (Luke vii. 44). The details in which the two scenes are similar are purely accidental. What is there in common between Simon the leper of Bethany and Simon the Pharisee of Galilee, except the name? But, only in the small number of individuals met with in the Gospel history, there are twelve or thirteen Simons; and yet it is said that there could not be two men with so common a name, at whose houses these two similar scenes would take place! The chief point of resemblance is, that both women wiped *the feet* of Jesus with *their hair*.

seven sons who were high priests, answered those who asked her to what she owed so great an honour: 'To the fact that the beams of my chamber have never seen the hairs of my head.'"

But the sinner wiped away *her tears* with which she had bedewed His feet, and after that spread perfume on them. Mary, on the contrary, had no tears to shed at a time like this, when she was enjoying the full satisfaction of possession, and only wiped away perfume, thus anointing herself as well as the Lord. This difference sufficiently separates the two women and the two scenes. Besides, Christian feeling will always protest against the identification of Mary of Bethany with a woman of bad character.

Vv. 4–6. "*Then*[1] *saith one of His disciples, Judas, son of Simon the Iscariot,*[2] *which would (shortly) betray Him, Why was not this perfume sold for two hundred pence, and the price given to the poor? Now he said this, not that he cared for the poor; but because he was a thief, and kept*[3] *the purse, and took what was put in it.*"—This burst of indignation on the part of Judas was undoubtedly occasioned by the reason pointed out by the evangelist; but, like his treason, it had a deeper source than avarice. For a long time (vi. 70) a gloomy displeasure at the part taken by Jesus (vi. 70, 71, comp. with v. 15) had filled his heart, and this feeling was only waiting for an excuse to show itself. In the Synoptists it is *His disciples* (Matt.), *some* (Mark), who remonstrate. It seems that on this, as on so many other occasions, Judas played among his fellow-disciples the part of the leaven which raises the flour.

In this passage we again find between St. John and the Synoptists the same relative difference which so frequently occurs. In the latter, the outlines are obliterated, in the former the individual and characteristic features are preserved. —Judas knows the exact price of this commodity, as if he were a trader.—On the value of the penny, see remarks on vi. 7. The sum, in the times of the emperors, was about ten guineas, and is stated at exactly the same amount in Mark. Several similar coincidences have already been noticed between these two evangelists (v. 3, vi. 7, 10).—Even independently of the fact of Judas' treachery, attested as it is by four evangelists,

---

[1] ℵ and B read δε instead of ουν.
[2] There are many various readings in the designation of Judas. ℵ B and L: Ιουδας ο Ισκαριωτης; T. R. with 10 Mjj. (A I K, etc.): Ιουδ. Σιμωνος Ισκαριωτης; D: Ιουδ. απο Καρυωτου, etc.
[3] ℵ B D L Q have εχων instead of ειχεν και.

it would be a very rash proceeding to attribute the accusation here made by St. John to the impure motive of hatred, as modern criticism has thought fit to do.—The word γλωσσόκομον (properly γλωσσοκομεῖον) literally means the *case* in which musicians kept the mouthpieces of flutes; hence: box. This purse was probably a small portable cash-box, in which the property of Jesus and the disciples was mingled with that of the poor (xiii. 29). This fund was furnished by voluntary gifts (v. 5; Luke viii. 1–3).—It may be seen from xx. 15 how easily the word βαστάζειν, generally used in the N. T. in the sense of *to bear*, changes its meaning for that of *to bear away, to purloin* (de Wette, Meyer). The former sense, without being absolutely impossible here, would nevertheless furnish a tautology with the preceding proposition. But why, it has been asked, did our Lord entrust Judas with an office so dangerous to his morality? We would not say, with Hengstenberg, that He thought fit thus to call forth a manifestation of his sin, as the only mode of effecting his cure. In thus acting, Jesus would, as it seems to us, have put Himself in the place of God in a manner unsuited to the reality of His humanity. And what proof have we that Jesus directly intervened in the choice of Judas as treasurer to the community? Might it not have been an arrangement between the disciples themselves, with which He did not wish to interfere?

Vv. 7, 8. " *Then said Jesus, Let her alone: against the day of my burial*[1] *hath she kept this. For the poor always ye have with you, but me ye have not always.*"[2]—We translate according to the reading of the T. R.; ἄφες is absolute: "*Leave her.* (in peace); cease to trouble her with your observations." According to the Alex. variation, the proposition which follows might be made the direct regimen of ἄφες, whether in the sense of the Vulgate, Meyer, Bäumlein, etc.: "Let her keep *it* (αὐτό, the rest of the perfume of which she had as yet used but a part) to embalm me on the day of my death, and not to sell it for the poor," or in that of Lange, Luthardt: "Allow her *to have kept* this perfume for this very day, which, by the act she has performed,

---

[1] T. R., with 12 Mjj. almost all the Mnn. Syr^{sch}, reads: αφις αυτην· εις την ημεραν τ. ενταφ. μου τιτηρηκεν αυτο. ℵ B D K L Q X Π, 4 Mnn. It^{plerique} V_g. Cop.: αφις αυτην ινα εις την ημ. τ. ενταφ. μου τηρηση αυτο.

[2] D omits ver. 8.

becomes, as it were, that of an anticipated burial." Rilliet, while accepting the Alex. reading, takes ἄφες in the absolute sense, which we must do in the T. R.: " Let her alone, *that* she may keep it for the day of my burial." The sense of Lange is grammatically forced; it would have required: ἄφες αὐτὴν τετηρκέναι, the expression ἀφιέναι ἵνα necessarily relating to the future. That of Meyer rests upon the idea that only a portion of the perfume had been used, a notion incompatible with the natural sense of ver. 3. And with what right can αὐτό be restricted to the portion thus assumed to be unused? Besides, the saying of Jesus, thus understood, has no connection with the objection of Judas, who had not disputed Mary's right to keep all or part of the perfume for the purpose of using it on some future appropriate occasion. The translation of Rilliet does not remove these difficulties, and we can but agree with Lücke and Hengstenberg, that this reading, however translated, does not present any passable meaning. It is an unfortunate correction by the hand of critics who were occupied with the notion that no man is embalmed before his death. The received reading, on the contrary, offers a sense at once clear and refined. Jesus bestowed on the act of Mary just what it lacked in the eyes of Judas—an aim, a practical usefulness. It is not for nothing, as your reproaches suggest, that she has poured forth this perfume. She has embalmed me beforehand, and has thus by anticipation made to-day, which precedes by so short a period that when thy treachery will so suddenly consign me to the grave, the day of my burial. Ἐνταφιασμός, embalmment and the usual preparations for burial. The word τετήρηκεν, *she has kept*, is full of subtle meaning. It is as though there had been on the part of Mary a long-formed plan, in accordance with that cold utilitarianism upon which the reproach of Judas was founded. —The meaning to which we are thus led perfectly suits that of the saying of Jesus in Mark: " *She is come beforehand to anoint my body to the burying.*"

Ver. 8 is wanting in D; hence, if this manuscript is alone correct, in opposition to all the other documents, it must have been imported by copyists from the Synoptists. But it is much more likely that this is one of the erroneous omissions so frequent in D. Its sense is: "If the poor are really the objects of your solicitude, you will at all times be able to exercise your liberality towards them; but my person will be soon removed from your zealous and tender care." The first proposition seems to contain an allusion to Deut. xv. 11.—The present ἔχετε, in the first proposition, results from πάντοτε, *always;* the second is introduced by the first.

Beyschlag justly observes on this passage: " It is asserted that the fourth evangelist delights in depreciating the twelve; but why then does he here set down all to the account of Judas only? It is also said that he entertained a special hatred for Judas; but it is forgotten that a writer of the second century could have had no reason for personally hating Judas.—The slight modifications introduced into the synoptic narrative by St. John are quite unmeaning from the *ideal* point of view, and can only be explained by his more exact knowledge of the fact, and by the more historical character of his delineation. We thus see how erroneous is that idea of *dependence*, with regard to the account of St. Mark, which Weizsäcker attributes to the fourth evangelist, because of the three hundred pence common to both narratives, and the coincidence of their expressions" (*Untersuch.* p. 290).

Vv. 9–11. "*Much people of the Jews therefore knew that He was there: and they came not for Jesus' sake only, but that they might see Lazarus also, whom He had raised from the dead. Now the chief priests consulted that they might put Lazarus also to death; because many of the Jews went away and believed on Jesus.*"—The pilgrims who came from Jericho with Jesus, had, on arriving at Jerusalem, spread the news of His approach. And those inhabitants of Judea, already spoken of in xi. 55, 56, who, many days before His arrival, had made Jesus the subject of their conversation, could not, when they learnt that He was staying in the neighbourhood, restrain their impatience to see Him, as well as Lazarus, the living monument of His power.—The term Jews here maintains the meaning which it bears throughout this Gospel, viz. the representatives of the ancient order of things. This was just the point which exasperated the rulers; the very people upon whom they had always depended to make head against those of Galilee, the inhabitants of Judea, and even of Jerusalem, were beginning to fall away.—Ὑπάγειν, *to retire,* but in a private manner, for some caution accompanied these visits to Bethany.—Thus was the solemn entry into Jerusalem prepared for. The people were quite disposed for an ovation, and Jesus had but to give the signal, and cease to restrain the enthusiasm of the multitude, and the hour of that royal manifestation, so long desired by His mother (ii. 4) and demanded by His brethren (vii. 14), would immediately strike.

II. *The Entry into Jerusalem.*—Vv. 12–19.

Till this day, Jesus had on every occasion laboured to repress all popular manifestations in His favour (vi. 15 ; Luke xiv. 25-33, xix. 11 sq., etc.). He now gave free course to the feelings of the multitude, and accepted the homage offered Him. What reason was there any longer for precautions? Ought He not, at least for once, to be acknowledged and saluted as the King of Israel? The hour of His death was at hand, hence that of His royal accession had arrived.

The tradition of the Christian church fixes our Lord's entry into Jerusalem on the Sunday preceding His passion. The most probable explanation of ver. 1 does not confirm this view, and it is more likely that it took place on the Monday. The evangelists do not point out the time of day at which it happened. But it seems to result from Mark xi. 11 : "*And Jesus entered into Jerusalem, and into the temple: and when He had looked round about upon all things, and now the eventide was come, He went out unto Bethany with the twelve,*" that it was during the second half of the day. This verse in fact means that, after having entered Jerusalem, Jesus did nothing of importance on that day, because it was already too late.

Vv. 12, 13. "*On the next day a great crowd of people that were come*[1] *to the feast, when they heard that Jesus was come to Jerusalem, took branches of palm trees and went forth to meet Him,*[2] *and cried,*[3] *Hosanna: Blessed is the King of*

---

[1] ℵ and ⅃ omit ο before ελθων.
[2] A K U Π, 50 Mnn. read απαντησιν instead of υπαντησιν (11 Mjj.). D C L X: συναντησιν.
[3] ℵ D L Q read εκραυγαζον instead of εκραζον. ℵ A D K Q X Π add λεγοντες.

Israel that cometh in the name of the Lord!"—The crowd spoken of in vv. 9–11 meant only *the Jews* of Jerusalem and its neighbourhood, whose defection had so alarmed the rulers. But that mentioned in ver. 12 contained great numbers of pilgrims, who had come from all parts to the feast, and who, hearing that Jesus was at Bethany, and about to come to Jerusalem, went out to meet and escort Him into the city. Some of them, as we have just seen, went as far as Bethany; others, who set out later, met Him on the road; hence, as He drew near, He was met by group after group of the rejoicing multitude. It is thus that St. John's account explains, completes, and gives preciseness to that of the Synoptists. The latter, not having mentioned His stay at Bethany, quite naturally represent Him as entering the city with the caravan of pilgrims who, like Himself, had arrived from Jericho. These latter certainly formed part of His escort, but St. John gives us to understand that it was composed also of many other persons,—viz., of numerous inhabitants of Judea, and all the pilgrims spoken of in xi. 55, 56, who had arrived long before our Lord.

This multitude seems to have been animated by a feeling of heavenly joy. Their aspirations and rejoicing were expressed by symbols and songs.—The palm was regarded in the East as the emblem of strength and beauty, and its branches as that of joy. In 1 Macc. xiii. 51, Simon returns to Jerusalem "*with thanksgiving and branches of palm trees, and with harps and cymbals, and with viols and hymns and songs, because there was destroyed a great enemy out of Israel.*" In Lev. xxiii. 40 it is said, in the institution of the feast of Tabernacles: "*You shall take . . . branches of palms . . . and ye shall rejoice before the Lord your God seven days.*" There was, on each day of this feast, a procession, in which palm branches were carried round the altar of burnt-offering. But on this occasion all was done spontaneously (comp. Rev. vii. 9).—The term βαίον alone, signifies *branches of palm*, but the complement τῶν φοινίκων was added by St. John for readers unacquainted with this technical term.

The cries of the multitude leave no doubt as to the meaning of this demonstration; it was, indeed, the Messiah whom the people welcomed and saluted in the person of Jesus.

The acclamations reported by St. John (ver. 13), and for which equivalents are given by the Synoptists, are taken from Ps. cxviii., especially vv. 25, 26. Numerous Rabbinic quotations prove this psalm to have been regarded as Messianic. Every Israelite knew these words by heart: they were sung at the feast of Tabernacles, in the procession made round the altar, and at the Passover, after the singing of the great Hallel (Ps. cxiii.–cxviii.) at the close of the repast. Hosanna (from הושיעה נא, *save, I beseech Thee*) is a prayer addressed to God by the theocratic people on behalf of its King Messiah; it is, if we may venture so to speak, the Israelite *God save the King*. It is more natural, as it seems to us, to refer the words *in the name of the Lord* to the verb *cometh*, than to the participle *blessed*. The expression, *that cometh in the name of the Lord*, designates, in a general and still a very vague manner, that Sent One from God upon whose person and work Israel implores the blessing of Heaven. After this comes the great word, whose meaning all can understand, the unequivocal title, *King of Israel*.—Of course, all in this crowd did not cry out in exactly the same manner, a fact which easily explains the differences in reporting the acclamations of the populace in the different evangelists.—As Jesus saw (vi. 5), in the arrival of the multitudes in the wilderness, the call of His Father to give a feast to His people, so does He now recognise the divine signal in the rush of these crowds to welcome Him with triumphant shouts. He perceives that, as the very psalm from which their songs were taken says: "*This is the day which the Lord hath made,*" and that it is a day on which to rejoice; and He responds to the salutations of the people by a truly Messianic sign.

Vv. 14, 15. "*Jesus having found a young ass, sat thereon; as it is written, Fear not, daughter*[1] *of Sion: behold, thy King cometh, sitting on an ass's colt.*"—The conduct of Jesus was necessitated by the nature of things. When once He consented to accept this homage, it was impossible for Him to continue any longer mingled with the crowd. On the other hand, He desired to appear upon the scene in the humblest manner, and in the form most appropriate to the

---

[1] T. R., with 8 Mjj. (א E G, etc.), reads θυγατηρ; 9 Mjj. (A B D, etc.): θυγατηρ.

essentially spiritual character of His royalty. In the East, the mule, as well as the horse, is regarded as a noble animal; the ass, on the contrary, is despised there, as it is here. Comp. Wisd. xxxiii. (xxxvi.) 25 (24). Hence the manner in which Jesus was mounted must not be compared with that of Solomon (1 Kings i. 38), when he made his regal entry into Jerusalem upon the mule of David his father. The prophet Zechariah has himself furnished a commentary on this symbol by saying (ix. 9): "*Behold, thy King cometh unto thee: just, and having salvation, and* LOWLY (Fr. *poor*)." But, at the same time that the ass represented the poverty of the Messiah, it also recalled the pacific nature of His reign: "*I will cut off the chariots of war; and this King shall speak peace to the nations*" (Zech. ix. 10). These two notions of peace and poverty easily combine, as do, on the other hand, those of riches and military power.—The expression εὑρών, *having found*, seems at the first glance incompatible with the synoptic account, that Jesus sent before Him two of His disciples with a special order to bring Him the ass. But εὑρών by no means signifies finding *without seeking;* witness the εὕρηκα of Archimedes! The word might be translated: *having procured;* nothing can be inferred from it as to *how* the finding was effected, and St. John might naturally intend to summarize in this brief expression the synoptic account which was already sufficiently known in the Church. He equally abridges the quotation from Zechariah, his sole concern here being to prove the general relation between the prophecy and its fulfilment. The expression *daughter of Sion* designates either the town of Zion itself personified, or the population of the town as protected by the royal hill. John substitutes *Fear not* for the *Rejoice* of the prophet; it is the same sentiment in a lower degree, such a king could not be a tyrant.—If Jesus had never entered Jerusalem in this fashion, this prophecy would equally have been fulfilled. His whole ministry in Israel was its accomplishment. But by *literally* realizing the image employed by the prophet, Jesus desired to render the true and spiritual fulfilment of the prophecy more evident. At the moment, however, the disciples did not so remember the prophecy as to grasp its reference to what was taking place before their eyes.

Ver. 16. "*Now the disciples understood not these things at the time: but after Jesus was glorified, then they remembered that these things were written of Him, and that they had done them to Him.*"—Hitherto, in fact, the disciples had not imagined that this prophecy was to be accomplished in so simple and natural a form. It was not till after the elevation of their Master to heaven that they understood all the greatness of the act that day performed. Hence there is no reason for banishing, as Reuss does, the natural meaning of ἐδοξάσθη, *was glorified*, and referring this term to the salutary effects of our Lord's sufferings.—What a charlatan is Baur's pseudo-John, amusing himself by throwing into his narrative this piece of information, for the sake of making himself appear to have been one of those disciples whom the ascension had enlightened!—Exception has been taken to the expression: *they had done these things to Him*, because, in the scene related by St. John, the apostles did nothing to Jesus. Several take ἐποίησαν in the indefinite sense in which it is used in ver. 2, and make the multitude its subject. But the subject of *they remembered* cannot be entirely different from that of *they had done*. If they are distinct, the first ought at least to be included in the second. What St. John means to say is just this, that the disciples afterwards perceived that they had *themselves* assisted in accomplishing a prophecy of which at the time they were not thinking. The co-operation of the disciples, hinted at in John, is described in detail in Luke xix. 29–36 and the parallel passages. We find here a fresh proof of the abridged character of the narrative, while its relation with that of the Synoptists is clearly brought out.—The words: *they had done these things unto Him*, show how mistaken is the notion of Keim, who affirms that the tendency of St. John's narrative is to represent Jesus and His disciples as passive during this scene, and that out of repugnance for the idea of the Jewish Messiah.

Vv. 17, 18. "*The multitude therefore that was with Him when*[1] *He called Lazarus out of his grave, and raised him from the dead, bare Him witness; and for this cause also*[2] *the multi-*

---

[1] Οτι (*when*) is the reading of ℵ A B G H M Q S U X Γ Δ Λ, 100 Mnn. and ς, while D E K L, It^{plerique} Syr. and T. R. read οτι (*that*).
[2] D E H Δ Λ omit και.

tude met Him, because they had heard that He had done this miracle."—St. John does not give us a complete picture of the triumphal entry, because his design in recording this fact is solely to show its relation, on the one hand with the raising of Lazarus (its cause), and on the other with the condemnation of Jesus (its effect); and it is this connection which he brings forward in vv. 17-19. If, with some important Mss. and the most ancient translations, we read (ver. 17) ὅτι, *that* (*bare Him witness that*), the meaning is, that the crowd, by accompanying Jesus, was celebrating among other miracles the raising of Lazarus, and it is thus unnecessary to suppose that the multitude of ver. 17 differed, as Lücke supposes, from that of ver. 18. It might be the same at two different moments, and the prodigy it was now celebrating by escorting Jesus (ver. 17) was the same which induced them to come and meet Him (ver. 18). But if, with the oldest Mjj., we read ὅτε, *when* (*that was with Him when He raised Lazarus*), the meaning is quite different. Then the multitude of ver. 17 comprises only the Jews who were in Bethany at the time of the raising of Lazarus, those said to have "believed" in xi. 45, and here pointed out as the true authors of the ovation now offered to our Lord. They were dispersed among the crowd, relating to all who would listen what they had themselves heard and seen. The circumstance which gives a preponderance in favour of this reading is the dramatic amplification: *when He called Lazarus out of his grave, and raised him from the dead*; for the former case, the mere mention of the fact would have sufficed. If we adopt the latter, the *therefore* of ver. 17 is connected with vv. 10 and 11, and the verb ἐμαρτύρει must be taken in an absolute sense: *bare Him witness.* Ver. 18 adds to ver. 17 the idea that not only was this miracle the chief subject of conversation among the crowd, but also that it induced the company of pilgrims, to whose knowledge it had come on their arrival at Jerusalem, to go and meet Jesus.—We find here a remarkable resemblance to the account of St. Luke: "*When He was come nigh, even now at the descent of the Mount of Olives, the whole multitude of the disciples began to rejoice and praise God with a loud voice for all the mighty works that they had seen.*" As usual, the synoptic narrative presents a vaguer picture, with more undecided features, while that of St. John gives sharper outlines.

Ver. 19. "*Whereupon the Pharisees said among themselves, You see that you prevail nothing; behold, the whole world is gone away after Him.*"—Vv. 17 and 18 brought out the influence exercised by the raising of Lazarus in the scene of the entry into Jerusalem; ver. 19 points out that of this scene upon the final catastrophe.—Πρὸς ἑαυτούς, instead of πρὸς ἀλλήλους, because, belonging to the same body, they were, as it were, speaking *to themselves*.—Ἴδε, *behold*, alludes to the unexpected spectacle they had just witnessed.—There is distress in the term ὁ κόσμος, *the world*: all these people, both natives and strangers; and in the Aorist ἀπῆλθεν, *is gone away*: it is an accomplished fact; we are alone!—Θεωρεῖτε may be taken either as a present indicative or an imperative. In either case, these Pharisees are, with a certain amount of bitterness, mutually reproaching each other with the uselessness of their half measures, and encouraging themselves to adopt without further delay the extreme measures advocated by Caiaphas. It is by these last words in particular that this passage is connected with the general design of this part of the Gospel.

"The more closely the narrative of St. John is studied, the more impossible is it to regard it as the accidental product of tradition or legend. Instead of that juxtaposition of anecdotes which characterizes the Synoptic Gospels, we find at every step traces of profound connection even in the very slightest details. With regard to this book, the dilemma, then, is: either it is a true history profoundly grasped and reproduced, or a romance powerfully conceived and very skilfully executed" (Baur).

III. *The Last Scene in the Temple.*—Vv. 20–36.

Among all the facts which took place between the solemn entry and the Thursday evening before our Lord's death, St. John has preserved but one, omitted by the Synoptists,—viz., the attempt of certain Greek proselytes to approach Him, and the discourse in which He expressed the feelings to which this unexpected circumstance gave rise.

If St. John so specially records this fact, it is by no means because it was his design to complete the synoptic narrative in this respect, but that, recognising in this memorable scene, on one side the close of our Lord's ministry, and on the other the prelude to the agonies of His passion, it hence formed an important link in his narrative. He does not tell us on what day this event took place. According to Mark (xi. 11), it could not have been on that of the triumphal entry. Besides, it ends with the decided rupture of Jesus with the people. Now we know that, during the days which succeeded the entry, Jesus dwelt in the temple, as in His palace, and exercised in it a kind of Messianic sovereignty. On the first of these days (Tuesday), He purged the temple from the presence of the sellers; on the next, He coped with the authorities, who demanded an explanation as to the source of the authority He assumed; and then successively with the Pharisees, Sadducees, and scribes, who approached Him with captious questions, putting to them in His turn, from Ps. cx., the great question concerning the divinity of the Messiah, which was to be the subject of His condemnation. In the evening, after pronouncing the malediction upon the rulers of the people, He retired to the Mount of Olives, where He unfurled before the eyes of His disciples the picture of the threefold judgment of the church, of Jerusalem, and of the human race. The words of ver. 36: "*These things spake Jesus, and departed, and did hide Himself from them,*" give us reason to think that the scene recounted by St. John also took place on the Wednesday evening, at the time when Jesus was leaving the temple to repair to Bethany (comp. the solemn farewell, Matt. xxiii. 37–39). In this case, Jesus would not have returned to Jerusalem on the Thursday morning at the time when the people were expecting Him in the temple, but have spent the whole of the day in retirement at Bethany (*He hid Himself from them*). If, however, this seems to make the Wednesday too full of events, it is possible, as the saying quoted by St. Matthew may have been pronounced in Galilee (Luke xiii. 34, 35), that Jesus returned for a few moments to Jerusalem on the Thursday morning, and that the scene related by St. John took place then. But in this case, the expression · *He hid Himself from them,* is not so well justified, assuming as it does a certain interval of voluntary absence.

Vv. 20–22. "*Now there were certain Greeks among them that came up to Jerusalem to worship at the feast, who came to Philip, who was of Bethsaida in Galilee, and desired him, saying, Sir, we would see Jesus. Philip cometh and telleth Andrew, and Andrew and Philip tell*[1] *Jesus.*"—These Greeks belonged to those numerous Gentiles who, like the Ethiopian eunuch (Acts viii.), had embraced the Jewish religion, and came to Jerusalem to keep its festivals. They must be carefully distinguished from those Jews, speaking the Greek language, who dwelt in heathen lands (ἑλληνισταί). The spacious court of the Gentiles was devoted to these proselytes, according to the words of Solomon (1 Kings viii. 41–43). If these strangers witnessed the entry of Jesus into Jerusalem, and were present at the expulsion of the sellers,—an act by which Jesus restored to its proper use the only part of the sanctuary open to them,—we can all the better appreciate their desire for nearer acquaintance with such a person. Assuredly they did not merely desire, like Zaccheus, to behold Jesus with their bodily eyes (Brückner); for such a purpose there was no need of Philip's intervention, since they might have seen Him as He passed through the court. Besides, the solemnity of our Lord's reply obliges us to attribute a more serious intention to this step. What they desired was to have a private conversation with Him on religious subjects. How do we know even whether, having witnessed the opposition He encountered from the rulers of His own nation, they did not desire to invite Him to turn to the Gentiles, who would better appreciate such a sage and teacher than these bigoted Jews? The ecclesiastical historian (Eusebius, i. 13) has preserved the memory of an embassy sent to Jesus by the king of Edessa, in Syria, to invite Him to take up His abode with him, and to promise Him such a royal welcome as should compensate Him for the obstinacy with which the Jews rejected Him. This fact is not without resemblance to that which now engages our attention, and in which we behold, in one of the first demonstrations of the heathen world in favour of the Gospel, the first indication of that attraction

---

[1] T. R., with 12 Mjj., reads, και παλιν Ανδριας και Φιλιππος λιγουσιν.—A B L reads, ερχεται Ανδρ. κ. Φιλ. και λιγουσιν.—א : και παλιν ερχεται Ανδρ. κ Φιλ. και λιγουσιν.—The Vss. also present several variations.

Son of man should be glorified."—Ἀπεκρίνατο is not absolutely synonymous with ἀπεκρίθη (see on ver. 19). This question rather gave rise to a meditation than to a direct reply on the part of Jesus.—The first words: *The hour is come*, contain the germ of the whole discourse which follows, and which is entirely devoted to disclosing the importance of the time then present. First, to Jesus Himself, it was the hour of His personal transformation, and of His return to the divine condition, by the painful passage of death. What had just taken place made him perceive that this was now imminent. " It is arbitrary here, as elsewhere, to apply the expression δοξασθῆναι, *to be glorified*, to the acknowledgment of Jesus as the Messiah, and to the extension of His kingdom among the Gentiles" (Lücke, Reuss). The last words of vv. 25, 26 show that Jesus was thinking first of all of the exaltation of *His Person* to heaven: His agency among the Gentiles would be only a consequence of this change (xvii. 1, 2, 5). The term: *Son of man*, is inspired by the feeling of His inseparable union with human nature, which is to be raised in Him, its representative, to the possession of the divine condition. It is then that He will be able to communicate without impediment with the Greeks and the whole world. At ver. 24 Jesus expresses by a figure, and at ver. 25 in plain terms, the painful condition upon which this glorification depends:

Ver. 24. *" Verily, verily, I say unto you, Except a corn of wheat fall into the earth and die, it abideth alone: but if it die, it bringeth forth much fruit."*—Jesus states what must happen to Him before He can respond to those needs of which the first symptoms have just been manifested. As long as a grain of wheat remains in the granary, it is indeed in safety, but is without the power of reproduction; as soon as it is cast into the earth, its coverings decompose, and it perishes as a grain, but only to be born again in a multitude of grains like itself. This figure was perhaps the more apt, inasmuch as the grain of wheat played a considerable part in the Greek mysteries. —The strong affirmation, *Amen, Amen*, refers to the contrast which Jesus knew to exist between this painful necessity and the glory of which His disciples dreamed.

Ver. 25. Application of the figure: *" He that loveth his life loseth it;*[1] *and he that hateth his life in this world shall keep it in life eternal.*"—From the connection of ver. 23 with ver. 24, and of ver. 24 with ver. 25, there can be no doubt that Jesus applied this sentence to Himself. He thereby declared Himself to be subjected to that fundamental law of human life which He had so frequently applied to His disciples (Matt. x. 39, xvi. 25; Mark viii. 35; Luke ix. 24, xvii. 33). By the expression *his life*, ψυχή, Jesus meant the breath of natural life, and all the faculties with which it is endowed. This physical and psychical life was good, inasmuch as it was the starting-point of human existence, and Jesus Himself possessed it. But it was not destined to maintain and perpetuate itself as such; it was to be transformed by a divine force into a better life, a life spiritual and eternal; and to reach this it must be given, sacrificed, immolated, renounced. Otherwise, after having flourished for a moment with more or less of satisfaction, it perishes and withers for ever. This law applies also to a pure being, and to his lawful tastes. All that is not given to God by an act of voluntary immolation bears within it the germ of death. Hence, suppose that Jesus, seeking only His personal safety, had now gone to the Greeks to play among them the part of a sage, or to organize the state like another Solon, He might indeed thus have *saved* His life, but would in reality have *lost* it. Not having given it up to God, He could not have received it from Him glorified (ver. 23). Thus kept by Him, it would have remained doomed to sterility and earthly frailty. It was by renouncing the part of a sage that He became a Christ, by renouncing the throne of a Solomon that He obtained that of God. Lange, with much depth of perception, points out that this saying included the judgment of Hellenism. For what was Greek civilization but human life cultivated from the view-point of enjoyment, and withdrawn from the law of sacrifice?—It is more probable that the present *loseth* (ἀπολλύει) was replaced by the future *shall lose* (ἀπολέσει) than the reverse. This substitution would take place under the influence of the following proposition. The expression *loses it* goes beyond that of ver. 24: *abideth alone.*—The term

---

[1] ℵ B L: απολλυει (*loses* it) instead of απολεσει (*shall lose* it), which is the reading of T. R. with the other Mjj.

μισεῖν, *to hate*, here includes the idea of a generous contempt, and well characterizes the noble ambition which aims higher than this world. The expression: *in life eternal*, opposed as it here is to: *in this world*, refers not only to the superior nature of this life, but also to the future epoch in which it shall be perfectly developed.—This moral axiom, by which the Master's life is ruled, applies also to that of the disciple:

Ver. 26. "*If any man serve me, let him follow me; and where I am, there also shall my servant be: if*[1] *any man serve me, him will my Father honour.*"—*Follow,* i.e. in the way of sacrifice, which is also that of glorious transfiguration. The expression: *where I am*, is a present of anticipation, referring to the Lord's state of heavenly glory, as the promise: *there also shall my servant be,* does to the faithful disciple's participation in that state (xviii. 24).—Τιμήσει, *will honour*, recalls the *should be glorified*, δοξασθῇ, of ver. 23 with respect to Jesus. The Father will as certainly honour the faithful servant as He has glorified the Master. This is in both cases truly to *keep* the life which they give. Perhaps Andrew and Philip had felt some carnal satisfaction at the sight of these strangers thus ready to do homage to Jesus. But He, who was so constantly accustomed to repress in His own case even the lawful aspirations of natural life, silenced them with a word in that of His disciples. He thus revealed to them, as Luthardt observes, the condition by which alone they could extend His kingdom among all nations, and that condition was their own death. But having thus announced the law which obliged them to die, He immediately felt in His whole being the reaction of this formidable thought.

Vv. 27, 28. "*Now is my soul troubled; and what shall I say? Father, save me from this hour: but for this cause came I to this hour. Father, glorify Thy name.*"—The *soul*, ψυχή, is the seat of the natural, as *the spirit*, πνεῦμα, is that of the religious emotions (see on xi. 33). Jesus here used the first of these terms, because it was the prospect of His personal sorrows which at this moment moved Him.—The perf. τετάρακται, *is troubled,* indicates the *condition* into which the Lord found Himself plunged. This inward trouble revealed itself to Him especially by the unusual hesitation which He ex-

[1] ℵ Γ D L X, It. Syr. omit καὶ before ἐάν τις.

perienced when about to pour out His feelings in prayer. Generally, He had a distinct view as to what He should ask of the Father; now this certainty was absent. Like the believer in the state described by St. Paul in Rom. viii. 26, He knew not what to pray for, and asks Himself: *What shall I say?* This question was, properly speaking, addressed neither to man nor to God, but to Himself. For His sacrifice was a voluntary one; He might yet, if He thought good, ask God to release Him from it. And the Father would now, as ever, have heard Him, even if He had had to send *twelve legions of angels*. But would not the prayer which rescued Him ruin the world? Jesus did not feel Himself at liberty to pray thus. He had advanced too far on the road to the cross to stop so near the end. Renouncing, then, the cry of nature, He gave utterance to the voice of the Spirit: *Father, glorify Thy name.* This was His real prayer, the definite request in which His filial heart entirely poured itself forth, and which restored His serenity: "Do with me what Thou wilt, provided Thou art glorified thereby!" The word *now* characterized His present anguish as an anticipation of that which awaited Him in presence of the cross, *now already*, though the hour is still distant.—After the question: *What shall I say?* there is nothing strange in the interrogative turn which we have given to the prayer: "Father, save me from this hour." This was the prayer to which nature prompted Him; He expressed it hypothetically, to teach His disciples to silence, in every similar position (ver. 26), the voice of the flesh, and always to let that of the spirit prevail before God. Lücke, Meyer, and Hengstenberg regard these words as a positive prayer: "Deliver me from the necessity of dying." But then how should we understand the next sentence, which would in this case be an immediate withdrawal of this request? So abrupt a transition of feeling is impossible. The prayer at Gethsemane is appealed to, but there Jesus began by saying: *if it be possible*, and also expressly designated the contrast between the two cries by the word πλήν, *nevertheless*, while here the contrast would be absolute and left unexplained. Luthardt feels this, and proposes to understand σῶσον, *save me*, not in the sense of: "Save me from death," but in that of: "Bring me victoriously through it." This expedient is, however, excluded by the adversative particle ἀλλά, *but*, which follows. For there is no opposition between: "to have come to this hour," and: "to go victoriously through it."—Thus, whatever turn we give to this phrase, we cannot help seeing in it a hypothetical prayer; it was the cry of nature, if Jesus had suffered nature to speak. In the words which follow He expresses, first, what really hindered Him from addressing such a request to God—it would be the negation of all that He had as yet done and suffered;—then the prayer in which His heart definitely found repose, the cry of the spirit which alone remained when once the moment of trouble had passed: *glorify Thy name*. Nothing can be more instructive than the sight of this contrast between the two factors which claimed the empire over His will. The struggle is like one of those fissures in its crust which enables science to fathom the bowels of the earth. It lets us read the very inmost depths of the Lord's being. And what do we discover? Just the reverse of that impassive Jesus attributed by criticism to St. John.

The expressions: *for this cause* and *to this hour*, seem to constitute a pleonasm. This proposition might be taken as a question: "Is it then for this cause that I am come to this hour?"—that is to say, to seek to defer it indefinitely; or the words *for this hour* might be made an explanatory apposition to *for this cause:* "It is for this cause that I came (here below)" —that is to say, for this hour. Both these meanings are forced—the first, because of the interrogations which precede; the second, because εἰς is not a natural iteration of διά, but rather the direct regimen of ἦλθον, in opposition to σῶσον ἐκ. Hengstenberg explains: "It is that my soul might be troubled that I came to this hour," which is still more forced. Lücke and Meyer refer the words *for this cause* to the idea of the prayer which follows: for the glorification of the Father's name. But this is doing violence beyond measure to the phrase; while it seems quite natural to understand the neuter τοῦτο, *this*, as a slightly mysterious expression of the *something* which had just plunged His soul into so much trouble, the gloomy and unspeakable events of the hour which was drawing near, and which He felt tempted to remove by prayer. It is because of (διά) this death which I am to undergo (τοῦτο) that

I have held on to this hour. What He had done and borne with a view to the cross would not suffer Him to relax at the moment when the hour of this terrible punishment was at length about to strike (comp. iii. 14).

M. Colani, in his criticism of Renan's *Vie de Jésus*, by a strange inadvertence puts into the mouth of our Lord the words : "Father, glorify *my* name," an expression which he says is unmeaning, except from the view-point of the doctrine of the Logos.[1] Nothing is better calculated to show the difference which exists between the profoundly human Jesus of St. John and the fantastic and metaphysical Christ imputed by criticism to this evangelist than this writer's involuntary alteration of the text of this prayer. If, after this, M. Colani can see in this sublime scene only "an emblematic and almost simulated agony," whose is the fault ?

The most admirable feature in this passage is the perfectly human character of the struggle between nature and spirit in the heart of Jesus; the next is the sincerity and candour with which He expressed His inmost feelings, *His weakness* (Heb. v. 2), before all the people, without fearing to let them witness His distress at the prospect of His approaching sufferings.— This scene was, as is generally acknowledged, the prelude to that of Gethsemane. The only difference is, that in the latter Jesus at the climax of His anguish really utters the cry: "Save me from this hour!" which He here hesitates to pronounce. This slight shade of distinction, so suitable to the difference of the two situations, proves the strictly historical character of both. As to the view that St. John omitted from his Gospel the scene in Gethsemane as incompatible with the divine character of the Logos, it falls of itself before the passage we are studying.

Lastly, how admirable is the gradation between Luke xii. 49, 50, John xii. 27, and the scene in Gethsemane !—a gradation which so naturally depicts the increasing emotion with which Jesus slowly drew near to the cross.

Renan observes on this passage: "Here are verses which exhibit an unmistakeable historical stamp. They give the obscure and isolated episode of the Greeks who applied to Philip. Notice the part played by this apostle; this Gospel is the only one which knows anything of it."

[1] *Revue de Théologie*, third series, vol. i. p. 382.

Vv. 28b, 29. "*Then came there a voice from heaven: I have both glorified it, and will glorify it again. The people then, that stood by and*[1] *heard, said that it thundered: others said, An angel spake to Him.*"—Each time that the Son performed a great act of personal consecration, the Father answered by a sensible manifestation of approval. What had happened at the baptism and at the transfiguration was renewed. Now—when the ministry of Jesus was ending, and He was devoting Himself to death—or never was the time for the Father to affix publicly to His work and person the seal of His satisfaction.

Lücke, de Wette, and even Hengstenberg, view this voice from heaven as a mere clap of thunder, to which Jesus, by reason of the coincidence of this natural phenomenon with His prayer, gave a free interpretation in the sense pointed out by the evangelist. The Rabbis gave to prophetic voices and mysterious inspirations, sometimes arising in the heart on the occasion of a word accidentally heard, the name of בת קול, *daughter of the voice.* But this name dates from an antecedent era, and is applied only to the human voice. Besides, according to St. John, this was not a stroke of thunder interpreted by Jesus as a voice from heaven, but, on the contrary, a voice from heaven taken by some of the bystanders for a clap of thunder. And, finally, can it be supposed that St. John—nay, that Jesus Himself (comp. vv. 31 and 32)—would transform a purely material sound into a positive divine saying? Some even among the crowd discerned articulate language in this sound, and the text will not suffer us to regard this phenomenon as other than supernatural.—The past, *I have glorified*, refers to the Lord's ministry in Israel, now drawing to its close; the future, *I will glorify*, to the approaching agency of Jesus upon the whole world, when from the midst of His glory He would be a light to lighten the Gentiles. Between these two great works which the Father effects by the Son, lies that hour of suffering and death which is the necessary transition from the one to the other. He would not then draw back from this hour.—And was it not well accompanied? "Before it ... the name of God glorified in Israel; after it ... the name of God glorified in the whole world;" this was indeed the most consoling answer to the filial heart

---

[1] ℵ D Cop. omit καὶ before ἀκούσας.

of Jesus (xvii. 1, 2, 4, 5).—The two καί, *both* . . . *and*, bring out the close relation between the work done and the work to be done: "I who have effected the one, shall be able also to accomplish the other."

The whole multitude heard a noise; but the meaning of the voice was only perceived by each in proportion to his spiritual intelligence. Thus, the wild beast perceives only a *sound* in the human voice; the trained animal discovers a *meaning*, a command, for example, which it immediately obeys; man alone discerns therein a *thought*.—Ὄχλος: "the greater number;" ἄλλοι: others, "in smaller number" (comp. Acts ix. 7 with xxii. 9, xxvi. 13, 14).—The perf. λελάληκεν, instead of the Aorist, signifies that in their eyes Jesus was from henceforth an individual *in possession* of a celestial message.

Vv. 30–32. "*Jesus answered and said, This voice*[1] *came not because of me, but for your sakes. Now is the judgment of this world: now shall the prince of this world*[2] *be cast out. And I, when I have been lifted up from the earth, will draw all*[3] *men unto me.*"—These words are the development of the promise just made by God, to glorify His name by Jesus in the future as He has glorified it in the past.—When Jesus said this voice was not heard for His sake, He does not mean that He had no need of being strengthened, but that He had no need of being so by a sensible manifestation. What the step of the Greeks had been to Him in making Him feel the gravity of the present hour to Himself, this heavenly manifestation was to be to them, by revealing to them the gravity of the present crisis to themselves, first with respect to the world in general (vv. 31, 32), and then more particularly with respect to Israel (vv. 35, 36).—As to the world, this hour was one of deepest revolution. It was the signal, first, of its judgment (ver. 31*a*), then of the expulsion of its ancient master (ver. 31*b*), and, lastly, of the accession of its new Sovereign (ver. 32). The word νῦν, *now*, at the beginning

---

[1] T. R. with 11 Mjj. (E F G, etc.): αυτη η φωνη, instead of η φω:η αυτη, in 7 Mjj. (א A B, etc.).

[2] א omits the words νυν ο αρχων τ. κ. τουτου, and replaces them by και (confusing the two του κοσμου τουτου).

[2] Instead of παντας, א D, It. Vg. read παντα (*each man* or *all things*).

of the first two propositions, expressly brings out the decisive nature of the present moment with respect to the human race.

To judge is to verify the moral condition. The judgment of the world is based upon the cross, inasmuch as this discloses, as completely as possible, the moral condition of man in his natural state. Man, by raising this throne for Jesus, judged himself, and manifested that rebellion and enmity against God which is in the depths of his heart. Having erected it, he judges himself still more decidedly by his relation thereto; for either by faith he finds therein his salvation, or by unbelief his condemnation. And of this choice, the final judgment would be only the ratification. Thus the judgment of the world dates from Good Friday. Its first external manifestation was the destruction of Jerusalem; its second will be the judgment of the church; its third, the last judgment. Comp. the discourses in Matt. xxiv. and xxv., delivered on the very evening of the day on which Jesus uttered the words with which we are engaged.

But, while the crime of the cross disclosed the moral condition of the world, it also filled up the measure of tolerance granted to the perversity of its prince. The crucifixion of the Son of God was the most odious and most unpardonable transgression of Satan; this crime put an end to the long-suffering of God towards him, and consequently to his dominion over mankind. The Rabbis habitually designate Satan *the prince of the world*, but place the Jews outside his kingdom, while Jesus includes them as well as the heathen therein (ch. viii.). *Out* signifies not only out of his office and power, but chiefly out of the world, his ancient realm, as is shown by the connection of these words with those which precede them, and the opposition between vv. 31 and 32 (ἐκ τῆς γῆς).

The overthrow of the throne of the former monarch coincides with the accession of the new Sovereign. Jesus declares Himself appointed to fill this part: κἀγώ, *and I*. But, strange to say, while substituting His power for that of Satan, it is not upon this earth, whence Satan is cast out, that He will establish His kingdom. He will not become, as the Jews expected, the successor of His adversary, and consequently another prince of this world; He as well as His rival will leave the earth; He will be raised from it, and above it, and it will be in a higher sphere that He will draw to Himself His subjects and realize His kingdom. However little familiar we may be with the language of Jesus, it is easy to perceive that the expression *to be lifted up* must be understood here in the same amphibological sense as at iii. 14 and viii. 28. His lifting up upon the cross, that throne of love on which the eyes of believers throughout the whole world are fixed, appears to Him as the gloriously ironical emblem of His elevation to the throne of glory. And this comparison is based upon a deep truth. For was it not the cross which created the abyss between Christ and the world (Gal. vi. 14), and rendered the purely heavenly form of the kingdom of God for the present necessary? The earth, after being moistened with the blood of the Son of God, could not be glorified till it had passed through destruction and renewal. Meyer alleges against the double sense of the term *to be lifted up*, the regimen ἐκ τῆς γῆς, *from the earth*, as proving that Jesus was thinking not of His death, but of His ascension. It is very evident that the expression *from the earth* does not refer only to the small distance between the ground and the feet of the crucified. *From* or *out of the earth*, designates an ignominious expulsion from earthly existence by *any* capital punishment. It is the word *to be lifted up*, which contains an allusion to the particular punishment of the cross. But who can fail to feel that the expression *out of the earth* would be out of place if referred only to the ascension? The natural regimen in this case would have been: *to heaven*.

The cross and the ascension united freed Jesus from all earthly ties and national obligations, and placed Him in a position to extend His agency to the whole world, to become the *Lord of all* (Rom. x. 12). "*I will draw all to Me;*" *all*, not Jews only, but all men, especially the Greeks. It is this word *all* and this future *will draw* which evidently contain an answer to the request that elicited this discourse. The hour for the call of the Greeks was undoubtedly at hand, but another hour must strike first!—Many restrict the *all* to the elect; others understand it in the sense of: "men of all nations." Meyer, on the contrary, seems to find in it the notion of final universal salvation. But ἑλκύειν, *to draw*, does not necessarily imply effectual drawing. The word may relate solely to the preaching of the cross in the whole world, and to the agency of the Holy Spirit which accompanies it. This heavenly drawing is not irresistible.—The last word, *to me*, brings out the personal situation of Jesus as the supraterrestrial centre of the Divine kingdom. Once raised to heaven, Jesus will draw around Him a new people, strangers to earth, and like Himself of heavenly nature, His spiritual body. He will Himself be both the author and the end of this divine attraction.

These two verses sum up the whole history of the Church, whether from the negative and polemic point of view, the destruction of Satan, or from the positive, the gradual establishment of the kingdom of God.

Ver. 33. "*Now this He said, signifying what death He would die.*"—This explanation of St. John is declared incorrect by many modern interpreters (Meyer, Reuss, etc.); for, in their opinion, the preceding saying refers not to the cross, but to the ascension. But the apostle does not say δηλῶν, *declaring*, but uses the term σημαίνειν, which signifies *indicating, giving to understand;* and we have just seen that, by giving His thought this form, Jesus really indicated the kind of death He was about to die. Hence St. John's remark attributes nothing to Jesus which was not really in His mind.

This passage, in which our Lord, after shuddering at the view of His cross, encouraged Himself by portraying in broad outlines the immense revolution it would effect, may be compared to the passage of St. Paul, Col. ii. 14, 15, in which that apostle represents Jesus as making a show of the infernal powers, despoiling them of their power and triumphing over them *upon the cross.* Comp. also the passage, 2 Cor. v. 14–17, according to which the death of Christ is the virtual principle of life for the whole human race, and the means of universal renewal: "*It is a new creation: old things are passed away; behold, all things are become new.*"

Ver. 34. "*The people answered Him,*[1] *We have heard out of the law that Christ abideth for ever: and how sayest thou, The*

---

[1] ℵ B L X add ουν to απεκριθη.

Son of man must be lifted up? who is this Son of man?"—According to the Jewish programme, the Messianic kingdom was simply a glorified earth, and the Messiah the perpetual Sovereign of this new Eden. And now Jesus—who, as the triumphal entry proved, aspired to Messianic dignity—was transporting the kingdom, together with His own person, to another sphere! This was to the multitude a contradiction not to be solved. "How sayest *Thou?*" *Σύ, Thou,* is here opposed to the law and those who explained it.—The passages to which the Jews allude are those in which the Messiah is represented as founding an everlasting empire upon the ruins of the Gentile kingdoms (Isa. ix. 6; Ps. cx. 2–4; Dan. vii. 14, etc.).—On the term *the law,* see vol. ii. p. 409.—To solve this difficulty, the objectors themselves put forth a supposition. Jesus was accustomed to call Himself the Son of man; could this name, in His mouth, designate some other individual than the Christ? This supposition has some resemblance to that which John the Baptist seems to have entertained in prison (see vol. ii. p. 168). The Jews, then, in asking: " Who is this Son of man ?" do not mean to say: "Is it thyself, or some one else?" (comp. ver. 23), but: "What is the *part* to be played by this individual, thus differing from the Messiah, in the final drama?" Comp. the "*Who art thou?*" of i. 19. Meyer understands, "What strange Messiah is this who is to depart?" But in this sense we should have had, not: "Who is this Son of man?" but: "What kind of Christ is this?"—This answer of the people proves that the title " Son of man " was not used in Israel to designate the Messiah, and that it must be regarded as originating with Jesus Himself (vol. ii. p. 180). On this point we agree with M. Colani.[1]

Vv. 35, 36. "*Then Jesus said unto them, Yet a little while is the light with you.*[2] *Walk while*[3] *ye have the light, lest darkness*

---

[1] *Jésus-Christ et les croyances messianiques de son temps,* p. 75 sqq. But how can this author say : "We must go back at least four months (viii. 28) to find this title of ' Son of man' in the mouth of Jesus"? He forgets ver. 23, which immediately precedes.

[2] T. R., with A E F G H S V Δ Λ, Mnn. and Syr., reads : μεθ᾽ υμων ; א B D K L M X Π, 20 Mnn. It. Vg. Cop. : εν υμιν.

[3] A B D K L X Π, 4 Mnn. have ως instead of εως, which is the reading of T. R. with 11 Mjj.

come upon you: for he that walketh in darkness knoweth not whither he goeth. While[1] *ye have the light, believe in the light, that ye may be the children of light. These things spake Jesus, and departed, and did hide Himself from them."*—It was no longer the time for instruction and discussion. Hence Jesus did not give a direct answer, but addressed a last appeal to their Israelite consciousness, and made them feel the seriousness of the present hour to themselves and the whole nation. This is the reason why St. John says εἶπεν, *He said, He declared*, instead of ἀπεκρίθη, *He answered*. The last hour of the day of salvation had arrived, the sun was about to set for Israel. Let each hasten to believe; for, once deprived of Jesus, the heavenly revealer, the nation would be like a traveller lost at night and wandering aimlessly. We have seen that vv. 31 and 32 contained the history of the church, this (ver. 35) sums up that of Israel after the time when Jesus spake. The preaching of the apostles was, it is true, yet granted to this people; but, when once launched upon the declivity of unbelief, how could they as a nation change their direction? And this last favour, the apostolic preaching, after having been welcomed by individuals only, was soon withdrawn from the nation. Since then, Israel has wandered in the wilderness of this world, like a caravan without a goal and without a guide. —Περιπατεῖν, *to walk*, to advance towards an end; and that by believing.—Of the two readings, ἕως, *while*, and ὡς, *as*, Meyer and Luthardt prefer the latter as the best supported: " Walk *according* as the light still enlightens you." Büumlein justly declares this meaning forced. We must then either give, as he does, the meaning of *while* to ὡς (according to Soph. *Ajax* 1117, and *Phil.* 635, 1330), or, as these examples are uncertain, prefer the reading ἕως, which is supported at ver. 35 by the *Sinaiticus*. The initial ε of ἕως may have been confused with the final ε of περιπατεῖτε. The notion of *while* naturally combines with that of: *a little while*, which prevails throughout this passage. The same may be said of ver. 36.—An equal solemnity pervades the statements both of ver. 35 and ver. 36, but in the first a tone of compassion, in the second a tone of affection, is in the ascendant. The last saying of the Saviour to His people was to be an invita-

---

[1] ℵ A B D L Π: ὡς instead of ἕως.

tion, not a threat: "While you still possess in me the living revelation of salvation (φῶς), acknowledge it, believe in me, and become (γένησθε) by me, the Light, *children of light.*" The man united to Christ is so saturated with light that he himself becomes luminous.

Such was the farewell of Jesus to Israel. The words: *These things said Jesus,* in this context, signify: "Jesus gave them no other answer." He then retired, and did not reappear on the morrow. This time it was no mere cloud which obscured the sun, but the sun itself had set.

THIRD SECTION.

XII. 37–50.—A RETROSPECTIVE SURVEY OF THE MYSTERIOUS FACT OF JEWISH UNBELIEF.

This passage, which closes the second part of St. John's Gospel, is regarded by many expositors as a summary of the history of our Lord's *public ministry.* Chs. v.–xii. are viewed as depicting His public, and chs. xiii.–xvii. His *private, agency.* But this mode of regarding them is superficial; for there is between these two parts a far deeper contrast, that of unbelief and faith—of unbelief on the part of the people, of faith on that of the disciples. Is it not very easy to see that the real object of the epilogue, which is about to claim our attention, is the fact of Jewish unbelief, and by no means our Lord's public ministry in general? It is the unexpected failure of the work of Messiah in Israel which engrosses the attention of the evangelist, and becomes for the time the object of his contemplation. In the first passage, vv. 37–43, he explains the *causes* of the fact whose history he has just recorded; in the second, vv. 44–50, he describes its seriousness and announces its *eternal consequences.*

I. *The Causes of Jewish Unbelief.*—Vv. 37–43.

If the Jews were the chosen people, destined by God to receive the Messiah, and to convey the knowledge of salvation to other nations, did it not follow from their unbelief in

Jesus Christ, that this individual was not really the Messiah ? Or, if not, how was this great paradox of history to be explained ? Chs. ix.–xi. of the Epistle to the Romans are devoted to the solution of this problem, which was in fact to be the great apologetic question of the Apostolic Age. This explains the fact that this passage of St. John contains so many thoughts which also form the basis of St. Paul's dissertation.

Vv. 37, 38. *" But though He had done so many miracles before them, yet they believed not on Him: that the saying of Esaias the prophet might be fulfilled, which he spake, Lord, who hath believed our preaching? and to whom hath the arm of the Lord been revealed?"*—However unreasonable might be the fact with which St. John was about to be occupied, it was nevertheless inevitable, for it was *predicted*, and prophecy must be fulfilled.—How many motives had not the Jews for believing in the appearance of Jesus, and especially in His miracles! There was then, as it were, some fatality in such blindness. Τοσαῦτα, *so many*, in our Gospels, is always applied to numbers and not to greatness (vi. 9, xxi. 11). This saying assumes that Jesus had done a far greater number of miracles than the six related in this book. Comp. also vii. 3, xx. 30. Hence St. John did not intend to relate all he knew.—The term σημεῖα, *signs*, recalls the striking nature, and the words ἔμπροσθεν αὐτῶν, *before them*, the entire publicity, of these works.—The imperf., *they believed not*, brings out the duration, the obstinate persistence of Israelite unbelief.

An impartial exegesis would not weaken the sense of ἵνα, *in order that*, by making this word synonymous with ὥστε, *so that*.—The passage quoted by John is Isa. liii. 1. The prophet, when describing the humiliation and sufferings of the Messiah, declares that this message, so out of harmony with their carnal desires, will not be favourably received by the people. Now, if the announcement of a suffering Messiah was rejected by them, how much more this Messiah Himself! It is on this *a fortiori* that the application made of this text by the evangelist to his contemporaries is based. The question: *Who hath believed?* shows that there would undoubtedly be believers, but in numbers so small that they might be counted.—According to Hengstenberg, the expression ἀκοή, *our hearing,* for *the thing which we hear,* signifies: "what *we* (prophets) *have heard* from the mouth of Jehovah." A more natural explanation is: "what *you* (men) *hear* from the mouth of us, the prophets." "It is then by no means the people who are supposed to ask this question" (Hofmann, Delitzsch, Luthardt). Otherwise, we should have to suppose that they did so after turning from their unbelief, which is forced. It is Isaiah, as representing the other prophets, who puts this question.—The first term: *what we preach,* is here applied by the evangelist to the teaching of Jesus; that which follows: *the arm of the Lord,* refers to His miracles, those acts of divine power which He performed in Israel.

But Jewish unbelief was not merely *predicted;* it was *willed* by God, who Himself co-operated therein.

Vv. 39, 40. "*Therefore they could not believe, because that Esaias said again, He hath blinded their eyes and hardened*[1] *their hearts; that they should not see with their eyes, nor understand*[2] *with their hearts, and be converted,*[3] *and I should heal*[4] *them.*"—The omnipotence of God was itself exerted to realize what His omniscience had predicted, and to cause Israel to commit the impossible. The gradation between ver. 37 and ver. 39 is as follows: *They did not believe* (ver. 37), *and they even could not believe* (ver. 39). The word πάλιν (*again*) shows that we have here a second idea which serves to explain and complete the first. The same logical relation also exists between the two prophecies cited by St. John. The διὰ τοῦτο, *on account of this,* bears, as it generally does in John (v. 18, x. 17), upon the following ὅτι, *because:* "And *this is why* they could not believe; *it is because* Esaias had in another passage (πάλιν) said . . ." The words are taken from Isa. vi. 9, 10, but are not exactly quoted either from the Hebrew or the LXX. According to the former, it is Isaiah who, at the command of God, is to blind the eyes and harden the heart of the people by His ill-received prophesying: "*Harden the heart of this people.*" In the latter, this

---

[1] The Byz. (Γ Δ, etc.) read πεπωρωκεν; the Alex. (A B K L X): επωρωσεν; א Π: επηρωσεν.

[2] K Π, and Chrys. have συνωσιν instead of νοησωσιν.

[3] א B D: στραφωσιν instead of επιστραφωσιν, which is the reading of T. R. with 10 Mjj.; 5 Mjj. (K L, etc.) have επιστριψωσιν.

[4] All the Mjj. except L Γ read ιασομαι instead of ιασωμαι.

hardening is mentioned merely as a fact which is laid to the charge of Israel: "*The heart of this people is hardened.*" The text of John agrees in meaning with that of the prophet, for the omitted subject of the two verbs, *He has blinded, He has hardened*, can be none other than God. The command intimated in Isaiah is represented in John as an accomplished fact. The passage proves that St. John was not dependent upon the Greek translation, and was acquainted with the Hebrew text (vol. i. p. 253).—Τυφλοῦν, *to blind*, signifies to deprive of intellectual light, of a sense for the true and even the expedient; πωροῦν, *to harden the skin*, the want of moral sensibility, of a sense for the good. Unbelief necessarily results from the inactivity of these two organs: the people may witness miracle upon miracle, hear testimony after testimony, but they will not recognise the Messiah. Ἰάσομαι, *I will heal*, the reading of almost all the Mjj., may signify: "and I will end by bringing them back to myself by means of this very hardening." But the καί, *and* . . . *and* . . ., are too closely connected to admit of such a contrast between the last verb and those which precede. The influence of the formidable ἵνα μή, *so that . . . not*, evidently extends to the end of the sentence. If we object to the indicative ἰάσομαι (depending on ἵνα, which is not in itself impossible), we may find in these last words an indication of the result which would have followed in the opposite case, but which is not to be: "lest they should be converted . . . and I will heal them," for: "in which case I would heal them."

If such, then, is the meaning of the words both of the prophet and evangelist, how is it to be justified? Such declarations would be inexplicable and profoundly revolting if Israel had, at the time when God thus addressed and treated this nation, been in its normal condition, and regarded by God as *His* people. But such was not the case; God, when sending Isaiah, said to him, "*Go and say to* THIS *people*" (Isa. vi. 9). And we feel that a father, when speaking of his son as *this* or *that* child instead of *my* child, means that the paternal and filial relation no longer exists. This is the point of view which we must occupy to understand the divine dealings, which here enter into the category of *chastisements*. The creature who has wilfully abused previous Divine favours, incurs the most terrible of punishments. It is degraded from the rank of *end* to that of *means;* from being person, it becomes matter. In fact, though man can refuse freely to glorify God by his obedience and salvation, he cannot hinder God from glorifying Himself by an exemplary punishment, which shall publicly show forth the hateful character of his sin. "God," says Hengstenberg, "has so constituted man, that, when he does not resist the first beginnings of sin, he loses the right of disposing of Himself, and must obey to the end the power to which he has surrendered himself." And God not only *permits* this development of evil, but *wills* it and *concurs* in it. But how, it will be said, is the holiness of God, thus understood, to be reconciled with His love? This it is which St. Paul explains to the Jews by an example in Rom. ix. 17: Pharaoh refused to hearken to God, and to be saved. He had a right to do so. But from that moment he was forced to subserve the salvation of others. For this purpose, God paralyzed within him both the sense of the true and the sense of the good; He rendered him deaf to the appeals of conscience, and even to the calculations of interest rightly understood; He gave him up to the suggestions of his insane pride, that the world might learn, by the example of the ruin into which he plunged himself, what are the consequences of wickedly resisting the first calls of God. Thus he, at least, contributed to the salvation of the world. The history of Pharaoh is exactly reproduced in that of the Jews. As early as the days of Isaiah, the mass of the people were so carnally minded that the prophet foresaw their unbelief in the Messiah, the man of sorrows, as an inevitable moral fact (Isa. liii.). Could such an Israel, without a change of heart, recognise the Messiah, and become the nucleus of the Messianic church? Certainly not; for that purely intellectual adherence, of which we see examples during the ministry of Jesus, not only would not have saved Israel itself, but would have fettered the Divine work in the whole world. God preferred total unbelief to this belief without moral reality; for the rejection of the Jews might contribute to the salvation of the world by more widely opening the door to the Gentiles; while we have only to remember their contentions with St. Paul to perceive what an insurmountable obstacle would have been placed in the way of the mission to the Gentiles by the entrance of the bulk of a carnal, legal, and Pharisaic Israel into the church. God, then, blinded Israel that the miracles of Jesus might be in their eyes as though they had never taken place; He hardened them, that His preaching might be to them as an empty sound (Isa. vi.). Hence, carnal Israel rejected *freely*, and might be *freely* rejected. This decided position did not really render Israel's lot the worse, but it had, as shown by St. Paul in Rom. xi., most beneficial results on the salvation of the Gentiles. Israel became by their punishment what they had refused to be by their salvation, the apostles of the world; and, like Judas, their true type, they had also to fulfil, whether willingly or unwillingly, their irrevocable commission. It is also evident that, amidst this national judgment, each individual was free to turn to God by repentance, and thus to escape the general obduracy. The 13th verse of Isaiah and the 42d of St. John prove that this was the case.

As to the relation of Jewish unbelief to the Divine prevision (vv. 37 and 38), St. John does not point out the metaphysical theory by means of which he was able to reconcile God's foreknowledge and man's responsibility, but simply accepts these two data—the one of the religious sentiment, the other of the moral consciousness. But if we reflect that God is above time,—that, properly speaking, He does not *foresee* a fact which, as far as we are concerned, is still future, but *sees* it absolutely as we contemplate one present,—that, consequently, when He announces it at any moment as well before as after its accomplishment, He does not *predict*, but describes it as a spectator and witness,—the apparent contradiction of the two apparently contradictory elements vanishes. Undoubtedly the fact, once predicted, cannot fail to happen, since the sight of God cannot show Him as *being* that which will not be. But the fact does not take place because God saw it; but, on the contrary, God saw it because it will be, or rather because in His eyes it *is*. Hence the true cause of that Jewish unbelief which God announced was not His foreseeing it. This cause in its ultimate analysis was the moral state of the people themselves. It was that state which, when it had once become permanent, necessarily involved the final unbelief of Israel, as being on the one hand its deserved punishment, and on the other the condition of the salvation of the Gentiles.

Ver. 41. "*These things said Esaias, when*[1] *he saw His glory, and spake of Him.*"—St. John justifies in this verse the application just made by him of the visions of Isaiah to Jesus Christ. The Jehovah of the O. T., the Adonaï whom Isaiah beheld in this vision, is the Divine Being who became incarnate in Jesus. St. Paul says the same thing in 1 Cor. x. 4, by calling Christ *the spiritual rock which followed our fathers*, and in Phil. ii. 6, by attributing to Jesus before His incarnation *the form of God*, the Divine state. Some expositors have endeavoured to refer the pronoun αὐτοῦ not to Christ, but to God. But the last words: *and spake of Him*, would in this sense be superfluous, and the whole remark purposeless, in the context.— The Alex. reading: "*because* he saw . . . and spoke," has against it the testimony of the most ancient versions and the general tone of the verse, to which this *because* would give the far too pronounced character of a dogmatic reflection. It might have been concluded from vv. 37–41, that not a Jew either had believed or could believe; but vv. 42 and 43, while completing the historical picture, remove this misconception.

Vv. 42, 43. "*Nevertheless among the chief rulers also many believed on Him; but because of the Pharisees they did not confess Him, lest they should be put out of the synagogue: for they loved the praise of men more than*[2] *the praise of God.*"—St. John mentions this exception not to mitigate the severity of his own and Isaiah's estimate of the condition of the people, but to show that, notwithstanding the exception he is about to point out, the truth of this general estimate is unimpeached. Even where faith was evoked, cowardice repressed its confession and hindered its development. These remarkable words, which furnish the key to the parables of ch. x., show how crushing was the yoke laid upon Israel by the Pharisaic spirit. The spiritual obduracy and blindness spoken of in ver. 40, consisted precisely in the total surrender of the people to the power of Pharisaic fanaticism. The words: *lest they*

---

[1] ℵ A B L M X, some Mnn. Cop. Sah. read ὅτι, *because*, instead of ὅτε, *when*, which is the reading of 12 Mjj. (D Γ Δ, etc.), the Mnn. It. Syr. Chrys.

[2] ℵ L X and 5 Mnn. read ὑπὲρ instead of ἤπερ.

should be put out of the synagogue, are an evidence of the reality of the decree mentioned in ix. 22.—Δόξα, at ver. 43, is used almost in its etymological sense: "opinion, approbation." The difference of reading (ὕπερ and ἤπερ) is probably due to *itacism* (the pronunciation of η and υ as ι). If we read ὕπερ, we have here two forms of comparison combined to bring out more strongly the odiousness of such a preference. Undoubtedly, men like Nicodemus and Joseph of Arimathea must not be reckoned, as they are by Lücke and Meyer, among these cowards. It is of those who remained attached to the Jewish system, of Gamaliel, and so many others who were the Erasmuses of those days, that St. John meant to speak. On the necessity of confession to salvation, see Rom. x. 10.

II. *The Responsibility of Israel.*—Vv. 44-50.

The gravity of Jewish unbelief was directly proportioned to the greatness of the Being towards whom it was displayed. Now this Being was He whose *person* was the pure manifestation of God (vv. 44-46), and whose *teaching* was the pure expression of the mind and will of this same God (vv. 47-50). If this were the case, to reject Jesus was nothing less to Israel than to reject God Himself and His word. This rejection was that supreme act of rebellion, which could not fail to draw down an unexampled judgment.

Such is the meaning and spirit of this paragraph.

Criticism rightly disputes the historical reality of the following discourse, alleging, and with good reason, the absence of occasion and of definite locality, and the lack of any new idea (see *e.g.* Keim). But it is a mistake to infer that it is therefore a fictitious composition of the evangelist (de Wette), a composition which proves that the discourses of Jesus in the fourth Gospel are merely the expression of its author's own ideas (Hilgenfeld).

How, indeed, can we admit that the evangelist could, at this point of his narrative, have intended to give another discourse of Jesus as actually delivered by Himself? It is true that this is admitted by those who make Him speak thus on quitting the temple (Lampe, Bengel), or when again returning to it after the departure mentioned in ver. 36 (Chrysostom, Hengstenberg), or in a private conversation with His disciples (Besser, Luthardt, 1st ed.). But the first two suppositions clash with ver. 36, which evidently indicates the close of His public ministry. A word of explanation would at least have been necessary after the terms which conclude this verse. The third, against which the term ἔκραξε (he *cried* out) especially testifies, has been withdrawn by Luthardt himself (2d ed.). Moreover, the idea of this being a discourse really delivered by Jesus is excluded by the fact, that it would then be the sole example in St. John of this kind of teaching without indication of either occasion, time, or locality.

It must not be forgotten that at ver. 36 the evangelist finishes his part of *narrator*, so far as this portion of the history is concerned, and that after ver. 36 he is contemplating the fact recorded, viz. the unbelief of the elect people, and *meditating* on its causes and effects. As in vv. 37–43 he was chiefly preoccupied with our Lord's *miraculous agency*, he is here recapitulating His *teaching*, for the purpose of showing to what they are exposed who reject the testimony borne by Jesus to His own Person and word. Hence we have here indeed a discourse composed by St. John, but solely as a *summary* of the whole of Christ's teaching. And this is just the reason that it contains, as has been said, no new idea. The Aorists (ἔκραξεν, εἶπεν) recall all the particular cases in which Jesus had uttered such statements concerning Himself; they should be rendered: "And nevertheless He had told them plainly enough. . . . He had cried out loudly enough. . . ." Bäumlein: "*Jesus hatte aber laut erklärt.*" This is, with slight tinges of difference, the prevailing interpretation, the result of which is that each of the following statements, cited by St. John, rests upon a certain number of passages contained in the preceding discourses.

Vv. 44–46. "*Now Jesus had cried, saying, He that believeth on me, believeth not on me, but on Him that sent me. And he that seeth me seeth Him that sent me. I am come a light into the world, that whosoever believeth on me should not abide in darkness.*"—In the appearing of Jesus no element of independent and purely human will had hindered the revelation of God. Hence to believe in Him was not to believe in man, as though

Jesus had come or had acted in His own name (ver. 43), but really to believe in God alone, since God alone appeared in Him. It is not therefore necessary to take the negation *not* in the diluted sense of not *only*.—The sight spoken of in ver. 45 is not that of the body; it is that which is developed together with faith itself, the intuition of the inward and moral being of the individual beheld with the bodily eye. It is by this sight that Jesus, the living revelation of God, becomes the light of the soul. He who does not attain to it remains in darkness (ver. 46). Comp. for vv. 44 and 45 the following passages: ver. 36, vi. 38, vii. 17, 18, viii. 28, x. 38, etc.; and for ver. 46 the following: iii. 19, viii. 12, xii. 5, 39. What responsibility, then, is attached to such an appearing! From His Person He now passes to His doctrine.

Vv. 47, 48. "*And if any man hear my words, and keep*[1] *them not, I judge him not; for I came not to judge the world, but to save the world. He that rejecteth me, and receiveth not my words hath one that judgeth him: the word that I have spoken, the same shall judge him at the last day.*"—Jesus being the pure manifestation of God, His word is the pure manifestation of God's mind, for nothing of His own is mingled with it. Hence it is to be the sole criterion at the day of judgment. It is true, indeed, that it will be Jesus who will judge us; but He will confine Himself to applying to each life the rule of His word (comp. iii. 17, v. 24. viii. 15). What, then, will be the fate of him who has rejected this instruction!—The reading: φυλάξῃ, *keep*, seems preferable to the received reading: πιστεύσῃ (" and *believe* not "), for the former term is less used than the latter, and applies here to the act of internal appropriation, which is nothing else than faith.

Vv. 49, 50. "*For I have not spoken of myself; but the Father which sent me has Himself commanded*[2] *me what I should say, and how I should say it. And I know that His commandment is life everlasting; therefore what I say, I say as my Father has told me.*"—These verses explain the absolute value attributed by Jesus to His word as the rule of judgment. His teaching is both as to its matter (τί εἴπω) and form (τί λαλήσω), purely and simply that of the Father. He receives in each case a special

---

[1] ℵ A B K L X several Mnn. It^{allq} Syr^{sch} read φυλάξῃ instead of πιστεύσῃ.
[2] ℵ A B M X und 30 Mnn. read δίδωκεν instead of ἔδωκεν.

mandate (ἐντολή), to which in teaching He faithfully adheres; and this obedience arises in His case from the perception which He has of the quickening and regenerating power of the word entrusted to Him by the Father, of the fact that from it proceeds life eternal for every soul. This is why (*therefore* in 50*b*) He delivers it to men as He receives it, without allowing Himself to make any alteration (comp. v. 30, viii. 16-18, and the passages already quoted).

It would be impossible to summarize the absolute value constantly attributed by our Lord to His Person and His words in better terms than is done by St. John in these few propositions. And it is said that such a summary is one of the discourses composed by the evangelist himself; that he drew up this formidable accusation against Israel, here on the ground of discourses which Jesus never delivered, and at ver. 37 sqq. on the ground of miracles which He never performed! Is not such a proceeding morally impossible? There is, however, one thing which is perhaps still more so—viz., that the evangelist should put into the mouth of Jesus the principle: "*I have said nothing of myself; my Father has commanded me what I should say, and how I should say it,*" after having made Him speak throughout a whole book after his own fashion, and continuing to make Him speak thus in these very words! Was such deception ever before conceived?

Lastly, we would remark that, in proportion as reflections like these are in place from one who had himself witnessed the development of Jewish unbelief, and who wrote at a time when the recently consummated rejection of Israel was a subject which still filled all minds, would they be inappropriate in a writer whom no personal circumstance would any longer interest in the matter, and at a time when the ashes of Jerusalem were cold, and the Jewish question relegated to the second class by new discussions, important for very different reasons, both to faith and the government of the church.

Before leaving this second part of the Gospel history according to St. John, let us take, as its author does, a retrospective glance. We have followed, throughout its dramatically related vicissitudes, the development of the national unbelief, and the separation gradually effected between a small minority of believers and almost a whole population excited to fanaticism by its rulers. Let us now try to reject in thought all this aspect of the ministry of Jesus, all these journeys and disputes in the very centre of the theocracy, which form the subject of chs. v.–xiii., as must be done by those who deny the authenticity of this Gospel. We are now in view of the final catastrophe, attested by the Synoptists as well as by St. John. How are we to explain this sudden and tragical catastrophe? Only by the collisions arising from some cures on the Sabbath day in a remote province of the Holy Land? No; an earnest historian, desiring to account for the events of the life of Jesus, cannot, even allowing for the triumphal entry, dispense with this whole series of scenes in Jerusalem which we have lately been considering.

THIRD PART.

XIII. 1–XVII. 26.

THE DEVELOPMENT OF FAITH IN THE DISCIPLES.

THE third part of this Gospel relates the last moments spent by Jesus with His disciples, and teaches us to behold the full development of faith in their hearts, by showing us the supreme manifestations of His love to them. St. John here opposes to the dark picture of Jewish unbelief the bright one of faith, in the future founders of the church. Christ effected this work in the heart of His disciples—1st, by two acts, the washing of their feet and the dismissal of Judas, by which He purged the apostolic circle from the last remnant of carnal Messianism; 2dly, by a series of *discourses*, by which He prepared His disciples for the approaching separation, imparted to them the instructions necessary for their future ministrations, and raised their faith in His Person to the highest degree which it could as yet attain; 3dly, by a *prayer* of thanksgiving, in which He set the seal to His now accomplished work. Under the power of these last manifestations, their faith reached its relative perfection, as fruit ripens under the warm rays of the autumnal sun. It underwent a twofold test, that of humiliation by their Master's deep self-abasement in washing their feet; and that of sacrifice in the prospect of a violent struggle to be encountered on the part of the world, and of a victory to be gained solely by the spiritual power of Christ. With such anticipations, what would become of the earthly hopes which they cherished? But the faith of the apostles came out of this trial purified and triumphant; it grasped the divine person of Christ, and exclaimed: "*We believe that Thou camest forth from God*" (xvi. 30). To which Jesus replied: "*Ye do now believe*" (xvi. 31), and poured forth abundant thanksgiving to God (ch. xvii.) for the eleven whom He had given Him.

Hence this part is divided into three sections :—

I. Ch. xiii. 1–30: The purification of the faith of the apostles by two definite facts.

II. Ch. xiii. 31–xvi. 33: The strengthening of this faith by those last instructions of Jesus which contain the supreme revelations of His person.

III. Ch. xvii.: Our Lord's thanksgiving for His now terminated earthly ministry.

FIRST SECTION.

XIII. 1–30.—THE FACTS.

I. The Washing of the Disciples' Feet—vv. 1–20;
II. The Dismissal of Judas—vv. 21–30.

I. *The Washing of the Disciples' Feet.*—Vv. 1–20.

This section contains a preamble (vv. 1–3), the fact (vv. 4–11), and the explanation of the fact (vv. 12–20).

1st. Vv. 1–3. The preamble.

We have already met with short introductions to certain narratives, describing the moral situation in which the event took place, *e.g.* ii. 23–25, iv. 1, 2, 43–45. Each of these preambles is, with respect to the narrative it precedes, what the general prologue (i. 1–18) is to the whole gospel. That which we are now about to consider is composed after exactly the same fashion as the chief prologue, its matter being entirely borrowed from the sayings of Jesus contained in the narrative which follows.

Ver. 1. "*Before the feast of the Passover, Jesus knowing that His hour was come,*[1] *when He should leave the world to go unto the Father, after having loved His own*[2] *which were in the world, He perfectly manifested all His love to them.*"—The

---

[1] The T. R. with the Byz. (E F G H, etc.) reads ελληλυθεν; the Alex. (א B K L, etc.): ηλθεν.

[2] א: Ιουδαιους (*the Jews*) instead of ιδιους !

words: *before the feast of the Passover*, are connected with the previous particular *six days before the Passover* (xii. 1). These two expressions must then have nearly the same meaning. *The Passover* in xii. 1 designated, as we have seen, the time of the Paschal meal, the evening of the 14th-15th Nisan; the feast of the Passover may likewise include the whole of the 14th. Hence the time indicated by St. John in the terms "*before* the feast of the Passover," is the evening preceding that on which the Paschal meal was eaten, viz. the evening of the 13th-14th Nisan. This is quite in accordance with the language of the O. T., which speaks of the 15th Nisan as the day after the Passover. See Num. xxxiii. 3 in the LXX. (Meyer). Expositors who, for the sake of identifying this last supper of Jesus with the Paschal meal of the Israelites, try to harmonize the meaning of St. John's narrative with that usually attributed to the Synoptists, understand these words: "*before the feast* of the Passover," in the very narrowed sense: *at the moment* preceding the Paschal supper, or even: *at the beginning* of this repast. But this is doing violence to St. John's expression. For in this case he ought to have said: before *the Passover* (the Paschal meal, comp. xii. 1), or more plainly: πρὸ τοῦ δείπνου τοῦ πάσχα: before the supper of the Passover. What follows confirms the first explanation.—For upon what verb does this chronological particular bear? Naturally on the principal verb: ἠγάπησεν, *He loved*. But since this verb expresses a feeling constantly present in the heart of our Lord, and not an historical act, several expositors reject this relation, and assert that St. John could not really mean to tell us that, before the Passover . . . Jesus loved His own. Hence this particular has been referred (Luthardt, 1st ed., and Riggenbach) to the part. εἰδώς, *knowing*, or to ἠγαπήσας, *having loved* (Wieseler, Tholuck). But this notice, standing as it does at the head of the whole paragraph, can only refer to the principal action: ἠγάπησε, *He loved;* and this relation, besides being the most natural, is also that which offers the best meaning. The verb ἀγαπᾶν, *to love*, here means, as shown by the Aorist, not merely the sentiment, but also its external manifestations, especially that about to be related: *He riseth*, etc. St. John means to say that it was just before the day on which Jesus was about to leave His own that He perfected the manifestation of His love, that He in some way surpassed Himself in His manifestation of this feeling.

With this chronological data, St. John connects a particular of a moral nature: "*Jesus, knowing that* . . ." These words show the prevailing thought of our Lord's mind during these highest manifestations of His love; He knew that the hour of His return to the Father, and His separation from His own, was at hand. Hengstenberg and others paraphrase the participle *knowing* in the sense of: "*Though He knew* . . .," as though St. John had intended to say that the prospect of His future exaltation *did not prevent Him* from testifying the whole extent of His love to His disciples. But this is self-evident, and what St. John would, on the contrary, tell us is, that it was just *because* He saw that the time of parting was at hand that He redoubled His tenderness towards those whom He had so faithfully loved. It is to this meaning of *knowing* that the relation between the expressions: "*to go out of this world*," and "*His own which were in the world*," also points, as well as the antithesis between the terms: *this world*, and *the Father*.—Meyer makes ἀγαπήσας, having loved, refer to μεταβῇ: "*depart unto the Father* . . . *having loved.*" This construction is clumsy, and the sense empty. The two participles, *knowing* and *having loved*, are parallel, and both bear upon the principal verb ἠγάπησεν, which they qualify each in its own manner.—Luthardt justly points out the contrast between the expression: "*His hour was come,*" and that which we have so frequently met with: "*His hour was not yet come.*" This contrast shows the gravity of the present time.

It was under the force of this contrast, which He so keenly felt, between the state in which He was leaving them and that which He was about to enjoy with the Father, that all His love at length overflowed.

St. John adds a third particular: "*Having loved His own . . .*," which does not mean: "as He had loved them, He continued to do so," but: "if He had loved them before, it was now that it was fully seen how much He loved them."—The expression *His own* expresses the value His heart attached to these beings given Him by the Father, whom He was about to leave in so critical a position.—Εἰς τέλος does not seem to have in Greek the meaning: *unto the end.* At least Passow does not give this meaning, nor does the N. T. seem to furnish an example of it. In the two passages Luke xviii. 5 and 1 Thess. ii. 16, we must translate: *at last,* or *to finish,* a sense which this phrase has also in classical Greek (Passow), but which is inappropriate here. The usual meaning of εἰς τέλος in good Greek is: *to an extreme, to the greatest degree;* and this is also the most suitable in this verse. At these last moments, the manifestations of His affection attained a degree of intensity which they had not hitherto reached; they went so far as to completely pour forth this feeling, and, in some sort, to exhaust it. This is the sense which we have endeavoured to give in our translation.[1]

As we shall find in ver. 2 a fresh introduction relating more particularly to the washing of the disciples' feet and the departure of Judas related in this chapter, this ver. 1 must be regarded as forming the preamble not of this chapter only, but of the whole of this part of the Gospel in ch. xiii.–xvii. It is in fact in the discourses in ch. xiv.–xvi., and in the prayer in ch. xvii., rather than in ch. xiii., that the subjects filling our Lord's mind, and summed up by St. John in the *knowing that* of ver. 1, are brought to light. Comp. xiv. 12: "*I go to my Father;*" xv. 18: "*If the world hate you, know . . .;*" xvi. 28: "*I leave the world and go to my Father;*" xvi. 33: "*In the world ye shall have tribulation;*" xvii. 11: "*I am no more in the world, but these are in the world, and I come to Thee.*" Comp. also xiii. 34, xv. 9, 11, 14, xvii. 23, 24, etc.

Vv. 2, 3. "*And a supper having taken place,*[2] *the devil having now put into the heart of Judas Iscariot, son of Simon, to betray Him;*[3] *Jesus,*[4] *knowing that the Father had*

---

[1] The saying of Penelope to Ulysses (Od. ψ, 214): "Be not angry that *I did not love you as much* (ὣδ' ἠγάπησα) at the first moment that I saw you, as now when I press you in my arms," may be cited as analogous to this sense of ἠγάπησα.

[2] Instead of γινομένου, which is the reading of T.R. with all the other Mjj. all the Mnn. and Vss. and Or. (once); γινομένου is the reading of ℵ (γίνομ.) B L X, Or. (four times).

[3] ℵ B L M X It^{aliq} Vg. Or. (seven times) read, τοῦ διαβ. ἤδη βεβληκ. εἰς τ. καρδ. ἵνα παραδῷ αὐτὸν Ἰούδας Σ. Ἰσκαριώτης. T. R., with 11 Mjj. the Mnn. It^{plerique} Syr. Or. (three times), reads, τοῦ διαβ. ἤδη βεβληκ. εἰς τ. καρδ. Ἰούδα Σ. Ἰσκαριώτου ἵνα αὐτὸν παραδῷ; ℵ B D: παραδοῖ instead of παραδῷ.

[4] ℵ B D L X do not here repeat ὁ Ἰησοῦς.

put[1] *all things into His hands, and that He was come from God, and went to God; . . . .*"—This second preamble, relating more especially to the two following scenes, also contains three particulars calculated to throw light on our Lord's mode of action.

And first a definition of time: "*a supper having taken place,*" for it is thus, as it seems to us, that the words δείπνου γενομένου should be translated. To translate, as many expositors do: "the supper being ended," we should need either the article before δείπνου, or that the context should clearly show that *the* supper *par excellence*, the Paschal supper, was intended, in which case the article would be unnecessary. But the first words of ver. 1: "*Before the feast of the Passover,*" are calculated to exclude rather than to originate such a notion. The Alex. read γινομένου, which would mean: "*When* the repast as a repast *began.*" This reading, though approved by Tischendorf and Meyer, is only a correction, intended to place the washing of the disciples' feet, as seemed natural, at the beginning of the repast, the time at which the performance of this act was customary.

The second particular, relating to the treachery of Judas, is expressed under two considerably differing forms in the Mss. and Vss. The Alex. text reads: "*The devil having already put into his heart that Judas Iscariot would betray him.*" Whose heart? That of the devil himself, says Meyer, by reason of the Greek phrase, "to put into the heart," signifying *to decide to.* But this meaning is insufferable. Wherever do we find Scripture speak of the *heart* of the devil? and how long has the devil had men so entirely in his power that, if he but *decides* to make one of them a traitor, he infallibly becomes one? We must then understand: put into the heart of Judas (Baümlein, Luthardt); but the term: *into the heart,* cannot be used in this absolute manner, and without its complement. Hence this reading must be rejected. It arose from the idea that the diabolic impulse was only exercised at the moment described in ver. 27. The Byz. reading says only: "*The devil having put into the heart of Judas to betray Him.*" This makes everything harmonize, for ver. 27 assumes that the treachery was already consummated in the heart of Judas;

---
[1] א B D K L Or. : ιδωκιν instead of διδωκιν.

while, according to the Synoptists, the bargain between Judas and the Sanhedrim took place at least one day before this repast.—What, we would next ask, is the purpose with which this particular is here brought forward? To bring out, according to Chrysostom, Calvin, and Luthardt, the long-suffering and love of Jesus; according to Meyer, to show the perfect certainty of mind with which He advanced to meet His fate; according to Lücke, to indicate that time pressed. To us it seems that St. John desired more especially to show the motive for the different allusions which Jesus was about to make to the presence of the traitor, during the whole of the ensuing scene (comp. vv. 10, 18, 21, 26, 27, 30), and to exalt the love which, notwithstanding the certain perception of this revolting fact, suffered Him to wash the feet even of Judas. The Alex. reading παραδοῖ instead of παραδῷ (T. R.) is explained by grammarians as either a contraction of the optative παραδοίη (see in Kühner's *Ausführliche Grammatik* a multitude of examples from Plato and other writers), or as a contraction of the subjunctive (as by Baümlein, after Buttmann). — As the first particular: "*a supper having taken place,*" answers to the first of ver. 1 ("*before the feast . . .*"), so does the reflection: "*the devil having put into . . .*," answer to that of ver. 1: "*having loved His own . . .*" The vilest malice is here the pendant to the tenderest affection.

The picture of both the external and the moral situation is completed by a third hint, which affords us a view of the inmost feelings of Jesus, and reveals the true meaning of the act of abasement which follows: "*Jesus, knowing that . . .*" This *knowing* corresponds with that of ver. 1, and here, even more frequently than in the latter passage, commentators are wont to paraphrase it as: "*though* knowing." But this is in our opinion a still graver misconception of the evangelist's meaning, as well as of that of Jesus Himself, than at ver. 1. It was not notwithstanding His divine greatness, but *because of* that greatness, that Jesus humbled Himself in the manner about to be related. Feeling Himself the greatest, He also felt that it was for Him to give the example of true greatness, by humbling Himself to fulfil the office of the lowest; for greatness in the Messianic kingdom, as He had come to establish it, would consist in voluntary abasement. This was a kind of greatness hitherto unknown in the world, and which *His own* were now to behold in Him, that His church might never acknowledge any other. It was therefore, *inasmuch* as He was Lord, and not *though* He was Lord, that He was about to fulfil the office of a slave. St. John borrows this idea from the succeeding discourse of Jesus (vv. 13, 14): " *You call me Master and Lord . . . If then . . .*" It is in this sense that the accumulation of propositions, recalling the different features of His supreme greatness, is to be understood; His sovereign *position:* all things are put into His hands; His divine *origin:* He came from God; His divine *destination:* He is going to God (notice the repetition of the word *God*). And it was His consciousness of this incomparable greatness (*knowing*) which induced Him to abase Himself as none other had ever done. Hence His example became decisive and irresistible to His own.

2d. Vv. 4–11. The fact.

Vv. 4, 5. " (*Jesus*) *riseth from supper, and laid aside His garments; and took a towel, and girded Himself. After that He poureth water into the basin, and began to wash His disciples' feet, and to wipe them with the towel wherewith He was girded.*"—Ver. 3 has already taught us the purpose of this act, and this alone might suffice to explain it. Hence Ewald and Meyer abstain from seeking any external motive. Generally, however, Jesus was not accustomed to act from mere inward impulse, but to obey the Father's signal. Several modern expositors (Lange, Hengstenberg) find this signal in the fact that the ablution of the feet, which should, according to custom, have taken place at the beginning of the meal, had been omitted either through the pride or negligence of the disciples. None among them had been willing to take the place of the slave whom they were without. Peter, or one of the others, had indeed, Hengstenberg thinks, washed the feet of Jesus, but had then taken his place at the table, and waited with his co-disciples of the higher order for some disciple of inferior rank to perform the same service for them. This provoked the dispute spoken of by St. Luke at the close of the meal, as to which of them was greatest, and to which Jesus put an end by rising and Himself fulfilling an office disdained by all. Of course all this would occur before the commencement of the meal. But the expressions: δείπνου γενομένου, "*a supper having taken place*" (ver. 2), and: "*He riseth from supper*" (ver. 4), do not favour this opinion, but rather lead us to think that the meal had already begun, and even that it was nearly concluded. Besides, in this case, the subject of dispute would have been, not who was the greatest, but who was the least, the lowest, whose part it was to perform the lowest office. Baümlein's supposition, that the dispute was provoked by the claim of each to occupy the chief place *at table*, is more probable. To us it seems certain that the dispute mentioned in Luke occasioned the washing of the disciples' feet, as seems almost necessarily to follow from the words of our Lord in that Gospel: "*The kings of the nations exercise lordship over them; . . . let it not be so among you. . . . For whether is greater, he that sitteth at meat, or he that serveth? . . . I am among you as he that serveth.*" But, according to these words themselves, this act must, like the dispute itself, have taken place during the course or at the end of the meal, which is also the natural meaning of the text of John. Probably the washing of the feet, not being commanded by the law (Matt. xv. 2), had, as no one had volunteered to perform this office for our Lord and His companions, been omitted at the beginning of the meal. Jesus had allowed this want of respect to pass unnoticed; but when, in the course of the repast, a dispute which pained Him to the heart, brought out in full light the notions of earthly greatness still prevailing in the minds of His disciples, He made use of the omission to give them the lesson they needed by subsequently repairing the deficiency—He took the dress of a slave: *Nihil ministerii omittit*, says Grotius. Each particular is a picture. Ἱμάτια, here the upper garment which He laid aside, keeping on only the tunic, which was the vesture of slaves. He girt Himself with the towel, to leave both hands free for carrying the basin. Νιπτῆρα, with the article: *the* basin, that vessel which was in the room and formed part of its furniture.

Vv. 6–11. "*Then cometh He to Simon Peter: and he[1] saith unto Him, Lord,[1] dost thou wash my feet? Jesus answered*

---

[1] ℵ B b omit ἐκεῖνος; ℵ omits κυριε.

and said unto him, What[1] *I do thou knowest not now; but thou shalt know soon. Peter said unto Him, No, never shalt Thou wash my feet. Jesus answered him, If I wash thee not, thou hast no part with me. Simon Peter saith unto Him, Lord,*[2] *not my feet only, but also my hands and my head. Jesus saith unto him, He that is bathed needeth not save to wash his feet,*[3] *but is clean every whit: and you, ye are clean, but not all. For He knew who should betray Him; therefore He said,*[4] *Ye are not all clean."*—This conversation with St. Peter is an unexpected episode in the transaction. Οὖν, *then* (ver. 6), in going from one to the other, in the order in which they sat. The natural inference from this *then*, is that Peter was not sitting next to our Lord (comp. ver. 24).— The feeling of reverence which called forth this resistance is expressed in the antithesis of the pronouns σύ, *thou*, and μού, *my*, and in the title *Lord*. Here, as in Matt. xvi. 22, it was respect which produced in this apostle's behaviour a want of respect.—The antithesis of ἐγώ ... σύ (*I ... thou*) (ver. 7) corresponds with that of σύ ... μού (*thou ... my*) (ver. 6).— Μετὰ ταῦτα, which we have rendered by *soon*, is referred by Chrysostom to the future ministry of St. Peter. But the relation between γνώσῃ, *thou shalt know*, and γινώσκετε, *know ye* (ver. 14), shows that Jesus was thinking of the explanation which He intended to give, as soon as He had completed the act in which He was engaged.

The gentleness of our Lord emboldened Peter: he had but questioned (ver. 6); he now positively refuses, and refuses for ever. Jesus answers him in the same categorical tone, and there is certainly in His *no part* an echo of Peter's *never*. How then is this threat to be understood? Are we to see (with Hengstenberg) a symbol of the forgiveness of sins through Christ's blood in this washing? There is nothing in the circumstances which gave rise to this act, nor in the explanation given of it by our Lord in ver. 12 sq., to lead us to attribute to it this meaning. Must we then consider that the resistance of Peter induced

---

[1] ℵ reads α εγω instead of ο εγω.   [2] ℵ omits κυριε.
[3] T. R., with A E G M S U Γ Δ Λ, reads, η τους ποδας νιψασθαι (save to wash his feet); B C K L Π: ει μη τους ποδας νιψασθαι (if not to wash his feet); ℵ C: νιψασθαι (needs not *to wash* but ...).
[4] B C L add οτι.

Jesus to attribute to this act a bearing beyond what He had at first intended? Such a notion is improbable. Would it not be more simple to suppose that Jesus regarded Peter's refusal to accept the service which He desired to perform for Him as a refusal to enter fully into the spirit of His work, as He was at that time inculcating it, as a proof of his obstinate persistence in that love of earthly greatness from which He was at that very moment endeavouring by this act to purify him? In fact, by rejecting the humiliation which his Master was imposing upon Himself with respect to him, Peter was rejecting that which he was one day to impose upon himself. Our Lord's answer, then, was a new and more forcible reproduction of the truth which He had in another form expressed to His disciples, on the occasion of a similar dispute: "*Unless ye be converted, and become as little children,*" not only none of you shall be greatest in the kingdom of heaven, but "*ye shall not enter it at all*" (Matt. xviii. 1–4).—$Μέρος$ $ἔχειν$ $σύν$, *to have part with*, is an expression frequently used in the O. T. to indicate the participation of an inferior in the riches and glory of his leader (Josh. xxii. 24, 25; 2 Sam. xx. 1).

Ver. 9 presents us with one of those sudden revulsions of feeling in St. Peter which we so often find reported of him by the Synoptists. We have here the same Peter who one moment rushes into the water, and the next cries out, "I perish!" who now smites with the sword and now flees, who goes even unto the High Priest's palace, and who denies his Lord. The perfect harmony of these scattered features, and the image so full of life which results from them, admirably prove in this case, as in others,—as Luthardt has so well shown,—the entire truthfulness of the Gospel history.—In reality, what Peter was thoughtlessly demanding was the repetition of his baptism. It is this which furnishes the key to the answer of Jesus. This answer has naturally a double meaning. As in His conversation with the Samaritan woman He passed with a rapid transition from the material to the spiritual; just as one who, having bathed in the morning, considers himself clean and does not repeat this total ablution at meal-time, but is contented with washing his feet on entering, to remove such accidental defilement as he may have contracted by the way; so he who, by sincerely attaching himself to Christ, has found pardon for his sins, needs nothing else than a daily and continual purification from the moral defilement of which he becomes conscious during the course of his life. Peter was clean because he sincerely believed in Christ. The purpose, then, of what Jesus was now doing for him was not to reconcile him to God, but to remove from him, by such an example of humility, that particular defilement, the desire for earthly power and greatness, which Jesus at that very moment observed in His own. With this evil tendency Peter could not labour in the work of God, nor even sit down one day at the table of Christ. Every Christian must then apply this saying to his daily purification from those evil inclinations whose presence he discovers within him. The word, the example, and the spirit of Christ are the means of this increasing purification, which is the necessary complement of preliminary justification.—The reading εἰ μή, *if not*, of some Alex. is a correction of ἤ, which is slightly irregular; ἤ, *than*, for οὐδενὸς ἄλλου ἤ, *nothing else than*. The omission of the words ἢ τοὺς πόδας in the Sinait. completely changes the meaning: "He who is bathed needeth not to wash, but is quite clean." This reading is a correction caused by the difficulty of distinguishing between bathing the whole person and a partial ablution.—The last words: *but is clean every whit*, must be explained as follows: "*but*, far from needing to bathe a second time, as thou dost request, his body is, generally speaking, clean. He has only to remove any defilement which his feet may have contracted."

But was this happy state of reconciliation indeed the condition of all? No, there was one who had either broken the tie which united him to Jesus, or in whose case it had never existed. It was he who really needed to be the subject of that inward operation whose symbol Peter had just demanded. This is the first hint at the treachery of Judas during this repast. The Saviour, by expressing the grief which He felt in thinking of the crime of Judas, made a last effort to bring him to repentance. If He did not succeed, He would at least show His disciples that He was not the dupe of his hypocrisy (ver. 19).

3d. Vv. 12-20. The Explanation.

Vv. 12–17. " *When then He had washed their feet,*[1] *and*[2] *had taken again His garments, and had sat down again,*[3] *He said unto them, Know ye what I have done to you? Ye call me Master and Lord:*[4] *and ye say well; for so I am. If I then, your Lord and Master, have washed your feet, ye ought also*[5] *to wash one another's feet. For I have given*[6] *you an example, that ye should do as I have done to you. Verily, verily, I say unto you, The servant is not greater than his lord; neither he that is sent* (Fr. *the apostle*) *greater than he that sent him. If ye know these things, happy are ye if ye do them.*"—The explanation just given of our Lord's conversation with Peter, not attributing to the act of washing the disciples' feet a meaning foreign to its primary intention, the discourse by which it was followed no longer presents any difficulty. Jesus feared nothing so much for His Church as hierarchical pretensions. The disciples knew that their Master was establishing a kingdom. The very word was calculated to excite within them notions of superiority in a temporal sense. This was the reason why He sought to show them, that in His kingdom the means of rising was to descend, and that the way to the highest position was unhesitatingly to choose the lowest.—At ver. 13, *you call me* properly signifies: you thus designate me when you address me. The title *Master* refers to teaching, that of *Lord* to His sway over the whole life. They were the titles of *Rabbi* and *Mar* given by Jewish pupils to their masters. It is from the words: *for so I am,* that St. John rightly derived the *knowing* of ver. 3. The Church has, since the fourth century, seen in vv. 14 and 15 the institution of a rite, and it is well known what this ceremony has become where it is still literally practised. But neither the term ὑπόδειγμα, *example,* nor the plural, *these things,* in ver. 17, agree with the notion of such an institution; while in this case our Lord ought to have said in ver. 15, ὅ, *what,* instead of

---

[1] ℵ reads αυτου instead of αυτων.

[2] ℵ A L, It^plerique Syr. omit και before ιλαβιν.

[3] ℵ B C, Syr. read και ανιπτισιν, and A L, It^plerique και ανατισων, instead of ανατισων.

[4] T. R. with 6 Mjj. (Byz.) reads ο κυρ. και ο διδασκ.; all the others (12 Mjj.): ο διδ. κ. ο κυρ.

[5] D, It^plerique Syr. read πoσω μαλλον before και υμεις.

[6] ℵ A K M Π: διδωκα instead of εδωκα (13 Mjj.).

καθώς, *as*. Self-abasement to serve, and service to save, these are the moral essence of the act, and its permanent elements. Its form was accidental, and derived, as we have seen, from the actual situation; hence it was but transitory. The washing of feet mentioned in 1 Tim. v. 10 was a duty of hospitality, and had only a moral relation to the precept of vv. 14 and 15.—The meaning of the sentence, ver. 16, which is also found, with a different application, in the Synoptists (Luke vi. 40; Matt. x. 24, 25; comp. John xv. 20), is here, as in Matt. x., that the inferior cannot find any act unworthy of him which his superior has consented to perform.—But the Lord knows that it is more easy to approve and admire humility than to practise it, and for this reason adds the saying of ver. 17. *Εἰ, if,* "if indeed," as was really the case, expresses the general supposition; *ἐάν, in case,* the more particular condition.—The happiness here promised is not merely the inward complacency which accompanies every act of voluntary abasement, but a really superior position in God's sight; we are greater in His eyes, and nearer to Him, in proportion as we humble ourselves to serve our brethren (Matt. xviii. 4).

Vv. 18, 19. "*I speak not of you all: I*[1] *know those whom*[2] *I have chosen: but it is that the Scripture may be fulfilled, He that eateth bread with me*[3] *hath lifted up*[4] *his heel against me. Henceforth I tell you before it come to pass, that when it is come to pass you may believe that I am.*"—The thought of the happiness of disciples walking in the way of humility calls forth in the heart of Jesus the feeling of a contrast: there was one then present whose unconquerable pride would deprive him of this happiness and bring a curse upon him.—Ἐξελεξάμην, *I have chosen,* has been referred to election to salvation. In this sense it would not apply to Judas, but vi. 70 shows that it here signifies election to the apostolate and includes the Twelve.—The words: *I know,* serve to justify the preceding statement: *I speak not of you all;* hence, if the *for* of 4 Mjj. is a gloss, it is a correct one.—*That* may be made to depend upon the verb *has lifted up:* "That the Scripture may be

---

[1] ℵ A K Π, 30 Mnn. It^alia Cop. Syr. read γαρ after εγω.
[2] ℵ B C L M, Or. read τινας instead of ους.
[3] B C L: μου instead of μετ' εμου.
[4] ℵ A U Π: επηρκεν instead of επηρεν.

fulfilled, he that eateth bread with me hath lifted up . . ."
In this case our Lord would be identifying the scriptural
quotation with His own words. But it is more natural to
admit an ellipsis, and understand either, with Meyer: "Nevertheless I have chosen him, that . . .," or, which seems simpler,
to supply: "This has happened that . . ." (comp. xix. 36;
Matt. xxvi. 36). This latter ellipsis refers the responsibility
of the choice of Judas to God, whom Jesus obeyed (see
remarks on vi. 64). Ps. xli., from the 10th verse of which this
quotation is taken, is but indirectly Messianic; its immediate
subject is the just man in affliction, but this ideal is only
perfectly realized in the suffering Messiah. Among the
troubles which befall the righteous, the psalmist (David
according to the title, Jeremiah according to Hitzig) places
in the front rank the treachery of an intimate friend. In the
mouth of David, this would refer to Ahithophel. This last
stroke, Jesus would say, cannot fail to reach me also, in whom
all the sorrows as well as all the virtues of the righteous
sufferer are combined. This is, in the context, the meaning
of the formula: "*That the Scripture might be fulfilled.*" The
sing. ἄρτον, *bread*, in agreement with the Hebrew, while the
LXX. has the plural ἄρτους, might speak in favour of the
use of the original text. The translation of the passage by
St. John seems, on the whole, independent of the LXX.[1] *To
raise the heel*, to kick, is emblematic of brutal malice, and not,
as some have thought, of cunning. Foreseen and foretold as
it was by the Lord, this treachery, which might otherwise
have been a stumbling-block to His disciples, was afterwards
to be transformed into a support to their faith. This is
the fact brought out by Jesus in ver. 19.—The understood
attribute of ἐγώ εἰμι, *I am*, is: all that I have declared
myself, and all that you believe me to be, your Lord and
Master.

Ver. 20. "*Verily, verily, I say unto you, He that receiveth
whomsoever I send receiveth me; and he that receiveth me
receiveth Him that sent me.*"—The relation between this saying
and that which precedes is so obscure, that Kuinoel and
Lücke propose to regard this verse as a gloss derived from

---

[1] The assent which I gave to Mangold's opinion on this question (Introd. p. 253) must be modified. Comp. the quotation, xii. 40.

Matt. x. 40. Others, as Lampe, connect it with ver. 16, thus making what intervenes a mere parenthesis. Meyer and Hengstenberg think that Jesus designed to encourage His apostles, in prospect of the treachery of Judas, by reminding them of the greatness of their mission. Bäumlein calls this verse "a fragment of a larger whole, to which, perhaps, belonged the institution of the Lord's Supper." If we regard vv. 18 and 19 as a parenthesis occasioned by the contrast between the fate of Judas and the happiness of the faithful disciples (ver. 17), we can scarcely fail to see in ver. 20 the salient point of the $\mu\alpha\kappa\alpha\rho\iota\acute{o}\tau\eta\varsigma$, the happiness promised in ver. 17 to the apostle who is humble and devoted like His Master. He had just said: "*The servant is not greater than his master;*" He now seems to say: "The servant is not less than His Master." To receive Him is to receive Jesus, and God Himself (comp. Matt. xviii. 4, 5, and parallel passages). In Luke xxii. 29, 30, Jesus said: "*I appoint unto you a kingdom, as my Father hath appointed unto me; and ye shall sit on twelve thrones, judging the twelve tribes of Israel.*" This promise remarkably agrees with this 20th verse. To have Jesus within, and God in Him, is not this to *reign* and to *judge* in the deepest sense of the words?

Bretschneider and Strauss look upon this narrative of the washing of the disciples' feet as of legendary origin. But, as Baur observes on the raising of Lazarus, if such a fictitious narrative, due to Christian consciousness, had really been in circulation in the Church, it would infallibly have appeared in the Synoptic Gospels. Baur therefore regards this particular as purposely invented by the evangelist for the sake of a moral idea. But it is very difficult thus to account for so simple and vivid a scene, and especially for the composition of the admirable dialogue between Peter and the Saviour. Even Schweizer well brings out the seal of historical truth impressed upon the whole scene. Keim thinks that Jesus would not on that evening have thus openly opposed the feelings of His disciples. But the question was to teach them, in some manner which could never be forgotten, in what spirit their future mission was to be fulfilled, and this was the last opportunity for so doing. Exception has been taken to this circumstance from its omission by the Synoptists. It is probable that the institution of the Lord's Supper, a fact of such supreme importance to the Church, may have eclipsed it in the oral tradition of this last supper. Hilgenfeld suspects that the evangelist here substituted a narrative of his own invention for the institution of the Lord's Supper, which he was desirous of excluding (Introd. p. 111), as though there were such a relation between these two facts that one could compensate for the other. In any case, the discourse in Luke against false greatness, at the close of the supper, assumes a fact of this kind. St. Luke found in his documents the discourse reported independently of the fact. He desired to preserve the sayings of Christ, and reproduced this unconnected passage as he found it, without either adding to or taking from it.

II. *The Dismissal of Judas.*—Vv. 21–30.

We have here another work performed by Jesus from love to His disciples. So long as Judas was present, His feelings were under restraint, and He could not give free course to the Divine treasures with which His mind was filled. Ver. 3 ⁞ vividly expresses the feeling of relief which He experienced at seeing the traitor depart, and it was then that those full effusions of His inmost heart, contained in chs. xiv.–xvii., took place. These last moments of friendly intercourse were necessary to our Lord's work.

In the circle of the Twelve, Judas had been the representative of that spirit of carnal Messianism directly opposed to that which Jesus had just sanctioned by washing the disciples' feet (vi. 64, 70). If he would not humble himself and renounce this spirit, he must depart; and it was the spirit of the false, of the Jewish Messiah, of antichrist, which departed with him.

Vv. 21, 22. "*When Jesus had thus said, He was troubled in spirit, and testified, and said, Verily, verily, I say unto you, that one of you shall betray me. Then*[1] *the disciples looked one on another, doubting of whom He spake.*"—The emotion of Jesus arose neither from the feeling of wounded

[1] B C L omit ουν.

affection nor from pity for the traitor. The regimen τῷ πνεύματι, *in spirit*, shows that it had its dwelling in a higher region than that of even the noblest natural sensibility. Here, as at xi. 33–38, it was a shock of a religious nature, a kind of horror felt by His pure heart at the sight of this satanic crime, and at the approach of its invisible author. On the difference between ψυχή, *soul*, and πνεῦμα, *spirit*, in this relation, see remarks on xii. 27. The words: "*When He had thus said*," connect this emotion with the preceding discourse, in which Jesus had twice alluded to the treachery of Judas. The expression: "*He testified*," opposes the positive statement which follows to the vague indications of vv. 10 and 18; and the "*Amen, amen*," denotes the Divine certainty of this testimony. Accordingly, we find the apostles in ver. 22 doubting each other, and their own hearts, rather than the word of their Master, each of them, according to Matt. xxvii. 22, with a touching humility asking: "Is it I?" The same evangelist tells us that Judas himself addressed this question to Jesus, a circumstance which has been regarded as incredible. But would he not have betrayed himself had he alone remained silent? The answer of Jesus: "*Thou hast said it*" (Matt. xxvi. 25), is only a summary of the following scene related by St. John. It was by the act narrated in ver. 26 that Jesus answered his question.

Vv. 23, 24. "*Now*[1] *there was leaning on Jesus' bosom one of His disciples,*[2] *he whom Jesus loved. Simon Peter beckoned to him, that he should ask who it was*[3] *of whom He spake.*"—The ancients rather lay than sat at table, each guest having his left arm upon a cushion so as to support the head, and the right at liberty for eating; the feet were stretched out behind. Thus the head of each was near the breast of his companion on the left; and this was the place of John with regard to His Master in this last supper. In fact, the unanimous tradition of the primitive church points out John

---

[1] B C L omit δέ.
[2] 11 Mjj. (א A B C, etc.) add εκ before των μαθητων.
[3] Instead of πυθεσθαι τις αν ειη (*to ask who it was*), which is the reading of T. R. with 12 Mjj. (A D Γ Δ Λ Π, etc.), most of the Mnn. Syr. Cop., we read in B C I L X, It^pleriq. Vg. Or., και λεγει αυτω ειπε τις εστιν (*and he saith to him, Say who it is*).—א combines the two readings: πυθεσθαι τις αν ειη περι ου ελεγεν και λεγει αυτω ειπε τις εστιν περι ου λεγει.

as the disciple to whom ver. 23 applies. This Gospel itself leaves no doubt of it, as we have already shown in the Introduction (I. p. 259). This is brought out by ch. xxi. 2, compared with 7 and 20–23. Among the seven disciples spoken of in ver. 2, Peter, Thomas, and Nathanael are naturally excluded, as sometimes mentioned by name in the course of this Gospel, while the disciple whom Jesus loved is nowhere thus indicated. The two last unnamed disciples appear not to have belonged to the circle of the Twelve. Hence there remain only the two sons of Zebedee, of whom, James being excluded by his premature death (comp. ver. 22 : "*If I will that he tarry till I come, what is that to thee?*"), John alone is left. The Byz. reading: "*to ask Him who it was,*" is very preferable to that of the Alex. and Origen: "*And he said unto him, Say who it is.*" If, indeed, we interpret this last expression as telling us that Peter said to John: "Tell me who it is," this *he said unto him* is in contradiction with νεύει, *he made a sign*, which assumes that the two apostles were too far from each other for speaking. Besides, how should Peter suppose that John already knew this secret? If we understand: "Peter said to John, Ask the Lord of whom He is speaking," we are obliged to give to *say* the unusual sense of *ask*, and to supply the pronoun αὐτῷ, *to him*, as the regimen of this verb, which is forced. The Alex. text seems to result from a gloss, at one time added to (*Sinait.*), at another substituted for (*Vatican*), the primitive text as maintained in most of the other documents.—Ver. 24 shows that Peter was not seated next Jesus, since in that case he could himself have asked the question.

Vv. 25–27a. "*He then*[1] *lying*[2] *on Jesus' breast saith unto Him, Lord, who is it? Jesus answered, It is he to whom I will give a sop, when I have dipped*[3] *it. And when He had*

[1] ℵ D L M X Δ, several Mnn. It^plerique Vg. read ουν instead of δε, which is the reading of T. R. with 7 Mjj. Mnn. It^aliq.—B and C entirely omit the particle.

[2] B C K L X Π, 20 Mnn. Or. read αναπεσων instead of επιπεσων.—10 Mjj. read ουτως after επι- (or ανα-) πεσων ; this word is omitted in the T. R. with ℵ A D Π.—K S U Γ Λ read ουτος instead of εκεινος.

[3] B C L: βαψω το ψωμ. και δωσω. T. R. with the others : βαψας το ψωμ. επιδωσω.

dipped[1] *the sop,*[2] *He gave it to Judas Iscariot, the son of Simon.*[3] *And after he had received the sop, then*[4] *Satan entered into him.*"—The received reading ἐπιπεσών, leaning, properly *casting*, indicates a sudden movement agreeing with the strong feeling which inspired it. The Alex. reading: ἀναπεσών, seems absurd, because *sitting to table* is not here spoken of, and could only be received with the adverb οὕτως, and in the sense proposed by Bäumlein: "As he was *thus* seated at table" (comp. ver. 23: "*leaning on Jesus' breast*"). But it is far more probable that this is a mechanical correction after xxi. 20, where ἀνέπεσεν is perfectly in place. In any case, the most inadmissible reading is that adopted by Tischendorf (8th ed.): ἐπιπεσὼν οὕτως.—In the course of the Paschal meal, the father of the family used to offer to the guests pieces of bread or meat dipped in a sauce composed of fruit boiled in wine, representing the fruits of the Promised Land. Jesus here recurs to this custom, and answers John in language intelligible only to himself. As a sign of fellowship, it was one more appeal to the conscience of Judas. If he had been heart-broken at receiving it, he might yet have found pardon. Hence the moment was a decisive one, and this is what we are given to understand by the τότε, *then* (ver. 27), a word of tragic solemnity.—The Alex. reading: "*He takes* and gives the morsel," can only mean: "He takes it *from the dish*," after having dipped it, which is superfluous.—"Hitherto," says Hengstenberg, "Judas had, in the interest of his passion, stifled his conviction of his Master's Divinity. But now the ray of Divine omniscience which, in preceding warnings (ver. 10), had but grazed the surface, penetrated to his inmost soul, when Jesus plainly told him, both by this sign and the words which followed (Matt. xxvi. 25: '*Thou hast said*'): It is thou who, having eaten my bread, hast lifted up thy heel against me! But, at the same time, He gave him to understand that he was still one of His own. He could, therefore, even then have returned. But he

---

[1] א B C L X Or.: βαψας ουν; T. R. with the others: και εμβαψας.
[2] B C L M X Or. add λαμβανει και after ψωμιον.
[3] The Alex. (א B C, etc.): Ισκαριωτου; T. R. with the others (A Γ Δ, etc.): Ισκαριωτη.
[4] א D L It^plerique omit τοτε.

would not, and the violent effort which he made to close his heart to the heavenly power opened it to the powers of evil. It was from these even that he had to seek strength to accomplish this last act of resistance. As it is said of David: '*he strengthened himself in God,*' so did Judas strengthen himself in Satan."—The indwelling of Satan in a human soul, as well as that of the Holy Spirit, has its degrees. In Luke xxii. 3, the phases distinguished by St. John (comp. ver. 2) are combined. The present moment was that at which the will of Judas was at last confiscated by the power to which he had gradually yielded himself. Till then, he had acted freely and tentatively. From this moment it would not have been possible for him to recede. It has been asserted that, according to St. John, this result was owing to the magical agency of the piece of bread, that this was a miracle by which Jesus "*demonized*" the soul of a disciple.[1] If St. John had intended to express such a notion, he would have written, not μετὰ τὸ ψωμίον, *after the sop*, but rather μετὰ τοῦ ψωμίου, *with the sop*. It has been asked, moreover: Who saw Satan enter into Judas?[2] We might perhaps answer: John; for the terrible struggle which was at that moment taking place within him could not be unperceived by the eye of one who was anxiously observing the traitor, and something infernal in the expression of his countenance may have borne testimony to the decided victory just gained in his heart by the devil.—Keim would find an excuse for Judas in the conduct of Jesus at this juncture, supposing it faithfully related by St. John.[3] But Jesus expressly spared Judas, by making him known to John only.

Vv. 27*b*-30. "*Then said Jesus unto him, That thou doest, do quickly. Now no man at the table knew for what intent He said this unto him. For some of them thought, because Judas had the bag, that Jesus meant to say to him, Buy the things that we have need of for the feast; or, that he should give something to the poor. He then, having received the sop, went immediately out: now it was night.*"—The saying of Jesus to Judas was not a permission (Grotius), but a com-

---

[1] *Revue de Théol.* 3d series, vol. i. p. 255.   [2] *Ibid.*
[3] "Freilich wenn Jesus ihn so prostituirte, wie bei Johannes, war Judas einigermassen entschuldigt," iii. p. 262.

mand. Our Lord has been reproached for pushing Judas over the precipice by thus speaking. But there was now no longer any reason for treating him with caution, because it was no longer possible to him to recede. The evening was already far advanced (ver. 30), and Jesus needed the little time which yet remained to Him, to finish His work with regard to His own disciples. Judas, in his pride, supposed that the Person of his Master was in his hands. Jesus lets him feel that he, like the new master whom he now obeys, is but an instrument. St. John says: "*None of those who were at table*" (ver. 28). Keim objects that, if Jesus had really given John to understand who was the traitor, he at least must have perceived the meaning of this saying. Undoubtedly he did; nor is there anything to say that John does not except himself in using this expression, he only besides Judas possessing the key of the situation. It is difficult to infer from this passage anything decided respecting the day of Christ's death. On the one hand, it is said that this could not have been the day on which the whole nation was celebrating the Passover. For how could purchases be made at that Sabbatic season? and how could they be made *for the feast*, if the Paschal meal, the essential act of the feast, had already taken place? On the other hand, it is said: If this evening were that of the 13th–14th, there would be the day of the 14th left for purchases, and the supposition of the disciples would be unmeaning. Neither of these arguments is decisive.—The skill with which Judas must have concealed his character and plans is surprising, for even at this last moment his fellow-disciples were utterly in the dark about him. As far as our Lord Himself is concerned, He could not with safety have unmasked him more openly; for, with the impetuosity of Peter, what might not have taken place between him and the traitor?—The whole of the scene related in vv. 27–29 was but the affair of a moment. The words: "*having received the sop*," ver. 30, are directly connected by οὖν with ver. 27: "*and when He had dipped the sop.*" Hengstenberg places the institution of the Lord's Supper between the participle *having received* and the verb *he went out*. But the εὐθέως, *immediately*, makes the second of these acts directly follow the first.—The last words: "*it was night*," help to reproduce a perfect picture of the situation which was indelibly imprinted on the memory of John, whose narrative is everywhere interwoven with similar details only to be explained by the vividness of personal reminiscence. Comp. i. 40, vi. 59, viii. 20, x. 23, etc. The symbolical meaning which some, including Luthardt (2d ed.), have tried to attribute to these words by connecting them with xi. 10, cannot be accepted as the explanation of this detail in so simple a narrative.

At which period of this repast are we to place the institution of the Lord's Supper?—In stating this question, we are accepting the view that this was indeed the meal at which our Lord, according to the Synoptists, instituted this rite? Bengel, Wichelhaus, and others, have, it is true, attempted to distinguish two repasts. The first, they say, took place (John xiii.) at Bethany, John xiv. 31 indicating the moment at which Jesus left this place to go to Jerusalem; while the second, that of the Synoptists, was on the following evening, at the time of the Jewish Passover.—But the prediction of Peter's denial in both, and the close connection between the narrative of the washing of the disciples' feet and the discourse Luke xxii. 24–30, make this hypothesis untenable. —We admit, moreover, that though the institution of the Lord's Supper is not mentioned in this Gospel, this was not because its author was either ignorant of or denied it. For we agree with Lücke, that either this author was St. John, and that the existence of this rite being, according to 1 Cor. xi., an undoubted fact, could neither be ignored nor denied by an apostle, or that the author was a pseudo-John of the second century. Now at this epoch the First Epistle to the Corinthians was universally known, and the Lord's Supper universally celebrated in the Church; so that the pseudo-John, by pretending to ignore this fact, or to deny it by his silence, would only have made his narrative suspected. Its omission, then, can be explained only by the idea that the author did not relate it, because, as it was already sufficiently known in the Church, he had no special inducement for introducing it into his narrative.

If, then, this is the case, where must the institution of the Lord's Supper be inserted? According to Keim, after xiv.

31, as the foundation of the discourse in xv. 1 sqq.: "*I am the true vine,*" etc.; but at this moment Jesus arose and gave the order for departure, and this does not seem a suitable situation for such a ceremony.—According to Olshausen and Luthardt, after xiii. 38 (the prediction of Peter's denial), and before the words: "*Let not your heart be troubled.*" This opinion might be accepted, but that the Synoptists are unanimous in placing the prediction of the denial *after* the institution, while two of them recount it as uttered on the way to Gethsemane. —Lücke, Lange, Maier, and others place it in the interval between vv. 33 and 34, after the words: "*Yet a little while,*" etc., and before the proclamation of the *new commandment*. And certainly there is between this last expression and the idea of the *new covenant*, so strongly brought forward in the institution of the Lord's Supper, a relation which gives some probability to this view. But opposed to it is the direct connection between the question of Peter: "*Lord, whither goest Thou?*" (ver. 36), and the saying of Jesus: "*Whither I go, ye cannot come*" (ver. 33); a ceremony of such importance could hardly be interpolated between these two sayings.—It is placed by Neander and Ebrard in the interval between vv. 32 and 33. But ver. 33 is the direct continuation of ver. 32 (comp. the *straightway* of ver. 32, and the *yet a little while* of ver. 33). Indeed, the whole discourse in vv. 31–35 forms so closely connected a whole, that it is very difficult to insert in any part of it so important a fact.

Paulus, Kahnis, and others decide for the interval between vv. 30 and 31, immediately after the departure of Judas. The words: "*when he was gone out, Jesus said*" (see ver. 31), are unfavourable to this opinion.—That of Hengstenberg (ver. 30, before the departure of Judas) seems to us incompatible with the expression: "*he went out immediately.*"—Stier is for the interval between vv. 22 and 23. But the sign made by Peter, in ver. 24, is too directly connected with the anxious questions of the disciples in ver. 22.—Bäumlein proposes the interval between vv. 19 and 21, where the somewhat isolated saying in ver. 20 is placed. And certainly the idea of *receiving* Jesus and God, is in itself closely related to the Holy Supper; only it should not have been introduced by the totally alien idea of receiving *him whom Jesus sends.*—The notion of

Beyschlag is perhaps the most probable of the kind. The first act of the institution (the bread) is by him placed before ver. 18, and in this Judas would participate. The second act (the cup) he places after ver. 30, and thus considerably later, *after supper*, as it is said in Luke xxii. 20 and 1 Cor. xi. 25, and in this Judas would not take part. This view requires the admission that the repast lasted till this moment. The objection to it is the very close relation between vv. 18 and 17, and the no less direct connection of ver. 31 with ver. 30. —Meyer says : only after ver. 30.

The narrative of St. Luke, and certain hints in that of St. John, lead me to place the washing of the disciples' feet quite at the close of the repast. Hence the institution of the Lord's Supper would precede this act, and it would be as far back as ver. 1 that I should place this solemn transaction. Perhaps there is an allusion to this supreme pledge of Divine love in the expression : " *He perfectly manifested all His love to them.*" The saying of St. Luke : " *after He had supped,*" which places the institution at the close of the meal, may be objected, while John xiii. 26 (the sop given to Judas) seems to assume that it was still going on. But undoubtedly they would remain at table after the supper properly so called (comp. Luke xxii. 20, 27). And this sign, given by Jesus, does not necessarily imply anything more. Sieffert, in his work on the first Gospel, is, as far as I know, the first author who has spoken in favour of the solution here offered.[1]

On *the behaviour of Judas* we would add some remarks to those already given at the close of ch. vi.—It was not for the satisfaction of his moral necessities (as a being *given, taught, and drawn by God*, vi. 39, 44, 45), but from political ambition and gross cupidity, that Judas had become a follower of the Lord. For in his eyes Jesus was the Messiah, His miracles proved it, and by joining his fortunes to His a brilliant career seemed open to him. But when, as he soon perceived, the way followed by this Christ was the very opposite of what he hoped and expected, he became from day to day more irritated and exasperated. He saw himself at once deceived concerning Jesus, and seriously compromised in the eyes of the chiefs of the hierarchy by being His disciple.

[1] *Ueber den Ursprvng des ersten kanonischen Evangeliums*, 1832.

Hence his treason proceeded both from resentment and a desire to regain the favour of the rulers of the nation. As soon as he perceived that this latter object had failed, despair took possession of him.—Judas is an example of the faith which does not originate in moral wants.

Lastly, we would consider *the relation of the narrative of St. John to those of the Synoptists* with regard to this scene. Two principal differences are found in them : 1st. In proportion as the synoptic account is vague and obscure on the subject of the indication of the traitor, is that of St. John luminous, particular, and exact. As Beyschlag remarks : " The obscurities of the synoptic narrative are dispersed by its dramatic clearness." 2d. In the Synoptists, the relations between our Lord and Judas are presented as a special narrative, forming a separate picture. In St. John these relations form an organic part of the description of the repast, and are presented under the form of a series of historical shades and gradations. They form a living element, mingling in the whole course of events during this last evening, and accompanying its different phases. Which, we would fearlessly ask of any intelligent man, is the truly historical representation ?

SECOND SECTION.

XIII. 31-XVI. 33.—THE DISCOURSES.

Jesus has just bid farewell, an eternal farewell, to Judas: "*Do what thou hast to do !*" He now turns to His own, and the farewell which He addresses to them implies a future meeting (Gess [1]). The departure of Judas has set His heart at liberty. His love is now poured forth in a series of conversations and instructions which complete the revelation of His inmost soul to His disciples. Touched as they were by the affection which He had just testified, humbled as they had never been before by His humility, the apostles, notwithstanding their ignorance and weakness, were now disposed to receive and to preserve these last words.

---

[1] See his excellent work, *Bibelstunden über Ev. Joh.*, chs. xiii.-xvii., 2d ed. 1873.

A series of conversations (comp. the questions of Peter, ver. 36; of Thomas, xiv. 5; of Philip, ver. 8; and of Jude, ver. 22) open these communications upon the most familiar footing. They naturally turn upon the approaching separation, which Jesus teaches them to regard as the condition of a speedy and eternal reunion (xiii. 31, xiv. 31). Ver. 31 of ch. xiv. divides these conversations from the discourses by which they are followed. From this point onwards, the form of instruction properly so called prevails; Jesus transports Himself in thought to the period when the promised reunion will be realized, and glances from this point of view at the future career of His apostles in the midst of a hostile world to be saved (xv. 1–xvi. 15). Then the form of the dialogue reappears, and with it His mind reverts to the point whence He started, the imminent separation. Here Jesus now finds the decisive words (xvi. 16–33) to inspire them with the courage which they need at this painful moment. Thus does a dying father, when he has gathered his children about him, begin by speaking of his end; then their future career claims his regards, and he tells them what they will have to do here below, and what the world will be to them. After which, returning to the present situation, he draws from the depths of his paternal heart those last words in which he bids them a long farewell.

This course of things is so natural, that we are forced to own that, if this situation really existed, and if Jesus spake therein, He could only have spoken thus. His tone is ever on a level with the situation; it is one of deep but repressed emotion. The logical connection is not for a moment broken, but it is never made prominent. Distinctness of intuition is united with inwardness of feeling, and we are carried gently onwards by that gentle undulation of thought which characterizes, in a unique manner, the sayings of our Lord in this section. We know of only two passages of Scripture which present any analogy with this, and they originate in similar situations. These are the last discourses of Moses in Deuteronomy, in which the great lawgiver takes leave of his people, and the second part of Isaiah, in which the prophet, transported in spirit beyond the future ruin of Israel, unrolls the picture of its restoration, and describes the work of the true Israel in the midst of the world.—Hilgenfeld contrasts these discourses with those last instructions of an eschatological nature given in the Synoptists (Matt. xxiv.; Mark xiii.). According to John, he says, Jesus expects only the reign of the Spirit on earth, while, according to the Synoptists, a visible return of Christ to this world is spoken of. But the notion of the reign of the Spirit is not absent from the Synoptists (parable of the talents, or of the pounds in Matthew and Luke, and that of the virgins in Matthew; also Matt. xxviii. 18–20; Luke xxiv. 48, 49, etc.). And, on the other hand, the idea of an external and glorious consummation is not, as we have seen, lacking in John. The testing and the spiritual reign do but prepare for the judgment and the external reign.

I. *After Separation, Meeting.*—xiii. 31–xiv. 31.

After some sayings uttered by our Lord under the immediate impression produced by the departure of Judas (vv. 31–35), He replies to the questions of Peter (ver. 36–xiv. 4), of Thomas (vv. 5–7), of Philip (ver. 8–21), and of Jude (vv. 22–24), and concludes with reflections inspired by the present situation (vv. 25–31).

1st. Vv. 31–35.

Vv. 31, 32. "*When, therefore,*[1] *he was gone out, Jesus says, Now has the Son of man been glorified, and God has been glorified in Him. If God has been glorified in Him,*[2] *God will also glorify Him in Himself,*[3] *and will straightway glorify Him.*"—These two verses sound like a shout of triumph from the heart of Jesus at seeing the traitor depart in the darkness. Several documents omit the οὖν, *therefore*, and connect the words ὅτε ἐξῆλθεν with the preceding sentence: "It was night when He went out." But this addition would be useless, and would weaken the gravity of the short proposition: "*now it was night.*" Besides, the next verb λέγει, *he says,*

---

[1] T. R., with ℵ B C D L X, several Mnn. It. Vg. Cop. Or., reads οτι ουν; while ς, with the other Mjj. 90 Mnn. Syr., omits ουν.
[2] ℵ B C D L X Π, 12 Mnn. It^plerique omit the words υ ο θεος ιδοξασθη εν αυτω, which are read in T. R. with 12 Mjj. (A F, etc.) Mnn. It^alia Vg. Cop. Syr. Or.
[3] ℵ B H Δ read εν αυτω instead of εν εαυτω.

must be connected with what precedes it. We must then read ὅτε οὖν, and make the proposition: "*when he had gone out*," bear upon: "*Jesus says.*" The νῦν, *now*, with which the following sayings begin, naturally connects them with the departure of Judas. This is also shown by the past ἐδοξάσθη, *has been glorified*, which includes the whole past life of Jesus down to the scene just terminated. Most expositors, on the contrary, see in this verb an anticipative expression of the future glory of Jesus, whether by His death (Meyer), or by His elevation to the right hand of God (Luthardt, Gess). But if this is the case, why did Jesus directly after pass to the future (δοξάσει, *will glorify*) in speaking of this glorification to come. At xvii. 10, Jesus Himself gives thanks that He *is* from henceforth glorified (δεδόξασμαι) in the hearts of His apostles. The act of washing their feet had completed His condemnation of that false human glory which had filled their hearts, and with the departure of Judas the spirit of carnal Messianism had at last disappeared from the apostolic circle. Jesus now reigns there supreme, and the true glory realized in His Person has definitely triumphed over the false. This is also the reason that He here calls Himself the Son of man, for it was by His very humiliation that He obtained this glory. Now, such a glory did not, like ordinary human glory, make Him an appropriator of that of God. For it consisted, on the contrary, in His ever giving, as He had done that very evening, glory to God: "*And God has been glorified in Him.*" To glorify God by voluntary self-abasement is the task of man, and such had been the work of the Son of man, —a work now in some sort accomplished. The first words of ver. 32: "*If God has been glorified in Him,*" are omitted by the Alex. This omission, wrongly approved by Luthardt, arises simply—as the reading ἐν αὐτῷ instead of ἐν ἑαυτῷ in many of them proves—from the confusion of the two ἐν αὐτῷ by copyists. Examples of similar omissions in the Alex. text are very numerous, especially in ℵ. The proposition: "*If God has been glorified in Him,*" is not only perfectly appropriate, but even necessary to explain the transition from the past *has been glorified* to the future *will glorify* in ver. 32. Jesus, the instrument of God's glory on earth, will be glorified by God in heaven. Could God do less than the Son of man has done for Him? If He has glorified God, God will *also* (καί) glorify Him. This καί, *also*, stands at the head of the sentence to give vivid expression to this correlation between the conduct of Jesus and that of God (comp. xvii. 4, 5). Such, too, is the meaning of the evident correlation between the two regimens: *in Him* (Jesus) and *in Himself* (God). When God has been glorified by a being, He draws him to His bosom and envelopes him *in* His glory. Thus was His future illuminated in the eye of Jesus by the holy light of His past. This future was at hand. The departure of Judas had shown Him that it was imminent. *Straightway*, said Jesus, alluding to His resurrection and ascension. The second καί is explanatory, "*and that* straightway."—And after having thus given vent to His own feeling, Jesus next turned to His disciples, and made them the sole objects of His care.

Vv. 33-35. "*Little children, yet a little while*[1] *I am with you. Ye shall seek me: and as I said to the Jews, Whither I go, ye cannot come; so now I say to you. A new commandment I give unto you, that ye love one another. By this shall all men know that ye are my disciples, if ye have love one to another.*"[2]—The term of affection, τεκνία, *little children*, is nowhere else found in the Gospels; it was inspired by the *straightway*, implying a speedy separation, of ver. 32. The disciples seem to Him like children soon to become orphans. Indeed, what a void must be produced in any human heart by the absence of Jesus! He Himself vividly felt what they would experience: "*You shall seek me*," you will desire to rejoin me. And for Himself, how greatly He could wish to take them with Him into that world to which He was about to return! But what He had six months before said to the Jews (vii. 34, viii. 21) still applied to His disciples: they were not yet ready to follow Him. There was, however, this difference between them and the Jews, that in their case the impossibility was but temporary (comp. xiv. 3: "*I will receive you to myself, that where I am there ye may be also*"). Meantime He leaves them a task, but one so pleasant that it will also be their comfort. This new duty, conformable with the new situation, is indicated in ver. 34.

[1] ℵ L X It*alla* add χρονον after μικρον.
[2] ℵ reads μετ' αλληλων instead of εν αλληλοις.

The expression ἐντολὴ καινή, *new commandment*, has perplexed expositors, because we are commanded in the O. T. to love our neighbour as ourselves (Lev. xix. 18), and it does not seem possible to love him more.—Or are we to say with Knapp, in his celebrated discussion of this subject, that Jesus taught us both by example and precept to love our neighbour more than ourselves? This is a notion more specious than correct. Must we then give to καινή, *new*, some unusual meaning: *illustrious* (Wolf), *always new* (Olshausen), *renewed* (Calvin), *renewing man* (Augustine), *unexpected* (Semler), *latest* (Heumann), etc.? This is unnecessary. The entirely new character of Christian love is brought out first by the words *one another*, and then still more clearly by the explanation which follows: "*as I have loved you.*" This love does not apply to the whole human family in general, as might be said of the law of charity written on the conscience, nor specially to the members of the Jewish nation, like the commandment in Leviticus, but embraces all believers neither more nor less. This is an entirely new circle. But on what does its existence depend? Upon the appearance of an entirely new centre of life and affection upon earth. The love of a Jew for his neighbour arose from his seeing in him a worshipper of Jehovah, a being beloved by Him; thus every Israelite was to him a second self. So, too, it was from the love of Jesus for the disciples that this love for each other resulted. From this new hearth there issued forth the flame of an affection very different from any which the world had hitherto known: *in Christ* is the true explanation of this word *new*. It is a family affection, and the family came into existence that very hour.—The proposition: "*as I have loved you,*" is not, whatever Meyer and Luthardt may think, an appendage to the first proposition: "*that you should love one another*," which would render the repetition of these words at the end of the verse entirely useless. After saying in a general manner: "*that you should love one another*," Jesus again gives this command with fresh emphasis, this time adding to it the characteristic definition: "I mean to say that, *as I have loved you*, you should also love one another." Comp. exactly the same construction at xvii. 21. Καθώς, *as*, means more than a simple comparison (ὥσπερ); it indicates a conformity, and characterizes the mutual love of believers as *of the same nature* as that which unites Jesus to the believer (x. 15), each returning to his brother the love with which Jesus loves him. To this pleasant duty Jesus adds the most exalted motive, His glory; for He well knows that they who feel themselves beloved by Him can have none more urgent.—'Ἐμοί is perhaps stronger as a dative than as a nom. plural: "disciples belonging *to me*, the new Master." This promise of Jesus was realized in the history of the primitive church: "They love before they know each other," said Minutius Felix of the Christians; and the railing Lucian declared: "Their Master makes them believe that they are all brothers."

2d. xiii. 36–xiv. 4.

Vv. 36–38. "*Simon Peter said unto Him, Lord, whither goest Thou? Jesus answered him,*[1] *Whither I*[2] *go, thou canst not follow me now; but thou shalt follow me afterwards. Peter said unto Him,*[3] *Lord, why cannot I follow Thee now?*[4] *I will lay down my life for Thy sake. Jesus answered him,*[5] *Wilt thou lay down thy life for my sake? Verily, verily, I say unto thee, The cock shall not crow till thou hast denied*[6] *me thrice.*"—What especially struck St. Peter in the preceding sayings was the thought: "Whither I go, thither ye cannot come." His mind dwelt on the thought: Jesus is going to glory; Peter had no doubt about it (ver. 32). Why, then, after having walked, like his Master, upon the waters, and ascended with Him the Mount of Transfiguration, could he not follow Him to His glory, and return with Him to earth when He should establish His kingdom?—Jesus declared the separation to be for the present inevitable. Was He thinking of the task which Peter had yet to accomplish by his apostolic ministry? The saying in xiv. 2, 3 leads us to think rather of reasons of another nature. In the first place, the road is not yet open, redemption not yet effected; then Peter himself is not yet prepared for heaven. On his part, Peter, imagining that Jesus spoke as He did because He thought

---

[1] B C L It^plerique Vg. Cop. omit αυτω after απεκριθη.
[2] ℵ D U add εγω before υπαγω.
[3] ℵ, some Mnn. Vg. Cop. omit κυριε.
[4] C D L X read νυν instead of αρτι.
[5] ℵ A B C L X: αποκρινεται instead of ατεκρ.θη αυτω.
[6] B D L X: αρνηση instead of απαρνηση.

him incapable of facing death, declared himself ready to undergo martyrdom (ver. 37). Jesus then follows him to this region, and declares that even in this respect he is as yet incapable of accompanying Him (ver. 38).—The prediction of his denial appears to have made a profound impression upon this apostle; he seemed, as it were, overwhelmed by it, and from this moment he did not speak again during these discourses.

xiv. 1, 2. "*Let not your heart be troubled. Believe in God, believe also in me. In my Father's house are many dwellings: if it were not so, I would have told you.*[1] *I go to prepare a place for you.*"—The division into chapters is here very faulty, for these words relate to the preceding conversation, and particularly to the saying of Jesus: "*Thou shalt follow me afterwards.*" He now extends this promise to all His disciples, and explains it to them by showing them the manner in which He will fulfil it. He will begin by preparing a place for them in heaven (ver. 2), then He will Himself transport them thither (ver. 3). This explains the exhortation to full confidence, notwithstanding the approaching separation, contained in ver. 1. This event, far from plunging them into trouble of heart, would, if they understood it aright, fill them with the most joyful hope. The two πιστεύετε agree better with the imperative ταρασσέσθω if they are both taken as imperatives: *Believe*, than if the first or both are regarded as indicatives: *you believe*. Besides, it would be very unmeaning to remind them that they do believe in God. To dispel their trouble, Jesus invites them to confidence, first in God, who has promised them a glorious future, then in Himself, who will be able to realize it. In the first member of the sentence, the verb *believe* is placed before the regimen (*in God*); in the second, the regimen *in me* precedes the verb, to bring out the antithesis of the regimens *in God* and *in me*. The first motive to confidence is pointed out in ver. 2: the heavenly home to which Jesus is going is destined also for them. The image is derived from those vast oriental palaces, in which there is an abode not only for the sovereign and the heir to the throne, but also for all the sons of the king, however numerous they may be. The term πολλαί, *many*, by no

[1] ℵ A B C D K L X Π, 20 Mnn. It^{aliq} Vg. Syr. Cop. insert ὅτι between ὑμῖν and πορεύομαι (*I would have told you that I go*).

means refers to a *difference* between these abodes (as though Jesus meant to allude to the different degrees of heavenly glory), but solely to their *number:* there are as many as there are believers; in this vast edifice there is room for all.—This heavenly abode is before all a spiritual state; it is the sublime and filial position granted to Christ in the Divine glory, of which He will make His faithful people partakers. But this state will be realized in a definite locality, in the place where God most conspicuously manifests His presence and glory, in heaven. Lange thinks that Jesus, in uttering these words, pointed to the starry sky; but xiv. 31 proves that both Himself and His disciples were still in the upper room.

The words which follow have been very differently explained, but are easily understood if we adopt the reading which places ὅτι, *that*, after ὑμῖν : " If it were not so, I would have told you *that* I go to prepare a place for you;" or, which comes to the same thing, if, rejecting ὅτι, we translate : " I would have told you, I go . . ." But this meaning seems to me incompatible with ver. 3, in which Jesus says that He is really going, and that to prepare. All the efforts of the Fathers, who generally give this explanation, have not succeeded in removing this contradiction. It has been attempted to take the words εἶπον ἂν ὑμῖν in an interrogative sense (so Ernesti, Lange, Ewald) : " *Would I tell you ?*" or, " *Would I have told you* that I am going to prepare a place for you ? " But this would make Jesus allude to a saying which he had previously or at that moment pronounced, and we find nothing of the kind either in this discourse or in the Gospel. Some expositors, while rejecting the ὅτι, also take the proposition in the interrogative sense : " If it were not so, *should I tell you ?*" In this form there would be a certain touch of *naïveté*, harmonizing with the affectionate invitation : " *Trust in me.*" But this meaning would require the imperfect ἔλεγον ἄν. As to the meaning : " *Would I have told you ?*" the same reason makes it inadmissible. We must therefore return to the most simple interpretation : " If it were not so, I would have told you." That is to say : " If our separation were to be an eternal one, I would have forewarned you ; I would not have waited for this last moment to declare it to you."

It is not enough that the Father's house is spacious; access to it must be open to them, and an abode there assured them. For this purpose Jesus will precede them. Comp. Heb. vi. 20, Christ as the πρόδρομος (*forerunner*). It is under this image that He teaches them to regard His death, first, as that which will open to them by its atoning efficacy an entrance into heaven, and then as His elevation to that Divine condition, in which He will make them sharers by the gift of Pentecost. Meyer, reading with the Alex. ὅτι before πορεύομαι, gives to this conjunction the sense of *for*, and makes this *for* bear not on what immediately precedes it, but upon the proposition: "*there are many mansions.*" But this relation is very forced; the proposition: "*If it were not so, I would have told you,*" being certainly too closely connected with the principal idea: "*believe also in me,*" to be a mere parenthesis.

Ver. 3. "*And if I shall go away and*[1] *prepare*[2] *a place for you, I will come again and will receive you to myself, that where I am, there ye may be also.*"—But how are they to reach that abode when He has opened its entrance to them? Jesus will take care for this also. The omission of καί, *and*, before ἑτοιμάσω ("*and shall* prepare") in some documents, makes no sensible alteration in the sense: "If I go ... I will prepare." The *and* must nevertheless be maintained, as it prevents the tautology between this and the preceding phrase. The reading ἑτοιμάσαι, *to prepare*, was an almost indispensable correction when once this *and* was omitted.—The two verbs, *I come again* and *I will receive to myself*, answer to the two verbs of the principal phrase, *I go away* and *I prepare*.—The present, *I come again*, indicates the imminence of the action. Several refer this promise to the Lord's second and glorious coming (the Fathers, Calvin, Lampe, Meyer, Hofmann, Luthardt). But the promise in the context was a promise given not to the Church in general, but to the disciples personally, to comfort them in their present trouble; and could Jesus have meant to speak to them of an event still future when we now speak of this promise? We seem utterly to forget that Jesus never affirmed that His second coming was at hand, but rather stated the contrary. Comp.: "*While the bridegroom*

---

[1] Καὶ is omitted by A E G K Γ Δ and 40 Mnn.
[2] D M, 60 Mnn. Syr.: ετοιμασαι instead of και

tarried" (Matt. xxv. 5); "*If the master come in the second watch, or if he come in the third*" (Luke xii. 38); and the parable of the leaven. On the other hand, it is not possible to apply this term *come* to the resurrection of Jesus (Ebrard); for how, then, could we explain the close connection of the ideas, "*I come again,*" and "*I will receive you to myself*"? Grotius, Reuss, Lange, Hengstenberg, refer the word *come* to the coming of Jesus at death to every believer; comp. the vision of St. Stephen. But would this same term ἔρχομαι, *I come*, be twice used in the same discourse in quite different senses? In ver. 18 it is applied, as even these exegetes allow, to the return of Jesus *by the Holy Spirit*. And this is also the case in this passage. There are different distances in this saying of our Lord. The first is His coming in the Spirit: "*I come again*" (vv. 3 and 18); the second is the immediate effect of this return: "*I will receive you to myself.*" The close and indissoluble union contracted between the believer and the Person of the glorified Saviour (πρὸς ἐμαυτόν), from the time when he receives the gift of the Holy Spirit, is the subject here spoken of. The third is the final result, the aim of that increasing union which comprises the whole life of the believer, his entrance into the abode thus prepared, the participation of the sanctified believer in the Divine glory of his Lord: "*that where I am, there ye may be also,*" xvii. 24. This includes the death of the faithful as the commencement, and the second coming of Christ as the completion, of this participation. Identity of place (*where, there*) implies identity of moral condition; otherwise the return of Jesus in Spirit would not be the necessary condition of this future reunion.—With what touching simplicity and what dramatic force are these ideas, at once so novel and profound, of the believer's heavenly glory, and of that spiritual union with Jesus in this world, which is its indispensable condition, here expressed! "*My Father's house,*" the *preparation* of a dwelling, the return, the word: "*I will receive you to myself;*" this familiar, this almost childlike language, sounds like soft music by which Jesus is trying to alleviate the agony of parting. Thus closes the first conversation elicited by the question of Peter: "*Why cannot I follow Thee now?*" Not even his martyrdom would suffice; the life of the Holy Spirit in the heart was what was needed.

But Jesus perceived that many questions were rising in their minds, and that they were agitated by many doubts; hence He challenges, as it were, their ignorance, by saying:

Ver. 4. "*And whither I go ye know, and the way ye know.*"[1] —The way, according to ver. 3, is communion with Him; and, according to ver. 6, it is Himself living in them. This way the apostles knew, because they knew Him. And did they not really know Him better than any one else? This is what Jesus meant when He told them that they knew the way. But, on the other hand, they did not yet know Jesus as the way, so that Thomas might with no less truth say: "*We know not.*" The Alex. variation attributes to the disciples the knowledge of the way only, and not of the end: "*And whither I go, you know the way.*" But, first, this construction is somewhat harsh, and then 14 Mjj., most of the Mnn., and the two most ancient Vss. (It. and Syr.) are in favour of the received reading; it was probably the confusing of the two οἴδατε which, as in so many analogous cases, gave rise to the omission. According to the T. R., which we have followed, Jesus attributed to His disciples the knowledge of the end as well as that of the way. This end was, according to ver. 2, *the Father's house*, or, as Jesus also said (comp. xiii. 32, 33), *the Father*. The disciples might therefore have known whither He was going, but that, their imaginations being still preoccupied with another end, the earthly reign of Messiah, they had not yet learned to transfer their hopes from the world to God, from earth to heaven. They thought, with the Jews (xii. 34): "*We have heard that Christ abideth for ever*" (on the earth, which He shall glorify): "*how sayest Thou, then, The Son of man must be lifted up?*" Comp. Acts i. 6. And this false end hid from their eyes the true, which they nevertheless knew in a certain sense. These two *you know*, which expressed a relative truth, incited them to seek that clearer knowledge on these two points which they were as yet without.

3d. Vv. 5–7.

Vv. 5, 6. "*Thomas saith unto Him, Lord, we know not*

---

[1] Instead of the words οἴδατε καὶ τὴν ὁδὸν οἴδατι, ℵ B C L Q X read οἴδατε τὴν ὁδὸν.

whither Thou goest; and[1] *how can we know the way?*[2] *Jesus saith unto him, I am the way, the truth, and the life: no man cometh to the Father but by me.*"—The first conversation, occasioned by the questions of Peter: "*Whither goest Thou? Why cannot I follow Thee now?*" had turned upon the final reunion, the end. The second, called forth by the question of Thomas, turned rather upon the ability of Jesus to bring them to the end, upon the way. It is Thomas who is here, as he generally is, the exponent of the feelings of doubt and discouragement by which the apostles were possessed (comp. xi. 16, xx. 24). He frankly declares that the end, as just revealed by Jesus, is, so far as he is concerned, still enveloped in obscurity, and that consequently the way by which it is to be attained is also so misty as to be imperceptible.— To explain *the end*, Jesus substitutes the Father Himself for the Father's house. For it is not in heaven that we are to find God, but in God that we are to find heaven. And when once God is pointed out as the end, it is easily understood in what sense Jesus declares Himself *the way*. Besides, He Himself explains this by adding to this figurative expression the two terms *the truth* and *the life*, which express its meaning without a figure. The truth is God *revealed* in His essential nature,—that is to say, in His holiness and in His love (vv. 9, 10); the life is God *communicated* to the soul, and imparting to it holy strength and perfect blessedness (ver. 23). And as it is in Jesus that this revelation and this communication of God to the soul are effected, it is also by Him that the soul comes to the Father, and finds access to the Father's house. To be in Jesus is to be in the Father, because He is Himself God possessed and manifested. The three terms, *way, truth*, and *life*, are not then co-ordinate (Luther, Calvin: beginning, middle, end); neither do they express a single notion: *vera via vitæ* (Augustine); nor does Reuss seem to me to quite accurately express their relation when he combines them, by defining *the way* as the means of arriving *at* truth and life. Jesus means to say: I am the means of coming *to the Father* (the way); *because* I am the truth and the life. M. Reuss, on the other hand,

---

[1] B C L It^{aliq} omit καί before πως.

[2] B C D It^{aliq}: ειδαμεν την οδον instead of δυναμιθα την οδον ειδεναι.

makes the very just remark upon the word *I am*, that this expression excludes the notion of any other parallel means. Gess says: "A man can at most show the way to others; he can *be* neither the way, the truth, nor the life."

Ver. 7. "*If you had known*[1] *me, you would have known*[2] *my Father also: and from henceforth ye know Him, and have seen Him.*"—This verse reproduces the idea of the last proposition of the preceding verse, that of coming to the Father by Jesus. If Jesus is the manifestation of God realized, to have known Him is to have attained the knowledge of God (pluperf. ἐγνώκειτε). Jesus seems at first to deny that they possessed this double knowledge; in fact, it was not till Pentecost that they fully possessed it (ver. 20). Then He partially concedes it, and that *from the present time*. Meyer takes this expression literally: "Since my preceding statement" (that of ver. 6), which is too constrained, and almost insignificant. Chrysostom and Lücke, on the contrary, see in it an anticipation of the future enlightenment of Pentecost, a sense which *from henceforth* does not allow. It was to all that had taken place during this last evening that Jesus alluded; the washing of His disciples' feet, the departure of Judas, all that He had already told them, was well calculated to throw light upon the true nature of God and of His kingdom. Undoubtedly the fruit of these last instructions would not perfectly ripen till afterwards, but the germ of true knowledge was already implanted within them. In disclosing to them His inmost being, Jesus had revealed to them for ever the nature of God. The reading of ℵ D, admitted by Tischendorf (8th ed.): "If you *have known me*, you *will* also *know* the Father," is well explained by Luthardt as arising from the scruple felt by copyists at making our Lord say that His disciples had not as yet known Him.

This last saying seems, like ver. 4, intended to evoke the expression of some uneasy feeling which Jesus perceived in their hearts. The words *you have seen Him*, in particular, challenge this hidden trouble to show itself. For was not to have become *beholders* of the Father (perf. ἑωράκατε) the very utmost that the apostles could desire. This privilege

---

[1] ℵ D: εγνωκατε instead of εγνωκειτε.
  B C L Q X have αν ηδειτε; ℵ D: γνωσεσθε, instead of εγνωκειτε αν.

had under the Old Covenant been to a certain degree granted to Moses and Elias. If Jesus could bestow it on them, their faith would be henceforth unassailable. For, had not Isaiah said, when speaking of the times of Messiah: "*The glory of the Lord shall be revealed, and all flesh shall see it*"? (Isa. xl. 5). This furnishes a natural explanation of the request of Philip: "Thou sayest: you have seen; we ask Thee: show us!"

4th. Vv. 8-21.

Vv. 8, 9. "*Philip saith unto Him, Lord, show us the Father, and it sufficeth us. Jesus saith unto him, I have been so long time*[1] *with you, and yet thou hast not known me, Philip! He that hath seen me hath seen the Father; and*[2] *how sayest thou: Show us the Father?*"—Gess takes occasion from these interruptions on the part of the disciples to point out how much they felt at ease with their Master, and how this kind of relation justifies His saying: "*I have called you friends*," xv. 15.—The desire of beholding God is an aspiration implanted in man's heart by God Himself. Comp. the request of Moses in Ex. xxxiii. 18. Philip here makes himself the exponent of this desire, with a simplicity which recalls that which he manifested at ch. vi. Undoubtedly by this request he denied what Jesus had just affirmed concerning His Person in ver. 6. A dazzling vision, a magnificent spectacle in the atmosphere, seemed to him the best means of so strengthening his faith as to make it henceforth immoveable. It was the view-point occupied by those who demanded of our Lord a sign from heaven. This request would have been well founded if the Divine nature consisted solely in power. But God is holiness and love, and hence the true Theophany could not be a splendid phenomenon, but must be a Person manifesting in word and act those features of the Divine character, a human, filial life, in which is displayed that relation full of dignity and tenderness which God maintains with the Being who calls Him His Father. Now this unique spectacle, this only true Theophany, this visible brightness of the Divine glory, had been before the eyes of the disciples for three years, and Jesus beheld with

---

[1] ℵ D L Q: τοσουτω χρονω instead of τοσουτον χρονον.
[2] ℵ B Q It^plerique Vg. Cop.: πως instead of και πως.

wonder and grief that they had not better appreciated the privilege which had been granted them. The ground of His human consciousness was in such wise the feeling of His divinity, that He could hardly understand that a knowledge of His true nature had not also been found in the heart of His disciples.—The appellation, Philip, served to bring this disciple to himself, for, as Hengstenberg remarks, he had by thus speaking become *alius a se ipso*. His words must, as Luthardt observes, be connected with the preceding phrase, which was addressed to the disciples in particular, and not with the subsequent one, which is a general maxim. The perfects ἔγνωκας, ἑωρακώς, ἑώρακε, *hast known, has seen*, oppose the permanent condition to the sudden and single act expressed by the Aorist δεῖξον, *show us.*—It is impossible to refer this answer to the mere moral union of Jesus with God. No Christian, even if perfected, could say: "He that has seen me has seen Christ." How much less, then, could a Jew, though perfect, have said: "He that hath seen me hath seen the Father"! The expression can only be understood inasmuch as the Son carries on in this world, and under the human form, that revealing function which as the Word He accomplishes under the Divine form.

Vv. 10, 11. "*Believest thou not that I am in the Father, and the Father in me? The words that I speak*[1] *unto you, I speak not of myself: and the Father that dwelleth in me, He doeth these works.*[2] *Believe me when I say that I am in the Father, and that the Father is in me; and if not, believe*[3] *because of these works.*"—Jesus points Philip to two signs by which he should have recognised and might yet recognise the presence of God in Him. Jesus did not mean to say that He is one and the same Person with the Father, for He often addressed Him in prayer as *Thou*. The union of which He was speaking was that in virtue of which they live *One in the Other* (comp. Gess). Such a relation necessarily had the Logos life for its background. The first sign of this community of life and action is His teaching. The expression: "*the words that I*

---

[1] B L N X Cop. read λεγω instead of λαλω.
[2] ℵ B D read αυτου after εργα, and omit αυτος; L X have ποιει τ' αυτος.
[3] We here omit μοι, according to ℵ D L It^{alia} Vg. Syr.

say," might refer solely to the preceding statements, especially that of ver. 9. But it is more natural to apply it to the teaching of Jesus in general, that living self-manifestation whose Divine character testifies to His intimate union with the Father. Jesus would say: "Believe in my teaching, especially in my statements concerning myself, because I have never spoken of myself. And if you suspect them because they have passed through my mouth, believe in my works, because it is always God Himself living in me who has wrought them." This, then, was the second sign to which He appealed. The negative form of the first proposition supposes an affirmative proposition understood; and the converse holds good of the second. Meyer is wrong when he sees in the latter a proof of the former (as though the works were to demonstrate the Divine nature of the words), words and works simultaneously demonstrating the intimate relation of Jesus with the Father.—"*I in the Father*" is the suppression, on the part of Jesus, of all thought, will, and power of His own in the accomplishment of His work. "*The Father in me*" is the communication, on the part of God, of all the fulness of His being to the Person of Jesus. The reading λαλῶ is better than λέγω. Jesus is but the instrument; it is God who speaks, Jesus who *announces.*—At ver. 11, Jesus demands faith in this relation with the Father,— which makes Him the true Theophany,—on the authority of His mere word, of the testimony He gives to Himself. In the second proposition, the imperative *believe* is absolute (according to the reading of א B L): "*Believe* (*in me*, not *me*) on the foundation of my works," by which Jesus evidently means His supernatural works, His miracles. The same thought occurs in x. 37, 38. His miracles would be a proof to those who did not believe in His words, because this Divine testimony did not pass through His mouth, but was purely objective.—Their true position in apologetics is assigned to miracles by this saying. The part played by these supernatural facts is real, but it is secondary.—The meaning, then, of our Lord's reply is: The true Theophany has long been before your eyes. But, He adds, there is another and a greater one, which, if you continue in the faith, shall soon be granted you. To this it is that the following passage refers.

Vv. 12-14. "*Verily, verily, I say unto you, He that believeth on me, the works that I do shall he do also; and greater than these shall he do, because I go to the Father.*[1] *And whatsoever ye shall ask in my name, that will I do, that the Father may be glorified in the Son. If ye shall ask*[2] *anything in my name, I myself*[3] *will do it.*"—The marvels of another Theophany, that which He was about to effect *in them,* here begin to be displayed. *Amen, amen,* announces the revelation of a new and unexpected truth. The expression: "*the works that I do shall he do,*" refer to those miracles like their Lord's which were wrought by the apostles; and the words which follow: "*greater than these shall he do,*" to works of a higher nature than bodily cures. That which was done by St. Peter at Pentecost, by St. Paul all over the world, that which is effected by an ordinary preacher, a single believer, by bringing the Spirit into the heart, could not be done by Jesus during His sojourn in this world. For, that such facts should take place, it was needful that the wall of separation between God and man should be destroyed, and that the Holy Spirit should be given to mankind (Gess), or, as is said at the close of the verse, that the glorification of Jesus should be accomplished: "*because I go to the Father.*" The branch united to the vine may thus bear fruit, which the vine alone could not as yet bear. The term *greater* does not, then, designate miracles of a more astounding character, but of a more exalted nature, and does not, as Lücke, Tholuck, Olshausen, de Wette understand it, refer only to the *extension* of the apostolic ministry beyond the limits of the theocracy, —a distinction here occupying only the second place,—but to the very nature of the works accomplished.

But if the disciple effects such works, it is not by his own might, but because his Master, having attained the fulness of His power, accomplishes them through him. In fact, this superiority of productiveness attributed to the disciples is based upon the higher position of Christ Himself: "*Because I go to the Father.*" Jesus here says *to the Father,* not *to my Father.* For God is presently shown to be the Father

---

[1] ℵ A B D L Q X Π It. omit μου after πατερα.
[2] ℵ B E H U Γ Δ. 30 Mnn. It^{aliq} Vg. Syr. read με after αιτησητι.
[3] A B L It^{aliq} Vg. Cop. read τουτο instead of εγω.

of believers as well as of Jesus Himself.— The sentence must not be made to terminate with these words, the following proposition in ver. 13 being its necessary complement. Prayer is there declared to be the disciples' part in these greater works. The believer asks, and the glorified Christ works from the throne of His omnipotence. It is not, however, to prayer in general, but to a special kind of prayer, *to prayer in His name*, that Jesus attributes this power. To ask in the name of another is, in ordinary language, to ask in his stead, and, as it were, on his behalf. This individual has, by position, by service rendered or favour enjoyed, a right to what is demanded; he who asks in his name, asks as if filling his place. To ask in the name of Jesus, is, then, to come before God in the assurance of our reconciliation with Him, and our adoption in Christ, and to ask as if we were the representatives of Jesus Himself. This formula has been very variously explained: invoking my name (Chrysostom), through my merits (Calovius), in the element of my life (Meyer), in my spirit and for my sake (de Wette). All these definitions are true, but they are all included in our explanation. Jesus so lives, thinks, wills, desires in us, as reconciled believers, that our prayers are in God's sight as His own. Hence, prayer in the name of Jesus necessarily assumes the Pentecostal gift of which Jesus speaks after ver. 15. Comp. xvi. 23, 24, 26.—Meyer objects to this explanation of the formula *in my name*, first, that we cannot in this manner pray for the pardon of our sins, and, secondly, that by reason of the words *I will do it*, we thus make Jesus hear His own prayer. But does not Jesus, we ask, intercede for the pardon of our sins? And may He not, as the organ of God's omnipotence, effect what He asks of God by the mouth of His people thus closely united to Himself? Comp. ver. 16: *I will pray*, and xv. 26: *I will send*.—And all this shall be, He adds, *for the glory of the Father* in the Person of the Son; for the Son has no notion of establishing a kingdom on earth which should belong to Himself alone, but disposes of both Himself and His people in the interests of His Father's kingdom. His motto is: *Thy* kingdom come! not: *My* kingdom come!

Ver. 14 is a confirmation of this astonishing promise. By

the words ὅ τι ἄν, *whatever*, Jesus gives an unlimited range to the Christian ambition of His disciples. Hence this: "Yes, I say it again, you have only to ask and . . ." The received reading: ἐγὼ ποιήσω, *I myself will do it*, is undoubtedly genuine. Certain Alex. have mechanically reproduced the expression of ver. 13. But Jesus purposely modified it by substituting ἐγώ for τοῦτο: *I*, who have never deceived you, who shall be reinvested with omnipotence, and be with the Father, *myself* engage to do it. So close will be the nearness effected by Him between earth and heaven, that while His disciples pray on earth in His name, and, as it were, in His behalf, He will act in heaven in the name and on behalf of God. "We feel certain," says Stier, "when reading those frequently-recurring words at the beginning of St. Paul's epistles: 'I cease not to make mention of you in my prayers,' that it was by prayer in the name of Jesus that the apostles brought forth the Church."—Jesus next explains what is the source whence this prayer in His name, by which such great works are to be effected, flows forth.

Vv. 15–17. "*If ye love me, keep*[1] *my commandments. And for my part, I will pray the Father, and He shall give you another support* (Fr. *soutien*), *that He may abide*[2] *with you for ever; the Spirit of truth, whom the world cannot receive, because it seeth Him not, neither knoweth Him:*[3] *but*[4] *you, you know Him; for He dwelleth with you, and shall be*[5] *in you.*"
—And first, ver. 15, we have the moral condition of this new state: In the name of the love you bear me, remain in the road laid down by my directions, and you will be in a position to receive that supreme blessing which I proclaim to you. These commandments are the orders He had given, and especially the instructions of this last evening (xiii. 14, 15, 34, xiv. 1). The Aorist imperative *keep* reminds them that they were free to keep or break this condition. The reading of B L: *you will keep*, is a correction arising from the future

---

[1] Instead of τηρησατε (*keep*), B L Cop.: τηρησητε (*you shall keep*), ℵ: τηρησητε.
[2] ℵ B L Q X It^{plerique} Cop. Syr.: η instead of μεινη.
[3] ℵ B a omit the second αυτο.
[4] ℵ B Q omit δε after υμεις.
[5] B D, 5 Mnn. It. Syr.: εστιν (*is*) instead of εσται (*shall be*) in all the other Mjj.

which follows: *and I will pray.*—Jesus next pointed out the objective condition or efficient cause of the Divine gift, His own intercession. As the *future* object of this intercession is the Pentecostal gift, it is not difficult to reconcile this saying with xvi. 26: "*I say not unto you, that I will pray the Father for you;*" this latter passage referring to the times which *will follow* this outpouring of the Spirit, the season when the disciples will be able themselves to pray *in the name*, and as though they were the mouth of Jesus.— The term παράκλητος, literally *called towards*, was taken by Origen and Chrysostom in the active sense of παρακλήτωρ, *Comforter* (Job xvi. 2 in LXX.); and this sense has, under the influence of the Vulgate, been transferred to our versions. It is now, however, acknowledged that this word of passive form should have a passive meaning: he who is called as a support; this is exactly the meaning of the Latin *advocatus* and our word *advocate*, the defender of the accused before a court of justice. The word always has this meaning wherever it is met with outside the N. T., as in Demosthenes, Diogenes, Laertes, Philo, and the Rabbinists (the *Peraclith*). St. John himself gives it this meaning in his First Epistle, ii. 1: "We have a Paraclete with the Father, Jesus Christ the righteous." It is also that which is most suitable in these last discourses of our Lord. The meaning *teacher* (Theod. of Mopsuestia, Ernesti, Hofmann, Luthardt) has no philological basis to rest on; and the expression: "*Spirit of truth*," ver. 17, is not sufficient to justify it. What Jesus will ask for them from the Father is then another support, always within reach, always ready to come to their assistance at the first appeal in their conflict with the world. From this fundamental meaning arise the following applications: support in moments of weakness, counsellor in the difficulties of life, consoler in affliction. In a word, it is He who is, in all kinds of different situations, to replace the beloved Master who is about to leave them. By that word *another*, Jesus by implication attributes to Himself also this title of Paraclete; hence it is an error to see in 1 John ii. 1 a doctrinal discrepancy between the evangelist and the author of the First Epistle. This gift of the Father will be the result not only of the prayer of Jesus, but also of His intervention. Comp. xv. 26 : "*The Paraclete whom I will send to you from the Father.*" As He prays for the Spirit on our part, so does He send the Spirit on the part of God. And He will not, like Jesus, come to depart some day, but will dwell with them for ever. Meyer understands εἰς τὸν αἰῶνα : "till the age to come." But the word αἰών, both in the N. T. and in classical writers (ἐξ αἰῶνος, δι' αἰῶνος, εἰς αἰῶνα), denotes an infinite duration, and when used with the article, eternity.—Can we conceive of the Holy Spirit, a Divine Being, sent by the Father to replace a mere man?

The apposition: "*the Spirit of truth*" (ver. 17), serves to explain the term Paraclete, which was as yet obscure to the disciples. Teaching by the medium of language could but give a confused idea of Divine things; however skilfully such a medium might be used, it could only produce an image of the truth in the mind of the hearer, hence Jesus compares the instruction He has hitherto given in this form to a parable (xvi. 25). The Spirit's teaching, on the contrary, makes Divine truth enter the soul, gives it entire reality within us, and makes it *the truth* to us. This is undoubtedly the meaning of the expression: "*the Spirit of truth.*" But to receive this Divine teacher, a moral preparation is needed. The soul in which He comes to dwell must have been withdrawn from the profane sphere. This is the reason that Jesus said at the head of this passage (ver. 15): "*Keep my commandments,*" and here also added: "*whom the world cannot receive.*" It was by no arbitrary act that the Spirit came down upon a hundred and twenty only, on the day of Pentecost, and not on all the inhabitants of Jerusalem, the former having alone undergone the indispensable preparation. Jesus explains wherein this preparation, which the world is without, consists: before receiving, they must have *seen* and *known* the Spirit. The Spirit identifies Himself too closely with our individual life to be merely a bestowed gift; if He is to dwell in us, He must be desired and summoned by us. And this is what we cannot do till we have beheld Him (θεωρεῖν) in some one of His external manifestations, and then perceived and acknowledged (γινώσκειν) His supreme excellence and holiness. This preparation had been effected in the disciples during the three years they had passed in association with

Jesus; His words, His life, had been a constant emanation of the Spirit, and their hearts had done homage to the exalted holiness of this manifestation. This had not been done by *the world*, by the Jews, who, when they heard His words, said: "He hath a devil," and when they saw His miracles attributed them to Beelzebub. They had thus remained aliens to the sphere and the influence of the Spirit, they were not in a condition *to receive* Him.—The preparatory operation of the Spirit upon the disciples is expressed by the words: "*He dwelleth with you;*" and the closer relation into which He would enter with them at Pentecost by: "He shall be *in you.*" Hence we must be careful neither to read with the Vulgate, μενεῖ (in the future), *he shall dwell*, in the first proposition, nor with some Alexandrines, ἐστί, *is*, in the second. The whole meaning of the phrase consists in the antithesis of the present *dwelleth* (comp. μένων in ver. 25) and the future *shall be*. The contrast of the two regimens *with you* (comp. παρ' ὑμῖν of ver. 25) and *in you* corresponds exactly with that of the tenses. Nor must the last proposition: "*and He shall be in you*," be made to depend on ὅτι, *because*, which gives no meaning. This last phrase expresses, on the contrary, a consequence, a progress. And thus (by reason of the knowledge of Him which you have already attained by my presence among you) He shall be *in you.*—This distinction between the preparatory operation of the Spirit *upon* man, by means of external manifestations, and His actual dwelling *in* man, seems at present almost effaced from Christian consciousness.—Hitherto Jesus living *with* them had been their support; henceforth they were to have the support *in their own heart* (Gess), and this support would again be Jesus Himself.

Vv. 18, 19. "*I will not leave you orphans: I return to you. Yet a little while, and the world seeth me no more; but you see me; because I live, ye shall live also.*" — The term *orphans* refers to the address, "*my little children*" (xiii. 33); it is the language of a dying father. The close connection of feeling between these sayings and the preceding is indicated by the absence of any logical particle between vv. 17 and 18. This alone would suffice to obviate any other explanation of the words: "*I return to you*," than that which refers them to the return of Jesus by the Holy Spirit (vv.

16 and 17), and is adopted by most moderns (even by Meyer and Luthardt, 2d ed.). Those who apply this promise to the appearances of Jesus after His resurrection (Chrysostom, Erasmus, Grotius, Hilgenfeld) are unable to account for vv. 20, 21, 23. Those who apply it to His second coming (Augustine, Hofmann, Luthardt, 1st ed.) cannot explain vv. 19 and 23. In fact, that *seeing Him again*, which is promised to believers, is to coincide with the fact of His non-appearance to the world; and, according to ver. 23, His return to His disciples is to be a purely inward one, while of His final coming it is said: "*Every eye shall see Him.*" Still, what may and must be granted is, that this spiritual return was *prepared* for by the appearances of the risen, as it will be consummated by the coming of the glorified Christ. —The Spirit is undoubtedly *another*, a different support from Jesus; but His coming is none the less the return of Jesus Himself, otherwise the promise of the Paraclete would have but imperfectly met the needs of the disciples, whose hearts were demanding union with their Master Himself. Tholuck concludes from the expression: "*I come again*," that the Holy Spirit is only the Person of Jesus spiritualized; and Reuss insists that, though literal exegesis pleads for a distinction of persons (between Christ and the Holy Spirit), practical logic forbids its admission. He has even ventured to express the opinion, that in the discourses of Jesus the abstract notion of the Word is replaced by the more concrete notion of the Spirit. St. John is, however, innocent of so serious a confusion. As no Old Testament writer would have used the terms "Spirit of God" and "Angel of the Lord" for each other, so neither can a confusion of the Word with the Spirit be admitted in any writer of the New. St. Paul says (2 Cor. iii. 17): "*The Lord is the Spirit.*" But he does not therefore confound the Person of the glorified Saviour with the Holy Ghost. This is a sphere in which it is of consequence to distinguish between different shades of meaning. According to xvi. 14, the Spirit is not the Lord, but the power which *glorifies* Him, which manifests Him, which makes Him live and increase within us, and that by taking of what is His and imparting it to us. Their parts are perfectly distinct. And they are quite as much so in the work of

Pentecost as in that of the Incarnation. The Holy Ghost did not become Christ by producing Him in the Virgin's womb, nor does the Spirit become Jesus by glorifying Him and causing Him to live in us. The Word is the principle of the objective revelation, the Spirit that of the subjective. Jesus is the object to be assimilated, the Spirit is the assimilating power. Without the objective revelation given in Jesus, the Spirit would have nothing to fertilize in us; without the Spirit, the revelation given in Jesus would remain exterior to us, and resemble a parable which is not understood. Hence it is in one sense true, that when the Spirit comes, it is Jesus who comes again; from one without, He becomes one within us. The completed work of the Spirit is *Christ formed* in the believer, or, to express the same idea in other words, it is the believer *come to the measure of the stature of the fulness of Christ* (Gal. iv. 19 ; Eph. iv. 13).

The words: "*Yet a little while*" (ver. 19), are in accordance with the present *I come*. They reduce, so to speak, the period of separation to nothing. If Jesus, when He said : "*You shall see me again,*" were thinking of His appearances after His resurrection, it was in any case only in a secondary manner, His mind really dwelling at this time on another fact. For these appearances were but temporary, while the seeing Him, of which He was here speaking, was to be permanent. It is that close intercourse described by St. Paul in the saying so like the present passage (2 Cor. iii. 18) : "*We with uncovered face behold the glory of the Lord,*" the inward view of the glorified Saviour produced in us by the Holy Spirit. While the world, which has known Jesus only after the flesh, sees Him no more after His bodily departure, He becomes from that time visible to His people in a spiritual and Divine medium, to which they are transported by the Spirit, and where they meet Him. This close intercourse is the source of all the Christian's strength in his conflict with himself and with the world. The next phrase may be understood in three different manners. First, that of Meyer and Luthardt: "*And you, you see me because I live, and you shall live also.*" " Christ and believers being transported, the former by glorification, the latter by the work of the Holy Spirit, into the same medium of life, they meet again, His living people see their living Lord." The idea is a noble one, but the contrast between the presents: *you see me, I live,* and the future: *you shall see me,* cannot be well explained with this interpretation, though Luthardt endeavours to account for it. It may be secondly explained: *you see me* (then), *because I live;* and (by reason of this sight of me who live) *you shall live also.* The spiritual *sight* of Jesus which is granted us results from His heavenly *life* as glorified, and our *life* results from this inward vision. This meaning is equally beautiful, but there is a third construction which seems to me preferable: *But you, you see me* (in opposition to *the world seeth me no more*), and *because I live, you shall live also.* They behold Him, and since He whom they behold is alive, their own life flows forth from this beholding.—In any case, Jesus, by His use of these presents: *I live, I come, I come again* (vv. 3 and 18), already transports Himself to that approaching time, when, death being finally overcome, He will live the perfect and indestructible life; from that time, beheld by His people in the light of the Spirit, His life will become theirs. The relation between *I live* and *you shall live* is the same as that between *I come* and *I will take* in ver. 3. The present denotes the principle laid down once for all, the future its daily, gradual, and eternal results.

The absence of any logical particle between the successive promises of vv. 16–21, betrays the emotion with which Jesus beheld and announced the decisive day of Pentecost.

Vv. 20, 21. *"At that day ye shall know that I am in my Father, and ye in me, and I in you. He that hath my commandments, and keepeth them, he it is that loveth me: and he that loveth me shall be loved of my Father, and I, I will love him, and will manifest myself unto him."*—The expression: *"that day,"* indicates a definite time. And as all the great events of His ministry were connected with Jewish festivals, as the feast of the Passover was to be the period of His death, and the time of great illumination was closely to follow that event, there is no reason why we should not suppose, whatever Lücke and de Wette, etc., may say, that the day of which He was here speaking was already in His view that of Pentecost. By the expression: *"that day,"* Jesus contrasted that time with the time then present, in which they found so much difficulty in forming a conception of their Master's relation to the Father (vv. 9 and 10). '*Tμεῖς, you:* "yourselves, by your own experience, and not only, as now, by faith in my words." The object of this spiritual illumination of believers will be first the union of Jesus with the Father; they will know Him as a Being who lives and acts in God, and in whom God lives and acts as in a second self. This direct consciousness of the relations between Jesus and God will proceed from the living consciousness they will receive of their own relation to Jesus—they will feel Him live in them, and will feel themselves to live in Him; and when they no longer know any other life than that which they derive from Him (*you in me*), and feel at the same time that all His life really enters into them (*I in you*), they will thence understand what He has revealed to them of what God is to Him, and what He is to God. The transcendent fact of the communion of Jesus with God will become to them an object of direct perception in the experience of their own communion with Jesus. These were the μεγαλεῖα τοῦ Θεοῦ, *the wondrous things of God*, which St. Peter and the disciples celebrated in new tongues on the day of Pentecost.

Ver. 21 defines the mode of this illumination. Jesus had briefly said in ver. 15: "*Keep my commandments, and I will pray the Father.*" He here enumerates in detail each link in this chain of graces. 1st, His word must be resolutely retained (ἔχειν) and practically observed (τηρεῖν). This is not done by the world, which hears but rejects it, and is therefore unfitted to receive this higher favour. 2d, He that does so (ἐκεῖνος, this exceptional individual) gains by his moral faithfulness the special character of *a friend* of Jesus (ὁ ἀγαπῶν με). 3d, He hence becomes the *beloved of the Father*, for the Father loves all who love the Son, the supreme object of His love. This love of the Father is not that spoken of in iii. 16: "*God so loved the world.*" There is between these two feelings the same difference as between a man's compassion for his guilty and unhappy neighbour, and the affection of a father for his child, or of a husband for his wife. 4th, The Son, seeing the eye of the Father rest with loving complacency on His disciple, feels Himself united to the latter by a new tie ("*and I will love him*"); whence ensues, 5th, The perfect *revelation* of Himself: "*I will manifest myself unto him.*" This is the highest fulfilment of the words, *you shall know*, in ver. 20. But this remarkable expression, ἐμφανίζειν, transposes the manifestation of the Messiah to the inward (ἐν), the spiritual, and consequently the individual sphere. And it was just this circumstance which called forth the question of Jude. Thus this last word, while terminating the conversation with Philip, gave rise to the conversation with Jude which now follows. Philip had requested a theophany. Jesus had answered: "Thou hast long enjoyed one" (vv. 9–11). Then, justifying the aspiration of the apostle, who was longing for something still more glorious, He said: "And thou shalt have that which is still better; a more excellent theophany awaits thee, that of my return within thee by the Spirit" (vv. 12–21). This is the climax of the second series of thoughts on the internal theophany, which the answer of Jesus to Jude is about to bring before us. Gess compares our Lord, in His manner of treating these interruptions on the part of His disciples, to a skilful pilot, who does not suffer himself to be diverted from his course by the waves which he encounters, but by a prompt stroke of the rudder restores the ship each time to the direction he desires to give it.

5th. Vv. 22–24.

Ver. 22. "*Judas saith unto him, not Iscariot, Lord, and*[1] *what has happened, that Thou wilt manifest Thyself unto us and not unto the world?*"—The mode of revelation, of which Jesus had just spoken, entirely perplexed the minds of the disciples, constantly turned as they were towards some external manifestation of the Messianic kingdom which should be visible to all. It was especially in the secondary group of the apostolic college, which was more or less influenced by the carnal spirit of Iscariot, that such notions were still maintained. The Judas or Jude here mentioned is only so called by St. Luke (Luke vi. 16; Acts i. 13). In the lists of Matt. x. 3 and Mark iii. 18, he is designated by the names (surnames) of Lebbeus and Thaddeus: *the bold* or *the*

---

[1] A B D E L X It^plerique (not ℵ) omit καὶ before τι.

beloved. He occupies one of the lowest places among the apostles. The explanation, *not Iscariot,* is intended to obviate the supposition of a return of Judas after xiii. 30.—By saying, "*What has happened?*" Jude requests to know the new fact which is the cause of so complete a change in the Messianic programme—a change of which he thinks he sees a proof in the saying of Jesus in ver. 21. The καί, *and,* before τί γέγονεν, is an expression of surprise; it is omitted, as superfluous, in several Mss. — *To us* here signifies: to us *alone.* The objection of Jude is connected with, and completes, the request of Philip. The latter was thinking of the great theophany which was to inaugurate the establishment of the Messianic kingdom; Jude, of the realization of the kingdom itself.

Vv. 23, 24. "*Jesus answered and said unto him, If any man love me, he will keep my words, and my Father will love him, and we will come unto him, and will make*[1] *our abode with him. He that loveth me not keepeth not my sayings; and the word which ye hear is not mine, but the Father's which sent me.*"—Jesus continued His discourse as though He had not heard the question of Jude; for the first part of ver. 23 is but a reproduction of ver. 21. He nevertheless answered the question by more forcibly reiterating the promise, as well as the moral condition, which had called forth the objection. Comp. an analogous kind of answer, Luke xiii. 41 sqq. To love Jesus, to keep His word, to be loved of the Father, these are the conditions of the promised revelation; now the world does not fulfil them, but is animated by opposite dispositions (ver. 24).—As to the conditions of the manifestation, Jesus abridges ver. 21; as to the manifestation itself, He more gloriously develops it. The manifestation of Jesus to the soul becomes an actual habitation, and this is a descent of heaven to earth, a true dwelling of God Himself in the believer. Here, as at x. 30, Jesus, speaking of God and Himself, says *we;* this expression, under penalty of being absurd, implies His consciousness of His deity.—The conception of the kingdom of God here met with is one not alien to the Synoptists. Comp. Luke xvii. 20: "*The kingdom of God cometh not with observation; the kingdom of God is within*

---

[1] ℵ B L X read ποιησομεθα instead of ποιησομεν.

you" (ἐντὸς ὑμῶν); and Matt. xxviii. 18–20. A similar image occurs in Rev. iii. 20: "*If any man hear my voice and open the door, I will come in to him, and I will sup with him, and he with me.*" The term μονή, *dwelling*, connects this verse with ver. 2. Here below, it is God who dwells with the believer; above, it will be the believer who will dwell with God. The first of these facts (ver. 23) is the condition of the second (ver. 3).

Ver. 23 explained the *to us* of Jude's question; ver. 24 answers the *and not unto the world*. The notion: "And it is no slight thing to reject my word, for (καί) it is that of God Himself," must be understood between the two propositions of ver. 24. The understood conclusion is: "How, then, with such a disposition, hostile as it is to the word of both the Son and the Father, is it possible to become their abode?" Comp. what is said of the world in vv. 15 and 17.—Thus have the various encouragements brought forward by the Lord gradually risen: "You shall be received with me into my Father's house. . . . In me you have already seen the Father. . . . You shall carry on my work below. . . . Another divine support shall give you power. . . . In this inward support I will myself return within you. . . . With me the Father Himself shall dwell in you. . . ." Was not all this enough to justify His "Let not your heart be troubled" (xiv. 1)? The next passage, with which this first outpouring on the part of Jesus closes, returns to the starting-point, but changes the *Be not troubled* into *Rejoice!*

6th. Vv. 25–31.

Vv. 25, 26. "*These things have I spoken unto you, being present with you; but the support, the Holy Spirit, whom my Father will send in my name, shall teach you all things, and bring back all things to your remembrance which I have said unto you.*"—These words might be directly connected with the preceding, since it is by the gift of the Holy Spirit that the great promise of vv. 22–24 will be fulfilled. But the perf. λελάληκα, *I have told you*, which denotes a teaching now concluded, and the words *being present with you*, which allude to the approaching separation, show that Jesus was returning to the idea from which He started, and the first discourse approaching its termination; and this is confirmed by all that follows. The sayings, then, of vv. 25-29 must be regarded as beginning the conclusion of this dialogue. What Jesus had just said concerning a future meeting above (vv. 1-3), and here below (vv. 12-24), is all that He can as yet reveal to them. If this future is to them still enveloped in obscurity, the instructions of another teacher shall dispel these mists, and explain all His promises by fulfilling them. Ταῦτα, *these things*, stands first, in opposition to πάντα, *all things* (ver. 26): "This is what I can tell you now, another shall afterwards tell you *all*."—The epithet *holy*, given to the Spirit in ver. 26, recalls that deep line of demarcation just drawn by Jesus in vv. 17 and 24, between the profane world and the disciples, already sanctified by their attachment to Him. As holy, the Spirit can dwell only with the latter. — The expression, *in my name*, should, according to Luthardt and Meyer, be explained by the general principle that all that is done for the accomplishment of the plan of salvation is done *in Christ*—that is to say, for the manifesting and glorifying of the name in which salvation is comprised. But is not this too vague? Jesus had just said that He who loved Him should be loved of His Father, and that the manifestation, which is the work of the Spirit, should proceed from this love. The believer's title, then, to this gift will be his love for Jesus, and the motive for this gift on the part of the Father will be His love for Jesus, and for him who loves Jesus. This is the exegesis of the formula: *in my name*. The pron. ἐκεῖνος, *He*, only brings into strong relief the instruction of the new teacher in opposition to that of Jesus, who is about to leave them (ver. 25). He will do two things: *teach all things*, and *bring to their remembrance* what they have been already taught. The two functions are closely connected: He will teach new truths by recalling the old, and will recall the old by teaching the new. The sayings of Jesus, the remembrance of which the Spirit shall revive within them, will be the matter of His instruction in all truth, the germ which He will fertilize in their hearts; as conversely this inward agency of the Spirit will incessantly recall to their memories some former saying of Jesus, so that, in proportion as they partake of His illumination, they will exclaim: "Now I understand this or that saying of the Lord!" Then, again, the brightness of this light will bring from oblivion other long-forgotten sayings. Such is even yet the relation between the teaching of the written word and that of the Spirit.—Of the two πάντα, *all things*, the first, the object of *shall teach*, embraces more than the second. The Holy Spirit will make the disciples understand *all*, by recalling to them one after another *all* the sayings of Christ. Of course, this *all* includes only the things of the new creation in Christ Jesus, of salvation. The first creation, nature, is not a matter of revelation, but of scientific study.

Vers. 27–29. "*Peace I leave you, my peace I give you: not as the world gives it, give I it unto you. Let not your heart be troubled, neither let it be afraid. You have heard how I said to you, I go away, and I come to you. If ye loved me, ye would have rejoiced because I said,*[1] *I go unto the Father, for my*[2] *Father is greater than I. And now I have told you these things before they come to pass, that when they come to pass you may believe.*"—The promises of vv. 25 and 26 aimed at tranquillizing the disciples with respect to the obscurity which hovered over their own, and their Master's future. Vv. 27–29 tend to reassure them concerning the *difficulties* to be encountered in this future. Meyer takes the word εἰρήνη in an objective sense: *salvation* (שלום, full prosperity). But the close of the verse: *Let not your heart be troubled*, favours the subjective meaning, which is also the natural signification of εἰρήνη: tranquillity, inward repose. Peace is the inward serenity based upon reconciliation with God. This is His legacy (ἀφίημι, *I leave*), a legacy derived from His own treasury: *my* peace. Their faith was not yet strong enough to produce in them a peace of their own, hence He invited them for the present to enjoy that which they beheld in Him. They were by faith in Him to make His calmness in the presence of danger their own. The verb δίδωμι, *I give*, agrees with τὴν ἐμήν (*my*); it is of his *own* that one *gives*. In Luke x. 5, 6, Jesus confers upon His disciples the power which He here exercises, that of imparting *their* peace.—The

---

[1] א A B D, 10 Mnn. It. Vg. Syr. Cop. Or. omit ειπον between οτι and πορευομαι (*because I go*, instead of *because I said I go*).

[2] A B D L X, 8 Mnn It^plerique Vg. omit μου after πατηρ.

contrast between the peace of Jesus and that of the world is generally referred to their *nature*,—the world's peace consisting in the enjoyment of a good which is but seeming; that of the Saviour in the possession of real and imperishable good. But the omission of the object, *peace*, in the second proposition (*not as the world giveth give I*), and the conj. καθώς (*in the manner of*), oblige us, I think, to place the contrast on the verb *give*, and not on its object: "My gift is real and efficacious, while the world, when it bids you farewell with the ordinary formula, Peace be unto you, gives you but empty words, a powerless wish." I cannot see in what respect this meaning is beneath the serious nature of the situation (Meyer). It was the peace which He at that moment imparted which was to banish from their hearts the *trouble* He still perceived there (μὴ ταρασσέσθω), and to preserve them at the same time from the danger of *being afraid*, δειλιᾶν, which would result therefrom.

But it was not sufficient for Jesus to see that they should be reassured and strengthened; He desired to see them even *glad* (ver. 28). And this they would really be if they understood aright the meaning of His approaching departure. The words: *if you loved me*, are exquisitely tender. The Saviour uses them to make their joy the duty of affection; He calls their attention to His approaching exaltation (comp. xiii. 3, 31, 32). What friend would not rejoice to see his friend raised to a position truly worthy of him? And if they rightly understood the extent of this change in their Master's situation, they would at the same time rejoice for themselves. This second idea is brought out by the fact that Jesus, while saying: "*I go away, I go to the Father*," adds: "*and I come to you.*" The first of these facts is the condition of the second. It is because Jesus is, by His departure, about to share in the omnipresence and the absolute life of the Father, that He will be able to manifest and impart Himself to His disciples, and to live with them everywhere (vv. 21 and 23). Matt. xxviii. 18-20 expresses the same connection of ideas. To Jesus, *to go away is to come again* in a truer manner. This meaning of ver. 28 seems to us to result directly from the expressions used and from the context. The explanation: God will be a better protector to you than I could be by my visible presence

(Lücke and De Wette after older expositors), ignores the personal character of the words: If you loved me.

The saying: *The Father is greater than I*, is in perfect agreement, whatever M. Reuss may say, with the premises laid down in the prologue; or rather, the thought of the prologue is but an echo of this statement and of so many like it in this Gospel. On the one hand, in fact, this saying assumes in Him who uttered it the most vivid consciousness of His participation in the divine nature. For how should nothingness institute a comparison between itself and God? The creature who should say: "*God is greater than I*," would blaspheme no less than one who should say: "I am equal with God." God alone can compare Himself with God. Hence the Arians have been guilty, to say the least, of great unskilfulness in relying on this saying. On the other hand, it is impossible to admit that it is solely as man, and not as Logos, that Jesus, as orthodoxy affirms, uttered these words. The unity of Christ's person must be maintained, and two distinct *egos* cannot be admitted in Him. The difficulty is solved by allowing that the *ego* of the Divine Logos fully entered into the human condition, but that in the course of His development, Jesus, at a given moment (that of His baptism), apprehended Himself in His oneness with the Divine Logos. It is, then, the Logos made man who, from the midst of His limited and relative existence, contemplates that divine absolute state of being in which He found Himself before His incarnation, and to the participation of which He is about, as man, to be re-exalted. Nothing could be more consistent with the views of the prologue.

At ver. 29 Jesus applies to His approaching departure what He had said, ch. xiii., of the treachery of Judas. This painful separation and this return of a purely spiritual nature, which they find it so difficult to receive, will, when these facts have taken place and the disciples remember the present sayings of Jesus, conduce to the establishment of their faith. And now at last He gives the order for departure, for which He has thus prepared them.

Vv. 30, 31. "*I will say little more to you; for the prince of this*[1] *world cometh, and hath nothing in me. But that the*

---

[1] Τούτου in T. R. is supported by only some Mnn. and It.

world may know that I love my Father, and [1] *that I act as the Father hath commanded* [2] *me, arise, let us go hence."*—Jesus felt the approach of His invisible enemy. He had a presentiment not only of the arrival of Judas, but also of the conflict with Satan himself which He was about to sustain in Gethsemane.

Two very different meanings may be given to these verses, though the results are in either case fundamentally the same. Either the καί, *and*, before ἐν ἐμοί must be taken in a concessive sense: *and indeed:* "He cometh, and indeed he hath nothing in me which can be a reason for his power over me; but for the love I have to my Father I willingly surrender myself to him. *Arise!*" Or we may take this καί in the adversative sense, in which it is so frequently used in St. John: "He cometh, *but* he has no hold upon me; nevertheless (ἀλλά), that the world may know . . . *arise!* and let us depart hence, that I may yield myself to this enemy." Οὐδὲν ἔχειν signifies to have neither right nor power over the object of his hatred. The saying implied in Him who pronounced it a consciousness of perfect innocence. *That* may be made to depend on ποιῶ, *I do:* "That the world may know . . ., I am about to do all that the Father has commanded me." But this construction is a forced one, by reason of the καί which precedes καθώς. Or *that* may be made to depend on a verb understood: "*It happens thus*, that the world may know that I love the Father, and *that* I do what He has commanded me." So Tischendorf. But how much more effective is a third construction, which makes *that* depend upon the two imperatives which terminate the sentence: "But that the world may know . . ., *arise*"! This manner of speaking much resembles the triumphant apostrophe of our Lord, preserved by the three synoptists, Matt. ix. 6 and parallel passages. *To rise* for the purpose of going to Gethsemane was, in fact, willingly to surrender Himself to the power of Satan, who was there preparing for a decisive conflict, the completion of that in the wilderness, and to the treachery of Judas, who was about to seek Him in that very place which he knew so well. Jesus knew that no one would come to take Him in the room which He and His disciples at that moment occupied.

---

[1] A E It^{alia} omit καί.

[2] B L X It. Vg. read ἐντολὴν ἔδωκεν instead of ἐνετείλατο.

The imperatives: *arise, let us go hence*, might certainly have produced no immediate effect; which is the supposition of Meyer, Luthardt, and all who consider that Jesus remained in the room till after the priestly prayer. But in this case, it is not easy to see why St. John should have so expressly mentioned this order, without at least hinting at this delay by a word of explanation, as in xi. 6. Hence Gess justly remarks: "Jesus having in ver. 31 given the signal for departure, we must regard the discourses of chs. xv. and xvi. as delivered on the road to Gethsemane." The opposition of Meyer and Luthardt to this view does not make us hesitate to do so. Comp. remarks on xvi. and xvii. 1.

According to M. Reuss, the questions of Thomas, Philip, and Jude arose from misconceptions so strange, and mistakes so gross, that it is impossible to regard them as having any historical value. Exegesis has, on the contrary, confirmed their perfect agreement with the view-point at that time occupied by the apostles. So long as Jesus was with them, they did not greatly differ from the rest of the people, except in attachment to His person. Intellectually speaking, they still shared the generally received ideas. It was their Master's death and ascension, and lastly, the gift of Pentecost, which radically transformed their notions of the kingdom of God. Hence there is nothing astonishing in the fact that Thomas should, like the Jews in ch. xii., declare that he can understand nothing about a Christ who leaves the earth and speaks of meeting His disciples in another world; or that Philip should, like those who demanded a sign from heaven, beg for a sensible theophany as a pledge of his Master's and the disciples' glorious future; or, lastly, that Jude should inquire with anxiety concerning the reality of a Messianic coming from which the world would be excluded.—Undoubtedly, the reproduction of the details of this conversation in so natural, and at the same time so exact, a manner, could only have been the work of one who had, like the author himself, stood on the confines of the two conceptions, that of Jesus and that of the disciples, thus brought into collision. Nowhere does the evangelist appear more completely initiated into the internal relations and characters of the individuals composing the apostolic circle. As to the answers of our Lord, they are so perfectly adapted to the situation, they bear such an impress of exquisite refinement of feeling and sublime spirituality of thought, that it is impossible to attribute them to any other than Jesus Himself, without making that other the equal of Him whom the church adores as her Lord and Founder.

II. *The Position of the Disciples in the World after the Effusion of the Holy Spirit.*—xv. 1-xvi. 15.

The preceding conversations referred to the approaching separation between Jesus and His disciples, and to the twofold meeting, both heavenly and earthly, which would terminate it. This meeting would take place by means of their future dwelling with Him in His Father's house, and previously by means of an event now close at hand, by His dwelling in them by the Holy Spirit. At ch. xv. Jesus transports Himself in thought to the period which will bind together these two meetings—the period in which His spiritual return will be consummated, but His people not yet exalted to His abode. The glorified Christ, possessed of His divine condition, has returned, and is living in His people. They are united to Him, and by Him to each other. Under His influence they work together like members of one body at the Father's work. Such is the new position, in view of which He now gives them the necessary directions, warnings, and encouragements. Like the branches of a fruitful vine, they are to offer good fruit to the world, which, instead of blessing them, will take up the axe to destroy this noble vine, this heavenly plant. This opposition, however, will have no other effect than that of making conspicuous to all, that divine power by which they are animated, and by which they will confound the world. Thus we have three leading ideas: 1st, The new condition of the disciples resulting from the Pentecostal gift, xv. 1–17; 2d, The consequent hostility of the world, xv. 18–xvi. 4; 3d, The spiritual victory to be gained over the world by the Holy Ghost, through their instrumentality, xvi. 5–15. The actors in this future drama are the disciples, the world, and the Holy Spirit, each of whom is successively predominant in the following discourse.

1st. xv. 1–17.

After the words: "*Let us depart hence,*" Jesus and His disciples left the upper chamber, which had just been to them, as it were, the vestibule of the Father's house. They passed in silence through the streets of Jerusalem, and soon found themselves alone in some retired spot on the declivity which descends into the valley of the Kedron. Surrounded by this little band of disciples, in view of Jerusalem, in which the Jewish people were assembled, and thinking of the human race represented by Israel, Jesus reflected on the mighty task which awaited His disciples in carrying on His work in the world. And in the first passage He chiefly devoted Himself to making them fully understand the nature of this new situation and the obligations attached to it. In this, then, we have first the *position*, in vv. 1–3 (*in me*); then the duty of this position, in ver. 4 (*to abide* in Him); and lastly, the *consequences* of fulfilling or neglecting this duty, in vv. 5–8 (*to bear fruit*, or *to be burned*).

Vv. 1–3. "*I am the true vine, and my Father is the husbandman. Every branch that beareth not fruit in me, He taketh away; and every branch that beareth fruit, He purgeth it, that it may bring forth more fruit. And as for you, ye are clean already because of the word which I have spoken unto you.*"—The pronoun ἐγώ, standing first, and the epithet ἡ ἀληθινή, the *genuine* vine, naturally lead us to suppose that Jesus was here intending to contrast His person with some other vine, which was not in His eyes the true. We ask, then, "What external circumstance was it which led Jesus thus to express Himself?" Those who hold that Jesus had not yet quitted the room decline to answer this question (De Wette), or have recourse, in explaining this image, either to the use of wine in the institution of the Lord's Supper (Grotius, Meyer); or to the shoots of a vine whose branches entered the room (Knapp, Tholuck); or to the golden vine which adorned one of the gates of the temple, the remembrance of which might present itself to the thoughts of Jesus (Jerome, Lampe); or, finally, to the representation of Israel under the figure of a vine, so frequent in the O. T. If it be admitted, as by us, that after pronouncing ver. 31 of ch. xiv. Jesus really left the room and the city, the explanation becomes more easy and simple. Jesus stops at a vine loaded with branches; His disciples gather around Him; He finds in this plant an emblem of His relation to them. This natural vine is in His eyes an image, an earthly copy, of the true, essential, spiritual vine, and He proceeds to develop the thought of His future union with His people, by borrowing from the object before His eyes, expressions which may render it intelligible to His disciples. "It is to be supposed," says Gess, "that on the declivity of the valley of the Kedron there were vines, before which Jesus stopped with His disciples." The word *vine* here comprises both the trunk and the branches, as the term ὁ Χριστός in 1 Cor. xii. 12 denotes Christ and the church. The point of comparison between Christ and the vine is that organic union by which the life of the trunk becomes that of the branches. As the sap in the branches is that which they draw from the vine, so will life in the disciples be the life they will derive from Jesus glorified. This comparison might undoubtedly have been borrowed from any other plant. But the vine has a special dignity, resulting from the nobleness of its sap and the excellence of its fruit.—The title of *husbandman* is given to God as at once *proprietor* and *cultivator*. He it was who possessed the theocracy, and this theocracy seemed now to be transformed into the little community by whom Jesus was surrounded. He it was who watched over the preservation of that divine organism, and directed its development on earth. While Jesus is its essential life, the Father cultivates it by His providential care. Jesus designs to impress upon them the value of this plant, which God Himself tends and cares for. What is here said by no means interferes with the fact that God effects this work by the instrumentality of the glorified Christ, only the figure employed does not allow this aspect of the truth to be brought forward. On the one hand, Jesus lives *in* His people by His Spirit, and it is in this respect that He compares Himself to the vine. On the other, He reigns *over* and *for* them as the organ of the Father, and His agency in this respect cannot be represented here by reason of the figure employed, but is mingled with the agency of the Father. St. Paul finds the means of uniting these two aspects in Eph. i. 22. The culture of the vine embraces two principal operations,—that by which every *unfruitful* branch is cut off (the αἴρειν), and that by which the *fruitful* branches are purged—that is to say, freed from barren shoots, that the sap may be concentrated in the cluster which is forming (the καθαίρειν). As this passage refers solely to the relation of Jesus to the true or seeming members of His church, the first of these images cannot be applied, as Hengstenberg thinks, to unbelieving Israel. If any historical example were present to the thoughts of our Lord, it would only have been that of Judas. But He was probably thinking of the future of His church, and was contemplating beforehand those professors of the gospel, who, while externally united to Him, nevertheless live in a state of internal separation from Him, whether in consequence of a decree which prevents their genuine conversion, or of their own neglect to sacrifice wholly their own life and to maintain the spiritual tie which unites them to Him.—’Ἐν ἐμοί, *in me*, may refer either to the word *branch: every branch in me* (united to me), or to the participle φέρον: *which beareth not fruit in me*. In any case, the term branch in itself already assumes that individuals who are in a certain sense united to Christ are here spoken of. By *fruit*, Jesus designates the *spiritual life*, with all its normal manifestations,—that life which the believer is called upon to produce and incessantly to develop, whether in himself, or, by the power of Christ living (Rom. i. 13) in him, in the case of his neighbour. It may happen that the believer, after a season of fervour, suffers his own life to predominate above that which he derives from the Lord, and that the latter is about to perish. Then the arm of the Father interposes. After tolerating for a time the presence of this dead member in the church of Christ, God severs the deceptive tie, at one time by allowing him to be subjected to a violent temptation, at another by death and the judgment which is to follow.

In describing the second operation, Jesus had in view not only the eleven disciples, but all future believers who should live in Him by the Holy Spirit. Ver. 3 teaches that it is first of all by the word of Christ that God will purge them from the shoots of their own life, which show themselves in them; then, when this proves insufficient, God will use other and more painful means, which will, like a sharp pruning-knife, cut to the quick of the natural affections and the carnal will. And thus the whole being of the disciple will at last be devoted to the production of the divine fruit which he ought to bear.

Jesus calms the minds of His disciples with respect to this second operation, by reminding them (ver. 3) that in their case it is, in principle, already accomplished. By their attachment to Christ, and by the word which He has spoken to them, "the old man has already received his death-blow" (Gess), although he has yet to die. The moral training which they had received from Jesus had deposited in them the principle of perfect purity. For the word of Christ is the instrument of a daily judgment, of an austere discipline, which God exercises by it upon the soul which remains attached thereto. On this part, attributed to the word of Christ, comp. v. 24, viii. 31, 32, xii. 48.—Διά (with the accus.) is not *by*, but *because of*.—'Υμεῖς, *you*, in opposition to those who were not yet in this privileged position.—From the nature of the position (*in me*), Jesus deduces the duty of this position: *to abide*.

Ver. 4. "*Abide in me, and I in you; as the branch cannot bear fruit of itself except it abide*[1] *in the vine, no more can ye, except ye abide*[2] *in me.*"—For a branch to remain united to the vine is the condition, the law of its life. All the conditions of fruitfulness are included in this. The imperative proves that this relation is maintained as it was begun, *freely*, by the faithful use of the means divinely offered. Ver. 7 will show that the fundamental means is the word of Jesus. —'Ἐν ἐμοὶ μένειν, to *abide in me*, expresses the continuous act by which the Christian lays aside all that he might draw from his own wisdom, strength, or merit, to derive all from Christ by the inward aspiration of faith. And this is so entirely the sole condition laid down for the agency of Christ's life in him, that Jesus omits the verb in the following proposition. Hence the: *and I in you*, appears to be in such wise the direct and necessary consequence of the former of these two acts, that where the first is accomplished the second cannot

---

[1] ℵ B L: μινη instead of μενη (T. R. with 14 Mjj.).
[2] ℵ A B L: μινητι instead of μεινητι (T. R. with 13 Mjj.).

fail to be realized. Thus the agency of Christ is, no less than our own, boldly placed under the control of our freedom. The close of ver. 4 justifies the duty pointed out; instant unfruitfulness would be the immediate result of the believer's separation from the vine. Here, as in ver. 19, ἐὰν μή is a simple explanation of the ἀφ' ἑαυτοῦ, and not a restriction appended to the principal idea.—The thesis here laid down is not that of the moral impotence of the natural man, but that of the unfruitfulness of the believer left to his own strength; still it is evident that the second of these truths is based upon the first.

The following verses, vv. 5–8, are, as it were, the *sanction* of the law of life and death which Jesus has just proclaimed. We have first the contrast between fruitfulness and unfruitfulness (ver. 5), with the terrible consequences of the latter (ver. 6), and then the glorious results of fruitfulness (vv. 7 and 8).

Vv. 5, 6. *" I am the vine, ye are the branches; he that abideth in me, and I in him, the same beareth much fruit, for apart from me ye can do nothing. If a man abide* [1] *not in me, he is cast forth as the branch and is withered; then they gather them* [2] *and cast them into the fire, and they burn."*—The first words of ver. 5: *" I am the vine, ye are the branches,"* are not, as has been said, either an idle repetition or a tardy development of the truth expressed in ver. 1. While continuing to contemplate the actual vine before Him, an increasingly vivid sense of the entire dependence of His disciples upon Himself possessed our Lord's mind: " Yes, this is indeed what I am to you, and what you are to me; I the vine, ye the branches!" The reason alleged: *"for without me ye can do nothing,"* seems, as a purely negative one, at the first glance illogical. But if Christ is in such wise *all* to the believer that he can do nothing without Him, does not this imply that he can do much if he remains united to his Lord ?

With the happy fruitfulness of the branch united to Him, Jesus contrasts the sad and terrible fate of the unfruitful branch.—The operation of pruning had just taken place in Palestine; perhaps, as Lange remarks, Jesus might at that

---

[1] ℵ A B D : μεινη instead of μεινη.
[2] ℵ D L X Δ Π, 20 Mnn. It^{aliq} Syr. : αυτο instead of αυτα.

very moment have been beholding the fire in which the recently lopped branches were burning. It is impossible to refer ver. 6 (as Hengstenberg does) to the Jewish nation and its destruction by the Romans; a believer who does not remain faithful is the sole subject of this saying, which is spoken as a warning to the disciples when they should have received the Pentecostal gift.—The aorists, ἐξηράνθη, ἐβλήθη, *has been withered, has been cast forth*, are, according to Bäumlein, to be explained in this passage, as in numerous other cases where this tense is employed to designate a fact of daily experience. Perhaps it would be better to say, with Meyer, that our Lord transported Himself in thought to the moment of the judgment just uttered. 'Εβλήθη, *cast out* of the vineyard.—The subject of συνάγουσι, *they gather*, is the vineyard labourers; in the application, the angels (Luke xii. 20; Matt. xiii. 41). The *fire* is the emblem of judgment; comp. another image in Luke xiv. 34, 35. Καίεται, *they burn*, is the present of duration, which here has its full force. The thought pauses at this unquenchable fire, . . . and then turns to the fruitful branch, which bears fruit to the husbandman's praise. Thus vv. 7 and 8 combine with ver. 5 in developing the glorious *results* of the believer's communion with Christ.

Vv. 7, 8. "*If ye abide in me, and my words abide in you, ye shall ask*[1] *what ye will, and it shall be done unto you. Herein is my Father glorified, that ye bear much fruit, and thus shall ye become*[2] *my disciples.*"—The parallelism of the two conditions in ver. 7 leads us to expect the expression: "*and if I abide in you.*" For this, Jesus substitutes the remarkable variation: "and if *my words* abide in you." In fact, it is by constantly remembering and meditating on the words of Jesus that the disciple remains united to Him, and that He can continue to act on and by His disciple. Jesus next adds an important idea, that of prayer, which is directly connected with the preceding. The words of Jesus, digested by meditation, nourish in the soul of the believer those holy desires which urge it to prayer. By meditating on them, he

---

[1] A B D L M X Γ, 50 Mnn. It^{aliq}: αιτησασθι, *ask*, instead of αιτησεσθι, *you shall ask* (T. R. with ℵ, 9 Mjj. etc.).

[2] B D L M X Λ: γινησθι, *that you may become*, instead of γενησεσθι, *you shall become* (T. R. with 11 Mjj. etc.).

better understands the holiness and beauty of God's work; he measures its length and breadth and depth and height, and, moved by this contemplation, he more fervently supplicates, in that definite manner which arises from actual wants, the advancement of this work. A prayer thus inspired is a child of heaven; it is God's promise transformed into petition; as such it is certain to be heard, and the absolute promise: "*it shall be done unto you,*" is no longer surprising.—The Alex. substitute the imperative *ask* for the future *you shall ask*, a correction which turns the promise into a moral precept. —The result of this fruitfulness of the disciples would be the glorification of the Father (ver. 8). What could more honour the husbandman than the abundant fruitfulness of the vine which he has taken care of with so much delight? Now the husbandman is the Father (ver. 1). Ἐν τούτῳ, *in this*, evidently bears upon ἵνα, *so that*, or *that*, which follows; this conjunction taking the place of ὅτι, because the idea of bearing fruit presents itself to the mind as an *end* to be attained.— The aorist ἐδοξάσθη, properly *has been glorified*, characterizes this result as one immediately attained whenever the condition, the bearing of fruit, is present. Winer and others make this aorist an aorist of anticipation, as in ver. 6.—Jesus, when contemplating with filial satisfaction the glory of the Father, which will from time to time be the result of His disciples' work, seems to press these beloved beings with redoubled ardour to His heart. By carrying on here below the work of their Master, whose only care was to glorify the Father, they will more and more deserve the title of His disciples. **Καί,** *and thus*. The Alex. read the subjunctive, *and that you may become* (γένησθε, dependent on ἵνα), instead of *you shall become*. Tischendorf himself rejects this reading, which is only a correction after φέρητε.—The dative ἐμοί is closer and more affectionate than the genitive ἐμοῦ: "You shall more nearly belong to me as disciples." We *are* not disciples once for all, but must always be *becoming* such.—As the vine does not itself directly bear fruit, and offers its clusters by the intervention of the branches, so Jesus will only diffuse spiritual life here below by the instrumentality of those who have received it from Him. By forming a church, He created a body for the effusion of His life, and the glorification of God upon earth. In this great work the Vine hides itself, and lets only the branches appear; it is for them in their turn to hide themselves, and to do homage to the Vine for all that they effect. The Epistles to the Ephesians and Corinthians show this same relation between Christ and His members under an entirely original form. The image of the *head* and *the body* in these Epistles corresponds with that of the vine and the branches in this passage. When St. Paul says of the glorified Christ, that "*in Him dwelleth all the fulness of the Godhead bodily*," and that "*we have all fulness in Him*," he does but formulate the meaning of the parable of the vine and the branches. This also explains why the diffusion of spiritual life makes such slow progress in the world. The vine effects nothing but by means of the branches, and these so often paralyse instead of promoting the action of the vine

The condition of abiding under the influence of Christ's love is to persevere in obedience to His commandments, that is to say, in brotherly love (vv. 9–17).

Vv. 9–11. "*As the Father hath loved me, I have also loved you; abide in my love.*[1] *If ye keep my commandments, ye shall abide in my love, even as I have*[2] *kept my Father's commandments, and abide in His love. These things have I spoken unto you, that my joy might be*[3] *in you, and that your joy might be full.*"—Jesus here substitutes the notion of abiding under the influence *of His love* for that of abiding *in Him*. In fact, it is the love of Jesus which forms the tie between Him and ourselves. In Him the fountain of divine love has welled forth upon earth: the love of the Father for Jesus, of which He gave assurance at His baptism, and which includes that wherewith He loved Him before His incarnation (xvii. 24), and then that of Jesus for His people, which is of like nature (καθώς, not ὥσπερ). In both these cases, the initiative of love was taken by the more exalted Being. On what condition, then, may the relation be maintained and strengthened? Solely by the inferior responding to this love. He has not to evoke it, he has but to remain under its beams. To do this he has only to abstain from forcing it, by unfaithfulness

---

[1] א omits the words ιαν . . . ιν τ. αγαπη μου (confusing this with ver. **9.**).
[2] א D It.: ιγω instead of καγω.
[3] A B D It. Vg. read η instead of μεινη.

and disobedience, to turn from him. Jesus points out that He imposes upon the believer no other condition with respect to Himself but that to which He had to submit with respect to the Father. His holiness was an act of continual submission to the divine injunctions, and without this submission He would have instantly ceased to be the object of the Father's complacence (viii. 29, x. 17). Such also is the position of the believer in respect of Christ's love to him. The expression *my love* can here, in fact, only denote the love of Jesus for His people; comp. the words: *as I have loved you*, and the development, vv. 13–16. The second proposition of ver. 9: *and I have loved you*, does not depend on καθώς, *as*: "As my Father has loved me, *and* I have loved you." For the principal verb would in this case be *abide*, which is impossible, because this idea is in no logical connection with the first of the two propositions of ver. 9: *As my Father has loved me.*—Jesus is certain that in thus speaking He is not imposing a burden, but rather revealing to them the secret of perfect joy (ver. 11). This constant enjoyment of the Father's love in the way of obedience constitutes His joy, which will in the same way be reproduced in His disciples. It is, then, indeed His joy into which He initiates them, and in the possession of which He associates them, in the words: "*These things have I spoken to you, that* . . ." *My* joy cannot then signify: the joy which I will produce in you (Calvin), or: the joy which I feel on your account (Augustine), or: the joy which you feel on my account (Euthymius); but the joy which He Himself experiences in feeling Himself the object of the Father's love. Comp. the analogous expression "*my peace*" in xiv. 27.—By obedience their joy will grow to perfect fulness. For every act of faithfulness will draw closer the bond between Jesus and themselves, as every moment of His life did the bond between Jesus and the Father. And is it not *perfect joy* to be included with the Son in the Father's love? The reading ᾖ seems preferable to μείνῃ. The notion of *being* is enough, that of remaining superfluous; comp. xvii. 26.

This obedience to His commandments, to which Jesus invites them, is concentrated in the exercise of brotherly love.

Ver. 12. "*This is my commandment, that ye love one another, as I have loved you."*—Comp. xiii. 34. Hengstenberg finds in vv. 1–11 a summary of the first table of the law, and in vv. 12-17 one of the second. The normal relation of each branch to the others assumes first of all its normal relation to the vine.

In vv. 13-16 Jesus exalts Christian love to its full height, by setting before it His own for its model. These four verses are a commentary on the words: *as I have loved you.* And first, ver. 13 states the point to which love carries its devotion, death; then vv. 14, 15 show the intimate character of the relation He has borne to them, the confidential intercourse of a friend rather than the authority of a master; and lastly, ver. 16 declares the free initiative which He took in establishing this relation: " If, then, you ask yourselves what limits you are to lay down to your mutual love, first ask yourselves what limits I set to the love I have shown to you!" or: "and if you want to know what it is to love, look at me " (Gess).

Ver. 13. "*Greater love hath no man than this,*[1] *that a man lay down his life for his friends.*"—Our Lord's meaning is clear; *in the relation of friends* there is no greater proof of love than the sacrifice of life. Undoubtedly there is, *absolutely speaking,* a greater proof of love, viz. to give it for enemies, Rom. v. 6-8. "Ἵνα preserves the notion of an end: "The highest point *to which* love in this relation can *aspire* is . . ."

Vv. 14, 15. "*Ye are my friends, if ye do whatsoever*[2] *I command you. I no longer call you servants, because the servant knoweth not what his lord doeth: but I have called you friends; for all things that I have heard of my Father I have made known unto you.*"—At ver. 14 the accent is not on the condition: *if you do,* but upon the statement: *ye are my friends,* as though Jesus meant to say, " It was not without a reason that I just now said : *for his friends* (ver. 13), for this is really the relation I have borne to you." And what is there more touching in domestic life, than a master who, finding a servant really faithful, raises him to the rights and title of a friend ?—Ver. 15 proves the reality of this statement. He had bestowed upon them an unbounded confidence, by com-

---

[1] ℵ D It. omit τις after ινα.
[2] The Mss. read either ο (B It[all 1]) or α 'ℵ D L X It[aliq] Vg. Cop.) or with T. R. οσα (13 Mjj. Mnn. Syr.).

municating to them all that the Father had revealed to Him regarding the great work for which He sent Him. Undoubtedly there were still many things of which they were not yet informed (xiv. 12). But it was not from want of confidence and love that He had not revealed these also, but to spare them in their state of weakness, and because another alone could fulfil this task. The title: *my friends*, used in Luke xii. 4, long before the present moment, has been adduced in objection to this οὐκέτι (I *no more* call you); as though the tendency to make them His friends had not existed from the very first, and could have failed to manifest itself from time to time! It has also been objected that the apostles continued to call themselves *servants of Jesus Christ*, as though, when the master chooses to make his servant a friend, the latter is not all the more bound to remind himself and others of his real condition!

Ver. 16. "*You have not chosen me, but I have chosen you, and appointed you, that you should go and bear fruit, and that your fruit should remain: that whatsoever[1] ye ask the Father in my name, He may give it you.*"—Jesus is conscious how great is the proof of love which He has given them in calling them of His own accord to the apostolate. It was Himself alone who took the initiative in calling them to the highest office bestowed upon man. By the expression: *I have chosen you*, Jesus alludes, as in vi. 70 and xiii. 18, to the solemn act of their election to the apostolate, narrated in Luke vi. 12 sqq. The word ἔθηκα, *have appointed*, denotes the endowment with spiritual light and power which accompanied this act, and enabled them to exercise such an apostolate. The expression ὑπάγητε, *that you may go*, brings out the kind of independence to which He had gradually raised them: "I have put you in a condition to walk alone." *Fruit* here, as throughout this chapter, denotes the communication of spiritual life to mankind; this fruit, unlike that produced by earthly labour, does not perish, but *remains*.

The second *that* is rather parallel with, than dependent, as Luthardt makes it, on the first; comp. the two ἵνα, xiii. 34, and for the meaning the two ὅτι, xiv. 12, 13. To the end of their election, Jesus adds the essential means by which the

---

[1] Instead of ινα ο τι αν and δω (or δωη), ℵ reads οτι αν and δωσιι.

apostles are to accomplish their task—a means which also enters into the end of their vocation, viz. prayer in His name. This latter proposition—depending as it does on the words: *I have appointed you*—signifies: "And I have put you into the glorious position of yourselves obtaining directly from the Father all that you ask of Him." This is the privilege which they owe to the free initiative of His love.

Ver. 17. "*These things I command you, that ye may love one another.*"—The pronoun ταῦτα (*these things*) can only refer to the ἵνα which follows: "I command *this, so that* you may love one another." For the plural proves that this expression comprises and sums up all the preceding instructions and exhortations since xv. 1. The work is all love: love in its hidden source, the love of the Father; in its first manifestation, the love of Christ; and lastly, in its full outpouring, the love of believers for each other. Love is its root, its stem, and its fruit. It forms the essential characteristic of the new kingdom, whose power and conquests are owing solely to the contagion of love. This is why our Lord left no other law than that of love to those who had by faith become members of His body.

Luthardt points out that not a single connective particle occurs in the first seventeen verses of this chapter. There is special solemnity in this long *asyndeton*. We have here the last wishes of Jesus as delivered to His own (see xvii. 24). Such a style could not be that of a Greek author, but must have proceeded from the Hebrew mind.

2d. xv. 18–xvi. 4.

In opposition to this spiritual body, whose inner life and external agency He has just described, Jesus beholds a hostile association arise, whose unifying principle is hatred of Christ and of God. This association, of whose hatred to believers Jesus gives a sketch, vv. 18–25, is the world, mankind in its natural state, which will declare war against the church, and was at that time represented by the Jewish people. Then, after encouraging His disciples by a passing indication of the assistance which will be afforded them, He reproduces in more vivid colours, ver. 26–xvi. 4, a description of the hostility of the world.

Vv. 18–20. "*If the world hates you, know that it hated me*

before you.[1] *If ye were of the world, the world would love its own: but because ye are not of the world, but I have drawn you out of the world, therefore the world hateth you. Remember the word that I have said*[2] *unto you, The servant is not greater than his lord. If they have persecuted me, they will also persecute you; if they have kept my word, they will keep yours also."*—Jesus desired not only to announce to His disciples that hatred on the part of the world of which they would be the objects, but also to strengthen them against it; and this He did first by saying: " It will hate you *as it hates me* (vv. 18-20), and then it will hate you *on my account*" (vv. 21-25). Nothing could better prepare for suffering than the certainty of suffering like Christ and for Him. Γινώσκετε is not indicative (*you know*), but imperative, like μνημονεύετε (*remember*), ver. 20. Consider what has happened in my case, and you will understand that all that happens to you is but natural. —By their union with Christ, the disciples would henceforth represent a new principle upon earth. This would be a strange and a wounding phenomenon to the world, which would try to get rid of it.—'Εξελεξάμην, *I have chosen*, here refers to their having been called to be believers, not apostles; and by it Jesus means to designate the act by which He withdrew them from the world, and not divine predestination. The idea of the close connection thereby formed between Jesus and His disciples reappears at ver. 20 in the expressions *servant* and *lord*. The axiom here cited by Jesus is used in the same sense as at Matt. x. 24, but in one differing from John xiii. 16. In ch. xiii. it was quoted as an encouragement to humility, here as a reason for patience.—It is natural to regard the two cases laid down by Jesus as both actual. The mass of the people will no more be converted by the preaching of the apostles than by that of Jesus. But as He had enjoyed the satisfaction of snatching *individuals* from ruin, so will this joy be also granted to them. This meaning seems to me to be preferable to that of Grotius, who gives to the second proposition an ironical signification; or to that of Bengel, who takes τηρεῖν, *to keep*, in the sense of to observe

---

[1] ℵ D It[plerique] omit ὑμῶν.

[2] Instead of του λογου ου εγω ειπον, ℵ reads τον λογον ον ελαλησα; D: τους λογους ους ελαλησα.

maliciously; or lastly, to the interpretation of Lücke, Meyer, De Wette, and Hengstenberg, who see in these two alternatives only abstract propositions, of which the apostles must discern which will be realized in their case.

Vv. 21–25. *"But all this will they do unto you*[1] *for my name's sake, because they know not Him that sent me. If I had not come and spoken unto them, they would not have sin; but now they have no excuse for their sin. He that hateth me, hateth my Father also. If I had not done among them works such as none other has done,*[2] *they would not have sin: but now they have seen and nevertheless have hated both me and my Father. But this is that the word might be fulfilled which is written in their law: They hated me without a cause."*—'Αλλά (ver. 21): "*But* be of good cheer, it is for my sake."—If Israel has not in this case recognised God as Him who sent me, it is because they have not in general the knowledge of God. Their idea of God is morally perverted, and this is why they have stumbled at my appearing. Jesus speaks only of their ignorance, but behind this ignorance He discerns hatred of good—of Himself as manifested good, of God the living good. Hence the following words, ver. 22. Their long resistance to God through the whole course of their history would certainly have been forgiven, as well as their individual transgressions, if they had at last surrendered in presence of this supreme manifestation. But rejection of Jesus characterized their state as one of invincible estrangement, as *hatred of God*, which is by its nature the unpardonable sin.—The idea differs somewhat from ix. 41.—Ver. 23. Jewish wickedness by hating Jesus clearly showed itself to be *hatred of God*, and was thus distinguished from mere ignorance, like that of the heathen. The words of Jesus (ver. 22), or if not these, His works (ver. 24), ought to have opened their eyes. He whose consciousness was not sufficiently developed to grasp the divine character of His teaching, had at least eyes to behold His miracles. On the two καί, see remarks on vi. 36. I cannot attach any value to the reasons adduced by Meyer against this meaning. His, if I am not mistaken, amounts to: "If I had not come,

---

[1] B D L It^{aliq} Syr.: τις υμας instead of υμιν. א omits the word.
[2] The Mss. are divided between πεποιηκειν (T. R. with E G H, etc.) and εποιησεν א A B D, etc.).

the Jews would not have rejected me and God in me, and would not, by this rejection, have filled the measure of their resistance to God." This idea might suit ix. 41, but is too weak for the present context.—Ver. 25. Ἀλλά: *But* this is not to be wondered at. The righteous man under the old covenant had already complained by the mouth of David, Ps. xxxv. 19, lxix. 4, of being the object of the *gratuitous* hatred of the foes of God. If their hatred was to be entirely laid to their own account, notwithstanding the *faults* and *follies* of the imperfect righteous man (Ps. lxix. 6), how much more might the perfectly righteous Saviour make this complaint, which was at the same time His comfort as well as the comfort of those who suffer like Him and for His sake! *So that* depends upon: "This has happened," understood.—On the term: *their law*, see remarks on viii. 17. De Wette sees a certain amount of irony in these words: "They faithfully observe their law." But this seems rather far-fetched.

Vv. 26, 27. "*But*[1] *when the Support is come, whom I will send unto you from the Father, the Spirit of truth, who proceedeth from the Father, He shall testify of me: and ye also shall bear witness, because ye have been with me from the beginning.*"—Jesus here points out, in only a passing manner, the power which will sustain them in their conflict with the world. This idea He develops in the following paragraph, xvi. 5–15, but now hastens to show His disciples the authority which they would have to oppose to that of the world. In saying: *I will send*, Jesus was necessarily thinking of His reinstatement in His divine condition; His saying, *from the Father*, taught His own subordination to the Father, even when He should have resumed that condition.—Jesus here designates the Spirit as the *Spirit of truth,* in opposition to the falsehood, the voluntary ignorance, of the world. The Spirit will disperse the obscurity with which the world endeavours to surround itself. It is difficult (with Luthardt, Meyer, and most moderns) to refer the words: *who proceedeth from the Father*, to the same fact as the former: *whom I will send to you from the Father*, as this would be mere tautology. Besides, the future πέμψω, *I will send*, refers to an historical fact to take place at an undefined period, while the present ἐκπο-

---

[1] א B Δ omit δὲ after ὅταν.

ρεύεται, *proceedeth*, seems to refer to a permanent, divine, and therefore eternal relation. The divine facts of revelation are based upon the Trinitarian relations, and are, so to speak, their reflections. As the incarnation of the Son is related to His eternal generation, so is the *mission* of the Holy Spirit to His *procession* within the divine essence.—The Latin Church, starting from the words: *I will send*, is not wrong in affirming the *Filioque*, nor the Greek Church, starting from the words: *from the Father*, in maintaining the *per Filium* and the subordination. To harmonize these two views, we must place ourselves at the Christological view-point of St. John's Gospel, according to which the homoousia and the subordination are both at the same time true.—The pronoun ἐκεῖνος, *he*, this Being, and He only, sums up all the qualities which have been attributed to the Holy Spirit, and brings out the authority of this divine witness. The expression: *shall bear witness of me*, must not be referred to the miracles effected by the Holy Spirit in attestation of the mission of Jesus; in which case we should have ὑπὲρ ἐμοῦ, *in my favour*, and not περὶ ἐμοῦ, *of me*, concerning me. Does, then, this witness borne to the person of Jesus consist in the *presence* of the Spirit in this world? Such a sense would suit neither the epithet *Support*, nor that of Spirit *of truth*. Or is the witness to be borne by the Spirit *in the hearts* of the apostles intended? This cannot be when the testimony spoken of is to be given before the world, and in answer to its hostile attitude. We conclude, then, that Jesus intended to speak of testimony to be borne by the *mouths* of the apostles, like that of Peter and the one hundred and twenty on the day of Pentecost.—But in this case, why did He afterwards distinguish it from the testimony of the apostles themselves: "*And ye also shall bear witness to me*," ver. 27? The difference is explained by the words which follow: "*because ye have been with me from the beginning.*" The apostles are by no means to be the passive instruments of the Spirit; they are to remain free personal agents. Side by side with the agency of the Spirit, they will have their special part in the testimony to be given. For they possess a treasure which is their own, and which the Spirit could not have imparted to them, their *historical* knowledge of the ministry of Christ from its commencement to its close. The apostles were to be the *witnesses* of the historic Christ. Now the Spirit does not teach historical facts, but reveals their true meaning. Hence the apostolic testimony, and the testimony of the Spirit, form but a single act, in which each contributes a different element, —the one the historic narrative, the other the internal evidence and the victorious power. This relation is reproduced in our own days in all living preaching derived from Holy Scripture. St. Peter equally distinguishes the two kinds of testimony, Acts v. 32 : "*And we are His witnesses of these things; and so is also the Holy Ghost, whom God hath given to them that obey Him.*" This shows us why, when the apostles desired to fill up the place of Judas, they chose two men who had accompanied Jesus from the baptism of John to the resurrection (Acts i. 21, 22).—Καὶ ὑμεῖς δέ then signifies : "*And you too, you shall bear your part in this testimony.*"

xvi. 1–4. "*These things have I spoken unto you that ye should not be offended. They shall put you out of their synagogues; yea, the hour cometh, that whosoever killeth you will think he offereth worship to God. And these things will they do unto you*[1] *because they have not known the Father nor me. But these things I have foretold you, that when their hour shall come, ye may remember*[2] *that I told you of them. These things I said not unto you from the beginning, because I was with you.*"— Having thus encouraged His apostles, Jesus comes to the most serious matter He had to communicate concerning the subject of which He was speaking. The former picture brought out especially the guilt of the persecutors, the present words dwell rather on the sufferings of the persecuted; the apostles, having always lived in expectation of the national conversion of Israel, might have felt their faith shaken at the sight of the impenitence of this people, and of their increasing hatred to the church.—Ἀλλά here, as frequently, is a term of gradation (2 Cor. vii. 11): *But* you must expect more. Ἵνα denotes that the contents of the hour are *willed* by God. The fanatic zeal of Paul at the time of Stephen's martyr-

---

[1] T. R., with ℵ D L, several Mnn. It^{plerique} Cop., reads ὑμῖν after ποιήσουσιν ; 12 Mjj. Mnn. It^{aliq} Syr. omit it.

[2] A B Π Syr. read αὐτῶν twice, after ὥρα (*the hour of these things*) and after μνημονεύητε. L. Mnn. It. Vg. read it after ὥρα and omit it after μνημονεύητε. D omits it both times.

dom is a striking example of the spiritual state described at ver. 2; comp. Acts xxvi. 9. The notion of ignorance at ver. 3 is introduced by the term δόξῃ, *will think*. Is it not really the height of *blindness* to think to serve God by the very act which is an expression of the most vehement hatred against Him? Ver. 4 returns to the thought of ver. 1. However terrible might be their sufferings, the apostles, by remembering their Master's predictions, would no longer find in them a reason for doubt, but a ground of faith; comp. xiii. 9. Hitherto Jesus had sought to spare them by not disclosing to them this gloomy prospect. As long as He was with them, it was upon Himself that the blow would fall. But now that He was about to leave them, He could no longer conceal from them the future that awaited them.—It seems to us impossible to reconcile this saying: " *These things I said not unto you at the beginning,*" with the place occupied in the discourse, Matt. x., by the positive announcement of the persecutions to which the church would be subjected. It cannot be said, with Euthymius and Chrysostom, that the sufferings here foretold are far *more terrible* (comp. Matt. x. 17, 21, 28); nor, with Bengel and Tholuck, that the present description is *more detailed;* nor, with Hofmann and Luthardt, that Jesus at this season of leave-taking made the announcement of these persecutions the more exclusive object of His discourse. All these distinctions seem to us too slight. It would be better to admit that St. Matthew, in the great discourse given in ch. x., combines all the instructions given to the Twelve at different periods on this subject, as he does in chs. v.–vii. all the new Christian law, and in chs. xxiv. xxv. all the eschatological predictions; and that, because in the composition of the *Logia* he attached more importance to *subject* than to *chronology*. This characteristic is explained as soon as the mode of composition of the first Gospel is understood. (See my *Etudes Bibliques*, II. pp. 18, 19, 3d edit.)

3d. xvi. 5–15.

Jesus now describes the victory which His disciples shall gain over a world in arms against them. He first points out the power which will gain this victory by their means, vv. 5–7; then describes the victory itself, vv. 8–11; and lastly, speaks to His disciples of that inward operation by which the Holy Spirit will prepare them to become His instruments in this conflict with the world, vv. 12-15.

Vv. 5-7. "*But now I go my way to Him that sent me: and none of you asketh me, Whither goest thou? But because I have said these things unto you, sorrow hath filled your heart. Nevertheless I tell you the truth: it is expedient for you that I go away: for if I*[1] *go not away, the Support will not come; but if I go, I will send Him unto you.*"—Vv. 5 and 6 form a natural transition from the idea of separation to the promise of the Paraclete, ver. 7; the departure of Jesus being the condition of the mission of the Holy Spirit. De Wette and Lücke propose placing ver. 6 between the two propositions of ver. 5. Such a proposal is useless, for the connection is perfectly clear: from the great conflict Jesus proceeds to the great promise. Grieved to see His disciples dwelling exclusively upon the approaching separation, and not also upon the glorious end to which His departure is to lead both Himself and them, He reminds them that if He goes away, it is to Him who sent Him; and to raise them from the deep dejection into which they had fallen, He invites them to ask the further information which He desires to give them concerning the glorious state into which He is about to enter, and the new agency He will then exercise. The friendly reproof: "*None of you asketh me: Whither goest thou?*" is not in contradiction with the questions of Peter (xiii. 36) and Thomas (xiv. 5), since which some considerable time had now elapsed, and which, moreover, related, one to the possibility of following Jesus, the other to the difficulty of knowing the way. As Hengstenberg says, Jesus would at such a moment have rejoiced to find in them the glad promptitude of hearts opening at the prospect of a new era, and putting incessant questions concerning all that it promised.

The words: *Because I have said these things to you* (ver. 6), after ver. 5, signify: "Because I have spoken of parting, conflict, and suffering." At ver. 7 Jesus appealed, as He did in xiv. 2, to their conviction of His truthfulness, and then announced some of those causes of rejoicing concerning which they had not been as forward as they should to inquire.

---

[1] T. R., with ℵ B D L Y It^allq, omits ιγω, which is found in 10 Mjj. 120 Mun. It^plerique Syr.

His departure was the condition of His restoration to His divine state, and this would enable Him to send the Holy Spirit. It is the same idea which we meet with in vii. 39: "*The Spirit was not yet, because Jesus was not yet glorified.*" That Jesus might send the Spirit, He must possess Him as His own personal life, and that as man, since it is to men that He is to impart Him. This supposes the complete glorification of His human nature.—It is surprising that no mention should be made in this passage of the *sacrifice* of the cross, which seems to be the first condition of the gift of the Spirit. Certainly, if it had been the evangelist who had put these words into the mouth of our Lord, this deficiency would not have existed (comp. the first Epistle of St. John ii. 1, 2, v. 6–8). That it does so is explained by the statement of ver. 12: "*I have yet many things to say unto you, but ye cannot bear them now.*"

Vv. 8–11. "*And when He is come, He will convince the world of sin, of righteousness, and of judgment: of sin, because they believe*[1] *not in me; of righteousness, because I go to my*[2] *Father, and you shall see me no more; of judgment, because the prince of this world is judged.*"—We have here a description of the moral victory to be gained over the world by the Holy Spirit, through the instrumentality of the disciples. The preaching of St. Peter at Pentecost, and its results, are the best commentary on this promise. The term ἐλέγχειν signifies to convince of fault or error, here of both at once.— The world in which such conviction is to be produced is not, as the Fathers, De Wette, and Brückner think, men decidedly lost, to whom the Holy Spirit will demonstrate the righteousness of their condemnation.—Ver. 11 proves that *the prince of this world* alone is *actually judged.* If the world is the object of the Holy Spirit's reproof, this is because it is still capable of salvation. The effect of the apostle's preaching in Acts shows that this reproof may lead the world to either conversion or obduracy; comp. 2 Cor. ii. 15, 16. The apostles, the instruments of the Spirit's agency, are not named. Their persons disappear in the glory of the Divine Being who works by their means. The absence of the article

---

[1] Some Mnn. It^plerique Vg. read ουκ επιστιυσαν.

[2] ℵ B D L, several Mnn. It^plerique Vg. Cop. omit μου after πατερα.

before the substantives sin, righteousness, and judgment, leaves these three notions their most indefinite meaning. Jesus defines their application by the three ὅτι, *because*, which follow.

Generally, when sin was spoken of in Israel, shameful crimes or gross infractions of the Levitical law were intended. The Holy Spirit would reveal to the world another sin, of which it thought nothing: that of not believing in Jesus. This He did by the mouth of St. Peter on the day of Pentecost (Acts ii. 22, 23, 36, iii. 14, 15); and those Jews who were sincere immediately acknowledged the truth of this reproof (Acts ii. 37).—This office is permanent. Jesus is the Supreme Good; to reject Him is to prefer evil to good, and wilfully to persevere in such a preference. This it is which the Holy Spirit is, by His instruments, continually making the unbelieving world feel.—Ἁμαρτίας ὅτι, not: will convince the world *of the sin which consists* in unbelief, but: *of sin* in general, and that because of its unbelief.

If the world, and especially the Jewish world, was in error as to its notion of sin, it was not less so in its manner of understanding *righteousness*. Its ideal of righteousness was an unexceptionable Pharisee, honoured by God and men. The Holy Spirit comes to show that this man, inasmuch as he believes not, may be a type of sin (ver. 9). On the other hand, He teaches the world what *righteousness* really is, by making it see its new and only true type, in the Person of One condemned as a malefactor by the righteousness of the age, but exalted by God to His right hand, and who, from the heaven into which He has vanished, acts with sovereign power. The Holy Spirit, in this respect, exercises in some sort the functions of a court of appeal. Good Friday had attributed sin to Jesus, and righteousness to His judges; Pentecost reversed the sentence. It was to the condemned that righteousness belonged, it was His judges who were malefactors. This meaning seems to us to result from the contrast between the terms *sin* and *righteousness*, and from the fact that, as in ver. 9 the Jews, the subject of the explanatory proposition, are at the same time the individuals to whom sin belongs, so in ver. 10 Jesus, the principal subject of the explanatory proposition, must be the individual to whom righteousness belongs. This righteousness cannot, then, be (Augustine, Calvin, Luther, etc.) that which *the believer* finds in Christ, or, as Lange thinks, that *of God*, who deprives the Jews, as a punishment of their unbelief, of the visible presence of the Messiah and of His earthly kingdom ("*you shall see me no more*").—Jesus says: "*because I go to my Father.*" The ascension, as the principle of Pentecost, was, indeed, the demonstration by fact of the righteousness of Christ. He adds: "*You shall see me no more.*" By the disappearance of His body, His departure acquired the glorious character of a heavenly exaltation. If the corpse had remained below, ignominy would still have rested on the supposed malefactor. The disgrace of punishment was washed away by the glorification of His body. This is the idea which St. Peter developes in Acts ii. 24-26, combining, as it were, in one view, the resurrection and ascension (vv. 32 and 33) as divine testimony to the innocence of Jesus.

It would seem that when *judgment* is spoken of after the contrast between sin and righteousness, it must be a judgment which, emanating from righteousness, would strike the sin just spoken of. It is not, however, anything of the kind. The judgment of which the Holy Spirit will give a demonstration to the world is not that of the sinful world, but of its prince. For the world may yet be saved, if it accepts the reproofs of the Spirit, while the prince of this world has now filled up the measure of his sin. Till Good Friday, Satan had only displayed his murderous hatred against the guilty. On that day he directed his attacks against the perfectly Righteous One. In vain had Jesus said: "*He has nothing in me;*" Satan exhausted upon Him his murderous rage (viii. 44 and 40). This murder, for which there was no excuse, brought forth an immediate and irrevocable sentence against him. From that moment he was actually judged (perf. κέκριται), and his ancient realm opened to the preaching of salvation. This invisible revolution, of which the cross was the principle, and whose results extend throughout the universe, was revealed upon earth by the coming and the powerful language of the Spirit; and every sinner, snatched from Satan and regenerated by the Spirit, is a monument of the condemnation henceforth pronounced upon him who was formerly called the prince of this world.

This passage differs only in form from xii. 31, 32; the three actors mentioned, the world, Satan, and Jesus, are the same, as are also the parts attributed to them. One idea alone is added, viz. that it is the Holy Ghost who will disclose to men the greatness of the invisible drama consummated on the cross. Henceforth, then, some will remain in the sin of *unbelief*, and share the judgment of the prince of this world; others will take the side of the righteousness of Christ, and escape the judgment pronounced upon Satan.—But if this victory of the Spirit is to be won by the apostles, the work of the Spirit must first have been accomplished *in them*. This is the reason that Jesus now passes from the agency of the Spirit upon the world *by* believers, to His agency *in* believers (vv. 12-15).

Vv. 12, 13. "*I have yet many things to say unto you, but you cannot bear them now.*[1] *When He, the Spirit of truth, is come, He will guide you into all the truth;*[2] *for He shall not speak of Himself, but whatsoever*[3] *He shall hear*[4] *that shall He speak, and He shall announce to you things to come.*"—Jesus begins by making room for the teaching of the Spirit beside His own. At that very time He had told His disciples so many things, which they could but half understand! Undoubtedly He had, in respect of confidence, hid nothing from them (xv. 15); but with regard to their spiritual incapacity, He had kept to Himself many revelations which were reserved for the teaching of the Spirit. These higher revelations comprise all which in the apostolic writings goes beyond the word of Christ in the Gospels: redemption by His sacrifice, the relation of grace to the law, the conversion of the Gentiles without legal conditions, the conversion of the Jews, the final apostasy, the destiny of the church till its consummation. In all these respects the teaching of Jesus had only sown the germs, which the Spirit came to fertilize.

[1] ℵ omits αρτι.
[2] T. R. with 11 Mjj. Mnn.: εις πασαν την αληθειαν. A B Y Or.: εις τ. αλ πασαν. D L It^plerique: εν τη αληθεια παση. ℵ: εν τη αληθεια.
[3] Αν is omitted by ℵ B D L, 4 Mnn.
[4] T. R. with 10 Mjj.: ακουση. B D E H Y Or.: ακουσει. ℵ L: ακουει.

The term ὁδηγεῖν, *to show the road*, at ver. 13, presents the Spirit under the image of a guide conducting a traveller in an unknown country. This country is truth. It is evidently only essential truth, the truth necessary to salvation, of which Jesus here spoke. That realm of the new creation, which He had only been able to show them at a distance, and by means of similitudes, should be disclosed to them by the Spirit in a direct and perfectly true manner. This truth, according to xiv. 6, is Jesus Himself, His person, His word, His work.—The reading εἰς suits the verb ὁδηγήσει better than ἐν.

The infallibility of this guide arises from the same cause as that of Jesus Himself (vii. 17, 18): the absence of all self-originated and consequently unsound productivity. Satan is a liar just because he speaks according to an entirely different method, deriving what he says from his own resources (viii. 44). The term ὅσα ἄν, *all things that*, leads to the notion of a series of separate acts. Every time an apostle needs wisdom, the Spirit will impart to him what is suitable. *Of the Father* or *of me* may be understood as regimen of the verb *shall hear*. Ver. 15 proves that these two ideas must be combined, and this most naturally explains the expression *shall hear:* He is present at the special communications between the Father and the glorified Son; He shares in the revelation which *God gives to Jesus Christ* (Rev. i. 1), to show unto His servants; and thus initiated into the divine plan, He instructs the disciples according to their needs. It is evidently an instruction in things as yet unknown upon earth (ver. 12), a *primordial* revelation, which is here spoken of. It is by this characteristic that apostolic inspiration is distinguished from that of simple believers. The latter is but a reproduction of the knowledge for which we are indebted to the former, and is consequently but indirectly included in this promise. It is effected by means of the word, in which the apostles deposited the wealth of the original revelation, which was their prerogative. The expression *all the truth* shows that, during the present dispensation, no new word of Christ will be heard upon earth.—To this teaching of the Spirit belongs also, as a specially important element, the revelation of the destiny of the church, *the things to come.*—Καί, *and even.* As Jesus is not merely the Christ who *is come,* but also the Christ *coming* (ὁ ἐρχόμενος, Rev. i. 4), these *things to come* (ἐρχόμενα) are still contained in His person. The saying xiv. 26 gives the formula of the inspiration of our Gospels; ver. 13 gives that of the inspiration of the Epistles and the Apocalypse.

Vv. 14, 15. "*He shall glorify me, for He shall take of what is mine, and shall show it unto you. All that the Father hath is mine; therefore said I, He shall take*[1] *of mine and shall show it unto you.*"—The asyndeton between vv. 13 and 14 shows that Jesus does but reproduce in ver. 14, in a new and stronger form, the thought of vv. 12 and 13. The definite work of the Spirit will be the glorification of Jesus in the hearts of the apostles. After the Father has personally exalted Christ to glory, the Holy Spirit will beam forth from above His heavenly image in the hearts of the disciples, and by their means in those of all believers. We have here a mysterious exchange, and, as it were, a rivalry of divine humility. The Son labours only to glorify the Father, and the Spirit desires only to glorify the Son.—The close relation between ver. 14 and what precedes shows that the revelation of the truth (ver. 13) is nothing else than the glorification of Jesus in the heart. Christ, His words and work,—this is the only text on which the Holy Spirit will comment in the souls of the disciples. Thus He will, by one and the same act, cause the disciples to grow in truth, and Jesus to grow in them.—To understand this word *glorify,* comp. the experience so admirably described by St. Paul in 2 Cor. iii. 17, 18. In calling the source from which the Spirit is to draw *mine,* Jesus uttered a paradox, of which He gives the explanation in ver. 15. In fact, He adds, "*all that the Father hath is mine.*" This wonderful saying reveals, as none other does, the consciousness He possessed of the greatness of His Person and His gospel. Christian *fact* is, in the consciousness of Jesus, the measure of the *divine* for human nature. There is nothing Christian which is not Divine, nothing Divine which is not Christian.—" *Therefore said I unto you*" here signifies: " Therefore I have been able

---

[1] T. R., with A K Π, some of the Mnn. It^plerique Vg. Cop., reads λήψεται (*shall take*). But B D E G L M S U Y Δ Λ Syr. and most of the Mnn. read λαμβάνει (*takes*). ℵ (confusing the two αναγγιλει υμιν) omits the whole of ver. 15.

to say."—There is more documentary authority for the pres. *takes* (ver. 15) than for the future *will* take. It is, besides, in relation with the presents *hath*, *is*, the future seeming a correction after ver. 14. *He takes*—this is His permanent function, the principle of His agency, whence it results that He will take in each particular case.—It is evident that there is no really divine inspiration which does not refer to Jesus Christ. St. Paul, too, makes the exclamation of adoration: "Jesus is the Lord!" the criterion of all true action on the part of the Holy Spirit (1 Cor. xii. 3). When it is remembered that the glorification of the creature is in the Scriptures the capital crime, it will be understood what is implied by such words.

All these discourses, and especially this masculine pronoun ἐκεῖνος, *He*, in ver. 14, are based upon the notion of the personality of the Holy Spirit.

III. *The Last Farewell.*—xvi. 16-33.

From these distant prospects Jesus returns to the event which so engrossed the present moment, to His approaching departure. It was natural that He should end with this, and that the conversational form should reappear.

Vv. 16-18. "*A little while, and you shall see me no more ;*[1] *then a little while more, and you shall see me, because I go to the Father.*[2] *Then said some of His disciples among themselves: What is this that He saith unto us, A little while, and you shall see me no more ;*[3] *then a little while more, and you shall see me? And, because I*[4] *go to the Father. They said, therefore, What is this*[5] *that He saith: A little while? We do not understand what He saith.*"—If the *seeing again* promised refers to appearances of Jesus after the resurrection, there is no connection between ver. 16 and the preceding verse. But the *asyndeton* leads us to suppose that there is a very deep connection

---

[1] ℵ B D L Λ read ουκετι instead of ου.
[2] ℵ B D L It^{alia} Cop. omit the words οτι... πατιρα, which are read in 13 Mjj. most of the Mnn. It^{alia} Syr. etc.
[3] ℵ (confusing the two μικρον και) omits the words μικρον και... παλιν.
[4] Εγω is omitted by ℵ A B L M Λ Π, 11 Mnn. It^{plerique}.
[5] Instead of τουτο τι... ο λεγει, B L Y It. Or. read τι ι. τουτο ο λ., and ℵ D τ. εστι τουτο.

between them. This proves that this seeing Him again refers to the illumination of Pentecost, which being admitted, the relation with what precedes no longer offers any difficulty. Full of the idea of His glorification by the Spirit in the hearts of His disciples, Jesus called this return a *seeing* of each other again (vv. 16, 22). It was by this living reappearance in the souls of His disciples that their approaching separation would be ended.—The first μικρόν, *a little while*, is that which ends at the death of Jesus; the second terminates at Pentecost. Four Alex. omit the words: *Because I go to the Father.* Probably it was not understood how the departure of Jesus could be the cause of His being seen again, especially when this seeing Him again was understood of the appearances of His risen body. But all is clear when this is referred to Pentecost. It was because Jesus ascended to the Father that He could manifest Himself anew by the Holy Spirit. Still, by expressing Himself as He did, Jesus proposed, as He was aware, a problem to His disciples. Those two short delays (*a little while*), which were to have opposite results, and that apparently contradictory notion: "you shall see me because I go away . . .," could not fail to be enigmas to them. We here again meet with the pedagogic process, which we have already observed in xiv. 4, 7. By these paradoxical expressions, He purposely provoked the disclosure of their last doubts, for the sake of entirely removing them.

The kind of *aside* which took place between certain of the apostles (ver. 17) could not be easily explained if they had still been gathering round our Lord, as when He uttered the discourse in xv. 1 sqq. It is therefore probable that at ver. 16 He continued His journey, the disciples following at a short distance. This explains how they could converse with one another, as related in vv. 17 and 18. The words: *I go to my Father*, were perhaps the signal to proceed.—The objections of the disciples were, from their point of view, natural. That which is quite clear to us was to them all mystery. If Jesus were about to found an earthly kingdom, why should He depart? If not, why should He return? Then how were they to understand these contradictory sentences, which were to be accomplished one after another? And, lastly : " I come because I depart . . . !" Had they not some reason for exclaiming: "*We do not understand what He saith*" (ver. 18) ? All this clearly proves the truth of the narrative; for how could a later author have ever thus placed himself in the very quick of the historical reality ? The last words of ver. 17 necessarily assume the reading of the T. R. at ver. 16.

Vv. 19, 20. "*Jesus then*[1] *knew that they desired*[2] *to ask Him, and said unto them, Do ye inquire among yourselves of what I said: A little while, and ye shall not see me; and again a little while, and ye shall see me? Verily, verily, I say unto you, that ye shall weep and lament, but the world shall rejoice; and*[3] *ye shall be sorrowful, but your sorrow shall be turned into joy.*"—Jesus here gives them a last proof of His superior knowledge, not only by showing them that He was conscious of the questions which were engrossing their thoughts, but also by solving in this last conversation all the enigmas by which they were tortured. But being unable to give them an objective knowledge of those great facts which were about rapidly to transpire, He described the opposite and sudden impressions of which they would themselves be the subjects. The greatest joy would succeed the greatest grief, and the latter would be but short—as short as the hour of travail to a woman; it would only last during the time of going to His Father and returning. It would be a terrible hour for them to pass through, but He could not spare it them, and afterwards their joy would be unmixed, and their power unlimited. These are the contents of vv. 20–24.—The tears and lamentations of ver. 20 find their explanation at ch. xx. in the tears of Mary Magdalen, and in the state of the disciples after their Master's death. The appearance of the risen Saviour only half healed this wound; perfect joy was not given till the day of Pentecost (ver. 22). The words: *and the world shall rejoice*, are not the true antithesis of the words: *ye shall weep*. They only form a kind of inserted contrast. This is why Jesus reproduces them in the words: *you shall be sorrowful*, to introduce the originally intended antithesis: *But your sorrow shall be turned into joy.* The δέ, *but*, after ὑμεῖς well expresses this return to the former idea.

---

[1] ℵ B D L omit οὖν after ἔγνω.
[2] ℵ : ἤμελλον instead of ἤθελαν.
[3] ℵ B D Λ It^{plerique} Syr^{sh} Cop. omit δὲ.

Vv. 21, 22. "*A woman when she is in travail hath sorrow, because her hour is come; but as soon as she is delivered of the child, she remembereth no more the anguish, for her joy that a man*[1] *is born into the world. And ye also now have sorrow;*[2] *but I will see you again, and your heart shall rejoice; and your joy no man taketh*[3] *from you.*"—The term of comparison is the sudden transition from the extremity of grief to the extremity of joy, and to this we must confine ourselves. The notion of the bringing forth of a new world as the result of this hour of anguish does not seem to have been in the mind of Jesus.—The expression: *her hour*, alludes perhaps to the terrible hour through which Jesus had Himself to pass (*my hour*). What they would experience would be but the rebound of what He had to bear. The word *a man* brings out the greatness of the event accomplished, and gives a reason for the mother's joy.

Ver. 22 applies the comparison. The connection of this verse with the following clearly determines its meaning. It is the event of Pentecost and not the resurrection which is here spoken of. The meaning of the words: "I will see you again," may be expressed as follows: "I will return to see you, to revisit you, to live again with you." These words are not exactly synonymous with: "*you shall see me again.*" His death not only separated His disciples from Him, but also *Himself* from His disciples. He no longer held, as during His life, the reins of their life. It is for this reason also that He, in the prayer which follows, entrusted them to His Father, so real was the separation on *both* sides. After Pentecost, on the contrary, He again guided His flock with His crook, and governed them from His heavenly throne. It is this change in His own situation which He expresses by: *I will see you again* (a change which the resurrection alone could not have effected). This explanation appears to Meyer *artificial*, and *I will see you again* is, in his opinion, identical with *you shall see me again*.—The present αἴρει, *takes*, is the true reading, Jesus transporting Himself in thought to that time.

---

[1] ℵ reads ο before ανθρωπος.
[2] A D L, 12 Mnn. It^aliq Cop. : εξετε instead of εχετε.
[3] B D Γ It^aliq : αρει (*will take*) instead of αιρει (*takes*).

Vv. 23, 24. "*And in that day ye shall no more question me on anything ; verily, verily, I say unto you, that whatsoever*[1] *ye shall ask the Father in my name,*[2] *He will give it you. Hitherto have ye asked nothing in my name ; ask,*[3] *and ye shall receive, that your joy may be made full.*"—This perfect joy (ver. 22) will be based upon a double privilege, which they will from that day enjoy,—*fulness* of knowledge (ver. 23a), and fulness of power (ver. 23b). They will no longer need to ask Him to explain what might seem to them mysterious or obscure, as they had but just now desired to do, ver. 19 ; they would have the Paraclete within. And, moreover, this inward source of light would make them participate in omnipotence, by conferring on them the new faculty of prayer in the name of Jesus (comp. xiv. 12-14).—The reading of A, ὅ, τι ἄν, *all that,* may well be the true one. After having changed this ὅ τι into ὅτι, *because,* it was necessary to add the pronouns ὅ or ὅσα, and the ὅτι was next omitted as useless (Meyer).—Ver. 24 does not absolutely require that the words *in my name* (ver. 23) should be connected with the verb *you shall ask,* rather than with *He will give.* This is, however, notwithstanding the Alex., their most natural relation.—Before the gift of Pentecost, the apostles could not pray in the name of Jesus—that is to say, as His organs; for this, it was necessary that He should live in their hearts. By saying: *ask* (pres. αἰτεῖτε), Jesus transports Himself to the great day announced. Then, says Meyer, will the deliverance described in ver. 21 be consummated, and perfect joy succeed extreme grief.

Vv. 25-27. "*These things have I spoken unto you in parables: but*[4] *the hour cometh when*[5] *I shall no more speak unto you in parables, but I shall speak*[6] *to you openly of the Father.* At

---

[1] Instead of ὅτι ὅσα ἄν, which is the reading of T. R. with 10 Mjj. Mnn., A reads ὅτι (probably ὅ, τί) ἄν ; B C D L Y It. Or.: ἄν τι ; ℵ: ὅτι ὅ ἄν; X and some Mnn. : ὅτι ὅ ἐάν ; Syr. : ὅσα ἄν.

[2] ℵ B C L X Y Δ Sah. Or. place ἐν τ. ὀνομ. μου after δώσει ὑμῖν (*will give in my name*).

[3] ℵ and some Mnn. read αἰτήσασθε instead of αἰτεῖτε.

[4] ℵ B C D L X Y It^plerique Or. omit ἀλλά.

[5] ℵ reads ὅπου instead of ὅτι.

[6] The Mss. are divided between ἀπαγγελῶ (ℵ A B, etc.) and ἀναγγελῶ (E G H, etc.).

that day ye shall ask in my name: and I say not unto you, that I will pray the Father for you: for the Father Himself loveth you, because ye have loved me, and have believed that I came forth from God."[1]—Ver. 25 takes up again and developes the idea of ver. 23*a* (knowledge), vv. 26, 27 that of 23*b* (power). Jesus during His whole teaching made use of figures; He had done so that very evening (the vine, the woman in travail, His return, their seeing one another again), because He could not just then express Himself plainly. It is the office of the Spirit alone to speak in language really commensurate with the truth. All teaching in words is but a parable, until the Spirit explains it. Παρρησία here signifies, *in appropriate terms*, which do not compromise the idea by exposing it to erroneous interpretation. On παροιμία, see remarks on x. 6.—It is not easy to decide between the two verbs ἀναγγέλειν (Byz.), *to declare* openly, and ἀπαγγέλλειν (Alex.), to *announce* as news.

V. 26 and xiv. 16 are harmonized by the fact that before Pentecost Jesus prayed for His disciples that He might send the Spirit to them; while after the Pentecostal gift, and in proportion as it worked in them, they themselves prayed in His name, and consequently He needed no longer to pray for them. As long, then, as they remain in this state of union with Him, the intercession of Jesus (Rom. viii. 34; Heb. vii. 25) is unnecessary. But as soon as they sin, they need *the advocate with the Father, Jesus Christ the righteous* (1 John ii. 1, 2). The expression: *I say not that I will pray*, is admirably adapted to this condition. *He does not promise that He will pray*, for as long as they remain in the normal condition they will not need it. In this condition He prays *by* them, not *for* them. But He does not say that He will not pray, for they may happen yet to need His intercession when some separation takes place between Him and them. Grotius and others understand the words: *I say not that* . . . in the sense: *not to say that* I also will pray for you. This is making Jesus say exactly the reverse of His thought, as shown by ver. 27.—On the words: *the Father Himself loveth you, because you have loved me*, comp. xiv. 21, 23. By saying: *and have believed*, Jesus comes back from Pentecost to the present state

---

[1] Instead of ἐμοῦ, B C D L X, 2 Mnn. Syr^sch Sah. read πατρος.

of His disciples. This is also shown by the present, *loveth*, and the perfects, *have loved* and *have believed*, as opposed to the futures which precede them. Jesus returns to the work already effected, the condition of that which still remained to be accomplished (that of Pentecost). And, in fact, the supreme moment was at hand. It was time to set the seal to the faith actually formed. For this purpose Jesus clearly states its essential contents: "You have believed *that I came forth from God*." Tischendorf himself rejects the Alex. reading: *from the Father*, instead of: *from God* (which is the reading of the Sinait.). Indeed, it was the *divine* origin and mission of Jesus, and not His *filial* relation to God, which it was needful at that moment to hold forth as the principal object of the apostles' faith. The case is quite different at ver. 28. The prepos. παρά, *from with*, and the verb ἐξῆλθον, *I came forth*, express more than the mere mission, which would have been designated by ἀπό and ἐλήλυθα, and characterize that divine sphere in general whence Jesus proceeds. They well bring out the heroism of the apostles' faith. They had recognised in this Being of flesh and blood, this feeble and despised man, one who came from the Divine abode.

Ver. 28. "*I came forth*[1] *from the Father, and am come into the world: now I leave the world, and go to the Father.*"— What the disciples could not previously understand was, that Jesus should leave the world, where He was, as they thought, to establish His kingdom. They had, besides, no clear notion of the place to which He was going. Jesus started from what was more clear, for the purpose of explaining to them what was less so. They believed and understood that His *origin* was divine; that behind His terrestrial existence was not nothingness, but the bosom of the Father (ver. 27); that consequently this world was to Him only a place of passage; that He came hither solely to perform a work. What more natural than that, having accomplished this work, He should leave this world, to which He came only for a purpose, and *return* to God, from whom He proceeded? The ascension is explained by the incarnation, and the divine future is illuminated by the divine past. The symmetry of the four propositions of this verse casts an unexpected light on the history

---

[1] Instead of παρα (*from with*), B C L X, 2 Mnn. Cop. Or. read ἐκ (*out of*).

of Jesus and on each of the four great phases in which it is summed up: self-abnegation, incarnation, death, ascension.—The Alex. reading ἐκ has, as Lücke himself observes, a too decidedly dogmatic flavour to be genuine. Παρά, *from*, here, as in ver. 27, includes both *origin* and *mission*. The idea of this first proposition is the renunciation by Jesus of the divine condition which He possessed with God. He here says *the Father*, instead of *God* (ver. 27). He was no longer speaking, as in ver. 27, of the contents of the apostolic faith. All the sweetness of His filial relation to the Father was present to His mind. The term πάλιν, *again*, which we have translated by *now*, indicates the correlation between His coming and returning, the former fully justifying the latter. The apostles understand why He goes away: because He came; and whither He goes: to God, because it was from God that He came.

Vv. 29, 30. "*His disciples said unto Him,*[1] *Lo, now speakest Thou plainly, and speakest no parable. Now we know that Thou knowest all things, and needest not that any should ask Thee: for this we believe, that Thou camest forth from God.*"—At hearing this simple and exact recapitulation of all the mysteries of His existence, past, present, and future, the disciples felt surrounded by unexpected light; a unanimous and spontaneous confession was pronounced by them; and the doubts which had from the beginning of these conversations tormented them, were dispersed. They seemed to have nothing more to desire in respect of illumination, and to have already arrived at that noonday of perfect knowledge which Jesus had just promised. Not that they had the folly to affirm, in opposition to the word of Him whose omniscience they were that moment proclaiming, that the promised time had already arrived; still the light was so bright that they could not conceive one more brilliant. By answering thus directly the thoughts which were secretly agitating their hearts, Jesus gave them a standard whereby to estimate the truth of all His sayings, and the certainty of all his promises.—They had just experienced, like Nathanael in the early days of His ministry, that He was omniscient, and like him, they thence inferred that He was Divine.—The relation of the words: *Thou needest not that any should ask thee*, to those of ver. 19, *Jesus*

[1] ℵ B C D A Γ, 2 Mnn. It^nlig omit αὐτῷ.

knew that they were desirous to ask Him, is indisputable; but it must be understood, as above, in a large sense, and one worthy this solemn scene (against Meyer).—The two ideas of Divine mission (ἀπό) and origin (ἐξῆλθες) are mingled in the confession of the disciples, as they are in the expression *Son of God*, i. 50.

Vv. 31–33. "*Jesus answered them, Now ye believe. Behold, the hour cometh, and is already*[1] *come, that ye shall be scattered, every one to his own home, and shall leave me alone: and yet I am not alone, because the Father is with me. These things have I told you, that in me ye might have peace. In the world ye shall have*[2] *tribulation; but be of good cheer; I have overcome the world.*"—The present was to Jesus a moment of unutterable sweetness; He had been recognised and understood by these eleven Galileans. That was enough; the Holy Spirit would complete the work of glorifying Him in them, and through them in mankind. He can now close this conversation and give thanks, for His earthly work is finished. St. John alone understood the greatness, and has preserved the remembrance, of this moment. We must be careful, therefore, not to take the words: *Now you believe,* in an interrogative sense, as though Jesus had cast any doubt upon the reality of their faith; nor must we set ἄρτι, *now,* in opposition to what follows: "Now indeed you believe, but what will you do shortly?" For how, in this case, could Jesus have poured forth such fervent thanksgiving to God for the faith of His disciples? Comp. xvii. 8. "*They have known truly* (ἀληθῶς) *that I came forth from Thee, and they have believed that Thou didst send me,*" words in which Jesus certainly alluded to this, ver. 30. The word *now* refers to the past, not to the future: "You have then reached the point to which I have so long laboured to lead you. At length you believe."

The tie, however, which is but just formed, is about to be subjected to a rude test (ver. 32). The bundle will be broken at least externally. But the centre will remain firm, and all the scattered members will return and group themselves around it.—Νῦν, which we have rendered by *already,* may have been

---

[1] ℵ A B C D L X Cop. omit νυν before ἐληλυθεν.

[2] Instead of ἑξετε (*you shall have*), which is the reading of T. R. with D, several Mnn. It^{plerique}, the other documents have ἐχετε (*you have*).

omitted by the Alex., because it seemed as though the time had not yet arrived.—The aor. pass. σκορπισθῆτε, *when you shall be scattered*, is more fitted to extenuate than to aggravate the fault of the disciples announced by the words: *ye shall leave me alone.* It is a violent blow, which will strike and stun them. This saying recalls the quotation from Zechariah in the Synoptists: "*I will smite the shepherd, and the sheep shall be scattered*" (Matt. xxvi. 31).—Εἰς τὰ ἴδια, to their respective dwellings. Gess remarks that this saying and that of ver. 33, uttered as they were at the moment when the disciples were about to forsake Him, contain beforehand the pardon of their unfaithfulness.

Ver. 32 reassured the disciples with regard to their Master's Person; ver. 33 aimed at setting them at rest as to themselves. —All that Jesus said to them during this last evening tended to inspire them with perfect repose by means of faith in Him (xiv. 1–xv. 17). Undoubtedly He could not conceal from them that they would have a conflict to maintain with the world (xv. 18–xvi. 4). But in presence of the tribulation by which this conflict would be accompanied, their peace must acquire the character of assurance, and become courage (θάρσος). For Christ has vanquished beforehand that hostile world with which they have to contend, has resisted its seductions and overcome its terrors. The cross which awaited Him, and which His obedience accepted, showed that henceforth the world had in Him its conqueror.—The two regimens, *in me* and *in the world,* are opposed to each other; they designate, the one the sphere of the inner life: peace; the other that of the outer life: tribulation. The last proposition points to the victory of the life in Christ over the changing fortunes of the earthly life—a victory whose principle is that of Christ's over the world. As yet this was only accomplished in Him who was speaking, but it would soon be so in their case also. Ἐγώ, *I*, emphatically brings out the idea of that unique personality whose victory is that of all the rest.

THIRD SECTION.

XVII. 1-26.—THE PRAYER.

It was with a shout of triumph that Jesus concluded His conversations with His disciples; but this triumph was an anticipation of faith. To transform the present reality into victory, nothing less than God's omnipotence was needed. And to this Jesus appeals.

This prayer is generally divided into three parts: first, prayer for Himself (vv. 1-5); secondly, prayer for His apostles (vv. 6-19); and thirdly, prayer for the church (vv. 20-26). But when Jesus prayed for Himself, He had in view not His own person, but the *work of God* (vv. 1, 2); when He prayed for the apostles, it was as the *instruments* and continuers of this same work; and when He commended to God believers present and future, it was as the *objects* of that work, and because their souls were to be the theatre on which the Father's glory was to be displayed. The framework of the prayer is indeed that indicated by the generally received division, but the leading thought which unifies it is the Father's work, or, which comes to the same thing, *the glory of God*. This prayer of Jesus is throughout inspired by His mission and His filial affection. He thanks God for what has already been given Him to do for His cause, and asks for the more effectual means which are henceforth indispensable to the completion of the work now begun.

This prayer is more than a mere meditation. Jesus had *acted* (ch. xiii.) and *spoken* (chs. xiv.-xvi.); He now used language which is at the same time action: He *prayed*. He not only prayed, He prayed aloud; which pr[...] while speaking to God, He was also speaking for th[...] Him. He desired to initiate them into that close [...] which He maintained with His Father, and, if pos[...] them *to pray with Him*. It is an anticipatory [...] that communion of glory which He asked for them "*That they may behold my glory which Thou ha[...] that they may be with me where I am.*" He rai[...] that divine sphere in which He Himself dwells.

This prayer has been called *priestly*. We have here, indeed, the act of the High Priest of mankind beginning His sacrifice by offering to God Himself and all His people, present and future. Beyschlag rightly brings forward a multitude of expressions in this prayer which would be inapplicable to the Logos *as such*, and which thus exclude the hypothesis that the theory of the Logos was the parent of this Gospel. (On its true theory, comp. Introd. pp. 187, 189.)

Vv. 1–5: Jesus prays for restoration to His divine glory.

Vv. 1, 2. "*These words spake*[1] *Jesus, and lifted up*[2] *His eyes to heaven, and said, Father, the hour is come; glorify Thy Son, that Thy Son*[3] *also*[4] *may glorify Thee: as Thou hast given*[5] *Him power over all flesh, that to all those whom Thou hast given Him, He may give*[6] *eternal life.*"—Jesus had spoken the preceding sayings on the road from Jerusalem to Gethsemane; He was therefore on the point of passing the brook of Kedron. At this decisive moment He paused for reflection and prayer.— He raised His eyes to *heaven*—a natural effort of the soul to escape from the prison of the body, an aspiration towards the living God, whose glory shines in the majestic spectacle of the heavens. How much better is this action understood out of doors than in a room! (comp. xi. 41; Mark vii. 34). The words: *and He said*, mark the moment when, beyond this visible heaven, His heart met the countenance of God, and in the God of the universe beheld His Father. The whole spirit of the prayer which follows is concentrated in this name of *Father* by which He addresses God. The tone which distinguishes it is that of confidence and filial affection. The Aramean word אבא (abba), *Father*, which was generally used by Jesus in prayer, and which expressed the holiest emotions of earthly heart, became sacred to Christians, and passed as such into the world-language of the New Testament (Rom. viii. 15; Gal.

was speaki
Ἐγώ, *I*, emp[]v instead of ελαλησεν.
sonality who.X, 7 Mnn. It^alid Vg. Cop: ιπαρας . . . ιιπιν instead of ιπηρι

omit σου after υιος (*the Son* instead of *thy Son*).

3 Mnn. It^plerique Vg. Syr. Cop. Or. omit και after ινα.

και instead of ιδωκας (this variation is almost constantly repeated s passage).

δωση αυτοις (T. R. with 7 Mjj.), 9 Mj^t. (B E H, etc.) have δωσω τω αυτω.

iv. 6).—The hour of which St. John and our Lord Himself had often said in the course of the Gospel, *that it was not yet come,* —the hour of death as that of a transition to glory,—had now struck. But if this was to be its result, the interposition of the Father, the manifestation of His arm in the glorification of the Son, was needed. Many, understanding by this glorification of Jesus *the moral perfection* which, by the Divine assistance, He would exhibit in His sufferings, give His prayer the meaning of: "Strengthen me, that I may honour Thee in the conflict which awaits me." Others, like Reuss, think rather of the *power of attraction* which Jesus would henceforth exercise upon men, and of His spiritual glorification in their hearts. These explanations are incompatible with ver. 5, which shows that Jesus was thinking of His *personal* restoration to that Divine condition which was His before His incarnation. This glory of Jesus must not be restricted, as it generally is by orthodox theologians, to the enjoyment of Divine *happiness* and glory. The result of His exaltation, thus understood, would not give any greater ability to glorify the Father in the future than He at present possessed; and yet the aim of His prayer was: "*that Thy Son may glorify Thee.*" It was for an increase of *personal* power, for new means of action, that He petitioned. His restoration to the possession of Divine omnipresence, omniscience, and omnipotence, the participation of His humanity in the Divine state (the $\mu o \rho \phi \grave{\eta}\ \Theta \epsilon o \hat{v}$, Phil. ii. 6); this was what He needed for continuing to glorify God, and for consummating that work of salvation of which He had already laid the foundation. He begged, therefore, for a very real change in His personal condition.—He spoke of Himself in the third person, as we do whenever we desire to draw the attention of one whom we address to what we are *to him.* There is, therefore, nothing suspicious in this third person which St. John puts into our Lord's mouth. It is, moreover, consistent with the manner in which He generally speaks of Himself in the Synoptic Gospels, where He habitually designates Himself the Son of Man. There would be more just cause for suspicion in the expression given by the Alex. reading adopted by Tischendorf: "That *the Son* may glorify Thee," —a reading which has a manifestly doctrinal tinge, and is not more probable than that of these Mss. at i. 18: "*God the only Son."*—The particle καί after ἵνα, that *also*, must, in spite of the same documents and of Tischendorf, be carefully maintained in the text. This little word well brings out the filial sentiment by which the request was inspired: "Glorify me, that I *in my turn* may glorify Thee."

Ver. 2 is an explanatory addition to ver. 1. In its first proposition, Jesus mentions what it is that gives Him the right to say to the Father, Glorify me. In thus praying He was only asking what was in conformity with the decree of God Himself: "*As Thou hast given Him* . . ." This decree is that by which God, when He gave Him His mission (x. 36), granted to the Son the sovereignty over the whole human race (*all flesh;* comp. Eph. i. 10).—The second proposition of ver. 2: "*that He may give life,*" is parallel with the second of ver. 1: "*that He may glorify Thee.*" The true means of glorifying God is the communication of eternal life. For this consists in *knowing God* (ver. 3). By presenting the aim of His supplication under this new aspect, then, Jesus was urging it on more pressing grounds: "Glorify me, that I, in conformity with the mandate Thou hast given me, may give eternal life to all believers." As much as to say: "Grant me the ascension, that I may execute the work of Pentecost."—Πᾶν, all, designates the future body of believers, the unity, the ἕν spoken of in ver. 33, xi. 52, and by St. Paul, Eph. ii. 14, which God beheld from eternity, and gave to the Son (Rom. viii. 28). Πᾶν is generally regarded as nomin. absolute; but is it not rather an inverted accusative? The writer was at the beginning of the sentence already conscious of the action of which this *all* would be the object; hence the accusative. Afterwards, when the verb comes,—a verb requiring a dative,—he completed it by the pron. αὐτοῖς; comp. vi. 39. This αὐτοῖς, *to them*, individualizes the contents of the totality, the πᾶν, which is the object of the giving. The act of giving refers to the whole; the communication of life is an individual fact (plu. *to them*).—The form δώσῃ in the T. R. is singular. It occurs in Rev. viii. 3 and xiii. 16, in some Mss. Is it a future conjunctive, a posterior form, of which some examples are, it seems, found in the N. T. (Bäumlein cites ὄψησθε, Luke xiii. 28; καυθήσομαι, 1 Cor. xiii. 3; κερδηθήσωνται, 1 Peter iii. 1; εὑρήσῃς, Rev.

xviii. 14)? Or may it be the conjunctive of an aorist form, ἔδωσα (a form unknown to the N. T.)? The second supposition is the more probable. In fact, it would have been difficult to say δώκῃ. The true reading, however, is probably δώσει (*Vatic.*), which it was thought necessary to correct on account of the ἵνα (comp. ver. 3, the reading γινώσκωσι). The reading δώσω in the Sinait. is incompatible with the third pers., which is used throughout the passage. The reading αὐτῷ, *to it* (the πᾶν), in the same Mss., is an evident correction.—The meaning of the expression: *all that Thou hast given Him*, is far less extensive than that of the term *all flesh*. If Jesus received power over *every* living *man*, it was in view of the believers whom He was to save. Comp. Eph. i. 22: "He has given Him *to the church*, which is His body, as *head over all things*."—Ver. 3 states the profound connection existing between the two ideas of *glorifying God* and *giving eternal life* (ver. 2).

Ver. 3. "*Now this is life eternal, that they might know Thee, the only true God, and Him whom Thou hast sent, Jesus Christ.*" —Jesus pauses to contemplate that eternal life which He is to bestow upon mankind; He fathoms its nature, and describes it in an expression of adoration.—Eternal life is a *knowledge*. This knowledge is not simply verbal and rational. Scripture always uses the word *know* in a deeper sense. When it is applied to the relation between two persons, it denotes the perfect intuition which each has of the moral being of the other, their near mutual approach in the same luminous medium. Jesus described in xiv. 21, 23, the revealing act which should, in the case of His people, result in this only real knowledge of God. It is the work of the Spirit glorifying Jesus, and with Him God, in us. The epithet *only* bears, as Luthardt says, upon the whole phrase: *true God*. The term ἀληθινός shows that this God alone perfectly answers to the idea expressed by the word God. One can hardly fail to see here, with Meyer, the opposition to the many gods, unworthy the name, of the dominant polytheism. Has not the term *all flesh* called forth the image of those nations, aliens to Israel, who compose the idolatrous portion of mankind? And does not the contrast of Jewish and Christian worship with that of the heathen in the second part of the verse find its complement in the contrast of the Messianic faith of the disciples with the unbelief of the Jewish people? The knowledge of the *only true God* and of *Jesus the Messiah* is thus that which will distinguish the new faith from all preparatory religions, whether within or outside the theocracy. Compare a similar contrast, iv. 21, 23. The opposition, then, of the expression: the *only* true God, is not to the person of Jesus. Could He be a mere creature, the knowledge of whom is in the following sentence joined to that of God, as the source, the very essence of eternal life? In the prologue the Logos is also placed in juxtaposition with God in ver. 1*b*, and the solution of the contrast immediately given in ver. 1*c*: "*And the Word was God.*" Meyer is certainly wrong in making the words: *the only true God,* the attribute of know: "to acknowledge Thee *as* the only . . ." We are thus led to give the word *know* too intellectual a meaning, in opposition to the part attributed in this saying to knowledge (the source of life). The expression: *the only true God,* is the apposition, not the attribute of *thee:* "*to know Thee, Thyself the only true God!*" Thus the word *know* maintains the deep and vital meaning which it ought here to have, while the contrast with polytheism, pointed out above, is by no means excluded.

If Jesus had been praying with a view to Himself only, He would have limited Himself to the words: "*That they may know Thee, the only true God!*" But He was praying aloud, and consequently with a view also to those around Him. And while worshipping God in their presence, as the source of eternal life, He was conscious of being the sole medium by which they could have access to this source, for it is in Him that God manifests and imparts Himself (xiv. 6). The enjoyment of eternal life, by all that is called man, is then identified in His eyes with the knowledge of Himself, Jesus, no less than with that of God. Full of gratitude towards the author of such a benefit to mankind, He proclaims Himself as *the way* prepared by God: *Him whom Thou hast sent,* and sums up this supreme dignity in the title *Jesus Christ (Jesus Messiah).* This form has been severely criticised since Bretschneider. Would Jesus, it is asked, have called Himself by His name, and that in prayer, and with the use of the title Christ in the technical form subsequently in use *(Jesus Christ)*? Is not this a proof of the fictitious composition of this prayer? The answer does not seem very difficult. Hitherto Jesus had avoided giving Himself the title of *Christ* before the people. Rather than use this term, subject as it was to so much misconception, He had had recourse, when He found the ordinary designation, Son of Man, insufficient, to the strangest circumlocutions (viii. 24, x. 24 sq.). He had acted thus in the circle of His disciples (xiii. 13–19). Once only, and exceptionally, in Samaria, in a non-Jewish land, He had openly taken the title of Messiah. In the Synoptics He behaves in the same manner. Thus at Matt. xvi. 20, while accepting the confession of Peter, He takes the opportunity of forbidding the apostles to proclaim Him publicly to be the Christ. But the time had now come when the new word of command for mankind, the glorious name formed by the union of the two words *Jesus Christ*, was to be published throughout the world. Was it not, then, necessary that the disciples should once at least hear it from His own lips? Could they have repeated this symbol of the new faith with such triumphant confidence to the very ends of the world, if their Master had to the end persisted in keeping apart the two words of which it was composed? And under what more favourable circumstances, in what more worthy or solemn form, could Jesus utter it than at this moment, in this last act of communion with His Father, while adoring Him in their presence for all that this name (*Jeshouah hammashiach, Jesus Messiah*) was about to become to them and to the world? St. John, then, is here guilty of no inadvertence. He has reproduced that inexpressibly serious and affecting moment in which he at length heard Jesus Himself consecrate, in a manner never to be forgotten, the conviction which had never ceased to grow within him since the day when he approached Him for the first time (i. 42). Would to God that all confessions of faith in the church had been as temperate as that contained in this verse, and that they had always been produced, as in the mouth of Jesus, under the form of devotion!—We must not translate: "That they may acknowledge Him whom Thou hast sent, Jesus, *as* the Christ," by making ὃν ἀπέστ. 'I. the object, and Χριστόν the attribute, of the verb know, which here also has not so cold and intellectual a meaning. The expression:

Him whom Thou hast sent, is the object; it is the pendant of σέ, *thee*, in the first proposition, and the name *Jesus Christ*, or Jesus Messiah, is an apposition (as were the words: *the only true God*): "to know Him whom Thou hast sent, Jesus Messiah."—Ἵνα is used instead of ὅτι, because knowledge is brought forward as an *end*, as the supreme good to be obtained.—After this outpouring, Jesus returns to the prayer of ver. 1; He mentions what He has already done towards establishing in the world this twofold knowledge, the source of eternal life to every believer, and reiterates the request of ver. 1, by asking for the restoration of His Divine condition, from the midst of which He will be able to complete the work thus begun (ver. 5).

Vv. 4, 5. "*I have glorified Thee on earth; I have finished*[1] *the work which Thou gavest me to do. And now, O Father, glorify Thou me with Thine own self, with the glory which I had with Thee before the world was.*"—Jesus would say: "I have done what I could to glorify Thee in the world, in my earthly condition (ἐπὶ τῆς γῆς). To carry on and complete this work, I need more potent means of action." It is an explanatory restatement of the words: "*Glorify Thy Son, that Thy Son may glorify Thee*" (ver. 1).—Jesus here expresses with sublime ingenuousness the feeling that His conscience is perfectly pure. He does not, at this supreme moment, perceive in His whole life any evil committed, or even any good omitted. The duty of each hour has been perfectly fulfilled. There has not been in that human life which is now behind Him, any spot, or even any deficiency.—The reading τελειώσας has the same meaning as that of the T. R., but aims too much at elegance.

These more potent modes of action, He can only obtain by recovering the condition which was His prior to the incarnation. This is the purpose for which He demands it, and there is no boldness on His part in addressing such a prayer to God, because this Divine glory is His own proper nature, which He voluntarily renounced to serve God here below.—By the words: *with Thine own self*, Jesus opposes the Divine sphere to that in which He at present lives (*upon earth*, ver. 4); xiii. 32.—The expression: *The glory which I had*,

[1] א A B C L Π, 5 Mnn. It^{alliq} Syr. Cop.: τελιωσας instead of ιτιλιωσα.

is opposed to another glory which He has now; see remarks on i. 14.—Reuss thinks that this verse does not imply absolute pre-existence, eternity, but only a certain priority with respect to the world. But in the scriptural point of view, *the world* embraces all that belongs to the sphere of *becoming*, and beyond this sphere there is only *being*. Comp. the opposition of γίνεσθαι and εἶναι, i. 1–3, viii. 58; and Ps. xc. 2.—Παρά σοι, *with Thee*, cannot have the purely ideal sense given it by the Socinians, and recently in a slightly differing form by Beyschlag: the ideal man existing in the Divine intelligence, and which, from the view-point of its realization in Jesus, appears to the consciousness of the latter as clothed in personality.[1] This theory, besides being artificial, does violence to the words of St. John. He who says: *I had . . . with thee*, lays no less stress upon *His* personality than on that of God (ver. 24). See, moreover, remarks on viii. 58.—Because Jesus said: "*before the world was*," and not: "*before I came into* the world," Schelling concluded[2] that the humiliation of the Logos began from the creation, and not merely with the incarnation. This conclusion is not exegetically tenable. For Jesus is here only opposing this glory to a glory which would have had some sort of beginning.

Vv. 6–19. Jesus prays for His apostles, and entreats the continuance and perfecting of their consecration to the Divine work.

It was with a view to the work of God that Jesus solicited the restoration of His glory, but He will accomplish this work only by means of the instruments whom He has chosen and prepared. Hence prayer for them naturally follows, and combines with that which He makes for Himself. This prayer is at first of a general character: *I pray for them*, ver. 9; but afterwards becomes more particular and definite in the two distinct petitions: τήρησον, *keep them*, and ἁγίασον, *sanctify them*, which are the pendant of δόξασον με, *glorify me*, vv. 1 and 5.—Vv. 6–8 prepare for the first general petition, for which vv. 9 and 10 give the full reasons.

---

[1] Beyschlag seems now to have modified his point of view, and to have adopted that which perceives two contradictory theories in this Gospel.

[2] In his oral courses.

Vv. 6–8. "*I have manifested Thy name unto the men which Thou gavest*[1] *me out of the world: Thine they were, and Thou gavest them me; and they have kept*[2] *Thy word. Now they have known*[3] *that all things, whatsoever Thou hast given me, are of Thee. For I have given unto them the words which Thou gavest me; and they have received them, and they have known*[4] *surely that I came out from Thee, and they have believed that Thou didst send me.*"—The general idea expressed in these words is that of the *value* which the apostles have acquired by the ministry of Jesus among them, and the success of this work. This prepares for the prayer in which Jesus commends them to His Father's care. The aorist ἐφανέρωσα, *I have manifested*, is connected with the similar aorists of ver. 4. The most important part of the work, on the accomplishment of which Jesus congratulated Himself, was the preparation and education of the Eleven. The *name of God*, which He revealed to them, denotes the reflection of the Divine Essence in the consciousness of the Being who knows it perfectly, in that of Jesus Himself. This consciousness, revealed in His word, had already become that of the disciples (Matt. xi. 25, 26). Jesus had revealed to them *the Father*, by revealing to them Himself as *the Son*. This is the reason that His testimony concerning Himself was, as we see in the Fourth Gospel, an essential element of His teaching.—Having stated what He has done on their behalf, Jesus proceeds to what God Himself has done for them. The apostles were *God's*. This is not here said of them merely as men, and as Jews, but by reason of the relation they already bore to God by inward disposition; comp. the expressions: *to be of God* (vii. 17, viii. 47), *to be of the truth* (xviii. 37), *to do the truth* (iii. 21), expressions used to designate the moral state of Israelites or heathens faithful to the lights of the law or of conscience. God had given to Jesus these beings who belonged to Him, and that by the drawing of the inward teaching so often spoken of, vi. 37, 44, 45, 65. This spiritual tie once formed, they had

---

[1] Here and elsewhere the Alex. read ιδωκας instead of διδωκας.
[2] ℵ: ιτηρησαν instead of τιτηρηκασι (B D L: τιτηρηκαν).
[3] ℵ: ιγνων instead of ιγνωκαν.
[4] Και ιγνωσαν is omitted by ℵ A D It^aliq.

faithfully maintained. Jesus here passes to what the apostles had themselves done for Him. They had kept intact and unaltered that name of God which had by His words been transmitted from His consciousness to theirs. Jesus says: "They have kept *Thy* word, not *my* word." This is explained in ver. 7: His word is only a faithful reproduction of the Father's. The disciples had been able to discern this profound relation, and to recognise in the teaching which Jesus had given them that which God Himself had given to Jesus. There is, at first sight, a tautology in the expressions: *which Thou hast given me*, and: *is of Thee*. But the first is derived from the consciousness of Jesus; the second is taken from that of the apostles: "They have perceived that all that I have imparted to them concerning Thee really came from Thee." And, in fact (ver. 8), Jesus never added aught to it from His own resources. From their perception of the absolutely Divine character of His word, they had risen to that of the Divine origin of His Person (*I came from Thee*), and of His mission (*Thou didst send me*). These sayings also breathe that sentiment of inward joy and lively gratitude which Jesus had but a few moments since experienced; for it was but quite recently that the glorious result for which He gave thanks to His Father had been obtained (xvi. 29–31). The harvest seemed undoubtedly scanty: eleven Galilean peasants after three years' labour! But it is enough for Jesus, for in these eleven He beholds the pledge of the continuance of God's work upon earth.—"*They have received:*" upon the authority of my testimony; "*they have known:*" by their own moral discernment; "*they have believed:*" by the surrender of their whole being. The forms ἔγνωκαν, τετήρηκαν, are Alexandrine; and the question here, as in so many other similar cases, is to know whether they were used by the apostles themselves or introduced by the Alexandrine copyists.—Having thus prepared for His petition, Jesus next states it, and then proceeds to bring forward further reasons for its being granted.

Vv. 9, 10. "*I pray for them: I pray not for the world, but for them whom Thou hast given me; for they are Thine. And all mine are Thine, and Thine are mine;*[1] *and I am glorified in*

[1] Instead of και τα ιμα . . . σα ιμα, ℵ reads και ιμοι αυτους ιδωκας.

them."—From the infinite value imparted by faith to the persons of the disciples, Jesus draws the conclusion: "*I pray for them.*" Ἐγώ, *I*, stands first: *I* who have so laboured to bring them to this point. Then immediately after, and before the verb, περὶ αὐτῶν, *for them: For them*, the fruit of my labours. This general prayer is equivalent to: I commend them to Thee. The antithesis: "*I pray not for the world*," is to be explained thus: Jesus has not the same reasons to bring forward in favour of the world, nor the same requests to make for it. Luther justly says: "What must be asked for the world is, that it may be converted, not that it may be *sanctified* or *kept*." Assuredly the statement of Jesus, that He prays not for the world, is no absolute one. He Himself said upon the cross: "*Father, forgive them!*" Was not this to pray for the world? Only He did not then, as He does now, bring forward as a reason: "*they have known*" (ver. 8), but on the contrary: "*they know not what they do.*" And instead of appealing, as in His priestly prayer, to the care of God for beings precious and belonging to Himself, He invokes His compassion for beings guilty and perishing. The saying in ver. 21: "*that the world may know that Thou hast sent me*," contains an implicit prayer for the world. Comp. also iii. 16. The statement of Jesus, that He prays not for the world, only becomes absolute in proportion as its moral characteristic of opposition to God is fixed, and as it becomes the association of "those who are not only enemies of God, but who desire to remain such" (Gess).— Before proceeding to the more special petitions contained in this general prayer, Jesus reproduces the two principal claims possessed by his disciples to the Divine interest: 1st. "*Thou hast given them to me;* watch therefore over Thine own gift; and the more so since, in becoming mine, they have not ceased to belong to Thee, but have even become more than ever *Thine*. For what I receive from Thee, I receive only to restore it to Thee, and to ensure to Thee its possession." Luther: "Any man may say: What is mine is Thine, but only the Son can say: What is Thine is mine." The present εἰσί, "*are* Thine," is purposely substituted for the imperfect ἦσαν, "*were* Thine," ver. 6, to express the idea that the gift of them to the Son has only confirmed their *being God's.* 2d. The second motive which commends them henceforth to the Father's care is, that they have become the depositaries of His Son's glory (perf. δεδόξασ-μαι). The expression: *I am glorified in them*, has been variously understood. There is no reason for departing from the constant meaning of the term: *to be glorified*. Notwithstanding His form of a servant, Jesus had appeared to their hearts in all His beauty as Son of God; even before having been restored to His glory, He had regained it in them by the fact that they had recognised Him for what He truly was, vv. 7, 8. — To this general commendation were added two special requests. The first: *Keep them*, is prepared for by ver. 11*a*, stated 11*b*, and the reasons for it brought forward in vv. 12–15.

Ver. 11. "*And I am no longer in the world, but these*[1] *are in the world, and I, I come to Thee. Holy Father, keep them in Thy name, them*[2] *whom Thou hast given me, that they may be one as*[3] *we.*"—While supplicating God's protection for His disciples, the mind of Jesus naturally turned to the dangers to which they would be exposed in the state of desertion in which His departure would leave them: "Keep them, these vessels so precious (vv. 6–10), and henceforth so exposed" (vv. 11–15). Jesus would no longer be with them in the world to keep them, and would not as yet be with the Father to protect them from the midst of His heavenly glory. There would be a sorrowful interval during which His Father must fulfil this office. This motive would be utterly incomprehensible if the fourth Gospel really taught, as Reuss insists, that the Logos is insusceptible of either abasement or exaltation, or, as Baur asserts, that death was to Him only the putting off of His corporeal semblance.

The appellation: "Holy Father," is in relation with the petition presented. With man, holiness is the consecration of his whole being to the task assigned him by the Divine will. In God, holiness is the free, deliberate, calm and immutable affirmation of Himself who is goodness, or of goodness which is Himself. The holiness of God, then, so soon as we are

---

[1] ℵ B read αυτοι instead of ουτοι.

[2] T. R. with only the Mnn. It^{aliq} Vg. Cop.: ους ; ℵ A B C E G H K L M S Y Γ Δ Λ Π, several Mnn.: ω ; D U X, 11 Mnn. Syr.: ο ; It^{plerique} omits all from ω (ους) to ημεις.

[3] B M S U Y, 12 Mnn. read και after ωμεν.

associated therewith, draws a deep line of demarcation between us and those who live under the dominion of their natural instincts, and whom Scripture calls the world. The term: *Holy Father*, here characterizes God as Him who has traced this line of separation between the disciples and the world; and the petition: *Keep them*, has in view the maintenance of this separation. Jesus begs His Father to keep the disciples in this sphere of consecration, which is foreign to the world's life, and of which God is Himself the centre. The words: *in Thy name*, make the revelation of the Divine character granted to the apostles the enclosing wall, as it were, of the sacred region in which they are to be kept.—The reading given by almost all the Mjj. would signify: "in Thy name *which* Thou hast given me." But where does Scripture speak of the name of God as given to the Son? The saying: "*My name is in Him*" (Ex. xxiii. 21), is quite different. We should prefer the reading ὃ δέδωκας, "*what* Thou hast given me," in the Cantabrig., making these words the explanatory apposition of αὐτούς, *them*, which follows, exactly as at ver. 2 (πᾶν ὃ δέδωκας ... αὐτοῖς) and ver. 24 (if the reading ὅ is genuine in this verse): "Keep them in my name, them, *that which* Thou hast given me." This reading (οὕς), while giving the same meaning as that of the T. R., easily accounts for the Alex. reading (ᾧ for ὅ, which was referred to ὀνόματι). The conjunction *that* may depend either on δέδωκας, or, which is the only possible sense with the readings ὅ and οὕς, on *Keep them:* "Keep them in the sphere of the knowledge of Thyself (them whom Thou hast permitted me to place therein), that they may remain one as we are, and that none of them may be lost in isolation, by breaking off from the bundle which my care has formed." What, in fact, would have become of Thomas, if, after the resurrection, he had persisted in keeping aloof from his brethren?—The words *as we* signify that, as it is by the possession of the Divine nature that the Father and the Son are one, it is by their common *knowledge* of this nature (*the name*) that the disciples also may remain closely united among themselves, and be each individually kept in safety.

Vv. 12, 13. "*While I was with them in the world,*[1] *I kept*

[1] ℵ B C D L It^plerique Vg. Cop. omit εν τω κοσμω.

them myself in Thy name: I have watched over those whom Thou hast given[1] *me, and none of them is lost, but the son of perdition; that the scripture might be fulfilled. But now I come to Thee; and these things I speak while I am in the world, that they may have my joy fulfilled in themselves.*"—The verses which follow support the petition: *Keep them,* by further developing the motive already shortly indicated in ver. 11*a*: They are *in need of* Thy protection.—"*When I was with them*" takes up the idea of ver. 11: "*I am no more in the world.*"—'Ετήρουν, *I kept them,* shows the result obtained: ἐφύλαξα, *I have watched,* refers to the means employed.—The reading ᾧ is still less admissible in this, than in the preceding verse.—By the term *son of perdition,* and its allusion to prophecy, Jesus desires to discharge Himself from responsibility, but not to lessen that of Judas. Prophecy had from the first set a limit to the effects of His vigilance, which it was not possible to pass over. As to Judas, he had freely played the part which prophecy had beforehand marked out. We may here compare what is predicted concerning antichrist. We know from prophecy that this individual will exist, yet this will not hinder the man who takes this part from doing so freely. Comp., pp. 86 and 87, the remarks on the relation between Divine foreknowledge and human freedom. In the Hebraic phrase: *son of* . . ., the term indicating the complementary notion of the word *son* personifies the abstract principle (light, darkness, etc.), which defines the moral life of the individual thus designated. The passage to which Jesus referred is Ps. xli. 10, quoted xiii. 18. Are we then to infer from this saying that Jesus reckoned Judas also in the number of those whom *the Father had* formerly *given Him?* The words εἰ μή, *if not,* do not oblige us to make this inference; comp. Matt. xii. 4; Luke iv. 26, 27.

The remark is parenthetical, and intended to justify the Lord's vigilance in respect of the loss of Judas. Jesus afterwards returns to the idea of His approaching departure, and declares that if he *speaks these words aloud*—for this is the meaning of λαλεῖν—before His disciples, it is that they may share in the joy with which He is Himself filled. It may be

---

[1] Instead of ους, B C L read ω (like ver. 11) and add και before ιφυλαξα; ℵ reads και ιφυλασσον instead of ους διδωκας . . . ιφυλαξα.

asked whether this joy was that caused by His assurance that the Father would take them under His protection, or that which He experienced from the expectation of His own speedy return to the Father? Both these grounds of rejoicing were mingled in His heart, and they ought to combine in theirs, and disperse, as in His, the last cloud of sadness.—The need in which they stood of protection is more particularly and urgently shown in the words which follow.

Vv. 14, 15. "*I have given them Thy word; and the world hath hated them, because they are not of the world, even as I am not of the world. I pray not that Thou shouldest take them out of the world, but that Thou shouldest keep them from the evil.*"— The word of Jesus, which they had faithfully received, had made them as much strangers to the world as was Jesus Himself. Like Him, they had become objects of the world's hatred. In such a condition, Jesus might easily have allowed Himself to entreat of God that they might be sharers in His departure. But since it was for the very purpose of preparing them for a mission to the world that He had separated them from the world (ver. 18), it was necessary that they should remain in it after His departure. Still the line of demarcation between them and the world must not be obliterated. While remaining in the world, they must be kept from the evil which prevails therein. Hence Jesus closes this passage by reiterating the petition which forms its background. Τοῦ πονηροῦ must certainly be taken in the neuter sense of *from evil*, and not *from the Evil One*. This is shown by the preposition ἐκ, *out of*, which relates to a *realm* out of which one is taken, rather than to an individual. The case is otherwise in the Lord's Prayer, where the prep. ἀπό and the verb ῥύεσθαι are used, two expressions which refer rather to a *personal* enemy (Matt. vi. 13). Reuss, then, is wrong in translating: "from the power of the devil." Hengstenberg points out that the form τηρεῖν ἐκ only occurs again in Rev. iii. 10.—From the prayer: *Keep them*, which refers to their *salvation*, Jesus passes to the second petition, which concerns rather their *mission: Sanctify* (or consecrate) *them*. This is prepared for, ver. 16; uttered, ver. 17; developed and justified, vv. 18, 19.

Vv. 16, 17. "*They are not of the world, even as I am not of the world. Sanctify them by Thy truth:* [1] *Thy word is truth.*" [2] —Jesus had raised them to that sphere of holiness in which He Himself dwelt; hence that *mission* to the world wherewith He could entrust them. Thus ver. 16 forms the transition from the first to the second petition. According to x. 36, the sending of Jesus upon earth was preceded by a consecration: " Him whom the Father *hath sanctified* and sent into the world." The same thing must take place in the case of the disciples. The word ἁγιάζειν, *to sanctify*, is not synonymous with καθαρίζειν, to *purify*. The *holy* is not opposed to the *impure*, but merely to the *natural* (without any idea of impurity). To sanctify is to consecrate to a religious use anything pertaining to common life. Comp. Ex. xxix. 1, 36, xl. 13 ; Lev. xxii. 2, 3 ; Matt. xxiii. 17. From an Old Testament point of view, consecration was an external and ritual act; under the New Covenant, where all is spiritual, the seat of consecration is first of all the heart, the will of the person consecrated. In saying, then, " *Sanctify them*," Jesus solicits for them a heart entirely devoted to the task they will have to fulfil in the world. Their whole strength, talents, life, must be dedicated to this great work, the salvation of men, which involves the renunciation of all self-gratification, however lawful, the absence of all interested aims and all self-seeking. This is the sublime idea of Christian *holiness;* but here, where the apostles are in question, it is viewed as about to be realized under the special form of the Christian *ministry*. Kept (now) themselves in this sacred sphere, they are hereafter to become the representatives and bearers of holiness among mankind.—We have in our translation given, as in i. 31, 33, the instrumental sense, *by*, to ἐν. Divine truth is thus designated as the *agent* of consecration. Meyer and others translate *in:* " *In this medium* of truth in which I have placed them." But why, in this sense, should Jesus have added : "*Thy word is the truth*" ? Is it not the aim of these words to represent truth as the *means* by which this consecration may be effected ? *Thy word* desig-

---

[1] σου, which is the reading of T. R. with 12 Mjj., almost all the Mnn. Syr. Cop., is omitted by ℵ A B C D L It^plerique Vg.; ℵ omits the words σου . . . αληθεια, confusing the two αληθεια.

[2] B reads η before αληθεια.

nates that which Jesus had in His instructions imparted to them (vv. 6 and 8). The pronoun σοῦ in the first proposition is wanting in the Alex. The testimony of the ancient Vss. (*Cop. Pesch.*) is, on the other hand, in its favour.—Jesus alleges, in support of this petition, two motives,—one taken from the mission He had conferred on His disciples (ver. 18), the other from the work which He had effected upon Himself, —for the purpose of obtaining what He was now asking on their behalf (ver. 19).

Vv. 18, 19. "*As Thou hast sent me into the world, so have I also sent them into the world. And for their sakes I*[1] *sanctify myself, that they also*[2] *may be sanctified in truth.*"—If Jesus asked that the spirit of their charge might be in them, it was was because He had already committed to them *the charge* itself (ver. 17). Ἀπέστειλα, *I have sent,* alludes to the name of *apostles* which He had long ago given them. But how could He say that He *sends them into the world*, when they were in the world already ? Because He had raised them to a sphere above the life of the world (ver. 16), and it was thence that He sent them into the world, as really as He had been Himself sent from heaven. And if He sent them thither, it was that they might continue the work commenced by Himself. This is the first motive which He urges for His petition : "*Sanctify them.*" The second is stated in ver. 19. The sense of καί, *and*, at the beginning of this verse is : " And in order to obtain for them this consecration which I ask, I begin by effecting my own." Jesus asks nothing from the Father without having done all that depends upon Himself for the realization of His request. It is by effecting His own sanctification that He demands and prepares for theirs. The word *sanctify* by no means involves, as we have seen, the removal of impurity, for it is not a synonym of *purify* (καθαρίζειν). Hence those interpreters are mistaken who find in this verse a proof of the existence of original sin in Jesus. On the other hand, however, those too much restrict the meaning of the word who apply it, like Chrysostom, Meyer, and Reuss, to His voluntary consecration to *death* as the condition of the gift of the Spirit. For this explanation obliges us to give to

---

[1] ℵ A omit ἐγώ.

[2] 10 Mjj. (ℵ A B C, etc.) It. Syr.: ωσι και αυτοι instead of και αυτοι ωσι.

the word *sanctify* entirely different meanings in the first and in the second proposition of the verse. We must confine ourselves to the natural sense of the word *to sanctify*, viz. to render holy (or sacred) by inward consecration to God. Our Lord possessed a human nature like our own, endowed with inclinations and dislikes as ours is, though of such only as are perfectly lawful. Of this nature He was continually making a holy offering; He constrained it to obedience: negatively, by sacrificing it where it was in contradiction with His mission (*e.g.*, in the cultivation of the arts and sciences, domestic life, etc.); positively, by devoting to His divinely-appointed task all His powers, all His natural and spiritual talents. It was thus that He, *by the Eternal Spirit, offered Himself without spot unto God* (Heb. ix. 14). When the question was to sacrifice a gratification, as in the desert, or to endure sorrow, as in Gethsemane, He ever subjected His nature to the work to which the will of the Father called Him. And this was not effected once for all. His human life received in an ever increasing degree the seal of consecration, till the entire and final sacrifice of death.—The pronouns *I* and *myself*, as well as the active *sanctify*, bring out the energetic action He had to exert upon Himself to obtain this result.—By such means did Jesus realize the perfect consecration of *human life*, and thus did He in His own Person lay the foundation for its consecration in His people.—" *For their sakes*," He said, and explained these words by the next proposition: "*that they also may be sanctified.*" The sanctification of each Christian is nothing else than the communication to him by Jesus of the human nature sanctified in His Person. This is the truth developed by St. Paul in Rom. vi. 1-12, and especially in viii. 1-3, where he shows that Christ began by *condemning* sin (condemning it to non-existence) in the flesh, that the (moral) righteousness exacted by the law might be realized in us. Jesus created a holy humanity in His Person, and it is the office of the Spirit, who has also the power, to reproduce in us this new humanity: "*The law of the Spirit of life, which is in Christ Jesus, has made me free from the law of sin and death.*" In this respect, as in all others, the part of the Spirit is to take of that which is Christ's (that perfectly holy human life) to give it unto us. If this holy life had not been realized in Christ, the Spirit would have had nothing to impart to us in this respect, and the sanctification of man would have remained a barren aspiration. We would remark finally, that, according to ver. 17, the apostles are here regarded not merely as Christians, but especially as *ministers* (ver. 18). Jesus Himself, while sanctifying Himself as *man*, and for the purpose of realizing human holiness, at the same time sanctified Himself as *Saviour*, and for that of restoring life to man. So also the task of the apostles would not be merely that of realizing that common consecration to which all believers are called. Jesus, by releasing them from every earthly vocation, and sending them into the world as His ambassadors, intended that their personal sanctification should be effected under the form of the apostolate.—This form is not more holy, but it has the character of a special service.—'Ἐν ἀληθείᾳ, *in truth*, must here be taken, seeing the article is omitted, in the adverbial sense of *in a true manner*, as opposed to the wholly external consecration of the Levitical priesthood.—Thus, from the general petition: "*I pray for them,*" have branched off the two progressive requests, "*Keep them* in holiness!" "*Consecrate them* by holiness to become the instruments of the world's sanctification!" It was natural that Jesus should thence pass to a prayer for the world itself, at least so far as its future believing part was concerned (vv. 20-26). Jesus prayed for *believers*, and asked for them spiritual unity, vv. 20, 21, and participation in His glory, vv. 22–24.

Vv. 20, 21. "*Neither pray I for these alone, but for them also who shall believe*[1] *in me through their word; that they all may be one, that as Thou, Father, art in me, and I in Thee, they also may be one*[2] *in us, that the world may believe*[3] *that it is Thou who hast sent me.*"—Having commended to God the *author* and the *instruments* of the work of salvation, Jesus prayed for its *objects*, the whole body of believers. We behold in the mirror of His prayer, the Church exalted by faith to unity in God and union with God, and thus rendered capable of possessing the glory of the Son. This is the realization of

---

[1] T. R. with D², several Mnn. It^plerique Vg. Sah.: πιστευσοντων (*who shall believe*). The 19 Mjj., all the other Mnn. Syr. Cop.: πιστευοντων (*who believe*).

[2] Ἐν before ωσιν is omitted by B C D It^alia Sah.

[3] ℵ B C: πιστευη instead of πιστευσῃ.

the end for which God created man, the contents of that *hidden wisdom which God ordained before the world unto our glory* (1 Cor. ii. 7). It is not, then, as is so often thought, the union of Christians with each other which is here spoken of, but above all that union which is its foundation, the union of the body of believers with Christ, and through Him with God. The Lord was contemplating the society of believers which would, by means of their preaching, gather around the apostles, and in which He would Himself dwell. The true reading is certainly the pres. πιστευόντων. But this present is anticipative, for as yet no believers had been won by the word of the apostles. Jesus was bringing before His mental vision all believers, absolutely speaking—believers of all times and places, whom in His prayer He was combining into a single body and transporting to glory.—This saying of Jesus assigned a capital part in the life of the Church to the apostolic *word*. Jesus did not recognise in the future any faith capable of uniting man to God, and of preparing him for glory, except that which should be begotten and nourished by the teaching of these eleven apostles. The term *word* (λόγος) does not designate, as that of *testimony* (μαρτυρία) might do, merely the narration of facts; it includes also the revelation of the religious and moral meaning of the facts, the contents of the Epistles as well as of the Gospels. There is no real coming to Christ at any time but by this means.

The first proposition, ver. 21: "*that they may be all one,*" summarily indicates the general idea. The words: *as thou, Father* . . ., which follow, depend, by an inversion similar to that of xiii. 34, on the subsequent, not on the former, *that*. The former word is returned to by way of explanation: "That they may be one, that, *I say*, as thou, Father . . . they also may be one in us." This construction has not the dragging character of that which makes *as* depend on the former *that*. Having thus petitioned for the unity of believers, Jesus describes it as a unity of the highest order, as sharing the *nature* (καθώς) of that of the Father and the Son. As the Father lives in the Son, and the Son in the Father, so the Son lives in believers, and, by living in them, causes them to live in one another. This sacred unity is the work of the Spirit, who alone has the power of overthrowing the barrier between different individualities without destroying them. Instead of: "that they may be *one* in us," some Mss. read. "that they may be in us." This reading is condemned by the context, which here requires the idea of the *unity* of believers. The ἕν has been lost in the ἐν ἡμῖν which precedes it.

A spiritual organism of this kind exercising its functions on the earth, is so novel a phenomenon, that the sight of it brings the world to *faith* in Him from whom it proceeds. This is the contents of the third *that* in ver. 21, the final end of the two preceding and parallel. The word *believe* is never used in the N. T. except in a favourable sense. Hence it cannot designate a forced conviction like that spoken of in Phil. ii. 10 sq. Jesus knows that there are still, in what He calls the world, elements capable of being won to the faith. And will not the effect produced upon the Jewish people by the sight of a local and transitory phenomenon, like that of the primitive Church at Jerusalem (Acts xxi. 20 : "*Thou seest how many thousands of Jews there are which believe*"), be repeated on a larger scale in the whole world by the same spectacle magnified. It may be that Jesus had more specially in view the conversion of the Jews in the latter days, when they should see the Church realized in all its beauty among the Gentiles. This supposition is confirmed by the words: "*that it is Thou who hast sent me,*" *i.e.,* "that I, this Jesus of Nazareth whom they have rejected, am indeed the Promised, the Sent One whom they were expecting," Rom. xi. 25, 31. Comp. 1 John i. 3; Eph. ix. 13.—Jesus now rises to His highest request, a share in *His glory* for His disciples. This petition is prepared for, vv. 22, 23, and then solemnly uttered, ver. 24.

Vv. 22–24. "*And the glory which thou hast given me I have given them; that they may be one, even as we are one :*[1] *I in them, and Thou in me, that their oneness may be perfect; and*[2] *that the world may acknowledge that Thou hast sent me, and that Thou hast loved*[3] *them, as Thou hast loved me. Father, I will that they whom*[4] *Thou hast given me may also be with me where*

---

[1] B C D L omit ιεμιν, and א εν εμιν.
[2] א B C D L X It^alia Cop. Or. omit και before ινα γινωσκη.
[3] D, 7 Mnn. It^alia Cop. : ηγαπησα (*that I have loved them*) instead of ηγαπησας.
[4] א B D Vg^alia Cop. : ο instead of ους.

I am; that they may behold my glory, which Thou hast given me: for Thou lovedst me before the foundation of the world."—Throughout this prayer, Jesus supports His petitions by what He has already done Himself towards the attainment of the end in view. Hence the ἐγώ, *I*, stands first. He had already begun that communication of His glory to the disciples of which He was soliciting the completion. What, then, we ask, is that glory which Jesus had already given to His own? Chrysostom understands thereby the honour of the apostolic office and miraculous gifts. But the mind of Jesus takes a higher flight, as is proved by the close of vv. 23, 24. Hengstenberg refers the term *glory* to the participation of believers in the oneness of the Father and the Son, an explanation which makes this tautological with the next proposition. Meyer understands by it the glory of the future kingdom; but if they did not as yet actually possess this, it was none the less their assured property. The prayer in ver. 24 only demanded that *right* should be exchanged for fact. This explanation is accepted by Luthardt (2d ed.). But our Lord appears to have had in mind a gift really effected, as a point of departure for a future gift. The end of ver. 23 leads us to a slightly different meaning. As the essence of the glory of Jesus consists in His dignity as the *Son*, and the *well-beloved* Son, so the glory which He has bestowed upon believers is the filial dignity, the state of *adoption* (i. 12), whereby they have *become* what the Son eternally *is*, children of God, and objects of His perfect love. This glory Jesus bestowed upon His own, by bringing matters to such a state that God could justly reflect upon them all the love which He has for Jesus Himself (ver. 26, xv. 9, 10). Thus the proposition which follows: "*that they may be one, even as we are one,*" is easily understood. Once objects of the same Father's love, and bearing in common the image of their elder brother, they form among themselves a closely united family (comp. Rom. viii. 29; Eph. i. 10). The foundation of this union is once more expressly recalled by the words: "*I in them, and Thou in me,*" which are not a new proposition, but, as Meyer says, an explanatory apposition of the subject *me* in the preceding phrase; or, as we would rather say of the predicate of this phrase: "*to be one as we.*" God living in Christ, Christ in each believer,—what is this but the Divine unity reproduced on earth? Hence a new *so that*. At the sight of this wonderful unity the world will not only *believe*, as was said in ver. 21, but will acknowledge. These two verbs cannot be synonymous. The term *acknowledge* undoubtedly includes the forced *conviction* of rebels as well as the *faith* of believers (ver. 21). The word κόσμος, *the world*, whatever Meyer (who here gives my explanation very lamely) may say, cannot designate believers only, but must have a more extended signification. In short, it is that universal homage, whether voluntary or involuntary, described in Phil. ii. 10, Rom. xiv. 10-12, which is here intended.

At beholding the glorious results of the work of Jesus, believers raised to perfect unity by that seal of adoption which they all bear, the whole intelligent universe will render homage to the Sent One of God, who, by transforming them into His own image, has succeeded in making them beloved of God as He is Himself beloved by Him. Thus is the ultimate end of God's dealings with the Church of Christ, the direct contemplation and enjoyment of the glory of the Son of God, who was willing to become its Head, prepared for. The repetition of the invocation: *Father* (vv. 21, 24, 25), reveals the increasing emotion of Jesus, in proportion as He draws near to the close of His prayer. The reading ὃ δέδωκας, "*what* Thou hast given me," by which expression Jesus would designate the body of the elect, the ἕν of whom He had just spoken (ver. 23), may here, as at ver. 11, probably be the true one.—Θέλω: Jesus no longer says, *I pray;* but, *I will!* This expression, which is nowhere else found in the mouth of Jesus, is generally explained by saying that the Son thus expressed Himself, because He felt Himself on this point so fully in accordance with the Father. But this He felt in every prayer, and this unique expression must be taken in its relation to the unique character of the situation. It is the saying of a dying man: "Father, my *last will* is . . ." It is truly His testament which Jesus thus deposits in His Father's hands.—In gathering disciples about Him, His one end had been, as He mentions in vv. 22, 23, to accustom them to the direct contemplation of His glory. This glory, according to His own explanation, is the love wherewith the Father eternally loves Him, and all its consequences. The words:

"*before the foundation of the world,*" necessarily indicate eternity. This expression is, among all the sayings of Jesus, that which leads us farthest into the depths of Deity. It points out to Christian speculation the road by which it must seek the solution of the Trinitarian relations; love is the key of this mystery. And this love being eternal, and therefore equally without end as it is without beginning, can form the permanent object of contemplation to believers who thus become initiated into the mystery of the nature of the Son and His eternal generation. And still more as being, through the complete community which the Son has succeeded in establishing, objects of a love like that which the Son enjoys, are they themselves thus introduced into the eternal movement of the Divine life. This is what is brought out by the word *behold*. A fact of this order is only beheld by being shared in. This is the height to which Jesus elevates the Church. Having drawn His spouse from the mire, from the midst of a world immersed in evil, He introduces her into the sphere of the Divine life, and places her with Himself upon the throne.

Meyer and Luthardt (2d ed.) deny that the glory of which Jesus here spoke can be that of His Divine state prior to the Incarnation. For that, they say, is not a *gift* of the Father's love, but inherent in the Person of the Son. The intention of the words: "*for Thou lovedst me before the foundation of the world,*" is not, they think, to explain *wherein consists* the glory of the Son, but to indicate the *motive* for which the Father is about to glorify Him by the ascension. The glory which the Father has given Him is thus that of the glorified *Son of man*. But the eternal love of the Father for the Son could not be the motive for the glorification of the man Jesus. According to the teaching of Jesus and His apostles, the reason for the exaltation of the Incarnate Christ was His perfect submission and absolute faithfulness to the will of God during His earthly life: x. 17, xv. 10, xiii. 32, xvii. 4, 5; Phil. ii. 9 ("*wherefore also* . . ."). Hence, if there is a glory which the Son owes to the eternal love of the Father, it is His eternal glory, His dignity as *Son*, His Divine condition prior to the Incarnation; comp. ver. 26: "The Father hath *given* Him to have *life in Himself.*" It is this inner mystery of the

Divine nature to the contemplation of which the faithful are to be admitted. "Ὅτι is then explanatory: "the glory which Thou hast *given me, in that* Thou lovedst me." Is not the love of which any one is the object his glory? The glory of the Son is the eternal love through which He is the Son.—Jesus has now come to the climax, and therefore to the close of His prayer. But He feels a desire again to justify such petitions. The *righteousness* of God is present to His mind. Does it not bar the way to an answer?

Vv. 25, 26. "*O righteous Father, the world, it is true, hath not known Thee: but I have known Thee, and these have believed that Thou hast sent me. And I have made known unto them Thy name, and I will make it known: that the love wherewith Thou hast loved me*[1] *may be in them, and I in them.*"—In thus transporting a church of sinners with Himself to His throne, how could He fail to feel the need of justifying to the *righteous* God the unheard-of privileges which He claimed for His people? The world had undoubtedly refused to know God, and, if the disciples had still been of the world, Divine justice would rightly have protested against His prayer. But He who presented Himself at their head *knew God*, and they too, by *recognising* Him as the Sent of God, had been introduced into the light of the *knowledge of God*. This light, it is true, had but dawned in them; but Jesus, who had caused its first rays to shine upon them, engaged to communicate to them in the time to come all His own knowledge of the Father, that thus they might become, with the same title as Himself, the objects of the Divine love, and that when His work was finished He might so truly *live in them*, that in loving *them* the Father *would be loving Him* still, and Him always. Hence Divine justice, far from having any pleas to raise against this step, should rather join her voice to that of love to support the petition of Jesus.—The title *Righteous* Father is not substituted without a purpose for that of *Holy* Father. It is not holiness, the love of goodness for its own sake, which is the property of this Divine attribute, still less the *equity* of God, that is to say, His mercy, which is here spoken of. The words: "*but I have known Thee,*" show that Jesus here places Himself in presence of the *retributive justice* of God,

[1] ℵ reads αὐτούς instead of μοι.

which, in *excluding* the world from glory, might or must have excluded the disciples also, if Jesus had not, by His work in them, found the means of making justice itself plead on their behalf. The καί, and (which we have rendered by *it is true*), before the word *the world* presents some difficulty. Meyer explains it (according to the frequent use of καί in this Gospel) as indicating an opposition. This καί would thus form an opposition to the idea of righteousness: "*righteous Father: and nevertheless* the world . . ." That is to say: "Righteous Father, for such Thou truly art, even though the world has not recognised Thee as such." And Jesus would then proceed to claim the favours which follow in the name of this justice (so also Luthardt, 2d ed.). But could the world's denial of God's righteousness be of such gravity, that Jesus should feel He could not greet His Father by the title of *righteous*, without thus expressly justifying the statement? It seems to me that, according to the general analogy of St. John's style, the construction is quite otherwise, and the intention very different. St. John delights in expressing contrasts by the correlation of two καί (vi. 36, xv. 24, etc.): "*both . . . and,*" for: "on the one side . . . on the other." Thus the first καί, put in the first place of the first proposition, before ὁ κόσμος, would announce an antithesis, and this is actually found in the *third* proposition: καὶ οὗτοι . . ., "*and these have known . . .*" The contrast then is as follows: "On the one side (καί), the world has not known Thee . . .; on the other (καί), these have recognised me as sent of Thee, and through me have learnt to know Thee." The relation of this moral contrast to the idea of retributive justice (*righteous* Father!) is as clear as possible. The world, it is true, deserves from Thee only rejection, for it has misconceived Thee; but these, by receiving me, and learning from me to know Thee, have become worthy of Thy blessing.—But it was necessary to introduce between these two terms of the contrast: "*the world . . . these,*" an intermediate notion, that of the part performed for the disciples by Jesus. For otherwise they would be confounded with the world. It was the appearance of Jesus which had given rise to the contrast. The world, by rejecting this appearance, had misconceived God; the disciples, by receiving Him by faith, had begun to know God, and had now the prospect of the perfect knowledge of Him. This is the reason why our Lord intercalates between the two terms of the original antithesis the words: "*But I, I have known Thee,*" which form a secondary antithesis (ἐγὼ δέ, *but I,* comp. xvi. 20). The καί of the first and that of the third propositions are then correlative; but the δέ, *but,* of the second forming an indispensable contrast with the first, the second καί is consequently at once the pendant of the first and the continuation of the δέ, which intervenes in a somewhat unexpected manner.[1] Such a construction could only occur in actual speech, and could not be explained in an artificial composition.—Meyer applies the words: *has not known Thee,* with regard to the world, to the blindness of mankind towards the revelation of God in nature, spoken of by St. Paul in Rom. i. 19, etc., a notion which has not the slightest relation to the context. What is there spoken of is unbelief with regard to the revelation of God in the Person and teaching of Christ.—The future: *I will make known,* refers to Pentecost and to the whole work of Christ in the Church subsequent to that day.—The closing words of the prayer: *and I in them,* act as a motive to the whole, but especially to the last thought: "*and that the love wherewith Thou hast loved me may be in them.*" The love of God in lighting on believers will not attach itself to aught that is defiled. For it will in truth light only on Jesus Himself, on Jesus living in them, and upon them as identified with Him and reflecting His holy image.

What simplicity, what calmness, what transparent profundity, prevail throughout this prayer! "It is, indeed," as Gess remarks, "the only Son speaking to His Father. All here is *supernatural,* because He who speaks is the only Son from heaven; but, at the same time, all is natural, for He speaks as a son to a father." The feeling which is the very soul of this prayer, an ardent zeal for the glory of God, is indeed that which is the soul of the whole life of Jesus. And are not these three petitions, that for His personal

---

[1] Meyer finds this explanation "*contorted.*" It seems to me to defend and justify itself. It approximates that of Bäumlein (which Meyer treats no better): ὁ κόσμος (μὲν) . . . ἐγὼ δὲ . . . καὶ οὗτοι ("*the world* undoubtedly . . . *but I* . . . *and these* also"*).

glorification, that for the consecration of His apostles, and that for the glorification of the Church, just the petitions in which this feeling must vent itself? In its details not a word is met with which exegesis cannot demonstrate to be perfectly appropriate and exactly suited to the situation. How, then, could it be possible to adopt Baur's view, that some Christian author, after more than a century, thus succeeded in recovering and reproducing the impressions of Jesus in all their holiness and exalted sublimity? It is the same as saying that there once existed another Jesus than Jesus Himself.

M. Reuss admits, as we do, that this composition is that of an immediate witness. But he finds in certain passages, *e.g.* ver. 3, a proof that the disciple freely reproduced the thoughts of the Master. He asks whether John had pencil and tablets in hand to take down word for word the prayer of Jesus. But we ask again, if John really regarded Jesus as the Logos, how could the respect which he must have felt for His words have suffered him to make Him speak, and especially to make Him pray, after his own fashion? Undoubtedly he had not pencil in hand, but were not the words of Jesus of such a nature as to engrave themselves more deeply and more distinctly than ordinary speech? Might not St. John, some short time after this evening, have committed to writing what he distinctly remembered of these conversations and of this prayer? Or, if not, might not his constantly renewed meditation on these words, graven as they were on the tablets of his heart, and continually refreshed by the agency of the Holy Spirit, have compensated for the use of external means? Is not this internal miracle—if calling it such is insisted upon—less inexplicable than the artificial composition of such a prayer?

But, it is asked, how is the calmness which pervades this prayer compatible with the agony of Gethsemane? Keim insists that John, by this narration, *annihilates the Synoptic tradition*. The conflict of Gethsemane exhibits the character of a sudden crisis, of a violent shock in some sort of a storm, after which calmness was restored to the mind of our Lord as quickly as it had been disturbed. The cause of this passing crisis was twofold; first, it was natural, viz. the unique impressionability of the soul of Jesus, of which we have already seen so many proofs in this Gospel, especially ch. xi. and xii. 27. By reason of the very purity of His nature He was accessible, beyond any other man, to every lawful emotion. His soul resembled a magnetic needle, whose mobility is only equalled by the perseverance with which, in every oscillation, it tends to recover its normal direction. Gethsemane was to our Lord not punishment, but the *acceptance* of punishment, and therefore the anticipation of the suffering of the cross. Such an anticipation is sometimes more terrible than the reality. The supernatural cause is pointed out by Jesus Himself in xiv. 30: "*The prince of this world cometh.*" Comp. Luke xxii. 53: "*This is your hour and the power of darkness.*" The satanic origin of this agony is betrayed by its very suddenness and violence. St. Luke finishes his account of the temptation in the wilderness with the words: "*The devil . . . departed from Him,* ἄχρι καιροῦ, till another favourable moment." The hour of Gethsemane was, in the eyes of the prince of this world, this other favourable moment.

The priestly prayer, which includes our Lord's act of thanksgiving for the work He had effected on earth, is the climax of the narrative of the *development of faith* in the disciples (chs. xiii.–xvi.). It thus forms, in this Gospel, the pendant to the passage, xii. 37–50, in which St. John summarizes the history of Jewish unbelief (contained in chs. v.–xii.).

FOURTH PART.

XVIII. 1–XIX. 42.

THE PASSION.

IT certainly was not the evangelist's intention to give, in the account which follows, as complete a narrative as possible of our Lord's Passion as though no other history of this event had existed side by side with his own. The most determined opponents of the authenticity of this Gospel (Baur, Strauss) are now in agreement with its most orthodox interpreters (Lange, Hengstenberg) as to the point that the fourth evangelist had constantly in view, the narratives of his predecessors. They only differ as to the intention to be attributed to the writer. According to Baur and Strauss, the pseudo-John derived from the Synoptists the materials indispensable for giving some air of probability to his romance of Jesus-Logos. According to the commentators of the opposite side, St. John was simply endeavouring to fill up the vacancies left in previous narratives, or to present facts already related in their true light.

It seems to us, as to these latter, that his choice of materials is often determined by a desire to complete the narratives already current in the Church. Thus, when St. John relates the examination of Jesus at the house of Annas, which is omitted by the Synoptists, and omits His appearance before the Sanhedrim, so fully related by the former Gospels, this intention appears evident. It is seen, also, in a multitude of other examples. On the other hand, the narrative of St. John has hitherto presented a character of too serious meditation and too profound elaboration, to suffer us to admit that the portion which now follows is governed by no ruling idea, but only obeys chance, as an account would do whose only motive it was to relate what others had omitted.

In St. John's history of the Passion, we again find that threefold point of view stated in the Introduction. Jesus makes His *glory* beam through the veil of ignominy with which it is covered, and that especially by the freedom with which He yields Himself to the lot awaiting Him. The *faith* of His own gathers up these scattered rays, and grows in the silence of grief. But especially—and this is, as we shall see, the ruling feature of the narrative—*Jewish unbelief*, by a series of hateful acts and disloyal sayings, passes judgment upon itself, and is then consummated by the murder of the Messiah.

There are three principal scenes:—
I. The apprehension of Jesus: xviii. 1–11.
II. His double trial, ecclesiastical and civil: xviii. 12–xix. 16.
III. His punishment: xix. 17–42.

FIRST SECTION.

XVIII. 1–11.—THE APPREHENSION OF JESUS.

Though St. John here omits the agony in Gethsemane, he clearly assigns its place to this fact by the words (ver. 1): "*where was a garden, into the which He entered.*" On reading these words, no Christian in possession of the three first Gospels could fail to think of their account of this scene. The reason for this omission, as well as that of the transfiguration, the institution of the Lord's Supper, and so many other matters, is that St. John knew this scene to be sufficiently well known in the Church, and that it had no special reference to the end which he had in view.

Strauss exclaims: "Every attempt to intercalate the agony of Gethsemane in the narrative of St. John between chs. xvii. and xviii. is a treason against the moral elevation and even the manly character of Jesus."[1] At this rate, St. John would be himself the first author of a treason of this kind; witness the scene in the temple (ch. xii.), especially the saying in xii. 27. Strauss concludes that we have in the synoptic

---
[1] *Das Leben Jesu,* 1864, p. 553.

narrative "a simple fiction, in that of St. John a more considered and calculating fiction." Thus, those who narrate lie in narrating, and he who omits lies in omitting! Such is the result at which criticism arrives by following its course to the end. It claims to restore the genuine edifice, it destroys the very soil on which it is to be reared.

Vv. 1–3 : The arrival of the band.—"*Having spoken these words, Jesus went out with His disciples to the other side of the brook Cedron,[1] where was a garden, into which He entered, as well as His disciples. And Judas, who betrayed Him, also knew the place; for Jesus had often met there[2] with His disciples. Judas then, having received the band with officers from the chief priests and Pharisees, cometh thither with lanterns and torches and arms.*"—The verb ἐξῆλθε, *He went out*, connected directly as it is with the regimen πέραν τοῦ χειμάρρου, *to the other side of the brook*, can only signify: "He went out from the town and suburbs of Jerusalem." This is acknowledged by De Wette, though he and many others consider that the discourses in chs. xiii.–xvii. were uttered in the supper chamber.—The received reading τῶν κέδρων would mean the brook *of the cedars*, and would evidently be an error on the part of St. John, for there are no cedars in the country, and the name Cedron comes from קדרון (Kedron), *dark*. In Josephus also the name κεδρών is a nomin. sing. (*e.g.* χείμαρρος Κεδρῶνος, *Ant.* viii. 1. 5). But it is sufficiently proved that the reading τῶν κέδρων, *of the cedars*, originated with ignorant copyists, who, taking Κεδρών for a genitive plural, placed the article τῶν before it. The true reading is τοῦ Κεδρών, *of the Cedron*, and this is preserved in the Alexandr. and the Sangallensis. The τοῦ has been kept in the Sinait. and Cantabrig., but the gen. sing. κέδρου, *of the cedar*, has been brought in after it. The same alteration is met with in several Mss. of the O. T. (see 2 Sam. xv. 23 and 1 Kings xv. 13).—The brook of Cedron rises half a league north of Jerusalem, and falls into the Dead Sea after a southward course of six or seven leagues. It is generally

---

[1] A S Δ It^{alia} Vg. and several other Vss. read τοῦ κεδρων; א D It^{alia} Cop. Sah.: τοῦ κεδρου; T. R. with B C E G H K L M U X Y Γ Λ Π, most of the Mnn. Or. and Tisch.: των κεδρων.

[2] 9 Mjj. (E G M, etc.) read και after συνηχθη.

dry during nine months of the year, and we were told at Jerusalem that for more than twenty years not a drain of water had been seen in it. Its bed is at the bottom of the valley of Jehoshaphat, between the temple hill and the Mount of Olives. After passing over the little bridge by which its dried-up bed is crossed, there is on the right hand a tract planted with ancient olive trees, and said to be the garden of Gethsemane. There is no reason worthy of consideration, whatever Keim may say, against the truth of this tradition. The word πολλάκις, *often*, at ver. 2, applies not only to the days immediately preceding, but to previous sojourns of Jesus at Jerusalem. This garden undoubtedly belonged to friends of Jesus, and generally served as a place of meeting for our Lord and His disciples (συνήχθη, the aorist: "the act of meeting") when they were returning from Jerusalem to the Mount of Olives and to Bethany, and desired to avoid passing together through the streets of the city. Comp. Luke xxi. 37, xxii. 39.—The term σπεῖρα always signifies in the N. T. the legion or part of the Roman legion which occupied the citadel Antonia, at the north-western angle of the temple. A detachment of Roman soldiers had seemed necessary to support the servants of the Sanhedrim. It was commanded by the tribune himself, the *chiliarch* mentioned in ver. 12. The art. τήν, "*the* band," is perhaps explained by the presence of this superior officer, who represented the whole. Although the Synoptists do not speak of this escort, the message of Pilate's wife shows that the governor had had to busy himself in the matter since the previous evening, and this circumstance confirms the participation of the Roman band in the apprehension of Jesus. If Keim chooses to speak ironically of "half an army," this poor piece of pleasantry is quite gratuitous. Bäumlein opposes the application of the term σπεῖρα to the Roman garrison. But an apprehension could scarcely have taken place, especially during the residence of the governor, without the participation of the Roman authorities.—The ὑπηρέται are, as in vii. 32, 45, the officers of the Sanhedrim or guards of the temple.—It was to them, properly speaking, that the order for our Lord's arrest was committed. Ver. 10 shows that servants belonging to the households of the chief priests had joined the band.—The meaning of the words φανοί and λαμπάδες is questionable. The former seems to us rather to designate lanterns, the latter lamps placed at the end of a long handle (Matt. xxvi. 1). All this apparatus: "lanterns and torches and arms," casts, by its very needlessness, an air of ridicule upon the scene. It was feared that Jesus might hide Himself, but He willingly gave Himself up; that He might defend Himself . . ., but where was the use of such arms if He had chosen to use His power? (ver. 6).

Vv. 4–9: The meeting of Jesus with the band.—"*Jesus therefore,*[1] *knowing all that should happen to Him, went forth, and said unto them,*[2] *Whom seek ye? They answered Him, Jesus of Nazareth. Jesus saith unto them, I am He. Now Judas also, who betrayed Him, stood among them. When then He had said, I am He, they drew back, and fell to the ground. Jesus asked them a second time, Whom seek ye? They said, Jesus of Nazareth. Jesus answered, I have told you that I am He: if therefore ye seek me, let these go away: that the saying might be fulfilled, which He spake: Of them which Thou gavest me I have lost none.*"—In advancing of His own accord to meet the troop, our Lord had a purpose which the sequel explains. He desired, by delivering Himself up, to provide for the safety of His disciples. The kiss of Judas, in the Synoptists, which is said to be incompatible with the narrative of St. John, must be placed at the moment when Jesus came out of the garden and met the band, therefore immediately before the question: "*Whom seek ye?*" Jesus having undergone this last act of treachery on the part of His disciple, turned to the band and addressed to them this question concerning their mission. He desired thereby to oblige them formally to declare what was the object of their search, for the purpose of sheltering His disciples. "*He went out*" might signify: "He advanced *from the midst* of His disciples, or from the depths of the garden" (Matt. xiv. 14). But the most natural sense is that He went out of *the garden itself*. Undoubtedly the kinsman of Malchus says at ver. 26: "*Did not I see thee with Him in the garden?*" But Jesus was walking boldly forward, while the disciples were keeping behind Him

---

[1] ℵ D L X It^{plerique} Syr. Cop. have δε instead of ουν.
[2] B C D It^{plerique} Vg.: εξηλθεν και λεγει instead of εξελθων ειπεν.

in the garden.—The intercalation in this place (ver. 5) of the remark concerning Judas has been variously explained. Luthardt justly says: "These words are placed between the saying: '*It is I*,' and the effect it produced, because they are intended to explain this effect." But how? The terror produced by the declaration: "*It is I*," which seemed to contain a threat from heaven, would first of all be felt by the perfidious disciple, and communicated by him to those who surrounded and followed him.—St. John has been accused of personal hatred to Judas, yet it is he alone among the evangelists who does not mention the kiss!—The same moral ascendancy to which the buyers and sellers in the temple yielded, caused the troop to draw back, and this sudden backward movement on the part of those who went first, caused the fall of a certain number among those who were following. The purpose of Jesus in this imposing display of His miraculous power is still the same; what follows shows that He desired to save the disciples from being apprehended.—In a milder tone, which summoned the officers to approach again, Jesus questioned them a second time. Their reply again showed that it was Himself alone whom they were sent to arrest; whereupon, ver. 8, He drew the conclusion at which He was aiming from the first, and, while giving Himself up as a prisoner, stipulated for the liberty of His disciples, thus fulfilling the beautiful image he had used, x. 12: "The shepherd seeth the wolf coming, and fleeth not, because he careth for the sheep." It was not only for the safety, but for the *salvation* of His disciples, as St. John truly felt, that Jesus was at this time solicitous, a fact which accounts for the remark in ver. 9. The example of Peter, the most courageous among them, shows what would have happened to the weakest if they had been at that moment called upon to share the fate of their Master. Jesus, who had before said: "*I have watched over those whom Thou hast given me, and none of them is lost*" (xvii. 12), was to realize all that was included in this saying, which bore upon the whole of His work on earth. This quotation is instructive. No one can suppose that St. John was ignorant of the spiritual meaning of this saying of our Lord; and yet he here applied it to a material fact, which only indirectly contributed to the salvation of the disciples.

Vv. 10, 11: Peter's attempt at defence.—"*Then Simon Peter having a sword drew it, and smote the high priest's servant, and cut off his right ear.*[1] *The servant's name was Malchus. Then said Jesus unto Peter, Put thy*[2] *sword into the sheath again: the cup which my Father hath given me to drink, shall I not drink it?*"—Was not St. John alluding to the natural character of Peter, by here giving him the name of Simon? Comp. xxi. 15-17.—Luke, xxii. 38, shows that the apostles had in fact brought arms with them.—Why, it may be asked, did St. John repeat this fact already related by the Synoptists? He desired to restore to it that precision which it had lost by oral tradition: the name of Peter had been omitted, very probably on purpose (see on xi. 2), that of Malchus forgotten.—These names are a constant source of embarrassment to critics. Again is the intention of humiliating Peter imputed to the writer, although the act attributed to him is wanting in neither faith nor courage! But as for Malchus? How can the slightest vestige of *idealism* be discovered in this name? Keim objects: "If these names were known, how could Mark and Luke have omitted them?" But because Mark and Luke were ignorant of them, was it impossible for one better informed to know them? How can we believe that an earnest Christian of the second century, writing at a distance from Palestine, either at Rome or Alexandria, or in Asia Minor, would have claimed a historical acquaintance with the name of a servant in the high priest's household! (ver. 26). Is such miserable charlatanism compatible with the character of the author of the discourses of the fourth Gospel? The trifling detail: "the *right* ear," found also in Luke, is, according to Strauss, a legendary amplification. To what a degree of childishness is not the evangelic narrative thus degraded?—The act of Peter, while testifying to a strong faith and to the sincerity of his declaration in xiii. 37, none the less by its imprudence compromised the cause of Jesus. Little was wanting to its depriving Him of the power of saying before Pilate (ver. 36): "*If my kingdom were of this world, then would my servants have fought.*" The answer of Jesus lays down for

---

[1] ℵ B C L X Y It. Vg.: ωταριον instead of ωτιον.
[2] Σου, which is the reading of T. R., is only found in several Mnn. and V$_G$ plerique.

the Church its line of conduct under persecution, viz. that passive resistance called, Rev. xiii. 10, *the patience of the saints.* —The image of a cup, used to designate a lot to be submitted to, recalls the similar expression in the prayer of our Lord at Gethsemane related by the Synoptists.—St. Luke alone mentions the miraculous cure of Malchus. If this fact had not actually taken place, one cannot see why Peter should not have been indicted for the act of rebellion which he had committed.

SECOND SECTION.

XVIII. 12–XIX. 16.—THE TRIAL OF JESUS.

I. The Ecclesiastical Trial, xviii. 12–27; II. The Civil Process, xviii. 28–xix. 16.

I. *The Trial before the Sanhedrim.*—xviii. 12–27.

The next portion contains an account of an appearance of Jesus before Annas, the ex-high priest, an account which is intermingled with that of the denial of St. Peter. This appearance is not mentioned by the Synoptists, who, on the other hand, relate a meeting of the Sanhedrim at the house of Caiaphas, at which Jesus was condemned to death, which is omitted by John. How, then, is this relation between the two chief forms of the Gospel history to be explained? Was St. John mistaken, as some think, in representing an appearance as taking place before Annas, which, according to the Synoptists, took place before Caiaphas? Or were the Synoptists, as others suppose, in error when they made the house of Caiaphas the scene of an event which really happened in that of Annas?

We would first of all remark, that when St. John says, ver. 13, that the band led Him away to Annas, he adds, πρῶτον, *firstly,* thus letting it be clearly understood that this appearance before Annas was followed by a second appearance. This could not have been that before Pilate. For we are positively told at ver. 24, that "Annas then sent Him bound *to Caiaphas* the high priest;" and at ver. 28, that "they led Jesus *from* (the house of) *Caiaphas* to the prætorium." Could

St. John more plainly indicate that a meeting had taken place in the house of Caiaphas, even though he omitted giving an account of it? Besides, the appearance of Jesus before Pilate necessarily supposes that *sentence of death* had been previously pronounced against Him by the Sanhedrim, the question being to obtain from the governor, the confirmation and execution of this sentence (ver. 31, xix. 7, 11, 16). Now nothing approaching a condemnation took place in the meeting at the house of Annas described by St. John. It was merely a simple preliminary inquiry, and followed by no kind of sentence. The narrative of St. John, then, implies a subsequent meeting of the Sanhedrim, as the high court of justice, for the condemnation of the accused, and consequently that meeting described by the Synoptists. If it is asked, what then was in this case the purpose of the appearance before Annas, we reply that not only might it serve to obtain from the mouth of Jesus some compromising words of a nature to procure His condemnation, for the lack of such was a matter of embarrassment, but that juridical usage absolutely required it. It is known that a capital sentence could not be pronounced by the Sanhedrim till the day which followed the appearance of the accused.[1] In the present case, this form could not be completely observed, because it had been decided to shorten the time. Still, to save appearances as much as possible, a semblance of a first preliminary meeting, followed by a second at which judgment should be given, was at least to be presented. The Synoptists have, in conformity with the nature of oral tradition, preserved only the remembrance of the meeting, which made a historical mark; St. John, as he usually does, has repaired the synoptic omission by relating the preliminary meeting, but has omitted the solemn sitting of the Sanhedrim as already sufficiently known. In fact, however impossible it is to deny that Jesus was condemned to death in the manner recounted by the Synoptists, it is, on the other hand, equally so not to admit that this condemnation was preceded by an inquiry intended to impart to it an appearance of legality, as related by St. John.

Langen[2] denies any appearance whatever of Jesus before

---

[1] Schürer, pp. 416 and 417, *d'après Sanhedrin*, iv. 1, v. 5.
[2] *Die letzten Lebenstage Jesu*, 1864.

Annas, and insists that the scene recounted by St. John in vv. 20-23 formed part of the meeting in the house of Caiaphas. He says that St. John, having omitted to state that Jesus had been led immediately from the house of Annas to that of Caiaphas, repaired this omission at ver. 24, where we must naturally translate the aorist by the pluperfect: "Now Annas *had sent* Him . . ." Langen admits that if this translation is impossible, his opinion is untenable. We defer this consideration till ver. 24.—M. Lutteroth settles matters in nearly the same manner,[1] solving the difficulty of ver. 24, however, by an expedient of another kind (see on this verse).—Beyschlag admits but *one* meeting at night taking place at the house of Annas, as described by St. John; then one in the *morning* assumed by St. John, and rightly placed and described by St. Luke in ch. xxii. 54, 66-71. St. Matthew and St. Mark, he says, also mention this latter (Matt. xxvii. 1; Mark xv. 1); but they have confounded the night meeting with that morning meeting when the appearance at the house of Caiaphas took place and Jesus was condemned by the Sanhedrim, an error which would make the morning meeting in their narratives utterly useless. We shall, I believe, see Beyschlag's mistake upon this latter point (see on xviii. 28); and with this mistake his entire hypothesis is overthrown.

Baur and Strauss see in the appearance before Annas only an invention of the author of the fourth Gospel, for the purpose of augmenting the guilt of the Jews by making the condemnation of Jesus to be pronounced not only by *one*, but by *two* of their high priests. But (1) St. John does not put any sentence of condemnation into the mouth of Annas; (2) he keeps a profound silence concerning that pronounced by Caiaphas!—Hilgenfeld thinks that the author, in his narrative, does but just glance at the meeting of the Sanhedrim, because the *Jewish Messiaship* of Jesus was too strongly dwelt upon in it for his anti-Judaic feeling.—But with the licence with respect to history which, according to these critics, he allowed himself, nothing could have been easier for him than to modify the narrative of this scene by making, *e.g.*, the sentence of Jesus turn solely on His assertion of His dignity as

[1] "Annas was informed *in passing* of the success of the apprehension," *Essai d'interprétation des dernières parties de l'Ev. de St. Matthieu*, 1876.

Son of God. Besides, if the idea of the Messianic office were so repugnant to St. John, why did he so expressly recall it side by side with his quality of *Son of God* in the summary of the Gospel with which this book concludes? (xx. 31).—Keim grows quite warm on the subject, and exclaims: "Who can be blind enough to seek for truth in a narrative which, after introducing the inquiry before Annas as a fact of a decisive nature, ignores in the most unpardonable manner that before Caiaphas!" (pp. 322, 323). But the meeting in the house of Annas had, according to St. John himself, nothing *decisive* about it. Its juridical result, to the great annoyance of the enemies of Jesus, who expected to derive therefrom some complaint against Him, to be brought before the great judicial meeting about to be held, was *nil.* Besides, this latter meeting is, as we have seen, by no means ignored. For St. John, while omitting its narration, most correctly assigns it its place (ver. 24), exactly in the same manner as he had done in the case of the scene in Gethsemane (xviii. 1). —Reuss, in his lately published work,[1] thus expresses himself: "John says nothing, and we may add, without deceiving ourselves, knows nothing, of the official inquiry and the trial before the court, because all this took place with closed doors." We have shown that St. John knew all, and that he makes any one who will read him carefully, clearly understand what it does not suit his purpose expressly to relate. Renan is unsparing in his admiration of this part of St. John's narrative. "Our author alone," he says, "makes Jesus appear before Annas, the father-in-law of Caiaphas. Josephus confirms the correctness of this account. . . . This circumstance, of which the two first Gospels afford not a notion, is a beam of light. How should a sectary writing in Asia Minor or Egypt have known of it? . . . It is a strong proof of the historical value of our Gospel" (pp. 522 and 407).

1st. Jesus led before Annas.

Vv. 12–14. "*Then the band and the tribune and the officers of the Jews took Jesus, and bound Him, and led Him away*[1] *first to Annas; for he was father-in-law to Caiaphas, who was*

---

[1] *Histoire évangelique,* 1876, p. 663.
[2] ℵ B D, 6 Mnn. have ηγαγον instead of απηγαγον.—ℵ B C D X Δ It^{aliq} omit αυτον.

*high priest that year.*¹ *Caiaphas was he who had given counsel to the Jews that it was expedient that one man should die*² *for the people."*—The word πρῶτον, *first*, contains a tacit confirmation of the synoptic account, according to which Jesus was led *directly* to Caiaphas; comp a similar remark, iii. 24.—Annas had himself been high priest in the years 6–15 of our era, that is, about fifteen years before. We see from Josephus that he was the influential man of the times. St. John, however, gives us to understand that the true reason for which Jesus was at that time led before him, was rather his relationship to Caiaphas the high priest. In virtue of this relationship, these two individuals were, so to speak, regarded as one. Comp. the expression in Luke iii. 2.—On vv. 13, 14, comp. xi. 50, 51. St. John would give us to understand by the remark in ver. 14 what kind of justice Jesus had to expect from such a judge.

2d. The first denial.

Vv. 15–18. "*And Simon Peter followed Jesus, and so did another disciple;*³ *and that disciple was known unto the high priest,*⁴ *and went in with Jesus into the court of the high priest. But Peter stood at the door without. Then went out that other disciple and spake to her that kept the door, and brought in*⁵ *Peter. Then said the damsel who kept the door to Peter, Art thou not also one of this man's disciples? Peter answers, I am not. Now the servants and the officers were standing there, having made a brazier, because it was cold: and they were warming themselves: and Peter*⁶ *was standing among them and warming himself."*—While the Synoptists relate consecutively the three denials of Peter, probably because they were, in the oral tradition of the Gospel, grouped in a single and separate narrative, forming one of the ἀπομονεύματα or traditional subjects, John separates them in the course of his history, passing

---

¹ Cod. 225 adds after πρωτον: απιστιιλεν ουν αυτον ο Αννας δεδεμενον προς Καιαφαν τον αρχιερεα. Syr^p adds the same words in the margin. Cyril reads after εκεινου: απιστιλαν δε αυτον δεδεμενον προς Καιαφαν τον αρχιερεα (comp. ver. 24).

² ℵ B C L X, 13 Mnn. several Vss. have απολυσιν instead of απελυσαι.

³ ℵ A B, 5 Mnn. and probably It. Vg. Syr. Cop. Sah., omit ο before αλλος ("an other disciple").

⁴ B C L X read ο γν. του αρχ.   ⁵ ℵ: εισηνεγκε instead of εισηγαγεν.

⁶ ℵ B C L X, some Mnn. It^plerique Vg. Syr. Cop. read και before ο Πετρος ("and Peter also").

alternately from Peter to Jesus and from Jesus to Peter. This less disjointed narrative certainly reproduces the real course of events, and there is nothing in this Gospel which more plainly discloses in its author the witness of the facts. "The same superiority," rightly exclaims Renan, "in the history of the denials of Peter! All is more circumstantial and better explained."

The art. ὁ, *the*, omitted by the Alex. before the words ἄλλος μαθητής, *other disciple*, ver. 15, must undoubtedly be rejected. This omission is confirmed by ancient versions and by the context. For nothing in what precedes justifies the use of the definite article. We must then translate: "*another disciple.*" Who, then, is it whom St. John thus designates? Himself? Such is the most usual answer. But the periphrasis used by St. John to designate himself, while maintaining his anonymous position, is: "*the disciple whom Jesus loved*" (xiii. 23, xix. 26). I endeavoured in my first edition to justify the absence of this expression, in the present case, by saying "that it was not the moment for using it" after the disciples had just forsaken their Master. I cannot, however, conceal from myself that this explanation is somewhat subtile. Why should not John designate by this phrase some other disciple, his brother James, for instance, whom he nowhere *names* in this Gospel any more than his mother? We do not know what were the relations which Zebedee and his sons might have with the household of the high priest. Perhaps the very calling of Zebedee might have given rise to them. Thanks to this relation, this disciple was allowed to enter with the band into the high priest's palace, and soon obtained admission for Peter also, who had undoubtedly claimed his good offices.

But of what high priest is St. John speaking when he says, ver. 15: "*into the court of the high priest*" (αὐλή, more probably here the inner court than the palace itself)? On the one hand, after it has been said: "*They led Him away to Annas*," it seems impossible to think of any other house than that of this individual. But, on the other hand, the title of ἀρχιερεύς, *high priest*, is not given to Annas either in this chapter or in any other part of this book. Undoubtedly, as Schürer has well proved, this term might designate, besides the high priest in office, all those who had previously filled this position, and even all the members of those few privileged families from whom the high-priesthood was generally recruited. For this reason it is that high *priests* are spoken of, and that Annas himself, though long since out of office, is called ἀρχιερεύς in the Acts of the Apostles (iv. 6). Only this is never done in this Gospel; and it would be difficult to believe that St. John, after opposing *the high priest* Caiaphas to *his father-in-law* Annas, as he does in ver. 13, should some few lines later have designated the latter by the title of *high priest*, without a word of explanation to his readers. If, then, it is the house of Caiaphas which is spoken of, we must conclude that, since acquaintance with the high priest Caiaphas and the members of his household opens the abode of Annas to the disciple, these two individuals must at this time have inhabited one and the same palace. The close connection by which they were united would explain this circumstance, and it was perhaps for this very reason that St. John mentioned this fact. Meyer, then, is certainly wrong in saying that the text furnishes not *the slightest indication* in favour of this opinion, to which, on the contrary, it directly leads.

The Hebrews very generally employed female doorkeepers (see Josephus, *Antiq.* vii. 2. 1; Acts xii. 13; 2 Sam. iv. 6 in the LXX.).—The καί, *also* (" Art thou not *also* "), shows that she well knew the anonymous disciple to be a disciple of Jesus. —The three denials of Peter have, as Luthardt observes, three distinct historical points of departure, which are in some sort distributed among the evangelists: 1st, the introduction of Peter into the court by a friend known to be a disciple of Jesus; 2d, the recognition of Peter by those who had seen him at the time of his Master's arrest; 3d, his Galilean dialect. But to these external circumstances, which called forth his trial, was added an internal one, which facilitated his fall,—viz., the remembrance of the blow which he had dealt, and which exposed him more than all the rest to be involved in the condemnation of Jesus. Fear thus allied itself to presumption, and the warning given him by Jesus: "*The spirit indeed is willing, but the flesh is weak,*" was verified.

The δοῦλοι, *servants*, ver. 18, designate the private domestics of the priestly palace; the ὑπηρέται, *officers*, are the official servants of the Sanhedrim charged with the guardianship of the temple.—The last words of ver. 18: "*Peter was standing with them and warming himself*," are literally repeated at ver. 25, where they are placed as a stepping-stone to the approaching resumption of the account of Peter's denials. The verbs in the imperfect are graphic, and signify that the situation described remains during the investigation about to be described.

3d. Appearance at the house of Annas.

Vv. 19–21. "*The high priest then asked Jesus of His disciples, and of His doctrine. Jesus answered him, I spake*[1] *openly to the world; I ever taught in open synagogue,*[2] *and in the temple, whither all*[3] *the Jews resort; and in secret have I said nothing. Why askest*[4] *thou me? ask them which heard me, what I have said unto them: behold, they know what I said.*"—Though this semblance of inquiry took place at the house of Annas, it was not he, as is generally thought, but Caiaphas, who directed the examination. The title of high priest which is given him in ver. 13, and again in ver. 24, immediately after, admits no other interpretation. This sitting was not entirely private, as is often said. It had its necessary place in the trial, and the term *officer* in ver. 22 supposes its official character. The duty of presiding over it therefore devolved on the high priest as such. It has been supposed that Annas acted here as *Ab-beth-din* (chief of the court of justice). But this dignity belonged to the high priest himself (Schürer, p. 413). Keim rightly says (assuredly not in the interest of John's narrative): "If Caiaphas was really the acting high priest, and at the same time the soul of the movement directed against Jesus, it was for him, and not for his father-in-law, to take knowledge of the matter and report to the Sanhedrim" (iii. p. 322). What meaning otherwise could attach to the description of Caiaphas in ver. 13? And when, at ver. 22, the officer says to Jesus: "*Answerest thou the high priest so?*" can we think of another than the acting high priest, the same who alone bears the title all through the chapter?

---

[1] ℵ A B C L X Y Δ: λιλαληκα instead of ελαλησα.
[2] T. R. reads τη before συναγωγη solely with Λ and some Mnn.
[3] T. R. with only some Mnn.: παντοθεν; ϛ with 10 Mjj. (Y Γ Δ Λ, etc.): παντοτε; ℵ A B C L X Π: παντις.
[4] T. R. with Byz.: επερωτας and επερωτησον; Alex.: ερωτας and ερωτησον.

Ver. 24 does not contradict this interpretation. The only change referred to there is one of locality.—The question put to Jesus was intended to extort from Him some answer fitted to be the ground of His condemnation. For embarrassment was felt as to the course to be followed in this matter, as is proved by the recourse had to false witnesses.—What is asked of Jesus is not the names of His disciples, as if a list of His accomplices was wanted; it is information about the number of His partisans, and the principles which serve as their watchword.—Jesus, knowing that all they seek is to drag from Him some utterance which they may turn to His disadvantage, simply appeals to the publicity of His teaching. He is not the chief of a secret society, nor the propagator of principles which fear the light of day.—$\Sigma v\nu a\gamma \omega \gamma \hat{\eta}$, without article: *in synagogal assembly;* the word $\iota \epsilon \rho \acute{o} v$, *temple*, has the article, because this edifice stands alone. When Jesus taught His disciples in private, it was not to tell them anything different from what He declared in public.—The testimony of the ancient Vss. decides in favour of the Alex. reading: "*all the Jews;*" not: "*the Jews everywhere* or *always.*"

Vv. 22, 23. "*When He had thus spoken, one of the officers which stood by struck Jesus with the palm of his hand, saying, Answerest thou the high priest so? Jesus answered him, If I have spoken evil, bear witness of the evil; but if well, why smitest thou me?*"—The answer of Jesus certainly contained a tacit rebuke. An officer, who wished to pay court to his master, takes occasion to remind Jesus of the respect due.—$'P\acute{a}\pi\iota\sigma\mu a$ signifies strictly: *a blow with a rod.* No doubt in Matt. v. 39 the verb $\rho a\pi\acute{\iota}\zeta \epsilon\iota v$ is taken in the sense of *buffeting.* But here the strict meaning seems preferable, because of the term $\delta\acute{\epsilon}\rho \epsilon\iota v$, *to flay*, ver. 23.—$M a\rho \tau\acute{v}\rho\eta\sigma o v$: "prove by lawful witness-bearing."—Jesus does not here literally fulfil His own precept (Matt. v. 39). His own innocence demanded this answer, so full of gentleness and dignity.

Ver. 24. "*Therefore*[1] *Annas sent Him bound unto Caiaphas the high priest.*"—This verse has always perplexed those who held that the previous sitting was that which took place at the house of Caiaphas, and which is related by the Synoptics.

---

[1] T. R., with B C L X ∆ It^aliq, some Mnn., reads: *ουν* (*therefore*); א Syr^sch, some Mnn.: δε (*then*); F, with 13 Mjj. (A, etc.), omits every particle.

This is what has led to the transposition of this verse in some documents after ver. 13 (see the critical note on this verse); it has also led several critics, such as Calvin, Lücke, Tholuck, de Wette, Langen, to take ἀπέστειλεν in the sense of the pluperfect, *had sent*. And as the particle οὖν, *therefore*, did not suit this explanation, they have been led thereby either to reject this particle or to transform it into δέ: " *Now* Annas had sent . . ." But the most probable text is certainly *therefore;* and this particle evidently makes the following sending *the consequence* of all that has just been related, and especially of the appearance at the house of Annas. The evangelist's object in inserting this notice here, is to indicate that this appearance must be distinguished from that which took place later at the house of Caiaphas before the Sanhedrim, and to assign its place to this well-known sitting which he does not relate. M. Lutteroth gives this verse a sentimental cast: " Now this Jesus, thus struck by the officer, stood with His hands bound, *as Annas had [previously] sent Him to Caiaphas !* " But this meaning does not harmonize with the uniform simplicity of the apostolic narrative. Besides, also, it supposes the meaning of the pluperfect given to the Aor., without any valid reason (see Meyer).—Jesus had no doubt been unbound during His examination; this scene over, Annas had Him bound anew to send Him to Caiaphas. Probably He was unbound a second time during the sitting of the Sanhedrim, and thus is explained why, Matt. xxvii. 2 and Mark xv. 1, He is bound anew when He is led away to Pilate.—" *Unto Caiaphas* " here signifies: " to the palace of Caiaphas; " there were the official apartments and a hall for the meetings of the Sanhedrim. This body had been called together in the interval. The members were at Jerusalem for the feast.

4th. Second and third denial.

Vv. 25–27. " *And Simon Peter stood and warmed himself. They said therefore unto him, Art not thou also one of his disciples ? He denied it, and said, I am not. One of the servants of the high priest, being his kinsman whose ear Peter cut off, saith, Did not I see thee in the garden with him ? Peter then denied again: and immediately the cock crew.*"—Till now, according to John, all has passed at the house of Annas; and it was consequently in the court of his palace that the fire was lighted beside which Peter denies Jesus. According to the Synoptics, who do not mention the appearing before Annas, the three denials took place at the house of Caiaphas. We have already stated the reasons which in our view support the supposition by which this contradiction is resolved, viz. that Annas and Caiaphas inhabited the same sacerdotal palace. This opinion is in keeping with oriental usage, according to which palaces are not only inhabited by the reigning prince, but also by all the members of his family. The marked connection of the first words of this verse with the last of ver. 18 shows that the second and third denials took place during the examination, vv. 20–23. The sending of Jesus to Caiaphas, therefore, followed immediately on this last denial. And so may be explained the look which Jesus cast on Peter, according to Luke (xxii. 61). Jesus was passing through the court which He had to cross to get from the apartments of Annas to those of Caiaphas. At that moment He heard the cock crow; and it was then that His look met that of Peter. The epithet δεδεμένον, *bound*, serves to explain better the impression produced on the faithless disciple by seeing his Master in this condition.

The subject of εἶπον, *they said* (ver. 25), is indeterminate. According to Matthew, it is a maid-servant who sees Peter approaching the gate to escape from the court to the front of the house. According to Mark, it is the same servant who had already given him trouble, and who denounces him to the servants gathered round the fire. In Luke, it is vaguely a ἕτερος, *another* person. It is probable that the porteress spoke of Peter to one of her companions, who denounced him to the assembled servants. From this group there rose instantly the question addressed to Peter.—After the second denial, Peter seems to have played the bravado, and to have set himself to speak more freely with the persons present. His Galilean accent was soon remarked, and drew attention more particularly from a kinsman of Malchus, which occasioned the third denial. John does not speak of Peter's imprecations which are related by Matthew. If, therefore, any one was animated with ill-feeling to Peter, it was not the author of our narrative, as is alleged, but rather the first evangelist.

This whole narrative would suffice to prove: 1st, how close

is the relation which is sustained by this Gospel to the previous Gospels; 2d, with how much less life and ease the facts were related by oral tradition than they have been by the pen of the eye-witness. The latter alone has reproduced the minutest links of the history; and M. Renan is not without reason in speaking of "its undulating features and lifelike points."

II. *The Trial before Pilate.*—xviii. 28–xix. 16.

Had the Romans, when they converted Judea into a province of the empire, taken away from the Jews the right of capital punishment? Our narrative says so positively, putting into their own mouths the words (ver. 31): "*It is not lawful for us to put any man to death.*" To this have been objected the execution of Stephen, Acts vii. 57 et seq., and the permission granted by Titus to the Jews to put foreigners and even Romans to death who passed beyond the enclosure of the temple court (Josephus, *Antiq.* vi. 2. 4). But the former is an act of extra-legal popular fury, and the permission given by Titus is expressly an exceptional case. According to the Talmud as well as John, the right of inflicting capital punishment did not now belong to the Sanhedrim. In the times which had followed the conquest, the governors had probably made use of concessions to the conquered people. But not long before this, perhaps since the governorship of the despotic Pilate, the Jews had been reduced to the common provincial law: the *jus gladii* had been withdrawn from them. "Forty years before the destruction of the temple," says the Talmud, "capital sentences were taken away from Israel."[1] It was, therefore, about the year 30 of our era, the year of Jesus' death. Hence the reason why the rulers were obliged to lead Jesus before Pilate, and to ask this Gentile magistrate to ratify and execute the sentence which they had just pronounced.— When we examine carefully the conduct of the Jews at this hearing, we discover in it a maturely-concerted and skilfully-followed plan. This circumstance proves, indeed, that after the judgment pronounced on Jesus at the house of Caiaphas, there must have been a new sitting, at which it was agreed

---

[1] *Sanhédr.*, fol. 24. 2: *Quadraginta annis ante vastatum templum ablata sunt judicia capitalia ab Israële.*

what course should be followed to get the sentence of death ratified by the procurator.[1] Moreover, the sentence, having been pronounced over night, required to be legally confirmed at a regular diet.[2] Finally, the Sanhedrim, wishing to conduct Jesus in a body to the governor, must have had a meeting-place somewhere. Such was the origin of the *morning* sitting, which took place very early, probably in the famous hall, paved with mosaic (*lischkath haggazith*), situated at the south of the temple. Comp. Matt. xxvii. 1; Mark xv. 1. Luke (xxii. 66 et seq.) has also preserved to us the account of it, perhaps mixing with it some details borrowed from the night sitting, which he passes over in silence. In any case, the examination and judgment of Jesus must have been summarily reproduced and ratified in this *plenary* (πάντες, Matt.) sitting of the Sanhedrim.

The Jews begin by asking Pilate to confirm their sentence *without examination* (ver. 30). This he refuses. Such is the first phase: vv. 28–32. They then frame a *political* accusation: He made himself a king. Pilate judges this accusation unfounded, after which he makes two attempts to deliver Jesus with the support of the people, but without success. This is the second phase: ver. 33–xix. 6. The Jews then advance a new charge of a *religious* nature: He made himself the Son of God. But, on hearing this accusation, Pilate endeavours all the more to deliver Jesus. This is the third phase: vv. 7–12*a*. At this moment, the Jews, seeing their prey on the point of escaping from them, put aside all shame and employ the odious means of *personal* threatening to bend the conscience of the judge; and in this way they allow themselves to be dragged into the denial of their most cherished hope, that of the Messiah; they subscribe themselves vassals to Cæsar. Such is the fourth phase: vv. 12*b*–16.

Ver. 28. "*Then led they Jesus from Caiaphas unto the hall of judgment: and it was early; and they themselves went not*

---

[1] Comp. especially the expression: ὥστε θανατῶσαι αὐτόν, Matt. xxvii. 1, that is to say: "*to seek the ways and means* best fitted to secure from the governor the execution of Jesus."

[2] Lightfoot, *Hor. Hebr.* in Matt. xxvii. 1. Keim: "The day sitting was required in point of legality to complete the night one. For the sittings of the Sanhedrim, especially in a case of capital punishment, required to be held during the day and in the morning, *before man has drunk or eaten*."

into the judgment hall, lest they should be defiled, that[1] *they might eat the Passover."*—The *prætorium* (*judgment* hall) was, properly speaking, the place where the prætor sat at Rome when he administered justice. This name had been applied to the palaces of the Roman governors in the provinces. Most critics hold that it denotes here the palace of Herod, which stood on the hill of Zion, in the western part of the upper city. They quote the passage of Josephus, *Bellum jud.* ii. 14. 8, but wrongly; for it is said there: "Florus *at that time* (τότε) dwelt in the royal palace,"—a clear proof that the Roman governor did not live there ordinarily. It is more probable that Pilate occupied a palace belonging to the citadel Antonia, where the Roman garrison was stationed at the northwest corner of the temple. There, at least, tradition places the starting-point of the *Via Dolorosa.*—Πρωΐ (T. R. πρωΐα), *early morning,* comprises the time from three to six o'clock (Mark xiii. 35). In general, the Roman courts did not open their sittings till nine o'clock; but, as we have seen, Pilate was forewarned the previous evening of what was passing, and he had consented to receive the Jews at this unusual hour.

The scruple which prevents the Jews from entering the governor's house brings us again face to face with the seeming contradiction between John's narrative and that of the Synoptics. If, as the latter seem to say, the Jews had already celebrated the Paschal feast on *the previous* evening, how are we to explain their fear that, defiling themselves by contact with leaven in a Gentile house, they should not be able to eat the Passover that same day? The defenders of what is thought to be the synoptical view had no other resource than to refer the expression *eating the Passover,* not to the Paschal feast properly so called, but to those sacred feasts which were celebrated daily during the festival, and which consisted of unleavened bread and of the flesh of the peace-offerings. It is in this general sense, they say, that the word *Passover* is taken, Deut. xvi. 2, 3: "*Thou shalt sacrifice the Passover unto the Lord, of the flock and the herd . . . : seven days shalt thou eat unleavened bread therewith*" (the Passover). Comp. the analogous expression, 2 Chron. xxx. 22 (literally): "*And they did eat the feast* (the sacrifices of the feast) *seven days, offering peace-offerings and*

---

[1] ℵ A B C Δ reject the second *ινα*.

praising the Lord;" 2 Chron. xxxv. 7-9 : "*And Josiah gave to the people, of the flock, lambs and kids, all for the Passover offerings, for all that were present, to the number of thirty thousand, and three thousand bullocks: these were of the king's substance. . . .*"

It is alleged further, that, according to the Talmud, the defilement which the Jews would have contracted by entering the prætorium would only have lasted to the end of the day, and would not have prevented them from eating the Paschal feast, which fell wholly on the following day.—But the passages quoted do not prove what they would require to prove. As in Deut. xvi. 5, 6 the term Passover is applied exclusively to the Paschal lamb, it follows that the expression: "*of the herd and of the flock,*" in ver. 2, is not an explanatory apposition to the word *pésach* (Passover), but an appendix by which there are *added* to the principal sacrifice all the secondary sacrifices required to complete it during the course of the holy week. And in any case, even if the word *Passover* could embrace *along with* the Paschal lamb all the other sacrifices of the feast, it would not follow that it could designate the latter *without the former*, as would be the case in the passage of John.—In 2 Chron. xxx. the name *Passover* is applied, vv. 15, 17, 18, *exclusively* to the Paschal lamb. Why does the chronicler in ver. 22 substitute for this special designation the general expression *the feast*, except because he now wished to speak of the sacrifices of the feast, *excepting* the Paschal lamb? Besides, the reading: "*and they did eat (vajokelou),*" is very doubtful. The LXX. had certainly read *vajekallou*, "*and they finished;*" for they translate καὶ συνετέλεσαν.—In the third passage (2 Chron. xxxv. 7-9), the distinction between lambs and kids intended to *form the Passover*, and the bullocks consecrated to the other sacrifices and feasts, is obvious at a glance.—But even supposing that in some passage of the O. T. the term *Passover* had received from the context a wider meaning than ordinary, would it follow that so common and technical a phrase in the N. T. as that of *eating the Passover* could all at once be applied to another than the Paschal feast? Here certainly Meyer has good right to protest against forced *harmonistic*.

As to the objection taken from the duration of the defilement which the Jews would have contracted: 1. It is impossible to conclude anything with certainty as to the times of Jesus, from a passage of the Rabbin Maimonides about the year 1200. 2. This passage refers to a case of defilement arising from contact with dead animals, etc., and not to defilement produced by leaven, and specially and directly connected with the feast itself. 3. The members of the Sanhedrim might perfectly, without incurring the penalty of death, have abstained from taking part in a sacrifice or feast of a general kind; for these acts were voluntary; the Paschal feast properly so called was the only one which did not admit of abstention.[1] 4. The defilement thus contracted would in any case have prevented the members of the Sanhedrim from participating in the *slaying* of the lamb in the afternoon.

For all these reasons, it is impossible for me to hold the view of the numerous and learned critics who refer the expression: "*eat the Passover*" in our verse to the peace-offering (the *chagigah*) which the Jews offered on the 16th Nisan (we shall only name among moderns, Tholuck, Olshausen, Hengstenberg, Wieseler, Hofmann, Lange, Riggenbach, Bäumlein, Langen, Luthardt, and Kirchner).

The pronoun αὐτοί, *themselves*, contrasts the Jews, in their Levitical purity, with Jesus, whom nothing could pollute more, so polluted was He already in their eyes. He was immediately given over to the governor and led into the prætorium. From this time Pilate must thus go from the Jews to Jesus, and from Jesus to the Jews. Keim judges this situation historically impossible, and is witty on the ambulant judge, the *peripatetic* negotiator who is presented to us in John's narrative. But the apostle himself clearly perceived the exceptional nature of the situation, and explained it definitely in ver. 28.

The first manœuvre of the Jews:

Vv. 29–32. "*Pilate then went out*[2] *unto them, and said,*[3] *What accusation bring ye against this man?*[4] *They answered*

---

[1] See the article of Andreæ, already quoted (at xiii. 1), in the *Beweis de Glaubens*, 1870.

[2] א adds ἔξω after Πιλατος, B C L X Syr. before προς αυτους, others after these words.

[3] א B C L X: φησιν instead of ειπεν.

[4] א B omit κατα.

and said unto him, If he were not a malefactor,[1] *we would not have delivered him up unto thee. Then*[2] *said Pilate unto them, Take ye him, and judge him according to your law. The Jews therefore said unto him, It is not lawful for us to put any man to death: that the saying of Jesus might be fulfilled, which He spake,*[3] *signifying what death He should die."*—Pilate was the fifth governor of Judea since the Roman domination. He was in office from 26 to 36 A.D., under Tiberius and Caligula. He was subordinate to the proconsul of Syria. His residence was Cæsarea; he went up to Jerusalem at the feasts; he loved on these occasions to display before the people the pomp of Roman majesty. Philo (*Leg. ad Caïum*) represents him as a proud, obstinate, impracticable man. But it is probable that the fanaticism of the Jews had also much to do with the endless embroilments which they had with him. "All Pilate's acts which are known to us," says M. Renan, "show him to have been a good administrator." This portrait is assuredly flattering; but it is confirmed in some measure by the picture of his government drawn by Josephus, *Antiq.* xviii. 2–4. Accused of false testimony and murder before his chief, Vitellius, governor of Syria, he was sent to Rome to answer for himself. Eusebius relates, on the testimony of pagan writers, that he committed suicide under Caligula.—Οὖν, *therefore* (then): because the Jews would not enter his court.

The answer of the Jews to Pilate (ver. 30) is clever. It is easy to see that it is premeditated. It unveils the attitude which they had decided to take up at the outset: they have *judged;* Pilate has only to *execute.* Thus the loss of the *jus gladii* came really to little. Pilate was the executioner; they were still the tribunal. Pilate understands them. He knows them. He plays check with them. Entering apparently into their view, delighted at finding this means of getting rid of the business, he answers them without hesitation: "Very well! Since you wish to be sole judges in this matter, be it so! Take the accused and punish him yourselves (of course within the limits of your competency)." The Sanhedrim had, indeed, certain disciplinary rights, such as excommunication,

---

[1] ℵ reads κακον ποιησας, B L κακον ποιων, instead of κακοποιος.
[2] B C omit ουν; A K U Π read δε.
[3] ℵ omits οιι μειν.

scourging, etc. There was no need of Pilate to apply such chastisements. Some critics have thought that Pilate really authorized them to put Jesus to death, but with this implied reserve: "If you can and dare" (Hengstenberg). But this is to make Pilate say yes and no at one and the same time. xix. 6 proves nothing in favour of this meaning, as we shall see.

This reply was not to the mind of the Jews, who wished at any cost to have Jesus put to death. It forces them, therefore, to avow their dependence in this case where capital punishment is in question (ver. 31). And this circumstance seems significant to the evangelist (ver. 32); for if they had been their own masters, or if they had allowed themselves to be carried away, as they did later in the murder of Stephen, to act as if they still were so, Jesus would have undergone the Jewish, not the Roman punishment. He would have been stoned, but not *lifted up from the earth* like the brazen serpent, as He had foretold (iii. 14, xii. 32).

The second manœuvre of the Jews:

Vv. 33–35. "*Then Pilate entered into the judgment hall again, and called Jesus, and said unto Him, Art thou the King of the Jews? Jesus answered him,*[1] *Sayest thou*[2] *this thing of thyself,*[3] *or did others tell it thee of me? Pilate answered, Am I a Jew? Thine own nation and the chief priests*[4] *have delivered thee unto me; what hast thou done?*"
—In John's narrative there is evidently a blank here. For there is nothing to explain the question of Pilate to Jesus: "*Art thou the King of the Jews?*" Such an inquiry supposes a saying on the part of the accusers giving rise to it. This supposition is changed into certainty when we compare the synoptical account, especially that of Luke: "*We found him,*" say the Jews accosting Pilate, *perverting the nation, and forbidding to give tribute to Cæsar, saying that he is the Christ the King*" (xxiii. 2). Luke has omitted the first phase of the accusation, that which John has just related; he begins his narrative at the point where the Jews come down to the humble part of accusers, and recognise fully the position of Pilate. It is evident that John, after supplying in the pre-

---

[1] 9 Mjj. (A B C, etc.) omit αυτω. [2] ℵ: ειπας instead of λεγεις.
[3] ℵ B C L: απο σεαυτου instead of αφ' εαυτου. [4] ℵ b e: ο αρχιερευς.

ceding part what the Synoptics had omitted, supposes in ver. 33 that the accusation mentioned by them is known. It comes out ever more clearly how intimate is the relation between his narrative and theirs.

To his question Pilate no doubt expected a ready, frank answer in the negative. But the position was not so simple as he imagined. There was a distinction to be observed. In the political sense which a Roman naturally gave to the term: "*King of the Jews,*" Jesus could repudiate the title; but in the religious sense given to it by every believing Jew, Jesus must accept it, whatever might be the consequences of His avowal. Otherwise He would have given occasion to the report that He had denied being the Messiah. Everything thus depended on the question whether the charge proceeded from Jewish or Gentile lips. Meyer's objections to this explanation seem to me of no weight. He sees in the question of Jesus to Pilate nothing but an explanation which He had *the right* to ask, that He might know the origin of the accusation. What! without any object whatever? Does Jesus in this scene then lavish His sayings uselessly? According to Tholuck and Luthardt, Jesus simply means to make Pilate aware of the suspected origin (*others*, the Jews) of this information. But why in this case not rather answer by a simple no? The really affirmative answer of Jesus in vv. 36 and 37 becomes a counter assertion. These two verses are incompatible with the question of Jesus, except on our explanation, which is that of Olshausen, Neander, Ewald, etc. —It must be concluded from this saying that Jesus had not Himself heard the accusation of the rulers, and that consequently He was already in the prætorium at the time when it had been uttered.

Pilate does not in the least understand this distinction. He gets out of patience: "What have I to do with all your Jewish subtilties!" There is supreme contempt in the antithesis: ἐγώ . . . Ἰουδαῖος . . . (*I . . . a Jew?*). Then, dismissing the Jewish jargon with which he had allowed the accusers to impose on him for a moment, he examines as an open, straightforward Roman: "Come, to business! What crime hast thou committed?"

Vv. 36, 37. "*Jesus answered, My kingdom is not of this*

world: if my kingdom were of this world, then would my servants fight, that I should not be delivered to the Jews: but now is my kingdom not from hence. Pilate therefore said unto Him, Art thou a king then? Jesus answered, Thou sayest that I am a king.[1] *To this end was I*[1] *born, and for this cause came I into the world, that I should bear witness unto the truth.*[2] *Every one that is of the truth heareth my voice."*—Jesus resumes the question (ver. 36) at the point to which it was brought by ver. 34. Ver. 36: in the Gentile political sense, He is not a king; ver. 37: in the Jewish religious sense, He is.—The phrase ἐκ τοῦ κόσμου, *of this world*, is not synonymous with ἐν τῷ κόσμῳ, *in this world*. The kingdom of Jesus is certainly developed here below. But it does not derive its *origin* from beneath, from human will and earthly force. Jesus alleges in proof of this, the way in which He has given Himself over to the Jews. His *servants* are that crowd of adherents who had surrounded Him on Palm day, and not merely, as they are understood by Lücke and Luthardt, hypothetical beings: the servants, whom in that case I should have. Of the meaning given by Bengel and Stier: *the angels*, Pilate could not even have had a glimpse.—It has been sought to give to νῦν, *now*, a temporal sense: "My kingdom is not now, but it will be later, of this world." But, at our Lord's advent, His kingdom will no more be *of* this world than it is to-day. *Now* ought to be taken, as it often is, in the logical sense: it contrasts the ever present reality of truth with the non-existence of error.

If in ver. 37 we read οὔκουν, *certainly not*, this word must be taken interrogatively: "Thou dost not then profess, as I thought, to be a king?" Pilate would thus make haste to take advantage of the denial of Jesus, ver. 36, to get rid of the business. But the end of ver. 36: "*My kingdom . . . ,*" and the assertion of Jesus, ver. 37: "*Thou sayest*," in which He resumes and appropriates the contents of Pilate's words, rather favour the accentuation οὐκοῦν: *then*. "Thou art a king then! Thou confessest it?"—The affirmative formula

---

[1] ℵ B L Y, 10 Mnn. It^{alia} omit one of the two εγω read by T. R., the one after ειμι, the other before εν τουτω.

[2] ℵ: μαρτυρηση περι της αληθειας.

used by Jesus: "*Thou sayest*," though unknown to classic Greek and even to the O. T., is common in the Rabbins. M. Reuss gives these words an impossible meaning when he makes Jesus say: "It is *thou* who sayest that I am a king; *as for me*, I have come into the world that . . .," which would signify: I am not a *king*, but a simple *prophet*. For this meaning, an adversative particle would have been required between the two propositions; and the well-known sense of the formula: "*Thou sayest*," does not admit of this explanation. —Ὅτι might signify *for*: "Thou art right in saying so; *for* I am." But it is more natural to explain: "Thou sayest well, *that* I am a king." The importance of the idea impresses Jesus with the need of expressing it at full length. —Hengstenberg entirely separates from this declaration the words following, which he applies exclusively to the *prophetic* office of Jesus Christ. But it is quite evident that Jesus wishes to explain by them in what sense He is *King*. He conquers the world by testimony borne to the truth, and His people are recruited from all men who have the sense of truth. The first ἐγώ, *I*, should be rejected. Jesus certainly did not say: "I am a king, *I* at least." The first no less than the second εἰς τοῦτο, *for this end*, bears on the following ἵνα (*in order that*), in opposition to the translation of Ostervald and Arnaud: "For this (to be a king) was I born."— "*I was born*" refers to the fact of His birth, which He has in common with all men, while the words: "*I came into the world*," bring out the mission for which He appeared below. —It is by His prophetic work that Jesus founds His kingdom among men. The truth, the revelation of God, this is the sceptre which He passes over the earth. The mode of conquest which Jesus here unveils to Pilate was the opposite of that whereby the Roman power was formed, and Lange very justly remarks that, as xii. 25 contained the judgment of the genius of Greece, this declaration of Jesus to Pilate contains the judgment of the genius of Rome by the Gospel. Here is the normal accomplishment of Paul's saying: "*The spiritual man judges all things*."—The phrase, "*to be of the truth*," is similar to iii. 21, vii. 17, viii. 47, x. 16, etc. It denotes that moral disposition whereby one is ready beforehand to receive objective truth, as soon as it is revealed in

Jesus Christ. By the word *whosoever,* Jesus was no longer addressing the judge, but man, in Pilate (Hengstenberg).

Ver. 38. "*Pilate saith unto Him, What is truth? And when he had said this, he went out again unto the Jews, and saith unto them, I find in him no fault.*"—Pilate's exclamation is neither the expression of an ardent thirst for truth (the Fathers), nor that of the despair of a soul which has long sought it in vain (Olshausen); it is the profession of a frivolous scepticism, such as is frequently met with in the man of the world, and especially in the statesman; witness the manner in which Napoleon used to speak of ideologues. If Pilate had seriously sought truth, this would have been the time to find it. He would not have turned away so abruptly from Jesus. But the conviction to which he has come now is, that the person before him is either a dreamer or a sage, but not a rival to Cæsar. With "that broad sentiment of justice and civil government which, as M. Renan says, the most ordinary Roman carried with him everywhere," he avows to the Jews his conviction of the innocence of Jesus as to the political accusation raised against Him. It was his duty now to dismiss Jesus, purely and simply absolving Him. But, fearing to offend the Jews, who had certain reasons for accusing him before the supreme government, he seeks to avoid such a measure, and has recourse to a series of expedients. The first was remitting the matter to Herod, on the pretext of the Galilean origin of Jesus; it is described by Luke xxiii. 6–12, and omitted by John, as a fact well known, and as not having led to any result. The second was that which John briefly relates, vv. 39 and 40, and which is given in detail by the Synoptics.

Vv. 39, 40. "*But ye have a custom, that I should release unto you one at the Passover: will ye therefore that I release unto you the King of the Jews? Then cried they all*[1] *again,*[2] *saying, Not this man, but Barabbas. Now Barabbas was a robber.*"—These words are immediately connected by John with those of ver. 38, because the sending to Herod was *preceded* as well as *followed* (Luke xxiii. 4, 14) by a declaration of the innocence of Jesus. These two declarations

[1] ℵ B L X, 15 Mnn. omit παντες.
[2] G K U Π, 50 Mnn. It. lerique Syr. Cop. omit παλιν.

might be blended in one. The very abridged account which John gives of the episode of Barabbas serves as a link of connection between his narrative and that of the Synoptics. The origin of the custom referred to in Pilate's offer is unknown. It is probable, since the custom was connected with the feast of Passover, that it contained an allusion to the deliverance of the Jews from their Egyptian captivity.—The words ἐν τῷ πάσχα, *at the Passover*, by no means contain the proof, as Lange, Hengstenberg, etc., allege, that the Passover feast was by this time celebrated. The 14th Nisan already formed part of the feast (see on xiii. 1). It is even more probable that the deliverance of the prisoner took place on the 14th than on the 15th, that he might be able to take part in the Paschal feast with all the people.—In making this offer to the Jews, Pilate counted on the popular sympathy for Jesus which had appeared so remarkably on Palm day. For it was to the entire people that the favour was granted; and Pilate knew perfectly well that it was *from envy* that the rulers wished the death of Jesus (Matt. xxvii. 18), and that the feeling of part of the people was against them.—In the designation: *"King of the Jews,"* irony prevails, as in ver. 14. Only the sarcasm is not addressed to Jesus, for whom Pilate from the beginning feels a growing interest and respect, but to the Jews. Their King? What! This, then, is the only rival whom this people with their national pretensions have to set up against Cæsar! But it is said in Mark xv. 11: "*The chief priests moved the people, that he should rather release Barabbas unto them.*" The friends of Jesus remained mute, or their weak voices were drowned in those of the rulers and their creatures. Some resolute agitators imposed their will on the multitude. Thus is explained John's πάντες, *all*, which corresponds to Luke's παμπληθεί.—The πάλιν, *again*, the authenticity of which is established by the principal documents of both families, is remarkable. Thus far in John's account the Jews have uttered no exclamation. It was otherwise in the Synoptics. Comp. Mark xv. 8: ἀναβοήσας ὁ ὄχλος, and Luke xxiii. 5, 10: "*They were the more fierce, saying . . . they vehemently accused Him.*" Here, again, John's narrative expressly assumes that of his predecessors.—Λῃστής does not always signify *robber*, but *a violent man* in general. According to Mark and Luke, Barabbas had taken part in an insurrection in which a murder had been committed. The gravity of the choice made by the people is indicated by one of those short propositions whereby John describes a crisis of peculiar solemnity. Comp. xi. 35, xiii. 30.—The name of the man who was set up along with Jesus for the choice of the people admits of two etymologies: *Barabbah, son of the father* (either God or any Rabbi), or *Bar-rabban, son of the Rabbin.* In the first case we must double the *b*, in the second the *r.* The Mss. and Talmudic orthography (Lightfoot, p. 489) favour the first etymology. The name is not infrequent in the Talmud.

According to Mark's narrative, there occurred at this point something like a rush of people demanding spontaneously the application of the custom whereby a prisoner was released to them; and Pilate sought to turn this incident to his purpose, the liberation of Jesus. In any case, whether this incident was suggested or simply turned to account by Pilate, thus to deliver Jesus was to commit a denial of justice. For He should have been released as innocent (ver. 38). This first weakness was soon followed by a graver. We come to Pilate's third expedient.

xix. 1-3. "*Then Pilate took Jesus, and scourged*[1] *Him. And the soldiers platted a crown of thorns, and put it on His head, and they put on Him a purple robe,*[2] *and said, Hail, King of the Jews! and they smote Him with rods.*"—Pilate had ascended his tribunal to pronounce the liberation of Barabbas. Then it was that he received his wife's message (Matt. xxvii. 19). Hengstenberg thinks that the washing of his hands ought also to be placed here. But this act must have accompanied the sentence of condemnation, which did not take place till later (vv. 13-16). After his two ineffectual efforts, Pilate has recourse to a third attempt. Scourging required legally to precede the death of the cross; it was the obligatory preliminary. This is proved by a multitude of passages from Josephus and Roman historians. Comp. also Matt. xx. 19, Luke xviii. 33, where Jesus, predicting His

---
[1] א L X Cop. Sah.: λαβων ... ιμαστιγωσι.
[2] א B L U X Λ Π, 20 Mnn. It^{plerique} Vg. Cop. Sah. here add και ηρχοντο προς αυτον.

Passion, does not disjoin scourging from crucifixion. Pilate, seated on his tribunal, now pronounces the condemnation of Jesus to the penalty of scourging. He does so in this case, in the hope of averting the extreme punishment, by conceding a measure of satisfaction to the less violent among the enemies of Jesus, and awakening the zeal of His friends and the compassion of the crowd.—Scourging, as practised among the Romans, was so cruel a punishment that the prisoner very often succumbed to it. The scourge was formed of switches or thongs armed at the extremity with pieces of bone or lead. The prisoner received the strokes while fastened to a small post, so as to have his back bent and the skin on the stretch. The back became quick flesh, and the blood spurted out with the first strokes.—As to the maltreatment described, vv. 2 and 3, it is solely the doing of the Roman soldiers. The crown of thorns, the purple robe, the "Hail, King!" this whole masquerade is a parody on Jewish royalty. The thorny plant is probably the *Lycium spinosum*, which grows in abundance round Jerusalem, and whose flexible stalk, armed with sharp spikes, can easily be plaited. The red robe was the soldier's common mantle, representing the purple robe worn by kings. These caricatures do not so much refer to Jesus personally, whom the soldiers do not know, as to the nation despised and detested by the Romans. It is its well-known Messianic hope which the soldiers ridicule in the person of one who passes for an aspirant to the dignity.

Pilate lets things take their course, and pursues his object.

Vv. 4–6. "*Pilate went forth*[1] *again and saith unto them, Behold, I bring him forth to you, that ye may know that I find no fault in him.*[2] *Then came Jesus forth, wearing the crown of thorns, and the purple robe. And he saith unto them, Behold*[3] *the man! When the chief priests therefore and officers saw Him, they cried out,*[4] *saying, Crucify, crucify him!*[5] *Pilate saith unto them, Take ye him, and crucify him: for I find no fault in him.*"—The scourging took place in the court of the

---

[1] ℵ D Γ It^plerique: εξηλθεν simply ; T. R. with 9 Mjj. (E G H, etc.): εξηλθεν ουν; 6 Mjj. (A B K, etc.): και εξηλθεν.

[2] ℵ: οτι αιτιαν ουχ ευρισκω.

[3] ℵ B L X Y: ιδου instead of ιδε.

[4] ℵ: εκραξαν.

[5] T. R. omits, with ℵ B L, some Mnn. Vg^plerique, αυτοι.

prætorium (Mark xv. 15, 16), probably so as to be seen from without. As soon as it is at an end, Pilate goes out, followed by Jesus. This spectacle could not fail, Pilate thought, at last to furnish him, through the favourable interposition of the people, with the point of support which he needed to resist the hatred of the priests. In the expression: *"Behold the man !"* there is a mixture of respect and pity for Jesus Himself, and a bitter sarcasm on the impossible part which is ascribed to Him. But once again Pilate is out in his calculation; no voice rises from the multitude in favour of the victim, and he again finds himself face to face with the fixed will of the rulers to push things to extremity, without contenting themselves with a half punishment. Concessions have only served to embolden them. At once indignant and full of vexation, Pilate then says to them: *"Take ye him, and crucify him !"* which in the context can only signify: " Do it yourselves if ye will, at your risk and peril; as for me, I shall take no part in such a murder !" This emotion was noble; it was destined, nevertheless, to remain barren. Thrice already Pilate had left the sphere of strict right, on which alone he could have kept his ground against the violent pressure which was brought to bear on him.

Of course the Jews could not think of using the impunity which was offered to them by Pilate. How could they provide for the execution? And without the fear with which the Roman power inspired the people, could the rulers hope to conduct this great affair successfully? The people might, by a sudden reaction, turn round violently against them and wreck everything. And so, prudently measuring the dangers of the offer, they have recourse to another expedient.

This is their third manœuvre.

Vv. 7–9. *" The Jews answered him,*[1] *We have a law, and by our*[2] *law he ought to die, because he made himself the Son of God. When Pilate heard that saying, he was the more afraid; and went again*[3] *into the judgment hall, and saith unto Jesus, Whence art thou ? But Jesus gave him no answer."*
—The Romans allowed conquered peoples in general to enjoy their laws and national institutions, precisely as the French

---

[1] ℵ It^{plerique} omit αυτω. ℵ omits παλιν.
[2] 10 Mjj. (ℵ D, etc.) It^{plerique} Or. omit ημων.

do at the present day with the Mussulmans of Algeria, to quote M. Renan's parallel. The Jews, taking their stand on this ground, appeal to the article of *their code* (Lev. xxiv. 16), which condemns blasphemers to death, and demand from Pilate the application of this article. They do not attempt hereby to regain the position which they had lost at the beginning; they state the offence, and submit it for the governor's investigation: "*He made himself the Son of God.*" Here there comes out palpably the difference, which is so often denied, between the meaning of this title and that of the designation *King of the Jews*, or *Messiah*. The inquiry regarding this latter claim had taken place; it was at an end. Now the question is of something entirely new.—But these words of the Jews produce an effect on Pilate for which they were not prepared. The saying gives strength to a dreadful presentiment which was gradually forming within him. All that he had heard related of the miracles of Jesus, the mysterious character of His Person, of His words, and of His conduct, the strange message which he had just received from his wife,—all is suddenly explained by the term Son of God. Was this extraordinary man truly a Divine being who had appeared on the earth? The truth naturally presents itself to his mind in the form of pagan superstitions and mythological legends. But it is well known how rapid the transition is from scepticism to the most superstitious fears. Feeling, then, the need of conversing with Jesus in private, Pilate leads Him back into the prætorium. The question: "*Whence art thou?*" cannot refer to the *terrestrial* origin of Jesus; Pilate knows perfectly that He is of Galilee. It certainly means, therefore: "Art thou of the earth or of heaven?" Wonder has been felt at the silence of Jesus. According to some, He keeps silence because He is unwilling, in giving the true answer, to keep up a pagan superstition in the mind of Pilate; according to others, He refuses to answer because here is a question of pure curiosity; Luthardt thinks that He will not, by revealing Himself to Pilate, prevent the plans of God from being accomplished. The true answer seems to us to follow from what precedes: Pilate knew enough of the matter as of himself to set Him free; he had already declared Him innocent! And besides, the Jews by changing their accusation as they suddenly did at this point, sufficiently condemned themselves. If, in such circumstances, he did not set Him free as a simple man, he had deserved the issue of crucifying Him as the Son of God. Such was at once his crime and his punishment. Furthermore, Hengstenberg rightly observes that His silence was in itself an answer. If the claim which the Jews accused Jesus of making had not been well founded, He would have expressly denied it.

Vv. 10, 11. "*Pilate saith unto Him,*[1] *Speakest thou not unto me? knowest thou not that I have power to crucify*[2] *thee, and have power to release*[2] *thee? Jesus answered,*[3] *Thou couldest*[4] *have no power against me, except it were given thee from above: therefore he that delivered*[5] *me unto thee hath the greater sin.*"—Pilate feels that this silence contains a reproach. He assumes all the hauteur of the Roman judge and governor. Hence the ἐμοί, *unto me*, foremost ("*to me*, if not to others"), and the repetition of the words: "*I have power.*"—T. R. puts the "*to crucify thee*" before the "*to release thee.*" For the idea of the imminent punishment of death is that which prevails in the conversation; but the opposite reading may also be defended (see Luthardt). Pilate speaks only of his power; Jesus reminds him of his dependence and responsibility. With the word *I have* is contrasted the term *given*. This time Jesus speaks. He also puts on His dignity; He takes the place of judge of His judges, and, as if He were already seated on His tribunal, He weighs Pilate and the Sanhedrim in His infallible judgment scales. The διὰ τοῦτο, *therefore*, is explained by the preceding words: "Because the power which thou exercisest is *given* thee, while the power of him who delivers me to thee is usurped." God Himself, by subjecting His people to the Roman power, had placed the Jews and their King under the imperial jurisdiction. But the Sanhedrim, in taking possession of the Person of their King, and giving Him over to the authority of the foreigner, arrogated to themselves a right over Him which God had not entrusted

---

[1] ℵ A, several Mnn. Syr. Cop. omit ουν.

[2] ℵ A B E Syr. read απολυσαι σε ... σταυρωσαι σε.

[3] ℵ B L It^{aliq} Syr. add αυτω.

[4] ℵ A L X Y Λ Π, 10 Mnn. Cop.: εχεις (*thou hast not*) instead of υχες (*thou wouldest not have*).

[5] ℵ B E Δ Λ It. Vg.: παραδους instead of παραδους.

to them, and committed an act of theocratic felony.—"*He that delivered me to thee*" is neither Judas—Jesus could not have said in this case: "*to thee*"—nor Caiaphas, who acts only in the name of the body which he represents, and who is not once named throughout the whole scene. It is the Sanhedrim which is meant, and the Jewish nation in whose name that body acts. —The explanation which we have given of those words of Jesus is nearly that of Calvin: "He who delivered me unto thee is the more guilty of the two, because he *criminally* makes use of thy *lawful* power." Some commentators think that Jesus means to distinguish between the function of judging, which is official, and that of informing, which is voluntary. This is less natural. The other explanations do not account for the *therefore*. Thus: Pilate is less guilty, "because he sins from weakness rather than wickedness" (Euthymius); "because he has less knowledge than the Jews" (Grotius).—Far from taking offence at this answer, Pilate is struck with the majesty which it breathes. Hence the fourth phase of the trial, Pilate's last effort to deliver Jesus, meeting with defeat from the fourth and last expedient held in reserve by the Sanhedrim.

Ver. 12. "*And from thenceforth Pilate sought to release Him: but the Jews cried out,*[1] *saying, If thou let this man go, thou art not Cæsar's friend: for whosoever maketh himself a king speaketh against Cæsar.*"—'Εκ τούτου, strictly: "after and in consequence of that word." Comp. vi. 66.—John seems to say that all Pilate's previous efforts to release Jesus were nothing in comparison with those which he made under the impression of the words which He had just heard from His lips. But the Jews had by them a weapon which they had resolved to use only at the last extremity, that of personal intimidation. The reigning emperor, Tiberius, was the most suspicious of despots. The accusation of high treason was always well received by this tyrant. *Qui atrocissime exercebat leges majestatis*, says Suetonius. The most unpardonable charge was that of having allowed his authority to be endangered. Such is the peril which the Jews call up before the dismayed view of Pilate. This equivocal term: "*King of the Jews*," with

---

[1] T. R. with 9 Mjj. (E H K, etc.): ἐκραζον; A I L M Y Π, 24 Mnn. Or.: ἐκραυγαζον; B, 13 Mnn.: ἐκραυγασαν; ℵ: ἐλεγον instead of ἐκραζον λεγοντες.

the political colour which it could not fail to have in the eyes of Tiberius, would infallibly make Pilate appear as an unfaithful adminstrator who had attempted to screen from punishment an enemy of the imperial authority; and his trial would be short. Pilate knew this well. True, to play this last move was, on the part of the Jews, to deny the very notion of the Messiah, and to subscribe themselves vassals of the Empire. Such a victory was a suicide. And so it is easy to understand why in their plan of operations they had kept this manœuvre to the last; it was the stroke of desperation. Its effect was immediate.

Vv. 13–16. "*When Pilate therefore heard these sayings,[1] he brought Jesus forth, and sat down in the judgment-seat, in a place that is called the Pavement, and in the Hebrew, Gabbatha. And it was the preparation of the Passover, and [2] about [3] the sixth [4] hour: and he saith unto the Jews, Behold your King! They cried out,[5] Away with him, away with him, crucify him. Pilate saith unto them, Shall I crucify your King? The chief priests answered, We have no king but Cæsar. Then delivered he Him therefore unto them to be crucified.*"—Before this threat (the plur. τῶν λόγων τούτων brings out its gravity more forcibly than the sing. of T. R., τὸν λόγον τοῦτον) the judge, who had long since renounced his part, lowers his head and gives in. Without saying a word more, he orders Jesus to be led out of the prætorium; for the sentence must be pronounced in presence of the accused; and he ascends his tribunal the second time.—The name λιθόστρωτον signifies *a place paved with stones.* There, probably, there was one of those mosaic pavements on which Roman magistrates were accustomed to place their judgment-seat. The Aramaic name *Gabbatha* is not a translation of the previous term; it is taken from the nature of the place. It signifies an *eminence* or *hill.*

John here inserts a notice of the day and hour when the

[1] T. R. reads, with K U Λ Π, some of the Mnn. Syr., τουτον τον λογον; all the rest: τουτων των λογων.
[2] T. R. with E H I S Y Γ Λ: ωρα δε; 9 Mjj. (א A B, etc.): ωρα ην; K: ωρα δε ην.
[3] The Mss. are divided between ως and ωσει (T. R. with 4 Mjj.).
[4] Instead of εκτη, L X Δ, 3 Mnn. read τριτη.
[5] Instead of οι δε εκραυγασαν, K Y Π: οι δε εκραυγαζον; B L X: εκραυγασαν.ον εκεινοι; א: οι δε ελιγον.

sentence was pronounced. With what view? Was it because of the solemnity and importance of this decisive moment for the lot of humanity? Or would he explain thereby the impatience of the Jews, which appears at ver. 15, to see this long trial at last come to an end, and the punishment of death exacted before the close of the day? The first solution is the more natural. "*It was the preparation of the Passover*," says John. The critics who try to bring John's narrative into accordance with the meaning usually assigned to the synoptical account, in regard to the question of the day of Christ's death, give to παρασκευή, *preparation*, the technical signification which it has sometimes in patristic literature, and even, according to them, in the N. T.: *the Friday*, as the day on which food was prepared for Sabbath, "the preparation *of the Sabbath.*" Comp. Matt. xxvii. 62; Luke xxiii. 54; and especially Mark xv. 42: παρασκευὴ ὅ ἐστι προσάββατον. They consequently explain the phrase παρασκευὴ τοῦ πάσχα, *the Friday of the Paschal week*. But though παρασκευή, taken alone (*the preparation*), became the name for Friday among the Fathers, it does not follow that when the word is succeeded by a complement like τοῦ πάσχα, *of the Passover*, it does not preserve its natural meaning: "*preparation of the Passover.*" Why otherwise add this complement: *of the Passover*, which carried absolutely no meaning to the reader; for what reader could fail to know that it was the Paschal week which was spoken of? How, besides, could Greek readers, who did not know the Jewish meaning of this word *preparation*, imagine on reading the words: "*preparation of the Passover*," that they signified the preparation *of the Sabbath* in Passover week, as we would say the *Friday* of holy week? It is evident that every one would be led to think, on the contrary, of the day of the 14th Nisan, as it was generally known that on that day preparation was made to celebrate the Paschal feast by slaying the lamb. This date agrees, therefore, with those of xiii. 1, 29, xviii. 28, and leads us, like all these passages, to the conclusion that the Paschal feast was not yet celebrated, but was to take place on the evening of this day (vv. 14, 31, 42).

According to John, sentence was pronounced on Jesus *about the sixth hour*, that is to say, about mid-day. It is difficult to harmonize this statement with Matthew's narrative, according to which at mid-day Jesus had been for some time on the cross, and still more with Mark xv. 25, where it is said that it was *the third hour*, that is to say, nine o'clock, when Christ *was crucified*. And if it were thought to reckon John's sixth hour from midnight, according to the Roman fashion, we should get six o'clock in the morning as the hour when the sentence was pronounced. But at this hour Jesus was only being led to Pilate. The sitting, far from being at an end, was beginning. The reading τρίτη, *third*, in some Mss. of John, is evidently a correction intended to harmonize the two narratives. Eusebius supposes that some old copyist had converted the gamma ($\Gamma'=3$) into a stigma ($\varsigma'=6$). This supposition is far from probable. Some documents at least would have preserved the true reading. Rather let it be remembered, (1) that the day as a whole was divided, like the night, into four parts of three hours each. This explains why mention is scarcely ever made in the N. T. of any hours except the *third, sixth,* and *ninth* (comp. Matt. xx. 1-5), and why also, as Hengstenberg remarks, the expressions *almost* or *about* are so frequent (Matt. xxvii. 46; Luke xxiii. 44; John iv. 6; Acts x. 3, 9). The ὡς, *about*, is expressly added by the author in our passage. It is therefore certainly allowable to take the mean here, both in Mark and John, especially if it be remembered that, as Lange says, the apostles had not watch in hand. As Mark's third hour may extend from eight to ten o'clock, John's sixth certainly includes from eleven to twelve. But, above all, (2) account must be taken of an important circumstance, which is also remarked by Lange, viz. that Matthew and Mark have given to the scourging of Jesus the meaning which it ordinarily had, and have regarded it as the *beginning* of the whole punishment. They have consequently identified the two judicial acts which are strictly distinguished by John, that whereby Pilate condemned Jesus to scourging, and that whereby he delivered Him over to the last penalty of death. It is easily conceivable that Mark, having lost sight of the entire interval between the two condemnations, has dated the pronouncing the sentence of death at the time which was properly that of the sentence of scourging.

There is a savage irony in the words of Pilate: "*Behold your King!*" But it is aimed at the Jews, not at Jesus.

Towards the latter Pilate constantly shows himself full of respectful interest, which towards the end goes the length of fear. Yet there is also a serious side to this sarcasm. Pilate perceives that if there is a man by means of whom the Jewish people are to carry out a great mission in the world, this is He. The rage of the rulers increases on hearing this declaration. The three imperative Aorists express their impatience and haste to have done. Pilate is henceforth resigned to yield, but first he wishes to have the pleasure of once more thrusting the dagger into the wound: "*Shall I crucify your King?*" He thus seeks to avenge himself for the act of baseness to which they compel him. The Jews thus find themselves driven to the decisive declaration whereby they pronounce with their own lips the abolition of the theocracy, and the absorption of Israel into the world of the Gentiles. They who cherish but one thought, the overthrow of the throne of the Cæsars by the Messiah, allow their hatred of Jesus to carry them so far, that they cry out before the representative of the emperor: "*We have no king but Cæsar.*"

After this they can say no more. Israel has denied herself; this is the price at which she obtains the delivery of Jesus to her. Αὐτοῖς, *to them*, says John, and not to the Roman executioners. For the latter are only the blind instruments of the judicial murder which is about to be committed.

Modern criticism (Baur, Strauss, Keim) regards this whole description of Pilate's conduct as fictitious. The author's intention is to personify in Pilate the sympathy of the Gentile world with the Gospel, and to throw on Israel almost the entire responsibility of the crime. But, 1. It is not really otherwise in the Synoptics, or the Acts, or the Epistles. In Matthew the governor *marvelled* (ver. 14); he knows that it is *for envy* that the rulers delivered Jesus (ver. 18), and strives to obtain His liberation from the people instead of that of Barabbas (vv. 17, 22). He asks indignantly: "*Why, what evil hath he done?*" (ver. 23). He sees *that he prevails nothing*, and ends by giving in, while declaring himself, by a solemn act, *innocent of the blood of this just man* (ver. 24). Thus is the condemnation of Jesus by Pilate described in the Judeo-Christian Gospel! Has it not the same meaning at bottom as that of John? It is the same with Mark's account, in which we see still more clearly than in Matthew the eagerness with which Pilate, in order to save Jesus, takes advantage of the spontaneous desire of the multitude to release a prisoner to them, and how he reckons confidently in his object on the popular sympathy (vv. 8–10). Luke adds to the other efforts made by Pilate his sending Jesus to Herod, and his twice repeated offer to let Him go at the cost of a simple scourging (vv. 16, 22). "*Wishing to release Jesus*" is the express statement, ver. 20. Then at ver. 22: "And he said to them *the third time*, Why, what evil hath he done?" In the Acts, whose conciliatory tendency is proclaimed in our day, Peter likewise charges the Jews with the entire responsibility of the murder: "Him *by* wicked *hands* ye have crucified," ii. 23; comp. iii. 15. Even James, addressing the rich of his nation, says to them: "*Ye have condemned and killed the just*" (v. 6). Finally, the Apocalypse designates Jerusalem as "the spiritual Sodom and Egypt where our Lord was crucified," xi. 8. The place (*where*), in such a context, implies the notion of causality and responsibility. 2. The second century, from Trajan to Marcus Aurelius, was a time of bloody persecution carried on by the Gentile world against the Church, and it would be very strange had an author at this epoch created a Roman governor more or less imaginary, to personify *the sympathy* of the Gentile world, and especially of the Roman power with the gospel! 3. The scene depicted by John carries in it its own defence. It is impossible to describe more to the life, on the one hand the astuteness, the perseverance, and the shameless suppleness of the accuser, who is determined to succeed at any price, and on the other the obstinate struggle in the heart of the judge between conscience and interest, between the fear of sacrificing an innocent victim, perhaps more dreadful than He seems to the eye, and that of driving to extremity a people already exasperated by crying injustices, and so to find himself accused before a suspicious sovereign who with *one stroke of the pen* (Reuss) can hurl him to destruction; finally, between cold scepticism and the transient influences of natural religiousness and even Gentile superstition. M. Reuss acknowledges that it is "the fourth Gospel which gives the true key to the problem" of

Pilate's inconceivable conduct: "Jesus was sacrificed by him to the exigency of his position" (p. 675). Excepting the natural blanks arising "from the fact that no witness saw the whole from beginning to end," the Gospel account (including John's) "bears, according to this author, the seal of entire authenticity" (*ibid.*). These two figures, indeed,—the one exhibiting a cool and diabolical malignity (Caiaphas, representing the Sanhedrim), the other a cowardice and vacillation deserving pity, and both contrasting with the calm dignity and holy majesty of the Christ,—form a picture which we do not fear to call the masterpiece of John's work, and which, taken by itself, could serve, were it necessary, to certify its authenticity.

THIRD SECTION.

XIX. 17–42.—THE CRUCIFIXION OF JESUS.

1st. The crucifixion, vv. 17, 18; 2d. The inscription, vv. 19–22; 3d. The parting of the raiment, vv. 23, 24; 4th. The Son's legacy, vv. 25–27; 5th. The end, vv. 28–30; 6th. The breaking of the legs and the spear-thrust, vv. 31–37; 7th. The burial, vv. 38–42.

John does not mean to present the full description of the crucifixion of Jesus. He states some circumstances omitted by his predecessors, and at once completes and gives precision to their narratives.

The crucifixion:

Vv. 17, 18. "*Then*[1] *they took Jesus, and led Him away.*[2] *And He, bearing His cross,*[3] *went forth to the place called the place of the skull, which is called in the Hebrew Golgotha: where they crucified Him, and two others with Him, on either side one, and Jesus in the midst.*"—These two verses are the very brief summary of the synoptical narrative. The subject of *they took* is the Jews (ver. 16*a*); it was they who executed the sentence by the soldiers' hands.—According to ancient

---

[1] The Mss. are divided between δε (T. R. with 11 Mjj.) and ουν (B L X).
[2] After τον Ιησουν, T. R. with A M U Γ: και απηγαγον; 9 Mjj., 130 Mnn.: και ηγαγον; B L X, several Mnn. It^plerique Cop. reject these words; א: *οι δε* λαβοντες τον I. απηγαγον αυτον.
[3] T. R. with 11 Mjj.: αυτου (εαυτου); B X: αυτω; א L Π: ιαυτω.

testimonies, the condemned had themselves to bear their cross. This is also implied by the figurative expression used by Jesus Himself in the Synoptics: "*If any man will come after me . . . let him take up his cross*" (Matt. xvi. 24 and parallels). John alone mentions this feature in the sufferings of Jesus. And herein he does not contradict the Synoptics, who relate that Simon of Cyrene was required to fill the office. For the participle βαστάζων, *bearing*, is closely connected with the verb ἐξῆλθεν, *He went forth*. When He set out, Jesus was subjected to the common rule; the episode relating to Simon did not happen till later, when Jesus from exhaustion began, no doubt, to delay the procession.—Moses had forbidden the execution of capital sentences within the enclosure of the camp (Lev. xxiv. 14; Num. xv. 35). And the Jews had remained faithful to the spirit of this law, by putting criminals to death outside the gate of their cities (1 Kings xxi. 13; Acts vii. 58). On this custom is founded the exhortation, Heb. xiii. 12, 13. Ἐξῆλθεν therefore signifies, *He went forth from the city*. The holy sepulchre lies now pretty far within the interior of Jerusalem; but the wall may have been displaced. Regarding the place of our Lord's execution and that of His burial, there exists no certain tradition.—The name, *place of the skull*, does not come from the executions which took place there (this would require the plural κρανίων, *skulls*); and such remains would not have been left uncovered among the Jews. The origin of the name was undoubtedly the rounded form and bare aspect of the hill. *Golgotha*: from גֻּלְגֹּלֶת, in Aramaic גֻּלְגַּלְתָּא, *skull*, from גָּלַל, *to roll*.—The word Ἑβραϊστί, which occurs four times in our Gospel, appears again twice in the Apocalypse, but nowhere else in the whole N. T.

The cross had the form of a T. It was of no great height (see ver. 29). The condemned man was raised to the desired elevation by means of cords (*in crucem tollere*); the hands were nailed to the transverse piece of wood either before or after he was raised. Keim quotes the following words from a Latin author: "*Patibulo suffixus in crucem crudeliter erigitur*," which show that the hands were usually nailed *before* its erection to the top of the cross. That they might not be torn by the weight of the body, the latter rested on a block of wood fastened to the shaft of the cross, and on which the prisoner sat as on horseback. There has been great discussion in modern times as to whether the feet were also nailed. The passages of the ancients quoted by Meyer (see on Matt. xxvii. 35) and Keim are decisive; they prove that, as a rule, the feet were nailed. Luke xxiv. 39 leads to the conclusion that it was so with Jesus. Sufferers lived usually on the cross for twelve hours, sometimes till the third day.

This sort of death combined in the highest degree the pains and infamy of all other punishments. "*Crudelissimum teterrimumque supplicium*," says Cicero (*in Verrem*). The growing inflammation of his wounds, his unnatural position, the constrained immobility and rigidity of the limbs caused thereby; the local congestions, especially in the head; the unspeakable anguish resulting from the disturbance of the circulation; a burning fever and thirst tortured the unhappy victim without killing him.—Was it the Jews who had demanded the execution of two other prisoners, in order to render the shame of Jesus more complete? Or are we to see here an insult put by Pilate on the Jewish people, and represented by the two companions in punishment set beside their King? It is hard to say.

The inscription:

Vv. 19-22. "*And Pilate wrote a title, and put*[1] *it on the cross. And the writing was, Jesus of Nazareth, the King of the Jews. This title then read many of the Jews: for the place where Jesus was crucified was nigh to the city: and it was written in Hebrew, and Greek, and Latin.*[2] *Then said the chief priests of the Jews to Pilate, Write not, The King of the Jews;*[3] *but that he said, I am King of the Jews. Pilate answered, What I have written I have written.*"—John here completes the very abridged account of the Synoptics. According to the Roman custom, the *cruciarius* himself bore, or there was carried before him on his way to execution, an inscription (*titulus*, τίτλος, ἐπιγραφή, σανίς, αἰτία) which contained the statement of his crime, and was afterwards affixed to his cross. Pilate took advantage of the custom to stigmatize the Jews by proclaiming this malefactor their king.—Tholuck and

---

[1] A K, 12 Mnn.: ἐπέθηκεν for ἔθηκεν.

[2] Instead of ιβρ., ελλην., ρωμ., B L X, 8 Mnn. Cop. Sah. read ιβρ., ρωμ., ελλην.

[3] ℵ omits vv. 20 and 21 as far as αλλ' οτι exclusive.

de Wette have thought that the ἔγραψε must be explained in the sense of *had written;* Meyer prefers to hold that Pilate wrote and sent this inscription afterwards, when Jesus was already on the cross. But the δὲ καί, *now also,* is a connection sufficiently loose to admit of our placing the act of writing at the time of condemnation, as is natural. The mention of the three languages in which the inscription was composed is found also in Luke, according to the ordinary reading; but that reading is uncertain. Hebrew was the national language, Greek the language universally understood, and Latin that of the conquerors. Jesus, in the lowest depths of His abasement, was thus proclaimed King in the language of the three principal peoples of the world.—The expression: "*the high priests of the Jews,*" ver. 21, is remarkable. It occurs nowhere else. Hengstenberg explains it as an intentional contrast to the term: "*King of the Jews.*" In reality, it was between those two theocratic powers that the struggle lay. And yet this explanation is far-fetched; the expression signifies more simply that they acted here as defenders of the honour of the theocratic people.—The imperfect: "*they said,*" describes the attempt, which fails. The present: "*Write not,*" is that of the idea. Pilate replies in the perfect, twice repeated: "*I have written.*" It is the tense of the accomplished fact. Here appears the Pilate who is characterized by Philo as *inflexible in character* (Hengstenberg).

The parting of the raiment:

Vv. 23, 24. "*Then the soldiers, when they had crucified*[1] *Jesus, took His garments, and made four parts, to every soldier a part; and also His coat:*[2] *now the coat was without seam, woven from the top throughout. They said therefore among themselves,*[3] *Let us not rend it, but cast lots for it, whose it shall be: that the scripture might be fulfilled, which saith,*[4] *They parted my raiment among them, and for my vesture they did cast lots. These things therefore the soldiers did.*"—Here again John completes the account of his predecessors, as to the description of the coat and the fulfilment of the prophecy. The Roman law, *De bonis damnatorum,* adjudged the garments of the condemned

---

[1] Instead of ὅτι ἐσταύρωσαν, ℵ: οἱ σταυρώσαντες.
[2] ℵ It^{aliq} Syr^{sch} omit καὶ τὸν χιτῶνα.
[3] ℵ: αὐτούς instead of ἀλλήλους.   [4] ℵ B It^{plerique} omit ἡ λέγουσα.

to their executioners. It is usually held that the entire company was composed of four men.[1] Keim thinks that each cross had its own company.[2] The soldiers performed two operations. They divided among them the various pieces of clothing, such as caps, girdles, upper garments, and the coats of two of them. Then, as the coat of Jesus could not be divided, and as it was too precious to go into one of the parts, they cast lots for it. This coat was no doubt a gift of the women who served Jesus (Luke viii. 2, 3; Matt. xxvii. 55). It was woven throughout its whole length, as was the garment of the priests, according to Josephus. Hence the use of the lot (*therefore*, ver. 24). Thus was realized to the very letter the description given by the psalmist when he draws the picture of Israel's King in the height of His sufferings. Criticism, it is true, declares that the two members of the verse quoted (Ps. xxii. 18) are entirely synonymous, and that John is the sport of his own imagination when he would distinguish either between the verbs *parting* and casting lots, or between the substantives ἱμάτια, *garments*, and ἱματισμός, *vesture*, in the LXX. But a more profound study of parallelism in Hebrew poetry proves that the second member always adds a shade or a new idea to the idea of the first. Otherwise the second would only be a needless tautology. It is not repetition, but gradation. Thus, in this verse of the psalm, the contrast between the plur. בגדים, *garments*, and the sing. לבוש, *vesture*, is obvious. The first term denotes the various pieces composing the upper dress; the second, the vestments properly so called, after the removal of which the person is wholly naked, the tunic. The passage of Job xxiv. 7–10 confirms this most natural distinction. The gradation between the two verbs is not less evident. It is a great humiliation to the prisoner to see his garments *parted*. Thereafter he may well say there is nothing left him but to die. But what humiliation greater than to see *lots* drawn for his garments, and so to become like a worthless plaything! David wished to describe these two degrees, and John remarks that in the sufferings of Jesus both of them are literally reproduced; not

---

[1] Philo, *in Flaccum*.
[2] Comp. Acts xii. 4, where we find four detachments, each of four men; doubtless one for each of the four watches.

that the fulfilment of the prophecy depended on this detail, but it came out the more clearly; and that, above all, because everything was done by the instrumentality of the rudest and blindest agents, the Roman soldiers. On this last idea John wishes to lay stress when he concludes the recital of the scene with the words: "*These things therefore the soldiers did.*" The Roman governor had proclaimed Jesus *the King of the Jews;* the Roman soldiers, without meaning it, indicated Him to be the true David.

Strauss thinks (new *Leben Jesu*, p. 579 et seq.) that when the Messianic pretensions of Jesus had been belied by the cross, the Church sought in the O. T. the idea of the suffering Messiah, and found it there, especially in Ps. xxii. and lxix. Thenceforth there was imagined in this programme a whole fictitious picture of the Passion. Thus facts first of all created the exegesis; then the exegesis created the facts. But, 1st. The idea of the suffering Messiah existed in Jewish theology before and independently of the cross (vol. i. pp. 421 and 439). 2d. It will always be difficult to demonstrate that *some* unknown righteous man in the O. T. could hope, as the author of Ps. xxii. does, that the effect of his deliverance would be the conversion of Gentile peoples, and the establishment of the kingdom of God to the very ends of the earth (26–32).

The filial legacy:

Vv. 25–27. "*Now there stood by the cross of Jesus His mother, and His mother's sister, Mary*[1] *the wife of Cleophas, and Mary Magdalene. When Jesus therefore saw His mother, and the disciple standing by whom He loved, He saith unto His mother,*[2] *Woman, behold thy son! Then saith He to the disciple, Behold thy mother! And from that hour*[3] *that disciple took her unto his own home.*"—John only relates this incident. Matthew and Mark simply say that some Galilean women stood at a distance from the cross, "*beholding afar off.*" It appears from John that some of them specially named, and particularly the mother of Jesus, accompanied by John, who supported her,

---

[1] Syr^{sch} and the Persian and Ethiopic Vss. read καὶ before Μαρια η τ. Κ. ("*and Mary the wife of Cleophas*").

[2] א B L X It^{alq} omit αυτου.

[3] A E, 40 Mnn. Sah.: ημερας instead of ωρας.

stood nearer the cross. This fact might easily be omitted in the synoptical tradition. Παρά does not mean *at the foot*, but *by the side of*; the cross was not very high (ver. 29).—We have already said in the Introduction (vol. i. pp. 30, 31), that Wieseler, adopting the reading of the *Peschito* (see critical note 1), finds *four* women, and not *three*, in this passage. Thus the difficulty is evaded of two sisters bearing the same name, the mother of Jesus and the wife of Cleophas. The unnamed sister of Mary the mother of Jesus was (according to Wieseler, Meyer, and Luthardt) Salome, the mother of John, mentioned by Matt. xxvii. 56 and Mark xv. 40 as present at the crucifixion. But (if at least the text of all our Mss. without exception is authentic) the absence of the καί, *and*, before the words: "*Mary the wife of Cleophas*," renders this explanation far from natural. If he omitted this word, the evangelist expressed himself in a wholly ambiguous manner. And how could it happen that throughout the whole Gospel history there should not be a single trace of so close a relationship between John and Jesus? It is simpler to hold that John abstained from mentioning his mother here, as he constantly keeps silence about the person of his brother. If he designates himself, it is only in an indirect manner. As to Mary the wife of Cleophas, see vol. ii. pp. 20–25.—Why do the Synoptics not mention the presence of Jesus' mother? It is difficult to say. Perhaps she left the cross immediately after the incident related by John. The Synoptics do not speak of the presence of the friends of Jesus and of the women till the close of the narrative.

Jesus, despoiled of all, seemed to have nothing left to give. Yet, from the midst of this deep poverty, He had already made some precious gifts: to His executioners He had bequeathed the pardon of God; to His companion in punishment, paradise. Could He find nothing to leave to His mother and His friend? These two loved ones, who had been His most precious treasures on earth, He bequeathes the one to the other, thus giving at once a son to His mother, a mother to His friend. This word, so full of tenderness, must have completely broken Mary's heart. She hasted to leave this place of grief.—The word " *to his own home,*" does not imply that John possessed a house at Jerusalem, but simply that he had a lodging there; comp. the same εἰς τὰ ἴδια applied to all the apostles, xvi. 32. From this time Mary resided with Salome and John, first at Jerusalem, afterwards in Galilee (Introd. vol. i. p. 37).—On the word: "*Woman*," see at ii. 4.

Keim, after Baur's example, regards this incident as an invention of the pseudo-John, intended to exalt the Apostle John and to make him the head of the Church, superior even to James and Peter. M. Renan also ascribes this fiction to the school of John, which yielded to the desire of making its patron the vicar of Christ. In the eyes of the man who has the sense of truth, a scene and sayings like these do not admit of such explanations. Besides, is it not Peter whom our evangelist describes as the great and bold confessor of Jesus? (vi. 68, 69). Is it not to the same apostle that John or his school (xxi.) ascribes the direction of the Church in a magnificent and thrice-repeated promise? (vv. 15-17). Finally, this supposition would imply that the mother of Jesus is here the type of the Church, a supposition of which there is not a trace either in the text or in the whole Gospel.

The death:

Vv. 28-30. "*After this, Jesus knowing*[1] *that all things were now accomplished, that the scripture might be fulfilled,*[2] *said, I thirst. Now*[3] *there was set a vessel full of vinegar: and they filled a sponge with vinegar, and put it upon hyssop,*[4] *and put it to His mouth. When Jesus therefore had received the vinegar, He said, It is finished: and He bowed His head, and gave up the ghost.*"—John completes with some important details the already well-known history of the last moments of Jesus.—Μετὰ τοῦτο, *after this*, should be taken in a wide sense, as everywhere in our Gospel. Between the preceding incident and this one comes the unspeakable anguish of heart under which Jesus exclaimed: "*My God, my God, why hast Thou forsaken me?*"—The phrase: "*All is finished*," refers to His task as Redeemer, so far as He could finish it during His earthly existence; and even in this restricted sense the word

---

[1] E G H K S Y Γ, 70 Mnn. Cop.: ιδων instead of ειδως.
[2] Instead of τελιωθη, א D^suppl, several Mnn.: πληρωθη.
[3] A B L X It^nin omit ουν; א reads δε.
[4] א B L X, some Mnn. Ital^iq Sah. read σπογγον ουν μεστον (ξους υσσωπω περιθεντες.

all should be limited by what follows. In fact, there remained yet a point of prophecy which was not fulfilled. Now the *scripture* formed part of that *all* which must necessarily be finished. Many commentators (Bengel, Tholuck, Lange, Meyer, Luthardt, and Bäumlein) make ἵνα, *in order that*, depend on τετέλεσται, "All is finished *that* the scripture may be fulfilled." This meaning seems to us inadmissible, first, because of the forced construction: "*finished, that;*" and next, because of ver. 30, where we find that Jesus could not declare *all was finished* in relation to the Scriptures, because to this fulfilment there was wanting a last feature of the prophetic description, that indicated in ver. 29. The *that* depends therefore on *Jesus saith*, which follows. So Chrysostom, Lücke, de Wette, etc. The object of Jesus in saying: "*I thirst*," was really to give occasion to the accomplishment of this last unfulfilled incident in the Messiah's sufferings: "*They gave me vinegar to drink*" (Ps. lxix. 21). The *therefore* (ver. 29), which is probably the true reading, precisely indicates the relation between this saying of Jesus and the fulfilment of the prophecy. Unquestionably Jesus had for a long time been tormented with thirst. This was one of the most cruel tortures of crucifixion. But He might have been able to restrain, as He had done up till now, the expression of that painful sensation. If He does not do so, it is that the last incident of the humiliations to which He was to submit may take place without delay. John says τελειωθῇ, and not πληρωθῇ (which some documents wrongly substitute). The subject in question, indeed, is *the finishing* of the fulfilment of the Scriptures as a whole, and not the fulfilment of this particular prophecy.—The drink offered to Jesus is not that which He had refused at the beginning of His crucifixion. The latter was a wine mixed with a bitter and stupefying liquor, such as absinthe (Matthew) or myrrh (Mark). The giddiness which this poison produced in the victim somewhat deadened the first pains. Jesus had refused it because He wished to preserve the perfect clearness of His mind to the end. The drink now offered to Him by the soldier is purely a vinegar prepared for the sufferers themselves, as is proved by the sponge and the stalk of hyssop. This last circumstance sets aside the common opinion of commentators who think that it was wine intended for the soldiers.—In the first two Gospels it is the cry: *" Eli, Eli ! ... My God, my God ! ..."* which leads the soldier to offer Him the vinegar. But John completes their narrative by referring to the cry: *" I thirst,"* which more immediately determined the soldier's action.— Hyssop is a plant not more than a foot and a half in height. Since a stalk of this length sufficed to reach the lips of the victim, it follows that the cross was not so high as is usually represented.—Ostervald and Martin are quite wrong in translating: *"* They put hyssop *round* [the sponge] ...," or *" surrounding* it with hyssop ..."

" I thirst " was the Saviour's fifth saying, and *" It is finished "* the sixth. The first three had reference to His personal relations: the prayer for His executioners (Luke); the promise made to the thief, His companion in punishment (Luke); the legacy made to His mother and His friend (John). The following three refer to His work of salvation: the cry: *" My God ..."* (Matthew and Mark), contains all the moral sufferings of the expiatory sacrifice; the groan: *" I thirst "* (John), sums up all its physical sufferings; the triumphant saying: *" It is finished,"* proclaims its consummation. The seventh and last saying is expressly related only by Luke: *" Father, into Thy hands I commit my Spirit ; "* but it is implied in John by the word παρέδωκε, *He gave up.* This word is by no means rendered by our phrase : *" to give up the ghost."* It expresses a free, personal, spontaneous act. *"No man taketh my life from me,"* Jesus had said; *" I have power to lay it down, and I have power to take it again"* (x. 18). Here, too, we have the meaning of that *loud cry* with which, according to Matthew and Mark, Jesus expired.—The word κλίνας, *" having bowed* His head," indicates that till then Jesus kept His head erect.

The breaking of the legs: vv. 31-37.

Ver. 31. *"The Jews therefore, because it was the preparation,*[1] *that the bodies should not remain upon the cross on the Sabbath day (for that Sabbath day* [2] *was an high day), besought*

---

[1] The words ιπει παρασκευη ην are placed by א B L X V, 10 Mnn. It^{plerique} Vg. Syr. Cop. Sah. immediately after οι ουν Ιουδαιοι, and not after εν τω σαββατω (T. R. with 12 Mjj.).

[2] Instead of εκεινη, the reading of T. R. with some Mnn. It^{aliq} Vg., εκεινου is found in all the other documents.

Pilate that their legs might be broken, and that they might be taken away."—John here traces a series of providential events omitted by his predecessors, which passed one after another, and which conspired to impress on the Person of Jesus, in His state of deepest abasement, the seal of Messiahship. The Romans usually left the condemned to perish on the cross; their bodies became the prey of wild beasts. But the Jewish law required that the bodies of criminals should be put out of sight before sunset, that on the following day the Holy Land might not be polluted by the curse attached to the lifeless body, a monument of condemnation (Deut. xxi. 23; comp. Josh. viii. 29, x. 26; Josephus, *Bell. jud.* iv. 5. 2). Ordinarily, no doubt, the Romans did not trouble themselves about this Jewish law. But in this particular case the Jews could not have borne the violation of it quietly, because, as John observes, the following day was not only a Sabbath, but a Sabbath of exceptional solemnity. Those who think that, according to John as well as the Synoptics, the Jewish people had already celebrated the Paschal feast on the previous evening, and that thus it was the end of the great Sabbatic day of the 15th Nisan, here give to the word παρασκευή, *preparation*, the meaning which it has in the Jewish calendar, that of *Friday*, and think that the peculiar solemnity of the Saturday, which was about to begin, arose simply from the fact that this Sabbath belonged to the *Paschal* week. Or they refer to the fact that it was on this day (16th Nisan) that the offering of the sacred sheaf fell to be made, a well-known act of worship with which the harvest opened yearly. But neither the one nor the other of these reasons can explain the extraordinary solemnity which John ascribes to the Sabbath of the morrow. The 16th Nisan was so little of a Sabbatic day, that, before cutting the ears intended to form the sacred sheaf, the deputies of the Sanhedrim were obliged to wait till the people called to them: "The sun is set;" this cry was the proclamation of the end of the 15th and the beginning of the 16th. Then only could they take the sickle. For from that moment work was allowed. So the 16th is called, Lev. xxiii. 11-15, "the day *after the Sabbath.*" How, then, could the coincidence of the Sabbath with this day, so purely a work-day, enhance the Sabbatic value of the Saturday which was about to begin? Besides, this technical meaning of παρασκευή, *Friday*, is here set aside by the absence of the article. Finally, there is an evident relation clearly indicated by the γάρ, *for*, which follows, between the idea of *preparation* and that of the solemnity of the Sabbath which was about to begin at six o'clock evening. We are therefore forced to hold that this exceptional solemnity of the morrow arose from the fact that that year the weekly Sabbath exactly coincided with the great and likewise Sabbatic day of the 15th Nisan. Hence it follows that, at the moment when Jesus died, it was still the 14th and not the 15th. Thus are explained the words (literally): "*for it was preparation*," on the one hand, undoubtedly preparation for the Sabbath (as being Friday), but, at the same time, preparation for the great Paschal day, the 15th Nisan. This day had in it, as it were, an accumulation of preparation, as the following had also in it an accumulation of Sabbatic rest. The *for* refers to the idea: "*that the bodies might not remain* . . .," as is indicated by the Alex. reading, supported by that of the old Vss. The evangelist hereby indicates indirectly that the essential act of preparation, the slaying of the lamb, took place in the temple at this moment, and that the Paschal feast was to follow that very evening.

Pilate, respecting the scruples of the Jews, consented to what was asked of him. The breaking of the legs did not produce immediate death, but its object was to make it certain, and so to allow the removal of the bodies. For it rendered all return to life impossible, because gangrene was the necessary and immediate result. The existence of this custom (σκελοκοπία, *crurifragium*) among the Romans, in certain exceptional cases, is perfectly well established (see the numerous passages quoted by Keim himself). M. Renan also says: "The Jewish and Roman archæologies of ver. 31 are exact." If Keim, notwithstanding, still raises difficulties, asking why the Synoptics do not mention the fact if it is historical, it is easy to answer: Because Jesus Himself was not affected by it. Now His Person alone was of consequence to them, not those of the two malefactors. Neither would John have mentioned it but for the relation of the fact to the prophecy which struck him so forcibly. Must we understand the ἀρθῶσι, *might be taken away*, of the taking *from the cross?* I doubt it very much. What concerned the Jews in making this demand, was not that the bodies should be unfastened, but that they should be removed out of sight. The law, Deut. xxi. 23, which dictated their request, had no reference to the punishment of the cross, a punishment unknown to Israel.

Vv. 32–34. *"Then came the soldiers, and brake the legs of the first, and of the other which was crucified with Him. But when they came to Jesus, and saw that He was dead already,*[1] *they brake not His legs: but one of the soldiers with a spear pierced His side, and forthwith came thereout blood and water."*—Ἦλθον, they came, here signifies *they approached;* for there is no reason to suppose that other soldiers are meant than those who had completed the crucifixion.—If the object for which the legs of the victims were broken was what we have said, this operation became useless in regard to Jesus, from the fact of His death. The soldier's spear-thrust was therefore a compensation, as it were, for the omitted operation; it meant: if thou art not really dead, here is something to finish thee. It would be absurd to demand precedents for such a fact, which had nothing judicial in it. Yet the saying of Quintilian may be quoted: "Cruces succiduntur, *percussos* sepeliri carnifex non vetat."— The verb νύσσειν denotes a thrust of a greater or less depth, in opposition to a cut. Homer uses it sometimes to denote even mortal wounds.—The fact of the effusion of blood and water might be regarded as a natural phenomenon. No doubt generally, when a corpse is pierced, no liquid comes from it; yet if one of the large vessels happens to be touched, there may flow from the wound a blackish blood with a coating of serum. Could this be what John called *blood and water?* This is far from probable. Ebrard supposes that the spear touched some deposits of extravasated and decomposed blood. Gruner (*Commentatio de morte Jesu Christi verâ*, Halle 1805) thinks that the spear first pierced some aqueous deposits which, during the long suffering on the cross, had formed round the heart, and then the heart itself. William Stroud

---

[1] ℵ : ιυρον αυτον ηδη τεθνηκοτα και ου, instead of ως . . . τεθνηκοτα, ου.

(London 1847) has recourse to phenomena observed in cases of sudden death caused by cramp of the heart. These explanations are not inadmissible, but they are all somewhat improbable. The phrase: "*blood and water,*" which naturally denotes two substances flowing simultaneously, but perfectly distinct, in the eyes of the spectator, finds no natural explanation on any of these suppositions. Baur and Strauss conclude for the necessity of a symbolical interpretation, and here again find the purely ideal nature of the narrative. The author meant, by this fact of his own invention, to express the abundance of spiritual life which was henceforth to flow from the Christ (Baur); the water represented more especially the Holy Spirit, the blood the Holy Supper, with allusion to the custom of mixing the wine of the sacrament with water (Strauss in his new *Vie de Jésus*). Are we entitled to ascribe such absurdities to the evangelist? And what notion must we form of the morality of a man who should affirm so solemnly that he *saw* (ver. 35) what he was conscious of never having beheld except *in idea?* In favour of this allegorical explanation there has been alleged the saying, 1 John v. 6 : "*He came not by water only, but by water and blood.*" But *water* here denotes the baptism of John the Baptist as opposed to the work of Jesus, who adds to the water of the baptism of repentance the *blood* of expiation and pardon. There remains but one explanation: the view that the fact lay beyond the laws of common physiology, and that it is related to the exceptional nature of a body which sin had never tainted, and which was destined to an immediate resurrection. From the very instant of death, the body of Jesus must take another way than that of dissolution, and enter upon that of glorification. Such is the meaning which the evangelist seems to have ascribed to this unprecedented phenomenon. Thus is explained the almost oath-like affirmation with which he certifies the reality of it in the following verse, which does not, however, mean that the affirmation of ver. 35 relates only to this fact. It refers also to the other two events which were mentioned, vv. 33 and 34 (the breaking of the legs and the spear-thrust).

Vv. 35-37. "*And he that saw it bare record, and his record is true:*[1] *and he knoweth that he saith true, that ye also*[2] *might believe.*[3] *For these things were done, that the scripture should be fulfilled, A bone of Him*[4] *shall not be broken. And again another scripture saith, They shall look on Him whom they pierced."*—Several (Weisse, Schweizer, Hilgenfeld, Weizsäcker, Keim, and Bäumlein himself) hold that in the words in ver. 35 the author of the Gospel expressly distinguishes himself from the apostle whose testimony he cites. The author speaks, indeed, of the witness: "*he that saw,*" in the third person, consequently as of a third person. And thus this passage, which had always been regarded as one of the strongest proofs of the Johannine composition of our Gospel, would be transformed into a positive denial of its apostolic origin. We have already examined this question, Introduction, i. pp. 93–95. We offer here the following remarks:

1. The school of Baur, while unable to refrain from catching at the bait presented to it by the verse when thus understood, has nevertheless felt the hook concealed beneath it (see Hilgenfeld's embarrassment on this question, *Einl.* p. 731). If, indeed, as the critics of this school allege, the author wished throughout his whole treatise to pass himself off for John the apostle, how comes he to distinguish himself expressly from him in this passage? Hilgenfeld's answer is that "he falls out of his part" (p. 732). Singular unskilfulness in a forger so able as the man to whom the composition of our Gospel is ascribed!

2. Neither the form of the phrase nor the pronoun ἐκεῖνος, *that man*, oblige us to regard the author of the writing as a different person from the apostle whose testimony he relates. When a narrator wishes to avoid speaking of himself in the first person, and regards himself objectively to the extent of designating himself in the third person, as happens so frequently, it is evident that he may employ all the forms which are used in speaking of another. So Jesus

---

[1] א: αληθης instead of αληθινη.
[2] 15 Mjj. (א A B, etc.), 25 Mnn. It. Vg. Syr. read και before υμεις ("that ye also might believe"); T. R. omits και with 7 Mjj. (E G, etc.), and the other Mnn.
[3] א B: πιστευητε, instead of πιστευσητε.
[4] א, 60 Mnn. It^{plerique}: απ' αυτου instead of αυτου (following Ex. xii. 46 in the LXX.).

does throughout the whole course of His ministry when calling Himself the Son of man. So Paul does in a remarkably striking way, 2 Cor. xii. 2: "I knew *a man in Christ who* . . ." Hilgenfeld does not believe that this mode of speaking admits of the use of the pronoun ἐκεῖνος, *that man*, which refers to a *remote* subject. But Steitz[1] has clearly proved that this pronoun, and that in St. John's Gospel, has a peculiarly emphatic and exclusive sense, but one which does not imply the remoteness of the subject to which it refers: *he*, he *precisely*, he *only*. Comp. i. 8, 18, 33, v. 39, etc. There is even a passage wholly analogous to ours (ix. 37): "Thou hast seen Him, and He that talketh to thee is *He*" (ἐκεῖνός ἐστιν, He precisely, and no other). Weizsäcker and Keim do not therefore insist on the philological question, but they appeal so much the more, as Keim says, to "rational logic," which does not allow us to hold "that a writer would describe himself objectively at such length."

But, 3. "Rational logic" is precisely what absolutely forbids our writer to affirm of John, as one distinct from himself, the fact which he attests here. What! a disciple of John declare to the Church that the apostle, his master, *saith true*, that is to say, that he did not lie or was not the dupe of an illusion! But the first of these attestations would be an insult, and the second an absurdity. And in general, if one may in certain cases become surety for the *veracity* of another, he can never act as surety for the *inner consciousness* which that other possesses of his own veracity, as would be done by the author here when he says of the apostle-witness: "And *he knoweth* that he saith true." If the writer really wished to distinguish himself from the witness, he should have said: "And *I know* that he saith true." Then he must have followed this up by saying: "that *we may believe*," and not: "that *ye may believe*;" for, excepting the *witness* who alone *saw*, all the rest, including the narrator himself, believe in consequence of this ocular testimony.

4. Hilgenfeld, Keim, and Bäumlein quote, as an analogy, xxi. 24: "*This is the disciple* (the loved disciple) *which testifieth of these things, and wrote of them: and we know that*

---

[1] See on the use of the pron. ἐκεῖνος in the fourth Gospel, Steitz, *Stud. u. Kritik*. 1859, pp. 497-506, and Buttmann, *ibid*. 1860, pp. 505-536.

his testimony is true." But there is a complete difference between the two passages. *The attester,* xxi. 24, is distinguished not only from the *witness,* but likewise from the *author* of the Gospel, whom he identifies with the witnessing apostle. And because he distinguishes himself from him, he uses the first person: "*we know*" (ver. 24), "*I think*" (ver. 25), and so does what the evangelist would have required to do in our passage if he had really wished to distinguish himself from the apostle.—We are persuaded that the time will come when this whole discussion will appear singularly unnecessary.

Μεμαρτύρηκε, *hath testified,* and that by this very narration which continues from that time forward (the perf.).—'Aληθινή, not a *veracious* testimony (ἀληθής), but a testimony which really deserves the name.—Καὶ ὑμεῖς, *ye also:* "ye, as well as I myself, the witness." In fact, the matter in question is not faith in the particular facts which have just been related, and to which the term *faith* would not apply in relation to him who bore witness to them. The subject in question is *faith* in the absolute sense of the word, faith *in Christ;* this ought in the case of all to derive confirmation from the facts mentioned above, which had already strengthened that of the witness himself. It is to this meaning of the word faith that the *for* of ver. 36 applies, since it refers to the manifestation of the *Messianic* character of Jesus by the fulfilment of the two prophecies quoted, vv. 36 and 37. —It follows, finally, from this connection of ideas, that the ταῦτα, *these things,* of ver. 36 embraces not only the effusion of the blood and water, but also the two facts which gave rise to it, the omission of the breaking of the legs in the case of Jesus, and the spear-thrust. The first prophecy is taken from Ex. xii. 46, not from Ps. xxxiv. 20, as Bäumlein thinks; for this latter passage refers to preservation of *life.*—The Paschal lamb belonged to God, and typified the Lamb of God. Hence the law sheltered it from all profanation, from all violent and brutal treatment. This is also the reason why the remains of it were to be burned immediately after the feast.

If prophecy was fulfilled by *what did not take place* in the case of Jesus (the breaking of the legs), it was equally so by what actually *took place* (the spear-thrust), ver. 37. Zechariah, xii. 10, had represented Jehovah as *pierced* by His people, in the Person of the Messiah. The death of the cross had realized this prophecy. But this fulfilment, to stand forth clearly, must take a yet more literal character (see on xii. 15, xviii. 9, xix. 24). The meaning of the Hebrew word (דקרו) *they pierced* was considerably weakened by the LXX., who no doubt thought the expression too strong to be applied to Jehovah, and translated it by κατωρχήσαντο, *they insulted*. The evangelist goes back here to the Hebrew text, as the author of the Apocalypse likewise does in the same quotation (i. 7). The term: "*they shall look on*," ὄψονται, refers to what shall take place at the time of the Jews' conversion, when in this Jesus rejected by them they shall recognise their Messiah. The look in question which they shall then cast on Him is one of repentance, supplication, and faith ; a striking scene magnificently described in that same prophetic view, Zech. xii. 8–14.

To understand what John felt at the moment which he here recalls, we must suppose a believing Jew, familiar with the O. T., seeing the soldiers approach who are to break the legs of the three victims. He asks himself anxiously what is to be done to the body of the Messiah, which is still more sacred than the Paschal lamb. And, lo ! simultaneously and in the most unexpected manner this body is rescued from the brutal operation which threatened it, and receives the spear-thrust, thereby realizing the spectacle which repentant Israel is one day to behold ! After such signs, with what feelings will this man leave the cross ? Will not what he *has seen* strengthen his faith, and soon also that of the whole Church ? Such is the meaning of John. Olshausen thinks that the water and blood are mentioned to prove the *reality* of Jesus' *body ;* Lücke and Neander, to prove the reality of His *death*. But the Docetæ did not deny sensible *appearances* in the person of Jesus; and these sufficed to explain what John perceived. As to His death, the fact related no more confirms than it invalidates its reality. The apostle therefore establishes, as we have said, the exceptional state of the body of Jesus, which was manifested at this time by an unexampled evidence. The *Holy One of God* was not to see *corruption*

(Ps. xvi.); and this promise must be fulfilled *perfectly* in the case of the *perfect* Holy One. Now it implied the beginning of the work of resurrection at the very moment when, in the case of every other death, the crisis of dissolution begins.

The entombment of Jesus: vv. 38–42.

John here fills up, as in the preceding passage, the narrative of his predecessors. He exhibits the part which Nicodemus took in the funeral honours paid to Jesus, and brings out the relation between the advanced hour of the day and the place of the sepulchre where the body was laid. He thus accounts for facts whose relation was not indicated by the Synoptics.

Vv. 38–40. "*After this,*[1] *Joseph of Arimathæa, being a disciple of Jesus, but secretly for fear of the Jews, besought Pilate that he might take away the body of Jesus: and Pilate gave him leave. He came*[2] *therefore, and took*[2] *the body of Jesus.*[3] *And there came also Nicodemus, which at the first came to Jesus by night, and brought*[4] *a mixture*[4] *of myrrh and aloes, about an hundred pounds. Then took they the body of Jesus and wound it in*[5] *linen clothes with the spices, as the manner of the Jews is to bury.*"—The request of the Jews, ver. 31, referred to the three victims; but, as John has observed, Pilate's order was executed only in respect of two of them. Joseph then appears before him with an entirely new request, which applies to Jesus only. Bäumlein: "Sometimes, especially on occasion of a feast, the corpse of the capitally punished was given up to the relations. Philo, *in Flacc.* § 10." Mark relates that, on hearing this request, Pilate was astonished that Jesus was dead already; a fact which, according to Strauss, would contradict the permission which he had himself given, ver. 31. But this operation, while involving death, did not bring it about immediately, as Strauss himself acknowledges; it served only to make it sure. And Pilate could thus express his astonishment that death had already taken place. Perhaps, also, Pilate's astonishment arose from the fact that Jesus was

---

[1] Δι is omitted by 7 Mjj. (א A B, etc.) It.

[2] Instead of ηλθιν and ηριν, א It^aliq read πλέον and ηραν.

[3] Instead of το σωμα του I., B L X Λ read το σωμα αυτου, א αυτον, It^plerique αυτο.

[4] א reads ιχων instead of φιρων; א B: ιλιγμα instead of μιγμα.

[5] א B K L X Y Π It^aliq Vg. omit. ιν before οθονιοις.

dead without the necessity of breaking His legs. For he required a detailed account of the manner in which the punishment had been carried out. This is attested by Mark himself, xv. 44: "*And calling the centurion, he asked him.*" *Arimathæa* might be the city *Rama*, situated two leagues to the north of Jerusalem, or another Rama, now called *Ramleh*, lying ten leagues to the north-west of the capital, near Lydda. But the place in question is more probably *Ramathaïm* (with the article represented by the syllable *ar*), in Ephraim, Samuel's native city (1 Sam. i. 1). In any case, Joseph was now settled in Jerusalem with his family; for he had a burying-place there, but very recently, no doubt, as the sepulchre had never yet been used.

In mentioning Nicodemus, John exhibits the contrast between the boldness of his present profession and the cautiousness of his former conduct. This man's faith recognised at this moment, in the crucified one, the Saviour typified by the brazen serpent which Jesus had explained to him beforehand (iii. 14). It is remarkable that these members of the Jewish aristocracy, Joseph and Nicodemus, are led to confess their faith in Jesus at the very moment of His deepest humiliation.—$T\grave{o}$ $\pi\rho\hat{\omega}\tau o\nu$ here denotes, as at x. 40, the beginning of the *ministry* of Jesus. If Nicodemus had been to John, as M. Reuss seems to hold, nothing more than a fictitious type (ch. iii.), how could he make him reappear here as a real acting person, and that while expressly recalling the scene of ch. iii. !—Myrrh is an odoriferous gum; aloes, a scented wood. After being pounded, they were made into a mixture which was spread over the sheet in which the body was wrapped. Probably this cloth was cut up into bandages to wrap the limbs separately. The words: "as the manner of *the Jews* is . . .," contrasts this mode of embalming with that of the Egyptians, who removed the intestines and secured the preservation of the corporeal wrappings by processes much more lengthened and complicated.—The hundred pounds remind us of the profusion with which Mary had poured the spikenard over the feet of Jesus, ch. xii.; it is a truly royal homage. The Synoptics inform us that the holy women intended also on their part to complete this provisional embalming, but *after the Sabbath* only.

Vv. 41, 42. "*Now in the place where He was crucified there was a garden; and in the garden a new sepulchre, wherein was never man yet laid.*[1] *There laid they Jesus therefore because of the Jews' preparation; for the sepulchre was nigh at hand.*"—According to the Synoptics, the sepulchre belonged to Joseph; and this was the reason of the use made of it. According to John, this tomb was chosen on account of its nearness to Golgotha, because the Sabbath was about to begin. These two reasons, far from contradicting, complete one another. What purpose would the proximity of the sepulchre have served if it had not belonged to one of our Lord's friends? And was it not the circumstance that Joseph owned this sepulchre near the place of crucifixion which suggested to him the thought of asking the body of Jesus?—John and Luke (xxiii. 53) observe that the sepulchre was new. Comp. Luke xix. 30: "*Ye shall find a colt tied whereon yet never man sat.*" These are providential facts which belong to the royal glory of Jesus. When a king is received, the objects devoted to his service are such as have never yet been used.—Might the phrase: "*the Jews' preparation,*" signify (as is thought by those who allege that, according to John as well as according to the Synoptics, the death of Jesus took place on the 15th): *the Jews' Friday?* What would be the object of this singular expression? Rotermund[2] answers, to explain how it happened that the morrow following the Sabbatic 15th day was also a Sabbath. But that has already been explained twice: vv. 14 and 31. Why this repetition and this new form: "*the Jews*"? When, in the space of thirty lines, the same thing is thrice repeated, there is not merely an affirmation expressed; there is the negation of the opposite idea. As at iii. 24, ii. 11, and iv. 54, John wishes tacitly to rectify some misunderstanding of the Gospel history. It was the hour when *the Jews* (so this supplement finds its explanation) prepared for their great national feast by killing the lamb. And they made haste, because with the setting of the sun the *work* day of the 14th would close, and the doubly Sabbatic day (v. 31) of the 15th begin; comp. Luke xxiii. 56.

[1] ‭א‬ B : ην τιθειμενος instead of ετεθη.

[2] In the remarkable article, "Von Ephraïm nach Golgotha," *Stud. u. Kritik.* 1876, first number.

Of the Day of our Lord's Death.

The evangelists are manifestly at one as to the day of the week on which the death of Jesus took place : it was a Friday. But they seem to differ about the day of the *month*, and consequently about that of the *Paschal feast* on which this event fell. The Jews celebrated the Paschal supper, the opening of the feast, on the evening of the 14th Nisan. This evening formed, strictly speaking, part of the 15th; the first and great day of the seven days of the feast, and one peculiarly solemn. For the law assimilated the 15th to the weekly Sabbath, so far as obligatory cessation from labour was concerned, with the single difference that it permitted the preparation of necessary food on this day (Ex. xii. 16), probably because on the evening before, the preparation of the Paschal feast having absorbed attention, it was impossible to provide the food of the 15th. Now it is generally held that, according to the synoptical narrative, it was on this Sabbatic 15th day that the Friday on which Jesus was crucified fell that year; which implies, of course, that on the evening before, Jesus had celebrated the Paschal feast with His disciples, in conformity with Jewish law and practice. And such seems really to be the force of Matt. xxvi. 17, and the parallel passages of Luke and Mark.

John's narrative, on the contrary, would lead to the conclusion, as we have seen, that the Friday of Jesus' death was the 14th Nisan, the day of *the preparation* of the Paschal supper and of the Paschal feast in general. In this case, it is obvious that He could not have celebrated the Paschal supper with the people generally; for He was dead some hours before this ceremony, and the last supper described by John is nothing more than an ordinary meal on which Jesus impressed peculiar solemnity by instituting the Holy Eucharist and uttering His last farewell.

Can these two forms of narrative be harmonized ? And, if not, which is to be preferred ?

From a very early date this question has occupied the Church. In a dispute which broke out about 170 at Laodicea, in Asia Minor, there were some who maintained that our Lord's last meal was the *real* Paschal feast, celebrated at the hour fixed by the law on the evening of the 14th, from which they concluded that the Church ought also yearly to celebrate on that evening the Holy Easter Supper, at the same time as the Jews celebrate their Paschal feast. Apolinarius, Bishop of Hierapolis, who opposed them, declares in substance " that, according to them, our Lord ate the lamb with His disciples on the 14th, and that He suffered death on the great day of unleavened bread (the 15th); and *that they thus explain the Gospel of Matthew.*"[1] We do not know what attitude was taken in this matter by *Melito*, Bishop of Sardis, who, Eusebius tells us, was the first to write a book on this controversy. But we have in the same collection some fragments of the works of *Apolinarius* and of *Clement of Alexandria*, which were called forth by that of Melito. " The 14th," says the former, " is our Lord's true Passover, the great sacrifice in which the Son of God, put in stead and place of the lamb, was to be given up to be crucified. . . ." These words are clear: they express John's view. Jesus did not eat the legal Passover; He died on the day on which they were preparing to celebrate it. Clement expresses himself to the same effect, but in a manner still more explicit: " In previous years Jesus had celebrated the feast by eating the Paschal lamb slain by the Jews. But on the 13th ($\iota\gamma'$) He taught His disciples the mystery of the type [the type of the lamb], when they asked Him, saying: 'Where wilt Thou that we prepare for Thee the Passover?' For that was the day on which took place the consecration of the unleavened bread, and the *pro-preparation* ($\pi\rho o\epsilon\tau o\iota\mu\alpha\sigma\acute{\iota}\alpha$) of the Passover. . . . And our Saviour suffered on the following day [the 14th]; for He was Himself the true Passover. . . . And hence the high priests and scribes, when bringing Him to Pilate, did not enter the prætorium, that they might not be defiled and might eat the Passover in the evening without hindrance." The disciples then asked our Lord, as is related in the Synoptics, not on the 14th, but on the 13th; and it was on the evening of the 13th that Jesus instituted the Supper, and consequently on the 14th that He died. This

---

[1] Fragments of Apolinarius (not Apollinarius) in the *Chronicon paschale* (a compilation of extracts from ancient authors, carried on from the fourth to the seventh century, and discovered in Sicily in the sixteenth; see *Le Jour de la Préparation*, by M. Lutteroth, p. 59).

is really John's view, and, besides, it is the first known attempt to harmonize it with the synoptical narrative.

After such discussions, it is not surprising that Chrysostom takes full account of the difficulty, and leaves his readers to choose between these two solutions: either John understands by *the Passover* the whole feast, which would allow us to hold that He was crucified on the 15th; or Jesus anticipated by a day the celebration of the Paschal feast, which would allow us to hold that He was crucified on the 14th. In these remarks Chrysostom has, as Meyer says, traced *the programme* of all the subsequent discussions down to our day.

We have treated this question briefly (Introd. i. pp. 209–211) in its bearing on the authenticity of our Gospel. We resume the subject here more fully from the exegetical and historical point of view.

I.

The conclusion to which we have been led is this: *According to the fourth Gospel, Jesus was crucified on the* 14*th Nisan, the preparation day of the feast of Passover.*

The most decisive passages in favour of this conclusion have been the following:—

1st. xiii. 1.—Again quite recently *Rotermund* (in his very interesting article, " Von Ephraïm nach Golgotha," *Stud. u. Kritik.* 1876) has alleged, as had been done before by Langen (on untenable grounds) and some others, that in this verse the *feast of Passover* meant the morning of the 15th, and that the phrase: "*before* the feast of Passover," must therefore mean the evening of the 14th, and so the hour of the Paschal supper (agreeably to the Synoptics). If John had said: " before the feast of *Unleavened Bread*," this meaning would have been admissible (Mark xiv. 1). But how can we for a moment imagine John placing the Paschal supper *before*, and consequently *outside* of, the feast of Passover? How can we hold that, writing for Greek readers, he designated the Paschal feast by saying: " Before the feast, a supper [or even : *the* supper] being ended," without designating this solemn feast more clearly ?

2d. xviii. 28.—All the learned efforts of *Kirchner* (*Die jüdische Passahfeier*, 1870) appear to me insufficient to overthrow the natural conclusion from this passage, so clearly recognised by Clement of Alexandria, as we have established it by our exegesis.

3d. xix. 14, 31, 42.—Neither Kirchner nor Rotermund has succeeded in convincing us that the translation in these three passages should run: "*the Paschal Friday . . . it was Friday . . . the Jews' Friday . . .*" That the day was a Friday is evident. That the word *paraskeué* (*preparation*) sometimes denotes in patristic language *Friday* cannot be disputed. But all this does not prove, as we have seen, that in the context John could give the word *preparation* this technical sense. As to Matthew and Mark, we shall examine the question afterwards. Rotermund himself cannot help making the following confession: "In truth, it is very surprising that the Gospels so expressly designate the day of the death as *that preceding the Sabbath*, if this day was itself the first day of the Paschal feast. . . ." So surprising, indeed, that it seems even impossible.

M. Lutteroth, in his pamphlet quoted above, is at one with us as to this impossibility. In his view, *the preparation* of the Passover signifies the preparation for the feast. But the Paschal feast began, according to him, on the 10th Nisan, the day on which the Jews *set apart* the lamb, five days before that on which they killed it. *And it was*, according to him, *on this* 10*th day of Nisan* that Jesus was crucified. He rose again after three *full* days and nights passed in the tomb, between the 13th and 14th; and His first appearances took place on the morning of the 14th. It is easy to see what superhuman exegetical efforts are needed to bring the texts into harmony with this wholly new chronology. It is overthrown especially by Mark xiv. 12, Luke xxii. 7, and Matt. xxviii. 1.[1]

After the observations of Kirchner and Luthardt, I do not insist on ranking xiii. 29 among the decisive passages, though

[1] Mark xiv. 12: "*And the first day of unleavened bread*, when *they killed the Passover . . .*" This expression may, according to M. Lutteroth, denote the 10th Nisan, because this day opened *the period* of the days of unleavened bread, which, according to the author, began five days before the 14th! As to the relative *when* (or *on which*), it does not refer to the word *day*, but to the complement *of unleavened bread:* the unleavened bread conjointly with which they killed the lamb!—Luke xxii. 7: "*Then came the day of unleavened bread, when the Passover must be killed. . . .*" This, he holds, is not a chronological determination (notwithstanding the parallels), but an anticipation purely of feeling: Fear not; the day of unleavened bread came afterwards [the 14th], when Jesus

it will always be difficult to understand how the apostles could have thought of *buying* on the night of the Passover. What shop would have been open in Jerusalem on that night, when every family, rich or poor, was gathered round the Paschal table?

II.

This Johannine date of the 14*th Nisan is not positively contradicted by any of the documents in our possession; it is confirmed by many of them.*

1st. *The Talmud.*—We have quoted in full, vol. i. p. 124, the passage of the Babylon *Gemara*, which says that " Jesus was suspended on the evening of the Passover (*beérev happésach*)," an expression which certainly denotes the *eve* of the Passover, as certainly as *the evening of the Sabbath* (*érev haschschalbath*) constantly signifies the eve of the Sabbath. No doubt against the trustworthiness of this Talmudic tradition there may be urged its late composition, and the erroneous statements which are mixed up with it in other passages where it is reproduced, for example, that " the son of Stada [Jesus] was *stoned*, and then hung *at Lydda*, on Passover eve" (*Sanhedr.* 67. 1). Yet it is remarkable that this point of time: *Passover eve*, reappears uniformly in those different Talmudic statements. Of two things the one or other: either a very positive tradition on this point had been kept up among the successors of Caiaphas and Gamaliel; or the learned Jews had borrowed this notice from our Gospels, which would prove that they understood them exactly in the sense which has seemed to be the meaning of John's narrative.

2d. *Saint Paul.*—Keim thinks that this apostle is a convincing witness against the opinion which fixes on the 14th, instead of the 15th, as the day of our Lord's death (i. pp. 127,

rose again; or, as M. Lutteroth now explains (*Essai d'interpret.* p. 410): The day was come when *Christ*, the *true* Passover, must be killed!—Matt. xxviii. 1, our author translates: "*Now after these things, on that one of the Sabbaths which dawns on the other of the Sabbaths,* Mary . . .," which signifies: on the 14th, a day of the Passover which reaches to a second Sabbath [the 15th]; as if the 14th had been a Sabbatic day!—But untenable as these explanations are, M. Lutteroth's treatise nevertheless remains a monument of earnest investigation and solid learning; and it cannot be denied that even for views so eccentric as the above, he has succeeded in discovering in patristic literature some apparent points of support (comp. pp. 60 and 76-77).

128, iii. p. 476). His argument is as follows: Paul envelopes the institution of the Holy Supper in the forms of the Paschal feast, which proves that in his view, as in that of the Synoptics, this institution coincides with the Jewish feast; that consequently Christ's last feast took place on the 14th, and not the 13th. This argument would tell if Keim could prove that Jesus was unable, with the foresight of His approaching death, to institute the Holy Supper, by borrowing the forms of the Paschal feast, on the eve of the day when it was legally celebrated. But this it will always be impossible to demonstrate. Perhaps some indications are to be found even in Paul of a view contrary to that which holds the 15th as the day of Jesus' death. In the narrative of the institution of the Holy Supper, 1 Cor. xi., he says: "The Lord Jesus, *the same night in which He was betrayed.*" If this night had been the solemn Passover night, would he not have characterized it a little more specially? When speaking of the different stages in the work of resurrection, Paul designates Christ as *the first-fruits* ($ἀπαρχή$). The term is that used to designate the sacred sheaf, gathered on the 16th Nisan, as the first-fruits of the harvest. Now this 16th day was precisely that of the resurrection of Jesus, if He died on the 14th and not the 15th. The most elevated spirituality did not prevent Paul from cherishing the most pious attachment to Jewish symbolism. Comp. the allusion to the Passover, 1 Cor. v. 7, 8, a passage written exactly at the time of this feast (xvi. 8).

3d. *The Synoptics.*—We shall not renew here a detailed discussion which has been so often taken up with opposite views in recent times, and at such length that it has become almost wearisome.—Could the priests and their officers go forth from Jerusalem to lay hands on Jesus in Gethsemane at the very time when the whole people were celebrating the Paschal feast within their dwellings? Yes, says the defender of the Synoptics, they certainly could. No, answers the defender of John, it was impossible.—Could sittings of tribunals be held and follow one another, one, two, three, during a Sabbatic night when, according to the Talmud, "everything reprehensible on Sabbath, such as climbing a tree, riding, *holding a court*, etc., is equally forbidden on *the feast day*"? (Beza, v. 2). Impossible, says the one. Quite possible, answers the other; for the law of the feast day is always less rigorous than that of the Sabbath; for a judicial sitting is allowed, provided there be no *writing* done at it; for these severe prescriptions were not formally set down till the Talmudic times, and there is nothing to prove that they were observed so early as the time of Jesus. —Is it possible to hold that Simon *came out of the country* on the morning of the Sabbatic day, the 15th (Mark xv. 21); that Joseph *bought* a winding-sheet that same day (xv. 46); that the women put off embalming the body that evening in order to rest, because the Sabbath was near (Luke xxiii. 56), if the very day on which these things took place was itself a Sabbatic day? No, says the one; by all these facts the Synoptics testify that the day of the death was a *work* day, and thus do homage consciously or unconsciously to the date of John, that of the 14th. Not at all, say the others; all is in perfect keeping with the 15th. Simon is a dweller in the country who is simply *repairing* to the city. The purchases are perfectly reconcileable with the Sabbatic rest, provided *payment* is not made the same day. Finally, the sanctity of the weekly Sabbath is always held higher than that of the feast day.

With such skilful and learned pleaders before us, it is prudent doubtless to pronounce no decision. Yet it is remarkable that the judge who betrays the most decided antipathy to John cannot help declaring that the 15th is the most difficult reading (Keim, iii. p. 475).

Besides these facts, the Synoptics also contain certain *sayings* which equally favour John's narrative; they are especially the three following passages:—

1. Matt. xxvi. 18, Jesus sends this message to the citizen of Jerusalem, at whose house He intends to eat the Passover: "*My time is at hand; I will keep the Passover at thy house with my disciples.*" M. Reuss says with perfect frankness: "The saying: '*My time is at hand,*' cannot well be interpreted otherwise than as an allusion to His death, though this communication *has no very intimate relation* to the commission given to the disciples." The connection sought is not established, indeed, unless the Lord meant to say: "I must make haste: to-morrow it will be too late; prepare everything therefore with my disciples, that I may eat the Passover at thy

house to-day with my own whom I am about to leave" ($\pi o\iota \tilde{\omega}$, the present). Thus understood, the message of Jesus has meaning, but a meaning which implies on our Lord's part the anticipation of the Paschal feast.

2. In Matt. xxvii. 62, the Saturday on which Jesus rests in the grave is described by the evangelist as "*the next day that followed the day of the preparation.*" Supposing that the word *preparation* was really used here in the sense of *Friday*, would it not be as strange an expression as if Sabbath were called *the day that followed Friday?* That would be like a riddle put to the reader. Is it not rather Friday which should be called *the day which comes before Sabbath?* Of two days which are related to one another, that which determines the designation of the other is evidently the more important of the two. There is in the case before us only one explanation of so strange an expression: As the day of *the death*, it was the so-called *preparation* day which for this time played the decisive part, and from which the designation of the Sabbath itself deserved to be taken. This phraseology therefore implies that the day was naturally a *work day*, and that its importance was entirely due to the fact that it was the day of our Lord's death.

3. Mark xv. 42 is often quoted as one of the passages opposed to John's date: "It was the *preparation* ($\pi a \rho a \sigma \kappa \epsilon v \dot{\eta}$), that is, the day *before the Sabbath* ($\pi \rho o \sigma \dot{a} \beta \beta a \tau o v$)." But does it follow that $\pi a \rho a \sigma \kappa \epsilon v \dot{\eta}$ really signifies *Friday?* What does Mark mean? That it was Friday? There was no need of two different terms to express this. The object of his remark is to convey to his Gentile readers the thought that every day having a Sabbatic character, whether the Sabbath or a feast day, was preceded by a day bearing the name of *preparation*, that is to say, of *pro-Sabbath*, because on that day everything was arranged so that the rest of the morrow might not be disturbed. Now this remark, with the accompanying explanation, was very important in the context. As is well said by Weiss (*Marc.* ad. h. 1.): "All work—and consequently also the taking down from the cross, which fell under this category—must terminate before sunset, otherwise the Sabbatic rest which was about to begin would have prevented its execution." Hence it follows not that the day of

Christ's death was a *Friday* (though it was so in reality), but that it was a *preparation* day in relation to some Sabbatic day or other which was about to follow. Would a Jew ever have characterized the 15th of Nisan thus, that day so essentially Sabbatic, if, as is alleged, Jesus really died on that day?

The only point at which the synoptical account seems really to conflict with that of the fourth Gospel, is the date of the disciples' question, Matt. xxvi. 17; Mark xiv. 12; Luke xxii. 7. But here everything depends on the precise time of the question put by the apostles. If it is supposed that it was put on *the morning* of the 14th Nisan, all possibility of harmony certainly disappears. For the evening which followed that morning, and on which the last supper of Jesus took place, could have been no other than that between the 14th and 15th, that of the Paschal feast among the Jews, which inevitably places the death of Jesus on the morrow following that feast, and so on the 15th. But Strauss has remarked,[1] that the procuring of the room and the articles necessary for the Paschal feast could not have been put off till the morning of the 14th. The number of pilgrims coming to Jerusalem was too considerable to admit of waiting till the morning of the day on which the feast took place to secure a room. Also Clement of Alexandria, to designate the previous day, that of the 13th, uses the term προετοιμασία, *pro-preparation*, or preparation for the preparation. The day of *preparation* (for the feast) was the 14th, but that on which the arrangements needed for this preparation were made was the 13th. Now, of these measures the most essential was to secure a room. It is therefore probable, to say nothing more, that it was on the afternoon of the 13th that the disciples referred to the Lord the steps to be taken with this view. Are the expressions used by the evangelists opposed to this idea? Luke says: "*The day of unleavened bread was come* . . ." These terms apply to the afternoon of the 13th, to the time of sunset, as well as to the morrow morning, and even better. For it was exactly at this time, on the evening of the 13th, between six and seven, that lamps were lighted to ransack the darkest corners of the houses, and to remove from them the last particles of leaven (Kirchner, p. 12).—Matthew

[1] *Das Leben Jesu*, 1864, p. 533.

says: "*On the first day of the feast of Unleavened Bread, the disciples came to Jesus.*" Mark says: "*The first day of unleavened bread, when they killed the Passover* . . ." Mark's somewhat more detailed expressions are solely intended to put Gentile readers more completely in possession of the object of the feast. They may, as well as those of Matthew, with which they are synonymous, refer to the last hours of the afternoon of the 13th, which, according to the Jewish mode of reckoning, began the 14th.

It is objected (Rotermund) that, notwithstanding the official mode of dividing days, reckoning from one evening to the other, in popular language (which is that of our evangelist) the *evening* of a day was always that of the day which *was closing*. But the proof of the opposite appears in the common expression: *Erev haschschabbath, Sabbath evening*, which denotes not Saturday evening, but *Friday* evening; and in the fact that the sacred sheaf of the 16th Nisan was cut not on the morning of that day, but on the eve of it. The deputies of the Sanhedrim arrived on the field accompanied by the people. " Has the sun set? they asked.—Yes, it has. Am I to cut? —Yes, cut! With this sickle?—Yes. Into this basket? —Yes." Then the work was accomplished. It belonged to the 16th, a work day, and not to the 15th, a Sabbatic day. Finally, when Hippolytus puts into the mouth of the partisans of the 14th this saying: " Christ celebrated the Passover *on the day on which* He suffered, I ought therefore to do likewise," is it not evident that they include in the 15th day the preceding evening, when the last supper took place? The objection is therefore unfounded.

An interesting coincidence, which can hardly be accidental, presents itself here. On the evening between the 13th and 14th Nisan, before the stars appeared in the sky, people went from every house to draw water from the fountain with which on the morrow to knead the unleavened bread. This custom no doubt explains the sign which our Lord gives to His two disciples, Peter and John, when, on sending them to the city, He says: " Behold, when ye are entered into the city, there shall a man meet you, bearing a pitcher of water; follow him. . . ." This coincidence fixes at the same time the hour when the disciples were sent; it was evening, when the stars were about to appear. The 14th had therefore begun. In reality, it was the beginning of the first day of unleavened bread.

What was our Lord's intention in giving these orders to the two disciples? The latter had asked His instructions for the morrow evening. In presence of the apostles, Jesus entered apparently into their thought. For He required to be on His guard against the treachery of Judas, who was watching all His steps. But when sending His two confidential disciples to the city, and giving them the message, which we know from Matthew, for the host on whom He reckoned, He gives them to understand that they were to prepare everything not for the morrow, but *for that same evening*. The mysterious nature of this message did not allow Judas to know beforehand the house where Jesus was to pass that last evening with His own.

It will be objected that it was rather late to buy and prepare the lamb. But from the 10th Nisan it must have been put aside and kept in a particular place. It was needed only to take and roast it, which could certainly be done between six and eight o'clock. The other necessary articles belonged to the furniture of the room, or might easily be procured by the host or His disciples.

But where, it will be said, is the ritual or sacerdotal *killing* of the lamb, such as took place in the temple on the afternoon of the 14th? It is to be remarked, first, that this whole ceremony of slaying in the temple was a human addition to the law. According to the Paschal ordinance and the example of the first Passover, every father of a household was himself to slay the lamb in his house, without the intervention of a priest. At this time, when the typical Passover was about to take end, it was surely allowable to return to its original simplicity. But more than this: the legal covenant verging to its close, the sacramental feast of that economy, the Israelitish Passover, resembled only a withered calyx, from the bosom of which there was about to blossom the sacramental feast of the *new covenant*, the καινὴ διαθήκη, as Jesus Himself says some hours later (Matt. xxvi. 28 and parall.). The lamb in the feast which was preparing had only a part to fill, that of giving place to the true Lamb, which was substituted for it with the words: "Do this henceforth *in remembrance of me.*" In such conditions the sacerdotal consecration was useless.

A difficulty remains, that of the *day*. Could Jesus change the legal day of the Paschal feast? Impossible, answer Keim and Luthardt resolutely, and this time in perfect harmony. But if Jesus could boldly declare Himself *the Lord of the Sabbath*,—and the transference of the Sabbatic day from Saturday to Sunday in His Church has proved that this was no vain word,—how should He not also be the Lord of the Passover? The Sabbath was the corner-stone of the whole Mosaic constitution. He who disposed of it freely, held in His hand the whole edifice.

We conclude: Many things lead, and not one is absolutely opposed in the Synoptics, to the date of John.

4. *The Paschal Controversies.*—The general fact on which this last contention rests is the following: The churches of Asia Minor celebrated the Paschal feast by fasting during the 14th Nisan, and taking the communion the evening of that day. The other churches of Christendom, with Rome at their head, fasted during the days preceding the Passover Sunday (the first Sunday after the 14th), and communicated on the morning of that day. In both cases the communion terminated the fast.

First phase of the discussion. About 155,[1] Polycarp in a visit to Rome converses on this subject with Anicetus. Each defends the rite of his church, on the ground of an *apostolical tradition* of which it is the depositary (proceeding at Ephesus from John and Philip, at Rome from Paul and Peter). There is nothing to prove that on this occasion the disputants penetrated to the exegetical and dogmatic domain of the question. The peace of the church remained unbroken. "Diversity in rite served rather, as Irenæus says, to establish harmony in faith."[2]

Second phase. Fifteen years after, in 170, there breaks out at Laodicea, in the very bosom of the church of Asia, a discussion on the subject of the Passover. There are people— who are they? we shall have to study the point—who, while

---

[1] Recent discoveries, due especially to M. Waddington, seem to prove that the martyrdom of Polycarp took place in 155 or 156, and not later, as used to be held.

[2] "Letter to Victor" (Eus. *H. E.* v. 24).

practising the Asiatic rite, found it expressly on the fact that Jesus instituted the Supper on the evening of the 14th, while celebrating the Paschal feast at the time prescribed by the law, in proof of which they allege Matthew's account, according to which our Lord celebrated the Paschal feast on the 14th, and was crucified on the 15th.[1] It is obvious that the controversy escapes from the domain of tradition, and lays hold from this time forth of the exegetical side of the question. Melito is the first who writes on this subject, we know not on which side. Then, *on occasion* of his treatise (ἐξ αἰτίας),—not in opposition to him, as is still alleged by Schürer,—Apolinarius and Clement of Alexandria take the pen. Both of them, judging from the fragments quoted in the *Chronicon paschale*, hold that Jesus celebrated His last feast and instituted the Supper not on the 14th, but on the 13th, and that He died not on the 15th, but on the 14th. They allege especially John's account in favour of this view.

Who are the adversaries combated by these two writers? Baur, Hilgenfeld, Schürer, and Luthardt answer: Simply the churches of Asia with their rite of celebration on the 14th. Apolinarius would thus be in Asia itself the champion of the western rite. It is difficult to believe this. 1st. Eusebius represents the churches of Asia as unanimous: "The churches *of all Asia* thought, according to an ancient tradition, that they were bound to observe the 14th in the celebration of the Holy Supper." If this consensus of all the churches of Asia had been broken by so considerable an exception as that of Apolinarius of Hierapolis, Eusebius, the declared adversary of the Asiatic rite, would not have failed to state it. But he says nothing of the kind. Undoubtedly Baur relies on the fact that a little later, Polycrates, when enumerating in his letter to Victor of Rome the illustrious persons who observed this rite, does not mention Apolinarius. But he names only the dead. Apolinarius might be included among those numerous bishops of whom Polycrates speaks without naming them, and who surrounded him at the time when he wrote his letter,

[1] Comp. p. 539, the polemic of Apolinarius and the words which Hippolytus, in his *Philosophumena*, puts into the mouth of his adversaries: "The Lord celebrated the Passover and suffered on that day [that is to say, on the day between the 14th and 15th]; *and therefore I should do as He did.*"

and gave it their assent. 2d. If Apolinarius had made a division in Asia, it is probable that the dispute would have broken out at Hierapolis in his own diocese, not at Laodicea. 3d. The adversaries of Apolinarius supported their position from Matthew, evidently in opposition to arguments drawn from other sources. Whence, if not from the fourth Gospel? Now is it not known, is it not obvious from the letter even of Polycrates, that John was constantly, whether from personal tradition or *by his Gospel*, the light of the churches of Asia?[1] And we should find them all at once making Matthew their patron, and that perhaps against John himself! The thing is impossible. 4th. The polemic of Apolinarius, in opposition to his Laodicean adversaries, does not really imply either a rupture with the Asiatic rite or adherence to the occidental. He might perfectly well remain faithful to the former, while justifying it otherwise than the Laodiceans, either exegetically or dogmatically. For we have seen that the latter likewise observed the 14th. As to the western rite, it is impossible to understand how the opinion of Apolinarius, which placed the death of Jesus on the 14th rather than on the 15th, favoured the view which placed the celebration of the Passover on the following Sunday! 5th. Schürer is entangled in an inconceivable contradiction: According to him, if the churches in Asia celebrated the 14th, it was without any relation to any fact whatever of Gospel history (whether the institution of the Supper or the death of Jesus); their rite arose solely from their having transformed the Jewish Paschal feast of the 14th into the Christian Supper and a celebration of redemption. Such is the result of his solid and remarkable work. And yet, on the other hand, the polemic of Apolinarius forces him to acknowledge that, if the Laodicean adversaries of this Father fixed the Supper on the 14th, it was to commemorate *the institution* of the ceremony on that day by Jesus Christ. How, then, can it be alleged that the latter are no other than the churches of Asia?

Thus it is easy to understand how Weitzel and Steitz, with

---

[1] See, besides the Asiatic literature of the second century, which rests on the writings of John (Polycarp, Papias, Ignatius, Melito, Theophilus, and Irenæus, comp. Introd. i. pp. 199-246), the letter of Polycrates, in which there is found indisputable allusion to John's Gospel.

whom are associated Ritschl, Meyer, Réville, etc., have been led to see in those Laodiceans a Judaizing party which arose in the church of Asia with the intention of preserving the *Jewish Paschal feast*, while adapting to it the Holy Christian Supper. Then the polemic of Apolinarius and Clement strikes home. These people say: "We wish to do *as the Lord did* [celebrate the Paschal feast on the 14th]." The two Fathers reply: "The Lord did not do so. He *replaced* the Paschal feast of the 14th by the Supper on the 13th,"—an opinion which does not prevent Apolinarius from remaining faithful to his church's rite; for, as Schürer himself acknowledges, the church of Asia did not celebrate the 14th as the day of *the institution* of the Supper. She celebrated the Holy Supper on that day as a memorial of redemption, thus translating into a sacramental Christian feast the Jewish Passover, which was instituted in memory of the Israelites' deliverance.

There are only two points on which I would dissent from Weitzel and Steitz: 1st. The Laodicean adversaries of Apolinarius I should hold to be less an Ebionite sect than a branch of the church of Asia with a more pronounced Judaizing tendency. 2d. The rite of the churches of Asia arose simply from the celebration of the 14th in Israelitish worship, not from the thought of maintaining that this day was that of *Jesus' death*. This consequence flows from the words of Eusebius: "The churches of Asia thought they should celebrate the 14th, *the day on which the Jews were commanded to kill the lamb;*" and especially from those of Polycrates: "And all my relatives (bishops before me) celebrated the day *on which the people took away the leaven.*" The Asiatic rite is expressly put into relation to *the day* of Christ's death only in two passages of the fourth and fifth centuries, the one in Epiphanius, the other in Theodoret (see Schürer, pp. 57 and 58), which shows that this point of view did not prevail in the beginning.

Third phase. Between 180 and 190 a certain Blastus (*Adv. hær.* of the pseudo-Tertullian, c. 22) seeks to transplant the Asiatic rite to Rome. Hence, probably, the reawakening of the controversy between the two churches of Rome and Asia, which are represented at this epoch by Victor and Polycrates. The latter, in his letter to Victor, no longer defends his cause merely by traditional arguments, as Polycarp had done thirty years before. "Before writing, he went over *all the Holy Scriptures* (πᾶσαν ἁγίαν γραφὴν διεληλυθώς)." And he declares that "his predecessors also observed the 14th *according to the Gospel* (κατὰ τὸ εὐαγγέλιον)." These words give rise to reflection. It has been sought to get rid of them by subtleties (see Schürer's embarrassment, p. 35). They evidently prove, as the preceding do, that Polycrates and the bishops of Asia had succeeded in establishing a harmony *of the Gospels* by means of which not only did those writings not contradict one another (τὸ εὐαγγέλιον, the *one* Gospel in the four), but such that they also agreed with the law itself (*all the Scriptures*). Such sayings imply, therefore, that Polycrates and his bishops had found the Asiatic rite confirmed at first by the law (the matter in question is the institution of the Passover, Ex. xii., fixing the Paschal feast on the 14th), next by the unanimity of the canonical Gospels, which has no meaning unless Polycrates harmonized the Synoptics with John by interpreting them as we have done ourselves; for to do the reverse (to bring John to the apparent meaning of the Synoptics) did not then occur to any one. Thus the words of Polycrates and the censure which Apolinarius pronounces on the opinion of his Laodicean adversaries are perfectly equivalent: "Wherefore not only is their opinion contrary to the law (which requires the lamb to be slain on the 14th), but there would also be in this case a disagreement between the Gospels [Matthew fixing the death on the 15th, John on the 14th]."

Polycrates therefore sets himself, in order to support the Asiatic rite, exactly at the same exegetical standpoint as Apolinarius does to combat the Laodicean party. This dispute was allayed by the efforts of Irenæus and several others, who interceded with Victor and stopped him on the way to violent measures.

Fourth phase. It is marked by the decision of the Council of Nice in 324, which enjoined on the Orientals to fall in with the western rite now generally adopted. "At the close of the controversy," says Eusebius (in his περὶ τῆς τοῦ πάσχα ἑορτῆς, Schürer, p. 40), "the Orientals yielded; and thus," adds he, "they broke finally with our Lord's murderers and joined their co-religionists (ὁμοδόξοις)." The Asiatic rite, from the fact of the Holy Paschal Supper falling simultaneously with that of the Jewish Passover, had become more and more the sign of a secret sympathy with the unbelieving Jews. This it was which decided its discontinuance. From this time, those only who, like the Laodicean Judaizers, maintained as the exegetical basis of their observation of the 14th the fact that the Holy Supper had been instituted on that day, kept their ground under the names of *Audians* and *Quarto-decimans*, who figure in the lists of heresies. Athanasius frankly confesses that they are not easily refuted when they advance the words of the Synoptics : " *On the first day of unleavened bread, the disciples came to Jesus . . .*" (Schürer, p. 45).[1] Here we come upon the first symptom of that preponderance which the synoptical narrative finally obtained over John's, and which held its ground through the Middle Ages and the Reformation down to modern times. The Synoptics, more popular than John, and apparently clearer, forming besides a bundle of three against one, and especially no longer encountering as a counterpoise the fear of mixing up the Christian Supper and the Jewish Passover, carried the day in general feeling. Of the Fathers, Jerome is the one who contributed most to this victory.

How, then, are we to explain the origin of the two observances, the Asiatic and the Roman, in the second century?[2] Paul had no fear of bringing into the Church the celebration of the Jewish Passover (Acts xx. 6; comp. 1 Cor. v. 7, 8, with xvi. 8). He transformed and spiritualized its rites, that is undoubted ; the Holy Supper was substituted for the Paschal feast of the lamb and the unleavened bread; but the time was the same; had not Jesus said, " Do *this* (the Passover) in remembrance of me " ? John did the same ; and thus it was that, under cover of his authority, there was introduced

---

[1] It is likewise to one of those obstinate and henceforth schismatic Quarto decimans that we must apply the words of Eusebius in the treatise quoted above (Schürer, p. 40) : "But if any one should say, It is also written, *On the first day of unleavened bread . . .*" It is easy to see that the same objection embarrasses Eusebius as well as Athanasius. But it no more proves the identity of the ancient churches of Asia with the Laodiceans of the second century than with the Quarto-decimans of the fourth (in opposition to Schürer).

[2] Schürer seems to us to have thrown real light on this important and difficult point, p. 61 et seq.

into Asia Minor the practice of celebrating the 14th Nisan by the Holy Supper. But the churches of the West, more estranged from Judaism, no doubt felt a certain repugnance to this close bond of unity *in time* between the Jewish feast and the Christian, and to the sort of dependence in which this simultaneousness placed the one in relation to the other. They therefore cast off the yoke; and, instead of celebrating the Holy Paschal Supper on the evening of the 14th, as they had already the institution of the weekly Sunday, this ceremony was fixed for the Sunday morning which followed the 14th Nisan yearly, or, to speak more correctly, the full moon of March.[1] Thus arose, no doubt, the western observance, which ended by carrying the day over the primitive observance. The Church is free in such matters.

The result of this long and complicated history, so far as concerns the subject before us, seems to be this: From the time that the Church occupied herself with the exegetical side of the question, she held to John's narrative. She made use of it, on the one hand, to refute by the pen of Apolinarius the exegetical basis which the Laodicean party pretended to lay for the observance of the 14th (by making that day, according to Matthew, the day of *the institution* of the Supper); on the other, to defend against Rome by the pen of Polycrates the Asiatic celebration of the 14th, by representing it as the Jewish Passover spiritualized, as the Christian feast of redemption, the counterpart of the Israelitish deliverance in Egypt. For the church of Asia, then, there was no question of celebrating the 14th Nisan as the day of *the institution* of the Supper, nor even, strictly speaking, as the day of Jesus' *death* (in opposition to Steitz). The meaning simply was *to christianize* the Jewish Passover. If, therefore, this observance contains any homage to John's narrative, it is not so of itself undoubtedly (for it has no direct relation to any particular fact in the life of Jesus); but it is so from the manner in which it was defended by Apolinarius on the one hand, and Polycrates on the other, for this double apology rests entirely on John's narrative.

[1] So it comes about, as Schürer rightly observes, that the name *Easter* (*Pâques*) is applied at the present day to the day of the resurrection rather than to that of the death.

5. *The year of our Lord's death.*—This year cannot be regarded as finally fixed. Science still oscillates between the year 29 (Ideler, Zumpt) and 35 (Keim), or even 36 (Hitzig). Yet, excepting the year 33 (Ewald, Renan), it is the year 30 which is condescended on at the present day by the majority of *savants* (Winer, Wieseler, Lichtenstein, Caspari, and Pressensé). It is the year which has always appeared to us also to combine the largest sum of probabilities on its side. Two astronomers, Wurm and Oudemann, have sought to determine which of those different years were those on which either the 14th or the 15th Nisan must have fallen on a Friday. They have found that in the year 30 the Friday of the Paschal week was the 15th, and not the 14th. This result, unfavourable to our interpretation, has been re-examined by Caspari, and he has attempted to show that Wurm's calculation, rightly understood, far from overturning our thesis, confirms it, and makes the 14th Nisan of the year 30 fall exactly on the Friday. The important fact is, that we find ourselves here face to face with the incalculable eventualities and subtleties of the Jewish calendar. Wurm feels this himself: he speaks simply of *probabilities*. He says also: "One will not be greatly mistaken if he calculates thus." He acknowledges that there always remains an uncertainty *of one or two days*, which in this question are of capital importance (Keim, pp. 498–500). It is therefore surer to operate on positive texts, as we have done, than on grounds so precarious. We think, consequently, that we may indicate *Friday the 14th Nisan, the 7th April* of the year 30, as the most probable date of the death of Jesus.

Thus, then, no historical fact really and duly attested lends itself to falsify the solution which we have presented.

III.

Let us now cast a rapid glance *at the other proposed solutions*.

1st. The *ideal* explanation of Baur and his school: The Johannine narrative is a fiction dictated on the one hand by the desire, *the real passion* (Keim) of the pseudo-John, to present Christ as the Paschal lamb, and on the other hand by the tendency to throw as much as possible into the shade the

Jewish Paschal feast.—But in thus putting himself in contradiction to the tradition received in the Church and the ancient Gospels, which had full authority within it, did not the forger run the risk of compromising the entire success of his work? And that for nothing; for the typical relation between Christ and the Paschal lamb was a point universally admitted in the second century, on the ground of 1 Cor. v. 7, xi. 24, 25, 1 Pet. i. 19, and the Apocalypse, and that abstracting from all chronological connection between the slaying of the lamb and the day of Christ's death. As to the Jewish Passover, it had already given place everywhere in the second century to the Christian Supper (Schürer, pp. 29–34); it was no longer necessary to reduce its importance.

2d. The interpretation of John which seeks to find in his narrative a meaning ordinarily attributed to the Synoptics (the death of Jesus fixed on the 15th Nisan). In spite of all the efforts of erudition and sagacity made by Hengstenberg, Tholuck, Wieseler, Hofmann, Luthardt, Lichtenstein, Lange, Langen, Riggenbach, Bäumlein, Oosterzee, Ebrard, Kirchner, and Rotermund, this explanation seems to conflict with the clear and precise texts of John, and to succumb to their force.

3d. Various attempts, tending either to put the Israelitish Paschal feast forward by an evening, or to hold two feasts, the one on the 14th, the other on the 15th, of which Jesus chose the former. The Jews this year held the Paschal feast a day earlier (Eusebius and Chrysostom; see Tholuck, p. 41); the Jews made it a day later this year to avoid celebrating two Sabbaths in succession (Friday, 15th, and Saturday, 16th), and Jesus abode by the legal day (Calvin, Beza, Scaliger, Casaubon); the Jews celebrated the Paschal feast every year, and legally on the evening between the 13th and 14th, and not the evening between the 14th and 15th (Frisch, Rauch); Jesus on this occasion followed the practice of some sect, the Karaïtes, for example, who celebrated the Passover on the evening between the 13th and 14th (Stier); in consequence of the great number of lambs to be slain in the temple from three to six o'clock (sometimes more than 250,000, according to Josephus), the Galileans (Ebrard) or the Jews of the Diaspora (Serno) celebrated the feast the evening before the legal day, and Jesus joined them. But there is no contemporary historical ground either in Josephus or Philo, or in the N. T., to support any one of these hypotheses whatever. And yet if ours is rejected, one or other of them must be accepted, unless we take the desperate course to which some condemn themselves :

4th. That of admitting a contradiction pure and simple between our Gospel narratives, and declaring it insoluble (Lücke, Neander, Bleek, de Wette, Steitz, J. Müller). Comp. also M. de Pressensé (*Vie de Jésus*, p. 593): "We regard the question up till now as insoluble, while holding John's account to be entirely correct." Undoubtedly this would be what should be done if the text of the Synoptics refused to be harmonized with the latter. But how explain such a contradiction on a point like this?

To sum up, we think that the difference between John and the Synoptics may be formulated and explained as follows:—

In editing the oral tradition, the Synoptics contented themselves, as it had done, with placing Christ's last Supper on the first day of unleavened bread, without *expressly* distinguishing between the first and second *evening* of that day. Now, as Jesus had wished to give to this last feast, celebrated on the evening of the 13th, the forms of the Paschal feast with the view of connecting with it the institution of the Holy Supper, while substituting the one of those sacred feasts for the other, a misunderstanding might easily arise; it might be thought that this feast had been the ordinary Paschal feast, a mistake which would necessarily result in displacing the day of our Lord's death by carrying it over to the 15th. John (as he had done in so many other cases in his Gospel) wished to rectify this misunderstanding and to dissipate the obscurity of the Synoptics, which might give it countenance. He therefore deliberately and clearly restored the real course of things, to which, besides, the synoptical narrative bore testimony at all points (comp. in modern times: Krummel, *Litteraturblatt* of Darmstadt, Feb. 1868; Baggesen, *Der Apostel Johannes*, 1869; Andreæ, *Beweis des Glaubens*, art. quoted).

FIFTH PART.

XX. 1–29.

THE RESURRECTION.

JEWISH unbelief had at once consummated and condemned itself in the trial and doom of Jesus. Now, the *faith of the disciples* reaches its full expansion through the highest earthly manifestation of the glory of Jesus—His resurrection.

John's narrative strikes out for itself a firm and sure way through the somewhat divergent narratives of the Synoptics, and without effort gives us a glimpse of their harmony. In a first piece (vv. 1–10), the evangelist relates how he himself attained to faith in the resurrection. Then, in the three following passages, he relates the appearances of Jesus by which this same faith was prepared, then established, and at last consummated in the apostolic circle. These are the appearances to Mary Magdalene (vv. 11–18), to the apostles on the evening of Easter day (vv. 19–23), and to the same, including Thomas, eight days after (vv. 24–29).

I. *Peter and John at the Sepulchre.*—Vv. 1–10.

Everything in this first passage tends to the words of ver. 8: "*And he saw, and believed.*" The part of Mary Magdalene is only that of the messenger who calls the two disciples to the sepulchre.

Vv. 1–3. "*The first day of the week cometh Mary Magdalene early, when it was yet dark, unto the sepulchre, and seeth the stone taken away from the sepulchre. Then she runneth, and cometh to Simon Peter, and to the other disciple whom Jesus loved, and saith unto them, They have taken away the Lord out of the sepulchre,*[1] *and we know not where they have laid Him.*

---

[1] ℵ, some Mnn. It^{alia} Cop. Sah. add ἀπο της θυρας (*from the door*) before ἐκ του μνημειου (ℵ) or του μνημειου.

Peter therefore went forth, and that other disciple, and came to the sepulchre."—In the phrase μία τῶν σαββάτων, there might be given to the word σάββατα the meaning of *Sabbath:* "the first day (μία) starting from the Sabbath." But Luke xviii. 12 proves that σάββατον or σάββατα signifies also the whole *week,* as forming the interval between two Sabbaths. So: "the first (μία) of the days of the week." The greater was the deliverance which Mary Magdalene owed to Jesus (Luke viii. 2; Mark xvi. 9), the more fervent was her gratitude, the more lively her attachment to His Person. John does not mention the purpose which brought her to the sepulchre, and which the Synoptics mention, that of embalming the Lord's body. Did she come alone? That is in itself far from probable. A woman would not have ventured to go alone to the sepulchre at so early an hour. Besides, the Synoptics inform us that her companions had the same intention as she had. Finally, the verb in the plural: *we know not,* in ver. 2, indicates positively that she was not alone. If she only is mentioned, it is because of the part which she plays in the following scene. Meyer objects the οὐκ οἶδα, *I know not,* of ver. 13, and alleges that this singular *counterbalances* the plural of ver. 2. A weak reason, which proves that if there is a *harmonistic* partiality, there may also be an *anti-harmonistic* passion. Alone with the angels, ver. 13, and naturally enough not speaking with them, but in her own name, she says here: "*I know not,*" and not: "we know not;" as she says: "*my Lord,*" and not: "*the Lord*" (ver. 2). Meyer attempts to explain the plural: *we know not,* by saying that Mary is speaking *in the name of the Lord's disciples* in general. But why, then, bring in all the believers here, not one of whom, according to Meyer, attested the opening of the tomb with her? Ewald and Luthardt hold that she arrived alone, and that the other women followed her. But is it not simpler to say that they came all together, and that, as soon as from a distance they saw the tomb open, Mary Magdalene made haste to bring the disciples word, while her companions remained in the vicinity of the sepulchre? When Mary returned with Peter and John, her companions had already gone back to the city. Comp. Luke xxiv. 22, 23: "Certain women of our company were early at the sepulchre, and when they found not the body," etc., and Mark xvi. 1-8.—There is only a slight chronological difference between John, Matthew, and Luke on the one side, who say: "*When it was yet dark,*" or: "*As it began to dawn,*" and Mark on the other, who says: "*At the rising of the sun.*" Perhaps there were several groups of women, whom each evangelist combines in one.— During Mary's absence, her companions approached the tomb and received the angel's message, which is related by the three Synoptics. As to the appearing of Jesus to the women mentioned by Matt. xxviii. 9, 10, it is certainly no other than the appearance to Mary Magdalene which is about to be described by John himself. Other features detailed coincide perfectly. The first Gospel applies to the whole group what passed in the case of one of its members. Thus is to be understood the account of Mark xvi. 1-8, and the words of the two disciples of Emmaus in Luke xxiv. 22, 23, implying that the women had not seen the Lord. In fact, Mary Magdalene not having seen the Lord at the tomb till later, and after the other women had returned to the city, the two disciples of Emmaus had set out from Jerusalem without having heard of this appearance. There were therefore in reality no other appearances on the morning of that day than that of the angels to the women and to Mary Magdalene, and that of Jesus to the latter. There is no occasion for the loud cries which are uttered by criticism (Keim, iii. p. 530).

The repetition of the preposition πρός, *to the house of*, ver. 2, may lead us to conclude that the two disciples had different homes, which is natural, if John lived with his mother and Mary the mother of Jesus.—The term ἐφίλει, *loved*, which has something more familiar in it than ἠγάπα, is no doubt used here only as a designation, without particular emphasis, Jesus Himself being absent.—The imp. ἤρχοντο, *they were coming, were repairing*, the fact pictured. This imperfect of duration reflects the feeling of inexpressible expectation which made the heart of the disciple and his companion beat.

Vv. 4-7. "*So they ran both together: and the other disciple*[1] *did outrun Peter, and came first to the sepulchre. And he stooping down, seeth the linen clothes lying;*[2] *yet went he*

---
[1] ℵ omits καὶ ὁ ἄλλος μαθητής.   [2] ℵ A X Syr. Cop. Sah. place κείμενα after ὀθόνια.

not in. Then cometh Simon Peter following him, and went into the sepulchre, and seeth the linen clothes lie,[1] *and the napkin, that was about His head, not lying with the linen clothes, but wrapped together in a place by itself."*—John, probably younger and more agile, arrives first. But his emotion is so great that he stops at the entrance to the sepulchre after looking in. Peter, of a more masculine and practical character, enters resolutely. These details are so natural, and so much in keeping with the personality of the two disciples, that they bear in themselves the seal of their authenticity. They remind us of the details of ch. i.—The pres. *he seeth* (ver. 5) contrasts with the Aor. *came* (ver. 4); the same contrast reappears between the verbs *he went into* and *he seeth* (ver. 6). John hereby brings out the contrast between the single moment of arrival, and the attentive and prolonged examination which follows it in either case. The θεωρεῖ, *considers*, includes observation and reflection on the fact. This linen displayed to view, did not lead to the supposition of a removal; the body would not have been taken away entirely naked. The napkin especially, wrapped together and carefully put aside, attested not a precipitate removal, but a calm and holy awakening. There was matter of reflection here for the two disciples.

Vv. 8-10. "*Then went in also that other disciple which came first to the sepulchre, and he saw, and believed. For as yet they knew*[2] *not the scripture, that He must rise again from the dead. Then the disciples went away again unto their own home.*"—The singulars, *he saw* and *he believed*, are remarkable. Till now, the two disciples had been spoken of; and in ver. 9 the plural is resumed: *they knew not*. What is meant in such a context by these two verbs in the singular, if they do not indicate an experience peculiar to this disciple? Here is an incident in the author's inmost life. He initiates us into the way by which he reached faith in the resurrection first of all, and then through it to complete faith in Christ as the Messiah and Son of God. The idea of believing cannot, in fact, refer solely, as some have thought,

---

[1] ℵ omits the end of ver. 5 from ου and all ver. 6 (confusion of the two τ. ε. κειμενα).
[2] ℵ It^{aliq}: ῃδει.

to the report of Mary Magdalene. On seeing the state of the tomb and the position of the linen clothes, the disciple arrived at this conviction: Jesus lives. And perhaps this is the explanation why there is no mention of any particular appearance of the Lord to His beloved disciple, while there is mention of appearances to Peter and James. On the other hand, we must not see in these two words, *he saw* and *he believed*, an eulogy which in this case would rather be a boast. They contain a reproach or, better still, a confession. For the following verse proves that we must paraphrase: "he saw and he believed *at length.*" John himself is amazed at the state of ignorance in which he, like Peter, had been plunged till then, in regard to the Scripture prophecies announcing the resurrection of the Messiah. He says ᾔδεισαν, which has the meaning of the imperfect, not the pluperfect. "*They knew not,*" not even then! It was the teaching of Jesus after His resurrection which opened the disciple's eyes on this point, as on so many others. Luke xxiv. 25-27 and 45.

As to Peter, the sight of the interior of the sepulchre did not yet bring him to faith. To gain this result fully, there was needed the Lord's appearance, which was granted him that same day (Luke xxiv. 34; 1 Cor. xv. 5).—The parallel of Luke xxiv. 12 is probably nothing more than a gloss borrowed from John's narrative. And hence we make no use of it.—This whole passage relating to the disciple whom Jesus loved and to Peter, presents one of the most striking instances of the autobiographic character of our Gospel.

The Tübingen school, followed in this by M. Renan and Strauss (in his second *Leben Jesu*), think that this narrative is a fiction intended to place John in all respects on a level with Peter. John, it is said, seeks systematically "to put himself above Peter" (M. Renan). How? Because he ascribes to himself more agile limbs, but less courage? Or Peter and John personify, the one the carnal Christianity of the Twelve, the other Johannine spiritual Christianity. How so? Does not John accuse himself of having required to see in order to believe? Does not all this Machiavellism ascribed to the evangelist vanish before the simple reading of this narrative? Is the sense of the true and pure really paralyzed in our critics?

M. Colani sees in the words, ver. 9 : " *they knew not the scripture*," a contradiction to the predictions of the resurrection put into the mouth of Jesus by the Synoptics. If those predictions were real, the evangelist would have said : "they knew not *the predictions of Jesus*."[1] But John has himself already explained to us (ii. 22), that scripture was the *medium* through which he came to understand the prophecies of Jesus regarding His Person : "*When He was risen from the dead* . . . *His disciples believed the scripture, and the words which Jesus had spoken.*" And then John had quoted no other prophecies regarding His resurrection than that of ch. ii. ; he was not, therefore, obliged to make special allusion here to such prophecies.

II. *The Appearance to Mary Magdalene.*—Vv. 11–18.

Mary Magdalene has just been the messenger to the two chief disciples announcing the empty tomb ; she is to become to them and to all the others the first herald of the living Jesus.

Vv. 11–13. "*But Mary stood without at the sepulchre*[2] *weeping : and as she wept, she stooped down, and looked into the sepulchre, and seeth two angels*[3] *in white sitting, the one at the head, and the other at the feet, where the body of Jesus had lain. And they say unto her, Woman, why weepest thou ? She saith unto them, Because they have taken away my Lord, and I know not where they have laid Him.*"—Peter and John withdraw, the one meditating, the other already believing ; Mary remains and weeps. Jesus, adapting His conduct, as He always did, to the wants of each of His own, reveals Himself to this suffering, loving soul. There is nothing to prevent us from taking the partic. pres. καθεζομένους, *sitting*, in its strictly grammatical sense. She sees the two angels at the time of their appearance. This fact does not contradict the previous appearance of an angel to the women who had first visited the tomb. Angels are not immoveable and visible

---

[1] *Jésus Christ et les croyances messianiques de son temps*, p. 112.
[2] Instead of προς το μνημειον, A B E G H L M Δ Λ, 60 Mnn. read προς τω μνημειω, ℵ εν τω μνημειω (rejecting εξω with A Itrlerique Syr.).
[3] ℵ omits δυο before αγγελους.

after the fashion of stone statues.—Mary answers the question of the heavenly ambassadors as simply as if she had been conversing with human beings, so thoroughly is she preoccupied with a single idea: to recover her Master. Who would have invented a touch like this?

Vv. 14–16. *"And when she had thus said, she turned herself back, and saw Jesus standing, and knew not that it was Jesus. Jesus saith unto her, Woman, why weepest thou? whom seekest thou? She, supposing Him to be the gardener, saith unto Him, Sir, if thou have borne Him hence,*[1] *tell me where thou hast laid Him, and I will take Him away. Jesus saith unto her, Mary. She turned herself, and saith unto Him,*[2] *Rabboni; which is to say, Master."*—Mary, after bending for a little over the sepulchre, raises herself and turns round as if to seek Him of whom she is in quest. His transition from His former to His new life, without destroying the identity of the body of Jesus, had yet wrought a change in His whole Person: He appeared ἐν ἑτέρᾳ μορφῇ, says Mark (xvi. 12). His own who saw Him again had an experience something like that which passes with us when we meet a friend after a long separation; we need a longer or shorter time to recognise him, and the simplest manifestation in such a case is often sufficient to make the bandage fall from our eyes.—It has been asked what garments Jesus wore, and it has been supposed that He had borrowed the clothes of the gardener. Are this question and answer in keeping with the conditions of the new existence of the glorified Jesus?—The most personal thing in human manifestations is the sound of the voice; it is thus that Jesus makes Himself known to her. The tone which the name Mary takes in His mouth expresses all that she is to Him, and all that He is to her.—It appears from the word στραφεῖσα, *turning herself back*, that she had again fixed her eyes on the tomb. For she was agitated, and sought first on one side, then on the other. And now, at the sound of that well-known voice, trembling with joy to the very depths of her soul, she in turn puts all her being into the cry: *"My Master!"* and casts herself at His feet, seeking to clasp them,

---

[1] ℵ: τι συ τι ο βαστασας.
[2] ℵ B D L O X Δ Π, 7 Mnn. It^(plerique) Syr. Cop. read ιβραιστι after αυτω.

as is shown by ver. 17.—*Rabboni*, which occurs only here and in Mark x. 51, is a form of the word *Rabban*.—The ι is either the ι paragogic or the suffix *my*. In the second case, it must have gradually lost its signification, which explains why the evangelist does not translate it.

Vv. 17, 18. *"Jesus saith unto her, Touch me not; for I am not yet ascended to my Father:*[1] *but go to my brethren,*[1] *and say unto them, I ascend*[2] *unto my Father, and your Father, to my God, and your God. Mary Magdalene comes and tells*[3] *the disciples that she had seen the Lord, and that He had spoken these things unto her."*—If we put ourselves at the standpoint of chs. xiv.–xvi., the words of ver. 17 do not present the great difficulties which have been found in them. Jesus had said: *"Ye shall see me, because I go to my Father"* (xvi. 16), which meant that it would not be till after His ascension and from the midst of His Divine glory that He would re-form the tie which His death was about to sever. His appearances as the Risen One were not therefore intended to establish the new state of communion between them and Him, but to prepare for it, to render it possible by laying the foundation of faith in the hearts of His own. This thought explains the words: *" Touch me not."* "Ἅπτεσθαι denotes a touch intended not to hold the object (κρατεῖν), but to possess or enjoy it: *to attach oneself to*. " It is not yet the time for laying hold of me, as if my promise to return to you were already accomplished." According to Luke xxiv., Jesus in one of His appearances uses this remarkable expression: *"While I was yet with you."* He *is* no longer with them: He only appears to them; but soon He will be in them. Then they will have Him anew. The regimen μου, *me*, is placed before the verb, with a certain emphasis: " Me, as I am here before thee in my human individuality." In this sense, the motive assigned by Jesus: *"for I am not yet ascended . . .,"* is easily understood. " I have not yet reached the state by means of which I shall be able to live with you in the communion which I promised you." Jesus does not use the Aor. ἀνέβην, which would signify: " I have not yet *done*

---

[1] א B D It^aliq reject μου after πατερα, and א D μου after αδελφους.
[2] א adds ιδου before αναβαινω.
[3] א A B I X: αγγιλλουσα for απαγγιλλουσα.

the act of ascending." It is not an act which is in question, but *a state*. Hence the perfect ἀναβέβηκα: "I am not yet in the state of one who has ascended; I have not yet acquired that supreme position which is the condition of our mutual meeting." We can see by this denial of Jesus that the disciples considered His death as having already realized the promise which He had made to them of ascending to the Father. Thus the resurrection disappeared; for death became the ascension itself; and if He was to reappear, it must be not as the Risen One, but as the Glorified One descending from the bosom of the Father. For the notion of the resurrection there was substituted that of a Parousia. Such was undoubtedly the figurative sense which the disciples instinctively had given to the resurrection promises related by the Synoptics. The surprise which the resurrection caused them is therefore perfectly compatible with the historic reality of these promises. In opposition to all these ideas, Jesus declares that *He is not yet ascended*, but that now only *He is about to ascend*. The resurrection is the first stage of His glorification, of His return to the Father, which, far from being finished, *begins* that very day (pres. *I ascend*).

As with the instant of His death His resurrection began (xix. 34), so from the moment of the resurrection dates the beginning of His ascension. Instead, therefore, of luxuriating in this moment of possession, as if Jesus were really restored to her, Mary must rise and go to tell the disciples what is passing. "*But go . . .*" is opposed to the act of staying to enjoy that which is about to be taken from her (as from the two of Emmaus). The message with which Jesus charges her for His own thus signifies: "From the time that I shall be in my state of glory, I shall make you sharers in it, and then nothing shall separate you more from me." Hence the expressions: "*my brethren,*" and "*my Father and your Father . . .*" They bring out the indissoluble unity which shall exist between them and Him in the new state upon which He is just entering. They shall be before God exactly in the same position as Himself. Calvin and Hengstenberg here refer to Ps. xxii. 23, where the Messiah, rescued from His sufferings, exclaims: "*I will declare Thy name unto my brethren;*" comp. also Matt. xxviii. 10: "Go tell *my brethren.*" He goes *to prepare the place* (xiv. 2, 3), to make the heart of His Father and His God to be the heart of their Father and their God. Col. iii. 3 : " *Ye are dead, and your life is hid with Christ in God.*" Jesus does not say: *our Father, our God,* because God is not their Father, their God, in the sense in which He is His. The word *Father* describes filial intimacy; the word *God* complete dependence. These two features which have characterized the worship of Jesus and His entire life, while preserving in Him an exclusive character, will henceforth be reflected in the life of His own. Comp. Gal. iv. 6 : " *Because ye are sons, God hath sent forth the Spirit of the Son into your hearts, crying, Abba, Father !* "

The explanation which we have just given is almost that of Calvin,[1] and approximates very nearly to that of de Wette, Gerlach, and Luthardt. The principal divergent explanations are : 1st. That of Beza, Bengel, and Hofmann : "*Stay not* to touch me, but *haste thee,* go and tell . . ." But the following words : " *I am not yet ascended,*" present absolutely no sense. 2d. That of Lücke and Hilgenfeld : " Do not *worship* me ; for I have not yet entered into my *Divine glory* ($\mathring{a}\pi\tau\epsilon\sigma\theta\alpha\iota$ in the classical sense of $\mathring{a}\pi\tau\epsilon\sigma\theta\alpha\iota$ $\pi o\delta\hat{\omega}\nu$, $\gamma o\nu\acute{a}\tau\omega\nu$)." But eight days later Jesus accepts the worship of Thomas. 3d. That of Neander : " Do not *hold* me thus ; I am not disposed to *escape* from thee." For this meaning $\kappa\rho\acute{a}\tau\epsilon\iota$ would be needed rather than $\mathring{a}\pi\tau o\upsilon$, and the explanation : "*I am not yet ascended,*" does not give a clear sense. 4th. That of Paulus, Schleiermacher, and Olshausen : " My body is still suffering from its wounds," or " is yet in a state of transformation ; do not *touch* it." But that very evening Jesus invites His disciples to touch Him (Luke xxiv. 39). 5th. That of Meyer : " Do not touch me thus to be assured that I am *corporeally* present; I have not yet returned to the state of pure spirit." But, in the Bible view, Jesus glorified does not become pure spirit. 6th. That of Baur : " Do not detain me ; for at this very moment I rise to my Father." Baur

---

[1] The meaning of these words is, that the condition of His resurrection will not be at all full or perfect until He is seated at His Father's right hand, and so that the women do wrong in that, contenting themselves merely with the half of His resurrection, they desire to have Him present in the world.

thinks that, according to our Gospel, the ascension must be placed on this very day, so that the following appearance, vv. 19–23, is posterior to that event. But there was no reason in that case to begin with saying: *"I am not ascended."* It would be necessary to say immediately: *"for I am ascending."* And how could the ascension have taken place that day, when in the appearance of the evening, and in that which took place eight days after, Jesus convinces His disciples of His sensible presence in the midst of them? When the glorified Saviour appears to Paul, He does not say to him: Touch me! Jesus wishes, therefore, to raise the thoughts of Mary and His disciples from this passing reappearance, which is only a means, to the permanent spiritual communion which is the end, and of which His perfect elevation to the Father is the yet uncompleted condition.— This warning applies to all the visits which shall follow, and is intended to console His own for the disappearances which terminate them.

The pres. *she comes* (ver. 18) expresses in all its vividness the surprise produced among the disciples by Mary's arrival and message.—The identity of this appearance with that related by Matthew appears from the words: "*Touch me not,*" compared with these: "They held Him by the feet . . .;" "*Go thou and tell my brethren,*" comp. with these: "*Go ye and tell my brethren.*" But what unprejudiced man could hold, with some of our critics,[1] that the scene in John is a poetical amplification of the short narrative of Matthew enlarged with some details from Mark and Luke? Is it not plain, on the contrary, that Matthew's account is only a vague and imperfect summary of tradition, while John's description reproduces the scene in all its primitive freshness and vividness?

III. *The First Appearance to the Disciples.*—Vv. 19–23.

The Lord proceeds gradually in His self-revelation. The appearance to Mary Magdalene, prepared for by that of the angels, prepares in its turn, by the message confided to her for

---

[1] Keim for example, iii. p. 558: "The evangelist of Christian mysticism borrows from Matthew the visit of Mary Magdalene to the sepulchre, and the message to the disciples . . ."

the disciples, for the appearing of Jesus in the midst of them. Three manifestations of the Risen One took place during the second half of that day, the appearance to the two disciples of Emmaus, that which was granted to St. Peter (Luke xxiv. 13-32, 34; Mark xvi. 12, 13), and that the account of which we are about to consider. This one must be identical with those related by Luke (xxiv. 36 et seq.) and Mark (xvi. 14); it took place in the evening, according to all the accounts.

Vv. 19, 20. "*Then the same day at evening, being the first day of the week, when the doors were shut where the disciples were*[1] *for fear of the Jews, came Jesus and stood in the midst, and saith unto them, Peace be unto you. And when He had so said, He showed unto them His hands and His side.*[2] *Then were the disciples glad, when they saw the Lord.*"—The phrase: "*the doors were shut*," can only be meant to indicate the miraculous way in which Jesus entered. Strauss goes the length of declaring, in opposition to Schleiermacher, that it needs a veritable induration against the real sense of the Gospel text to maintain the contrary. Calvin and M. de Pressensé suppose that the doors opened miraculously (comp. Acts xii. 10). Yet the natural sense of the expression is that the doors were and *remained* closed, and that Jesus *appeared* rather than entered. In truth, the body of Jesus was still that which had served Him as the organ of His activity during His life (ver. 20); but, as is proved by His walking on the waters, this body before His death was subject to the power of the Spirit (vi. 16-21); and now it was still more assimilated to the nature of the spiritual or glorified body (1 Cor. xv. 44). Now the characteristic of the latter is its being subject to the free disposition of the Spirit. Hence the word ἔστη, which occurs also in Luke's narrative: "*He stood there*," without any one having seen Him enter. We can understand the terror of the disciples and their supposition: it is *a spirit* (Luke xxiv. 37). To this mode of appearing there correspond the sudden disappearings (Luke xxiv. 31: ἄφαντος ἐγένετο).—The salutation of Jesus is the same in Luke and John: "*Peace be unto you.*" It is the ordinary Jewish form,

---

[1] T. R. adds συνηγμενοι, omitted in א A B D I Λ, 6 Mnn. It*alliq* Syr.

[2] א A B D I: τας χειρας και την πλευραν αυτοις; A L: και τας χειρας.

but serving here to express an entirely new thought. Jesus invites His disciples to open their hearts to the peace which He has just secured for them by His redeeming work, and which He brings them as the Risen One. All the painful emotions through which they have passed, the fear which they still feel, all their former and present trouble, must give place to complete serenity in the certainty that God is for them; comp. Eph. ii. 17: "*He came and preached peace.*"—The words: "*When He had so said*" (ver. 20), are intended to bring out the relation between this prayer and the following act. To convince them of the bodily reality of His appearance is to give them, by the greatest of miracles, the transcendent proof of Divine good-will toward their Master and toward themselves. Besides, from the moment they have satisfied themselves of the identity of His Person, their terror is changed not only into peace, but into joy.

Vv. 21-23. "*Then said Jesus*[1] *to them again, Peace be unto you: as my Father hath sent me, even so send*[2] *I you. And when He had said this, He breathed on them, and saith unto them, Receive ye* [*the*] *Holy Spirit. Whosesoever*[3] *sins ye remit, they are remitted*[4] *unto them; and whosoever sins ye retain, they are retained.*"—It is not only in regard to their past and to them as believers that Jesus wishes to communicate peace; it is also in view of their future and of their apostolic calling that He assures them of it. Hence the repetition of the prayer: "*Peace be unto you.*" They must face their ministry with that peace of reconciliation which they are to preach to the world (2 Cor. v. 20). On the foundation of the work accomplished by Him, Jesus confers on them the *office* (ver. 21*b*), then communicates to them the *gift* of the ministry, in so far as He is able to do so in His present position (ver. 22); and finally He reveals to them the greatness of the work which they have to accomplish (ver. 23).

Strictly speaking, there is only one mission from heaven to earth, that of Jesus. He is *the Apostle* (Heb. iii. 1). That of

---

[1] T. R. reads Ιησους before παλιν, which is omitted by ℵ D L O X It^plerique Vg. Cop.
[2] Instead of πιμπω, ℵ : πιμψω; D L O : αποστιλλω.
[3] Instead of τινων, B It^aliq : τινος.
[4] The Mss. are divided between αφιωνται, in T. R. with 11 Mjj. (E G I, etc.), and αφιωνται (A D L O X).

the disciples is embraced in His, and completes its realization. Hence it comes that Jesus, when speaking of Himself, uses the most solemn term ἀπέσταλκε: His is an *embassy;* while in passing to them He makes use of the simpler term πέμπω: they are *envoys.*

As there is but one mission, that of Jesus, so there is but one *power,* that of the Holy Spirit whom Jesus communicates. The words: "*when He had so said,*" serve, like ver. 20, to connect the following act closely with the preceding words. After conferring the office, Jesus conveys the gift. There are two extreme opinions as to the value of the act described in this verse. According to Chrysostom, Grotius, and Tholuck, it is simply a symbol, a promise. But is this meaning compatible with the imper. λάβετε, *receive?* There would be needed: *ye shall receive.* This phrase implies an actual communication. On the other hand, Baur alleges that here is Pentecost itself, so far as it was known to the evangelist. But the absence of the article before πνεῦμα ἅγιον could not well be explained in this sense. The natural meaning of the words of Jesus is: "Receive an effusion of the Spirit." What Jesus gives them is not a simple promise, but neither is it the fulness of the Spirit; it is an earnest. Raised Himself to a degree of higher life, He hastes to make them sharers in it as far as that is possible. This communication is to the resurrection what Pentecost will be to the ascension. As by Pentecost He will initiate them into His ascension, so by breathing on them now He associates them with His life as the Risen One. Some commentators, M. Reuss for example, see here an allusion to Gen. ii. 7: "*The Lord breathed into his nostrils the breath of life.*" Jesus would thus stand forth as the author of the new spiritual creation which is to sanctify and consummate the natural creation. But perhaps His thought is rather related to the future than to the past, and He means: "When the promised day shall come on which you shall feel the mysterious breathing, ye shall recognise in that breath of the Spirit the gift of your glorified Master." What was the immediate fruit of that preparatory communication, that anticipatory Pentecost? Luke informs us when he says (xxiv. 45): "*Then opened He their understanding, that might understand the Scriptures.*" The meaning of the whole theocratic work and word was unveiled to them. It may be said that the Gospel of St. Matthew is the fruit of this first inspiration.

The commission and the gift point to a work to be realized. This work is presented in ver. 23 in all its grandeur: it is the salvation, or, if not, the condemnation of humanity. Henceforth men will no more have to do, as in the Old Testament, with a provisional pardon or a rejection which may be revoked. With Pentecost, the world enters into the domain of absolute and immoveable realities. It has been sought to limit the meaning of the words used by Jesus in this verse to the *offer* or *declaration* of pardon, as well as to the *threatening* of damnation by the preaching of the Gospel. But the words of which He makes use involve positive action, real efficacy. We only need to remember that the ministry of the word (ver. 21) is carried out in the power of the Spirit (ver. 22). It is this Divine force which through its human organ *looses* or *binds*, removes or seals sin. Peter and Paul did not merely speak to the world of salvation or damnation. They consummated the double work of the salvation of the Gentiles and the rejection of the Jews, and thus presented to the Church the most striking example of the fulfilment of these words. Comp. Acts x. 34 et seq., xiii. 45 et seq., xxviii. 25 et seq. The pres. ἀφίενται (literally, *are pardoned*) indicates a present effect; the perf. ἀφέωνται, found in several Alexandrines, would signify: "are and remain pardoned." This perfect has probably been introduced to render this proposition symmetrical with the following (κεκράτηνται). The copyists did not understand that, in the former case, a *deed* is in question, which is accomplished at the instant when the Divine act emancipates the believer; while, in the second, Jesus is speaking of a *state* which is the consequence of unbelief itself, and which continues. The order of the two propositions indicates that the first of those two effects is the true object of the mission, and that the second is not destined to be realized save in those cases in which the first fails.

IV. *The Second Appearance to the Disciples.*—Vv. 24–29.

A last leaven of unbelief remained still in the circle of the

Twelve. It is rooted out, and the development of faith reaches its goal in all the future witnesses of the Christ.

Vv. 24, 25. "*But Thomas, one of the Twelve, called Didymus, was not with them when*[1] *Jesus came. When therefore*[1] *the other disciples said unto him, We have seen the Lord, he said unto them, Except I shall see in His hands the print*[2] *of the nails, and thrust my hand into His side, I will not believe.*"—On δίδυμος, *twin*, see xi. 16. We have learned to know Thomas from xi. 16 and xiv. 5; the impression made on him by his Master's death does not surprise us. It could not fail to be that of deep discouragement. "I told Him so," this no doubt was what he kept repeating to himself. His absence on that first day could not be without relation to that feeling of bitterness, and this is confirmed by the manner in which he receives the testimony of his brethren. There is tenacity even in the form of his utterance, especially in the deliberate repetition of his phrases. And so we need not hold, with Tischendorf, the reading τόπον, *the place*, instead of the second τύπον, *the print;* this reading takes away precisely from the denial of the disciple its marked character of obstinacy. Thomas does not speak of the feet; this is perfectly simple in the circumstances, and it is ridiculous to conclude from it, as some commentators do, that the feet were not nailed.

Vv. 26, 27. "*And after eight days again His disciples were within, and Thomas with them: Jesus came, the doors being shut, and stood in the midst, and said, Peace be unto you. Then saith He to Thomas, Reach hither thy finger, and behold my hands; and reach hither thy hand, and thrust it into my side: and become not faithless, but believing.*"—The disciples spent the whole Passover week at Jerusalem; that was natural. At the utmost stretch, they might have set out for Galilee on the Sunday which followed the second Saturday of the feast. What was it that detained them still on that day? Is it not allowable to suppose that it was the fear of abandoning Thomas, and of losing him if they left him behind in the state of mind in which he had passed the

---

[1] ℵ adds ουν after οτι, and rejects it in ver. 25 after ελεγον.

[2] A I It^{plerique} Vg. Syr. Or. read τοπον (*the place*) instead of τυπον, and ℵ: εις την χυραν (sic) αυτου (*except I put my finger into His hand, and except I put my hand into His side*).

week?—In His salutation Jesus includes this disciple also; nay, it is to him that He addresses it specially, for he is the only one who does not yet enjoy the peace which faith gives. —The almost literal reproduction of the disciple's rash words is intended to make him blush at the grossness and carnality of such exactions.—By the expression: "*become not*," Jesus gives him to understand that he is now at the critical point at which the two routes diverge: that of decided unbelief, and that of perfect faith.

Vv. 28, 29. "*Thomas answered*[1] *and said unto Him, My Lord and my God. Jesus saith*[2] *unto him, Because thou hast seen me,*[3] *thou hast believed: blessed are they that have not seen,*[4] *and yet have believed.*"—What produces so profound an impression on Thomas is not merely the conviction of the reality of the resurrection, but also the proof of omniscience which the Lord gives him by repeating the words which he thought he had uttered in His absence. And it is this immediate contact at once with the Divine attribute of omniscience, and with victory over death, which inspires him with the cry of adoration which goes forth from his heart. This scene recalls that of Nathanael (ch. i.). As in the case of that disciple, the light shines at this supreme moment with sudden splendour to the very depths of Thomas' soul; and by one of those reactions frequent in the moral life, he rises at a single bound from the lowest depths of faith to its very pinnacle, and proclaims the divinity of his Master in a more categorical form than had ever passed from the lips of any of his colleagues. The last becomes for the time the first, and the faith of the apostles, as professed by Thomas, attains at length to the full height of the Divine truth formulated by the prologue. It is in vain for Theodore of Mopsuestia and others to attempt to apply to God, and not to Jesus, Thomas' cry of adoration. In that case, it should not be εἶπεν αὐτῷ, "*he said to Him;*" and the word *my Lord* can only refer to Jesus. To this the

---

[1] 7 Mjj. (א B C D I, etc.) It^plerique reject και before απεκριθη.
[2] Instead of λεγει, א: ειπεν δε.
[3] All the Mjj. 150 Mnn. It. Syr. reject Θωμα after εωρακας με. Instead of it, א reads και.
[4] א Syr. read με after ιδοντες.

monotheism of Thomas is objected. But it is for the very reason that the disciple understands that henceforth he bears toward Jesus a feeling which transcends all that can be accorded to a creature, that he is forced by his very monotheism to place this being in the heart of Deity.—The objective validity of this feeling in Thomas is attested by the manner in which Jesus receives the expression of it. The Lord does not repress this outburst, like the angel of the Apocalypse, who says to John: "*Worship God.*" He answers, on the contrary: "*Thou hast believed.*" In an article of the *Lien* (May 1869), it is objected that this approving answer relates not to the exclamation: "*my God,*" but to his faith in the fact of the resurrection. But the two convictions of the resurrection of Jesus and of His Divine character are absolutely confounded in the impression of Thomas: the one is involved in the other; and it is this faith with its full object, as Thomas has just expressed it, which Jesus hails. Otherwise he could easily have removed the alloy while preserving the pure gold.

The perf. πεπίστευκας does not signify merely: Thou hast performed an act of faith, but: Thou art henceforth *in possession* of complete faith. These words, like those of Jesus to Nathanael, i. 50, and to the disciples, xvi. 31, may be taken as an affirmation. But Meyer observes, not without reason, that the side of rebuke emphasized by the words: "*because thou hast seen,*" comes out better with the interrogative form. In the last words Jesus describes the entirely new character of the era which is beginning, the era of a faith which shall have to content itself with the apostolic testimony, without claiming, like Thomas, to check it with its own eyes. The words thus close the history of the development of faith in the apostles, while opening the history of the Church. Baur alleges that Jesus is here contrasting with faith in *external facts* that which seeks its contents only in itself, in the *idea* of which it is henceforth fully conscious. It is easy to see that vv. 30 and 31 are entirely opposed to this view. And so Baur declares them interpolated, though they are not wanting in any document. The contrast which Jesus indicates is that between a faith which, to accept the miraculous fact, insists on *seeing* it, and a faith which consents to accept it on the foundation of *testimony*. In the first way, faith would be possible for the world only on condition ot miracles being renewed unceasingly, and appearances of Jesus being repeated to every individual. Such was not to be the course of God's operation on the earth, and hence Jesus calls those blessed who shall believe by the solitary means of that faith to which Thomas insisted on adding the other.—The Aorist participles ἰδόντες, πιστεύσαντες, are taken from the standpoint of one who places himself at the goal of the development of the Church, and casts his eyes backwards on the way in which all the glorified have attained to faith, and thereby to life (ver. 31).

These words of Jesus, which indicate the goal of the development of faith in the apostolic circle, and the point of departure for the history of faith on the earth, are the normal conclusion of a Gospel like John's, which rests on this thought: the manifestation of the *glory of Jesus* producing on the one hand *unbelief*, which separates from God, and on the other *faith*, which unites to Him.

Of the Resurrection of Jesus.

Here, as Strauss says, is "the decisive point at which the naturalistic school must retract all its previous assertions, or succeed in explaining faith in the resurrection without bringing in a corresponding miraculous fact."[1] It is no longer possible to have recourse to the customary expedients, "the secret forces of spontaneity," "the contact of an exquisite person," etc. For no human being took part in the resurrection of Jesus. If He really left the tomb after being laid there dead, it was indubitably Divine power which broke forth in this central fact of history; and, as Peter says, "GOD hath raised up Jesus." "*What, do you think it impossible that God should raise the dead?*" asked St. Paul of King Agrippa and the Governor Festus.—Yes; for it is contrary to the laws of nature.—But if the laws of nature were in this case the very element ordering the fact which you deny in their name? Does not the same natural law, in virtue of which sin separates from God and kills, require that

[1] *Das Leben Jesu*, 1864, p. 288.

holiness should unite to God and vivify? Is not this moral effect as necessary as the physical effect of wholesome nourishment to strengthen the body, or of a poisoned drink to destroy it? If Jesus was free from all sin, and supported Himself here below only on holiness, if He *lived on God* (John vi. 57), is not life the crown which should await this bold, this unequalled conqueror at the close of His career? And if, to fulfil the law which condemns sinful humanity, He gives Himself up voluntarily to death, will not this blow, falling upon a nature perfectly sound, both morally and physically, and reaching it only from without, meet,—will it not awake even, in this exceptional organism powers of reaction which are also exceptional, and from which Divine power will draw forth life as legitimately and necessarily as death is evolved from the action of sin? Certain symptoms in the body of Jesus betrayed, as we have seen, an unexampled vital reaction at the moment when dissolution commences in every other body. And that loud final cry with which He gave up His life and left it, not to be wrung from Him like the sinner, is another evidence, at once physical and moral, of an exceptional state fitted for the triumph of life over death, strength over weakness.

In these circumstances, then, the laws of physical and moral nature, far from protesting against the resurrection of Jesus, imperiously demand it.

Is it possible? If it is morally necessary, it must be possible, unless we are to affirm an irreconcilable dualism between *being* and *virtue*, which would be the destruction of monotheism. The essence of being, and consequently also of matter, is will; and as the law of the Divine will is virtue, it cannot be allowed that any part of being whatever escapes from the law of virtue. The will which made matter appear in relation to free being did not abdicate its power in relation to it, but reserved to itself the means of always ruling it and making it subserve the education and final destiny of free being. "Every historian," says Strauss, "should possess philosophy enough to be able to deny miracles here as well as elsewhere." "Every true philosopher," we shall reply, "should be sufficiently initiated into the secrets of history to understand the possibility of a miracle here as elsewhere."

There are four ways of getting rid of the miracle of the resurrection of Jesus Christ:—

1st. The oldest and simplest is to suppose a fraud on the part of the apostles, they in some way or other making the body of Jesus disappear (Matt. xxviii. 12–15). This is the plan to which the Jews who devised it had recourse, and following them Celsus, the *Wolfenbüttel Fragments*, and others. It is positively rejected by Strauss. A premeditated deception is indeed incompatible with the discouragement into which the disciples were plunged after the death of Jesus, and with the triumphant faith which they drew during their whole ministry from the conviction of their Master's resurrection.

2d. The second plan consists in asserting that Jesus was not entirely dead when He was laid in the tomb, and that the vital force was reawakened by the influence of the spices and of the coolness of the sepulchre. Paulus and Schleiermacher are the chief defenders of this hypothesis. From this point of view, the appearances of Jesus are real, but natural facts. Strauss has disposed of this hypothesis also. How, indeed, could Jesus appear in a room the doors of which were closed? How, after a punishment like that of the cross, could He make a long journey on foot with the disciples of Emmaus, to disappear suddenly thereafter, and reappear in the evening at Jerusalem? How, some days later, could He undertake the journey to Galilee? But above all, how could a half-dead being who had dragged Himself miserably from the tomb, whose life depended on every sort of care and nursing, and who after some time could not fail to succumb to His sufferings, have been able to produce on His disciples the impression of a conqueror of the grave, a Prince of life? How could such a sight have transformed their sadness into enthusiasm, their confidence into adoration? Here is puzzle which no serious historian will ever explain.

3d. The third and boldest plan is to acknowledge that the disciples believed in the resurrection, that without this faith the founding of the Christian Church was an impossibility, but to explain this faith by a purely mental phenomenon, a series of hallucinations in the holy women and in the disciples. "No one in reality," says Strauss,[1] "was a witness of the fact of the resurrection." Besides, none of our Gospels being authentic, we have not a single directly apostolic testimony. And then the accounts of the different appearances contradict one another in our Gospels. Finally, the notion of the risen body of Jesus presents contradictory characteristics; on the one hand it is raised above the laws of space and gravity, and on the other it can assimilate honey and fish. It must therefore be held that, in consequence of a morbid disposition of Mary Magdalene, and of a state of exaltation produced in the disciples by their return to Galilee, in the places where they had lived with Jesus, His memory reawoke in their hearts with extraordinary vividness, and became transformed into visions. They believed they saw Him, heard Him, touched Him; and this illusion produced the same moral effect on them as would have been produced by the objective fact.—Of course the date of the *third day*, indicated by the narratives, is not historical; we are to regard it only as a misapplication of a proverbial phrase and of some Scripture expressions. As to the body of Jesus, it was cast on the dunghill like those of the two malefactors; and when, six weeks later, at Pentecost, Peter for the first time publicly proclaimed the resurrection, it was impossible to use it to undeceive the disciples and annul the powerful effect of their testimony.—Such is the explanation of Strauss, shared in its leading features by Baur and M. Renan.

That the *fact* of the resurrection had no immediate witness is certain; but if the appearances of the Risen One are established, this proves nothing against the fact itself.—If even it were true that we are not possessed of any authentic Gospel, we should not be without all direct apostolic testimony to it. Does not the Apocalypse, in which Strauss recognises the work of John, put into the mouth of the glorified Jesus the following words: "*I was dead, and, behold, I am alive. . . . I have the keys of hell and of death*" (i. 18); "*These things saith He who was dead and is alive*" (ii. 8)? Besides, Strauss acknowledges that the apostolic preaching which founded the Church implies faith in the resurrection. The passage 1 Cor. xv. 1–11 would prove it unanswerably; for it ranks the

[1] *Das Leben Jesu*, 1864, p. 602 et seq., pp. 312, 316 et seq., and elsewhere.

testimony of the Twelve to this fact among the fundamental points of tradition proceeding from their lips, and that at a time when Peter, John, and the most of the Twelve were yet alive and preaching (1 Cor. ix. 5).—Divergences of detail between the Gospel narratives serve only to bring into brighter light their substantial unanimity, and, as Reuss says (*Histoire évangélique*, p. 698), to prove that the faith of the Church on this point is not "the product of an arbitrary and conventional combination;" for in this case, certainly, "men would have come to a uniform and stereotyped report." The differences are easily explained, if account is taken of the special circumstances which determined the mode of each of our Gospel narratives. Matthew's, agreeably to the character of his whole narrative, is summary as to its history, and aims solely at the proclamation of the Messiah and the royal instructions addressed by Jesus to the Twelve in His last discourse (Matt. xxviii. 18-20). These words are the counterpart of the first word of the book (i. 1): "*Jesus the Christ, the son of David, the son of Abraham.*" They show the programme drawn in this preface as realized: Jesus as the Jewish Messiah, and at the same time as the Saviour of all the families of the earth. As such, Jesus charges His apostles to make the conquest of the world in His name, by preaching and baptism. The fact of the resurrection is established by the appearing; this is all that was needed in this narrative. The historical delineation is only the frame designed to contain the teaching on which the mission is based. Luke's narrative has also in this last part a very abridged character, as is shown by the words: "*And He saith unto them*," frequently repeated without any indication of the precise situation, which is contrary to all Luke's antecedents. The reason of this fact, different from that which concerns Matthew, is, that the author proposed to give all historic details in opening the second volume of his work, the Book of Acts. As to Mark's Gospel, the conclusion of his treatise is wanting.—The contradictions which are pointed out between the different characteristics of the risen body of Jesus fall to the ground if account is taken of the words of Jesus Himself: "*I ascend*," ἀναβαίνω (xx. 17). It is a transition time, during which our Lord's body in certain respects still belongs to the present order of things, and yet already possesses, in a certain measure, the qualities of the *spiritual body;* that is to say, a body which has as its principle of life not a human soul merely, but the Spirit (1 Cor. xv. 44, 45). We must acknowledge, besides, the mystery which such a state presents, a mystery on which we have no experimental datum.

The hypothesis of Strauss himself is beset with difficulties otherwise insurmountable.[1] 1. The first question, supposing a hallucination on the disciples' part, is, What became of *the Lord's body?* "It was cast to the dunghill," says Strauss, or, as others express themselves, friends and enemies left it neglected. But the fact is, that our biblical accounts are unanimous in relating that it remained in the hands of friends of Jesus, and the Roman law is perfectly in keeping with this mode of procedure. If it is so, the supposition of hallucinations becomes impossible; they must have vanished in presence of the dead body. We should thus have to return to the hypothesis of fraud, which Strauss himself had so vigorously set aside. But if it is alleged, despite the unanimity of the records, that the body remained in the hands of the enemies of Jesus, how did they not use it to bring those poor misguided minds to reason? For if it was at Pentecost that Peter preached for the first time, it was nevertheless from the *third* day that the conviction of the resurrection sprang up in the disciples. This date is established not only by the four records, which diverge on so many other points, but also by the positive declaration of Paul, 1 Cor. xv. 4. So he had learned the fact from the lips of Peter and James (Gal. i. 18, 19). To escape this date, and to endeavour to form a gulf between the faith of the disciples and the terrible instrument of conviction deposited so near them at Jerusalem, Strauss makes them flee to Galilee on the day of the death or the day after, and there give themselves up to the dreams of their imagination. But this is a pure romance. According to all the accounts, the first appearances took place at Jerusalem, and that even according to Matthew, the most *Galilean* of the evangelists;

[1] Some of them have been vigorously exposed by Keim (iii. pp. 594-602), though there is an unmistakeable desire in this critic not to close this retreat against himself absolutely, if his present position (see below) should become scientifically untenable.

comp. xxviii. 1-10. If so, the disappearance of the body can only be explained by the voluntary leaving of His tomb by Jesus, and the faith of the disciples only by this mode of disappearance.

2. The idea of a hallucination is incompatible with the disciples' *state of mind*. None of them expected the return of the body to life. The women repaired to the sepulchre to embalm it. The disciples shared their feeling. Now, hallucination can only be the fruit of expectation, the child of desire. If the disciples expected anything, as we have seen, it was the heavenly reappearance of Jesus glorified. It is with this meaning that the two of Emmaus say: "*And this is now the third day*" (Luke xxiv. 21); and the thief: "*Remember me when Thou comest into Thy kingdom*" (xxiii. 42). Such, without doubt, is the application which the disciples had sought to give to the promises of Jesus in relation to His resurrection. As to the return of His body to a terrestrial existence, no one had a glimpse of it. They expected the Parousia, not the resurrection. Now, in this disposition of mind, how would they have interpreted simple hallucinations as bodily appearances? They would rather have done the very reverse, that is to say, interpreted real appearances as simple spiritual visions. And is not this what they really do when they believe that they see in Jesus who has appeared a pure *spirit*, and when Jesus endeavours to convince them of the contrary, and rebukes them on this point for their unbelief? (Matt. xxviii. 17; Mark xvi. 11-14; Luke xxiv. 25, 26, 37, 38, 42, 43; John xx. 20, 27.)

3. If there was nothing in question but simple subjective visions, it would be necessary to hold a real contagion, a nervous epidemic, which, originating with one or two of the faithful, Mary Magdalene and Peter, had gradually spread to the whole community, and finally issued in the most inconceivable paroxysm, in a hallucination not only of two or eleven, but of five hundred persons simultaneously (1 Cor. xv. 6). This supposition is improbable enough in itself, and Keim rightly meets it by pointing to the calm self-possession, the thoroughly practical energy of will, all the signs, in fine, of a perfectly sound intellectual and moral disposition, which characterized the founders of the early Church, and which are

incompatible with a state of visionary and morbid excitement. We could understand a time of intoxication being succeeded by coolness. But the simultaneousness of the two opposite states is morally impossible.

4. The very *nature of the appearances* is irreconcilable with the idea of purely subjective visions. If the object contemplated were some luminous appearance floating between heaven and earth, and soon vanishing into the azure of the sky, one might be forced to explain it by a hallucination, though it would be difficult to understand how it could be common to various persons. But we have to do with a personage who shows Himself very near, who invites men to touch Him, who gives distinct orders to gather, for example, on a mountain which is named, to baptize the nations, to preach the gospel to every human creature, to remain from that day forward at Jerusalem, etc., who has detailed conversations with the two of Emmaus, with Thomas, Peter, etc. Here we have a series of instructions and promises which, though scattered through the four records, form a whole which has admirable appropriateness and gradation.[1] Hallucination is not compatible with features so particular and precise. It is absolutely necessary to charge the narratives with being legendary, and even fictitious. But what, then, are we to say of Paul, who, during the lifetime of the apostles, alludes to them in the most express manner? (1 Cor. xv.)

5. But the last and greatest difficulty is that which Keim first brought out prominently: *the sudden end* of those alleged visions. At the end of a few weeks,—after eight or nine appearances,[2] which Paul, following oral tradition, counts, so to speak, on his fingers, and to which the narratives of our evangelists perfectly correspond,—on a well-marked day which the Church designates by the name of the Ascension, the excitement all at once calms down. Those 500 visionaries have suddenly returned to coolness. The Montanist excitement,

---

[1] Comp. the fine development of this remark in Gess, *Christi Zeugniss*, etc., pp. 198-204.

[2] Four on the first day (Mary Magdalene, the two of Emmaus, Peter, and the eleven); one eight days after (Thomas); three during the following weeks (on the shore of the lake of Gennesaret; on the mountain in Galilee, probably the same as that mentioned by Paul to the 500; and James); the last (ascension).

though much less creative, lasted a whole half-century. . . . Here, at the end of six weeks, everything returns to order. For it is evident that the visions of Peter and Paul in the sequel of the Acts—except that on the way to Damascus, which fills a place by itself—do not belong to the same category; they have no relation to the earthly existence of Jesus. They are not signs of His victory over death, but manifestations proceeding from the midst of His heavenly glory. As to the appearance of the Risen One, it is as if a charm had been broken. They take end for ever. The fact is incomprehensible, unless an external fact controlled both those few strictly-counted manifestations and their sudden cessation.—The hypothesis of visions is therefore as untenable as the preceding. M. Reuss rightly says: "Recourse to a visionary illusion is impossible, in view of the universality and firmness of the convictions within the Church" (p. 701).

4th. *Keim* has advanced another explanation already proposed by *Weisse* and defended by *Fichte* (the son): The appearances of the Risen One are true and real *manifestations of Jesus, as glorified Spirit*, to *the spirit* of the disciples. The objectivity which the preceding explanation denied to the appearances is granted to them in this, which at the same time accounts more easily for the small number of those miraculous facts, and for their prompt and abrupt cessation.— It may be said that as the apostles, in their expectations, substituted the Parousia for the resurrection, Keim's hypothesis identifies the resurrection with Pentecost. For what is the work of the Spirit, except the spiritual revelation of Jesus glorified to the hearts of believers? There is here a first step in the way of return to the explanation which the Church has always given of the fact. But this step is not enough, and that for the following reasons : 1st. This hypothesis does not explain any better than the preceding the disappearance of the body of Jesus and the empty tomb. 2d. What are we to think of Jesus, who, being *pure spirit*, ate before His disciples and called them to feel Him with their hands, to prove to them that He was not pure spirit; of Jesus, who, being *pure spirit*, rebukes them for their unbelief, which leads them to think that they have to do with a pure spirit ! 3d. How could the disciples, so little expecting a resurrection properly so called, have come to substitute for those purely spiritual visions the idea of bodily appearances? Keim's hypothesis succumbs to these insoluble contradictions.—We shall take up the two theatres of the appearances (Judea and Galilee) when we come to deal with the fact related in the following chapter.

Strauss had the good sense to acknowledge, that without the faith of the apostles in the resurrection of Jesus the Church would never have been born. We think we may add with no less truth, that without the *fact* of the resurrection, the *faith* of the apostles in that event would never have been born.

THE CONCLUSION.

XX. 30, 31.

THE evangelist here closes his narrative; for he tells his reader of the way in which he has proceeded in composing it (ver. 30), and of the aim of his work (ver. 31).

How are we to explain this so abrupt termination? If his aim had been to write *the history of Jesus*, could he rationally close his narrative with the conversation between Jesus and Thomas? Evidently not; this termination has no meaning except in so far as this conversation, with the exclamation in which it ends and the declaration of Jesus which follows it, is in close and essential connection with the purpose which has prevailed throughout the whole narrative—with the very *idea of the book*. This cannot be understood unless we acknowledge that the author's purpose was to describe *the development of the disciples' faith and of his own*. It is obvious in this case that the exclamation in which Thomas at length pays homage not only to the Messiahship, but to the personal divinity of Jesus, is the normal close of such a work, as the first testimony of John the Baptist relative to the Person of Jesus, and which resulted in the visit paid to the Lord by John and Andrew, was from this standpoint its equally normal commencement. The *birth* of faith was the starting-point of the narrative, the *consummation* of faith must be its close.

We need not therefore wonder at not finding in such a Gospel the account of the *ascension*, any more than at not finding that of the *baptism* of Jesus. Both of these events lie beyond the limits which the author has marked out for himself, the one on this side, the other on that. And it is easily seen how unfounded are the consequences which have been drawn from this silence by an unwise criticism, whether in the way of disputing the author's faith in these events, or the reality of the facts themselves.[1] If John believes in the reality of the bodily resurrection of Jesus,—and the preceding chapter leaves no doubt on this head,—and if he cannot have thought that this raised body was anew subjected to death, there remains only one possibility, namely, that he ascribed to it as its mode of departure the ascension, as this was held by the whole Church. This is further proved by the words which he puts into the mouth of Jesus, vi. 62 and xx. 17. And this would be proved if need were by his very silence, which excludes every other supposition.—The author's declaration about his *method* (ver. 30) and about his *aim* (ver. 31) is in harmony with this view.

Vv. 30, 31. "*And many other signs truly did Jesus in the presence of His disciples,*[2] *which are not written in this book: but these are written, that ye might believe*[3] *that Jesus is the Christ, the Son of God; and*[4] *that believing ye might have life through His name.*"—It is not a complete picture of what he has seen and heard that John meant to draw. From the mass of facts which he acknowledges to be true, and part of which already form the subject of other works than his, he has set himself to make a selection appropriate to the object which he has in view.—The particle μὲν οὖν, *it is true*, might be paraphrased thus: "There may be wonder, no doubt, that from a life so rich as that of Jesus I have related only so small a number of facts. But these suffice for the end which I have had in view." How, with this declaration of the author before us, can serious critics argue thus: John omits—therefore he denies or knows not!

The facts which he has omitted differ from those which he has adopted in his narrative not only as to *quantity* (πολλά, *in great number*), but also as to *quality* (ἄλλα, *other*). Consequently, if he has not given specimens of all the kinds of miracles,—if, for example, he has not related cures of lepers or of possessed persons, it will be positively in opposition to his intention to conclude from this silence that he meant thereby

---

[1] Keim, iii. p. 616: "John knows nothing of a visible ascension, though Jesus speaks once of it in one of His sayings (vi. 62)."
[2] Αυτου is omitted by A B E K S Δ, 12 Mnn.
[3] א B : πιστευητε instead of πιστευητε.
[4] א omits και before ινα, and with C D L T^d, 12 Mnn. It^{aliq}, adds αιωνιον to ζωην.

to deny them.—According to many commentators, from Chrysostom to Baur, the words: "*the signs which Jesus did,*" denote merely the appearances related in the foregoing chapter as *signs* or proofs of the resurrection; whence it would follow that these vv. 30 and 31 are the conclusion not of the Gospel, but only of the account of the resurrection. This opinion is incompatible, 1st, with the term ποιεῖν, *to do:* an appearance is not *done;* 2d, with the epithets *many* and *other:* the appearances were not so numerous and diverse; 3d, with the expression *in this book*, which shows that the contents of the whole book, and not of one of its parts, are in question.—Why does John refer only to the signs and miracles, and not also to the discourses which he has related? No doubt because the discourses are usually in this Gospel the mere expansion of the miracles which serve as their theme.

The phrase : "*in the presence of His disciples,*" brings out the part assigned to the Twelve in the foundation of the Church. They were the *chosen witnesses* of the works of Jesus not only with a view to their personal faith, but also with a view to the establishing of faith throughout the whole world; comp. xv. 26, and Acts i. 21, 22. The position of the word τούτῳ after βιβλίῳ (*this book*) gives it peculiar force, which, whatever Luthardt may say, seems to indicate an allusion to other βιβλία (*books*) which already contain the things omitted in this one. The phrase, thus understood, harmonizes with all the proofs which we have found of the acquaintance which John already had with our Synoptics. If it is so, the apostle in these words ratifies the contents of those Gospels anterior to his own, and gives it to be understood that he merely wished to complete them in certain respects.

But if his *method* did not consist with writing as complete a history of the ministry of Jesus as possible, what *end* then had he in view? Ver. 31 answers the question. He has related what he thought best fitted to guide his hearers to the faith which fills himself. And for this end, as we have shown, he has simply selected from the life of his Master those facts and testimonies which had most powerfully contributed to the formation and strengthening of his own faith. From this selection sprang the Gospel of John. When he says *ye*, the apostle addresses certain known Christians; but they, as Luthardt says, represent the whole Church. They *believe* already, no doubt, but faith ought always to be making progress, and at every step the previous faith appears as no longer deserving the name of faith (see ii. 11 and elsewhere).—The position of ἐστίν, *is*, in the text, can only be rendered by our translation: "is *really*." John characterizes Jesus, so far as He is the object of faith, so as to remind us of the two phases which we have observed in the development of his own: first the *Christ*, and then the *Son of God*. The first of these terms refers to the fulfilment of the prophecies and of the theocratic hope. It was in this character that the faith of the disciples had first welcomed Him (i. 42, 46). The solemnity with which this notion of the *Messiah* is referred to in this verse, which is a summary of faith, absolutely sets aside the idea of any tendency in the author of the fourth Gospel hostile to Judaism. But the acknowledgment of the Messiah in Jesus was only the first step of apostolic faith. From this John and his colleagues were soon raised to a more sublime conception of Him in whom they had believed. In this Messiah they recognised *the Son of God*. The first title referred to His *office*; the latter refers to the Divine character of His *Person*. Especially from ch. v. of our Gospel does this new light begin to penetrate the souls of the disciples, under the influence of the declarations of Jesus. It reached its consummation in the words of Thomas: "*My Lord and my God*," which has just closed the Gospel.—If John desires by his narrative to make his readers sharers of this faith, it is because he knows by experience that it gives life: "*that believing ye might have life.*" By receiving Jesus as the Son of God, the heart is opened to the Divine fulness with which He is Himself filled, and man enters into that perfect communion with God which is *life*, human existence saturated with blessedness and strength. The words: *in His name*, depend on the phrase: *having life*. The *name* is the acknowledgment of the dignity of Jesus in the heart, His essence as the Son of God written in letters of fire in the believer's soul.

Either the author who speaks thus of the aim of his book is deceiving us, or his work is not a work of religious speculation. His aim is not to produce knowledge, but faith, and by faith life. He has not laboured as a romance-making philosopher; his work as a historian is included in his apostolical commission. It is the testimony to which, in all ages, the faith of those shall be able to cling who *have not seen.* Such is the real aim of the fourth Gospel.

APPENDIX.

XXI. 1-25.

IT seems to us impossible to doubt that this chapter is a piece composed independently of and posterior to the Gospel, but one which was closely connected with it before the time of its publication. The former of these facts follows: 1st. From the conclusion, xx. 30, 31, which evidently closes the original narrative. All the efforts of Hengstenberg, Hölemann, Hilgenfeld, etc., have not succeeded in effacing this final period, placed at the end of his work by the author's hand. 2d. From the relation which we have established between the scene with Thomas and the governing idea of the Gospel. The goal is reached, the work finished, the plan exhausted! Lange and Hölemann see in this chapter an epilogue intended to form the counterpart of the prologue. "As," says the former (*Leben Jesu*, iv. p. 752), "the evangelist depicted in ch. i. the ante-historical reign of the Christ . . ., so he now draws the picture of His post-historical reign to the end of the world." But this parallel is more ingenious than real. In the following account it is the apostles who are on the scene much more than the Lord Himself; and it is their future lot which is described, much more than the reign of their glorified Lord. The counterpart of the prologue, from the point of view indicated by Lange, is not ch. xxi., but the Apocalypse. Weitzel has made a remark which may appear somewhat better founded.[1] The three other Gospels, says he, close each with a piece relating to the activity of the apostles after the departure of Jesus; comp. Matt. xxviii. 19, 20; Mark xvi. 20; Luke xxiv. 53. With the same right as those passages, ch. xxi. forms, according to him, an integral part of our Gospel. But though the observation were more just than it is (it cannot be held either in the

[1] "Das Selbstzeugniss des vierten Evangelisten über seine Person," *Stud. u. Kritik.* 1849, p. 579 et seq.

case of Mark or Luke, and scarcely in the case of Matthew), no conclusion could be drawn from it in regard to the fourth Gospel, composed as it is on a special plan. The insertion of the conclusion contained in vv. 30 and 31 of ch. xx. will always remain inexplicable from this point of view.

This piece, composed *separately from*, was certainly composed *after*, the Gospel. Ver. 14 (" *this was now the third time* . . ."), which supposes the narratives of the resurrection, excludes all doubt on this head. The same appears also from ver. 24: " This is the disciple which testified of *these things*," evidently of all the facts contained in the Gospel.

At the same time, and independently of the proofs which may be gathered from the contents of the piece, we have ground to think that this appendix was joined to the Gospel before it was put into public circulation. Otherwise there would undoubtedly have been formed, as in the case of Mark's Gospel, two families of copies, the one a faithful reproduction of the original text, without the appendix, the other derived from the completed text. We must therefore place the addition of this chapter between the time of the composition of the Gospel and that of its publication. M. Renan's judgment is almost to the same effect. " I close," says he, " the first work at the end of ch. xx. Chapter xxi. is an addition, but an almost contemporary addition, either by the author himself or his disciples " (p. 534).

It remains now to be seen, 1st, by whom and with what view this piece was *edited ;* 2d, by whom and with what view it was *joined* to the Gospel. The solution of these questions supposes the previous study of the piece.

This narrative may be regarded as containing two distinct scenes, which are expressly divided by the remark of ver. 14 ; the one general, referring to *all the disciples* present, vv. 1–13 ; the other particular, referring specially to the two principal of them, vv. 15–23.—Vv. 24 and 25 form the conclusion of the appendix, and at the same time bind it indissolubly to the work as a whole.

I. *Jesus and His Disciples.*—Vv. 1–14.

This first general scene comprises two descriptions, that of the *fishing* and that of the *repast*.

The fishing: vv. 1-8.

The theatre of this narrative is remarkable: it is the shore of the sea of Tiberias, in Galilee. The Johannine tradition, therefore, from which in any case this account proceeds, related other appearances besides those which took place in Judea, and which were related in ch. xx. This notion is in keeping with the Gospel of Matthew, which places the great Messianic appearance in Galilee on a mountain, perhaps Tabor, where, by a mistaken tradition, the transfiguration was afterwards placed. Thus the bond is established between Matthew, who (excepting the appearance to the women at Jerusalem) speaks only of the Galilean appearance, and Luke, who relates only the appearances which took place on the first day at Jerusalem, and on the last, near the Mount of Olives. The *forty days* of which Luke speaks in Acts i. 3 give, indeed, the necessary margin for a reconciliation. But it is our narrative which furnishes the harmony itself, by proving that the Johannine tradition related appearances on both theatres. The disciples then had returned to Galilee, and had there for the time resumed their old mode of life. Then towards the end of the forty days they returned, no doubt at the bidding of Jesus, to Jerusalem, where they were to begin the work of public preaching; and it is to this sojourn that the Lord's command refers not to leave Jerusalem till the coming of the Holy Spirit (Luke xxiv. 49, comp. with Acts i. 3, 4). "Harmonistic expedients!" exclaims Meyer. "Anti-harmonistic passion" is our answer.—According to Matt. xxvi. 31, 32, and xxviii. 7-10, all the believers (*the flock*; *ye*, addressed to the women) were to assemble anew in Galilee after the death of Jesus, and there see Him again. The appearances in Judea, by gathering the apostles, commenced this reunion of the flock; through the obstinacy of Thomas, a whole week elapsed before this first object was reached. Only thereafter could the apostles return to Galilee, where Jesus appeared to them, first by the sea-shore, afterwards on a mountain designated by Him (comp. Matt. xxviii. 16). Though Matthew speaks only of the leaders of the flock, the Eleven, because to them was given the missionary instruction which follows, we understand from 1 Cor. xv. 6 that this was the reunion of all the Galilean believers, to the number of more than *five hundred*, which Jesus had in view before His death.

Vv. 1, 2. "*After these things Jesus showed Himself again to the disciples*[1] *at the sea of Tiberias ; and on this wise showed He Himself. There were together Simon Peter, and Thomas called Didymus, and Nathanael of Cana in Galilee, and the sons of Zebedee,*[2] *and two other of His disciples.*"—The transition μετὰ ταῦτα, *after these things*, is frequent in John (v. 1, vi. 1, vii. 1, etc.). It obviously serves to join the appendix to the narrative of the last appearance, xx. 29, and to the Gospel. The phrase ἐφανέρωσεν ἑαυτόν is equally agreeable to John's style (vii. 4 : φανέρωσον σεαυτόν ; xi. 33 : ἐτάραξεν ἑαυτόν). Till now Jesus had manifested *His glory*, now He manifests *Himself;* for His Person even has entered from this time forth into the sphere of invisibility. The name *sea of Tiberias* is in the N. T. a purely Johannine name (vi. 1).—The Synoptics say *sea of Galilee* (Matt. iv. 18), or *lake of Gennesaret* (Luke v. 1). The O. T. knows neither the one nor the other of these expressions; Josephus uses them both.—The proposition : "*and on this wise . . .,*" is by no means superfluous. It impresses us with the solemnity of the following scene.—Of the seven persons indicated in ver. 2, the first five only are apostles ; the last two belong to the number of the *disciples*, in the wide sense which so often belongs to the word in our Gospel (vi. 60, 66, vii. 3, viii. 31, etc.). If it were otherwise, why would they not have been expressly named as well as the former ? Hengstenberg asserts that " every one must understand that it was Andrew and Philip!" The other reasons alleged have as little weight. The *sons of Zebedee* then occupy the last place among the apostles properly so called. The fact is the more remarkable, because, in all the apostolic catalogues, they are immediately joined to Peter, who is uniformly put first. We know of only one reason which can explain this striking circumstance: it is that the author of the narrative is himself one of Zebedee's two sons. It has been said, " But John never names either himself or his brother." That is true ; and exactly by this designation he avoids the proper name, while yielding to the necessity of

---

[1] D H M U X Γ, 40 Mnn. It^plerique Syr. Cop. add αυτου to μαθηταις.
[2] ℵ D E read οι υιοι instead of οι.

pointing to himself in view of the following scene.—On Thomas Didymus, see on xi. 16.—The explanation : " *of Cana in Galilee*," had not been given in ch. i. The author here repairs that omission.—Might the two unnamed disciples not be that Aristion and that presbyter John of whom Papias speaks as old *disciples of the Lord* (μαθηταὶ τοῦ κυρίου), living at Ephesus at the time when John wrote, and having almost the rank of apostles ?

Vv. 3, 4. " *Simon Peter saith unto them, I go a fishing. They say unto him, We also go with thee. They went forth,*[1] *and entered into*[2] *a ship immediately ;*[3] *and that night they caught nothing. But when the morning*[4] *was come,*[5] *Jesus stood on*[6] *the shore : but the disciples knew*[7] *not that it was Jesus.*"— After their Master's ministry, the disciples returned to their old profession. As usual, Peter takes the initiative. There is something abrupt in the apostle's words, which seem to indicate an uneasiness, a presentiment. The εὐθύς, *immediately*, wrongly rejected by some Mss., confirms this impression.— The word πιάζειν, used in vv. 3 and 10, occurs six times besides in our Gospel, nowhere in the Synoptics (Hengstenberg). Bäumlein : The *asyndeta* λέγει, λέγουσιν, ἐξῆλθον, etc., are in John's style.—That long night of fruitless toil must have reminded the apostles of that which had preceded their calling to be preachers of the Gospel (Luke v.).

Vv. 5, 6. " *Then Jesus saith unto them, Children, have ye any*[8] *meat ? They answered Him, No. And He said unto them, Cast the net on the right side of the ship, and ye shall find. They cast therefore,*[9] *and now they were not able*[10] *to draw it for the multitude of fishes.*"—The term παιδία, *young people*, *boys*, is not strange to John's language (First Epistle, ii. 14, 18). It is quite natural for Him not to use here the term of endearment, τεκνία, *my little children*, as in xiii. 33 ; for He

---

[1] A P It^allq add και before, ℵ G L X, ουν after εξηλθον.
[2] T. R. with Δ Λ : ανεβησαν ; almost all the Mjj.: ενεβησαν.
[3] ℵ B C D L X Δ, some Mnn. It. Vg. Syr. Cop. omit ευθυς.
[4] ℵ, some Mnn. It^plerique Vg. Syr^sch omit ηδη.
[5] A B C E L, 10 Mnn.: γινομενης instead of γενομενης.
[6] ℵ A D L M U X read επι instead of εις (τον αιγιαλον).
[7] ℵ L X : εγνωσαν instead of ηδεισαν. [8] ℵ omits τι.
[9] ℵ D Cop.: οι δε εβαλον instead of ε αλον ουν.
[10] ℵ B C D L Δ Π, 10 Mnn. It^plerique Vg.: ισχυον instead of ισχυσαν.

could not do so without betraying Himself. He makes use of the word of a master speaking to his workmen.—The meaning of the interrogative form, μή τι . . ., is analogous to that of vi. 67 : *Ye have nothing then* . . . ? Why this question ? The sequel will explain. Jesus is contemplating not merely a take of fish, as in Luke v., but a *repast*. We need not therefore think, with Tholuck and others, that Jesus appears as a merchant desiring to buy fish.—Προσφάγιον denotes, like ὀψάριον, what is added to bread at a meal. So in this case fish : only the second of the two terms reminds us of the cooking (ὀπτάω, *to roast*).—The apostle thinks that this stranger is acquainted with fishing, and that he has observed some symptom of a nature to give rise to his advice. Is the opposition between the left side of the ship, where they vainly cast the net the whole night through, and the right side, where they are about to take their magnificent draught, intended to symbolize the contrast between the failure of the work of evangelization in Israel and its unspeakably rich fruits in the heathen world ? This is not sufficiently indicated, and seems contrary to what is related in Acts ii.-v. and xxi. 20 (μυριάδες). It is safer to hold to the general idea of the immense successes which will be gained in the world by preaching, if the apostles take direction from the Lord in the course of their work. This meaning could not escape them, however little they might remember the terms of the original call: "*I will make you fishers of living men.*" They did not understand it, however, till after recognising Jesus.

Vv. 7, 8. "*Therefore that disciple whom Jesus loved saith unto Peter, It is the Lord. Now when Simon Peter heard that it was the Lord, he girt his fisher's coat unto him (for he was naked), and did cast himself into the sea. And the other disciples came in a little ship*[1] *(for they were not far from land, but as it were two hundred cubits), dragging the net with fishes.*"—How characteristically do the two apostles appear in these simple incidents ! John contemplates and divines; Peter acts, and that with impulsive energy. While recording these details, the author doubtless thought of the part subsequently taken by each of them in the evangelization of the world.—The garment called ἐπενδύτης is one intermediate

[1] ℵ reads αλλω before πλοιαριω ("with *the other* boat !").

between the χιτών, the under dress, the shirt, and the ἱμάτιον, the upper dress, the coat; it is the workman's *blouse*. After taking it off, Peter was really *naked*, except for the *subligaculum*, the *apron*, demanded by decency.[1] Yet Meyer thinks that he wore an under garment, which, in Greek usage, does not prevent the use of the term γυμνός, *naked*. The word διεζώσατο, literally *he girt himself*, here evidently includes the two ideas of *putting on* the dress and *fastening* it.—While Peter casts himself into the water and swims to the Lord, John remains with the other disciples in the boat. This detail has also its meaning, as we shall see. Πλοιαρίῳ, local dative (Meyer), or rather instrumental: by means of the boat (in opposition to Peter, who had taken to *swimming*), and while dragging the net. The *for* explains how they could in this case have recourse to dragging: "*they were not far from the shore*." Two hundred cubits are a little over 100 yards. Ἀπό, remarks Hengstenberg, is only used to measure distance in our Gospel (xi. 18), and in the Apocalypse (xiv. 20). The same author observes that the terms πλοῖον and πλοιάριον alternate in this piece, as in vi. 17 et seq.

Strauss thinks that this miracle is a fictitious enhancement of the two legends Luke v. and Matt. xiv. (the walking of Peter on the waters). Only he is embarrassed by the fact that swimming is not *more* but *less* miraculous than walking on the sea. But he does not suffer this to trouble him. For, says he, in this case "all the surroundings are supernatural." And so in this case the excess of the supernatural produces the return to the natural!—The suppleness of criticism is inexhaustible in devices.

The repast: vv. 9–14.

Vv. 9–11. "*As soon then as they were come[2] to land, they saw a fire of coals there, and fish laid thereon, and bread. Jesus saith unto them, Bring of the fish which ye have now caught. Simon Peter went up,[3] and drew the net to land[4] full of great fishes, an hundred and fifty and three: and for all*

---

[1] Meyer, in his note directed to me, p. 668, forgets that I made this exception. Nothing more common in the East than to see men in the state here described.

[2] ℵ H : ανεβησαν, Λ : επεβησαν, instead of απεβησαν.

[3] ℵ L : ενεβη instead of ανεβη.

[4] ℵ A B C L P X Δ Π : εις την γην instead of επι της γης.

there were so many, yet was not the net broken."—If this draught is to the disciples the symbol and pledge of the success of their preaching, the repast is undoubtedly the emblem of the spiritual and even temporal assistance on which they may reckon from their glorified Lord so long as the work shall last. Grotius, Olshausen, and others (I myself in my 1st ed.), have thought that, in contrast with the sea which represents the field of labour, the land and the repast represent heaven, from which Jesus gives aid, and to which He receives the faithful after their labour. The first meaning is simpler, and we are more naturally led to it by the question which opens the narrative: "Ye have nothing to eat then?" —'Ανθρακιά, *brazier*, is found only here and in the account of Peter's denial, and in *John's* account of the denial only, xviii. 18 (Mark and Luke: πῦρ and φῶς).—The sing. ὀψάριον, *roasted fish*, must certainly be taken to the letter, whatever Meyer and Luthardt may say: *a* fish. In ver. 10 Jesus bids Peter bring some of the fish which they had just taken, simply because the quantity prepared is not sufficient. The plural of the word is used by John v. 10 and vi. 9 (δύο ὀψάρια). —Whence came this bread and this fish? Luthardt traces them to the ministry of angels; Bäumlein, to the activity of Peter. The disciple might indeed have lighted the fire; but whence could he have procured the bread and the fish? Lampe thinks that Jesus received these provisions from some fisher in the neighbourhood. Anyhow, He did not create them; this course would be contrary to all His antecedents (ii. 7, vi. 9; comp. vol. ii. pp. 7 and 207). Does not the word of John himself: "*It is the Lord*," make it superfluous to occupy ourselves with this question?—The food prepared by the Lord must be completed by the product of their own fishing. Such a detail is incomprehensible unless it has a symbolical meaning. Jesus means to teach them that the satisfying of their wants will constantly depend on the concurrence of two factors: His blessing and aid on the one hand, and their faithful work on the other; as it is written, Ps. cxxviii. 2: "*Thou shalt eat the labour of thine hands.*"

The number of one hundred and fifty-three has been made the text of the strangest commentaries. Some Fathers have seen in it the emblem of God and of the Church (100, representing the Gentiles; 50, the Jews; 3, the Trinity). Hengstenberg explains it by an allusion to the 153,600 Canaanitish proselytes who were received into the theocracy at the time of Solomon (2 Chron. ii. 17). According to an explanation somewhat prevalent among critics at the present day, this figure originates in the idea received among naturalists of that time, that the entire number of the kinds of fish was 153. Köstlin, indeed, has quoted a passage from Jerome (*Comment. on Ezekiel*, xlvii.) which seems to prove the existence of this idea among the *savants* of the day from the words of a Cilician poet called Oppian, who lived under Marcus Aurelius: "Those who have written on the kinds of animals . . ., and among them the very learned poet Oppian of Cilicia, say that there are 153 kinds of fishes, which were all taken by the apostles, and none of which remained uncaught."[1] The figure, according to him, would naturally designate the totality of the Gentile nations. Hilgenfeld, to complete the interpretation, holds that the fish and the bread prepared by Jesus represent the Jewish people. But, 1st. Strauss himself (*Leben Jesu*, 1864, p. 414) remarks that Oppian does not indicate the total 153, but that he merely makes a not very clear enumeration, the sum of which may as probably be a number larger or smaller as that number itself. Then, 2d. Oppian's work is later than John's, and the terms used by Jerome would appear to signify that John's figure has rather been taken advantage of to support this scientific fable. As to Hilgenfeld's idea (*Einl.* p. 718), how are we to suppose that a sensible writer would represent the Jewish people under the figure of a roasted fish and bread?[2]

The mention of this number is not at all more astonishing

[1] "Aiunt qui de animantium scripsere naturis et proprietate, qui ἁλιευτικά tam latino quam græco didicere sermone, de quibus Oppianus Cilix est poeta doctissimus : CLIII. esse genera piscium, quæ omnia capta sunt ab apostolis et nihil remansit inceptum."

[2] We shall merely indicate in passing the still more fantastic explanations of some moderns, who find the key to this number by calculating the letters in the name Peter; thus Egli, following the Hebrew form : *Schimeon Jonah* (Simon, son of Jonah); Volkmar (*Himmelf. Mose*, p. 62), taking the form : *Schimeon* (71) *bar* (22) *Jonah* (31) *Képha* (29), total 153; and finally Keim himself (*Gesch. Jesu*, iii. p. 564), under this other form : *Schimeon* (71) *Jochanna* (53) *Képha* (29).

than that of the number of men who were fed, and of the baskets filled with fragments after the multiplication of the loaves, John vi. It is the simple fact recorded to prove two things: 1st. The largeness of this draught; 2d. The eager interest with which the apostle fishers counted the take.— The unbroken net is perhaps mentioned as a symbol of the Lord's special protection vouchsafed to His Church and to all those whom it contains.

Vv. 12-14. *"Jesus saith unto them, Come and dine. But*[1] *none of the disciples durst ask Him, Who art Thou? knowing that it was the Lord. Jesus cometh,*[2] *and taketh bread, and giveth them, and fish likewise. This is*[3] *now the third time that Jesus showed Himself to His disciples,*[4] *after that He was risen from the dead."*—A feeling of respectful fear prevents the disciples from approaching this mysterious personage. Jesus invites them to eat; and even then they dare not address Him. Their relations are no longer the familiar ones of former days.—Ἔρχεται (ver. 13): *approaches* the brazier.—The use of the terms τολμᾶν and ἐξετάζειν cannot be established in John. But as to the former, it is evidently a pure accident. As to the second, it is the notion of *informing oneself,* and not the more ordinary one of *inquiring* (ἐπερωτᾶν), which is meant to be expressed here.

The indication given at ver. 14 divides the narrative in two; for it is evident that the words of ver. 15 : *" So, when they had dined,"* connect the following conversation with the scene of the repast, ver. 13. The author undoubtedly meant hereby to separate what in this appearance had a general character, and referred to the work of evangelization represented by the disciples present, whether apostles or simple believers, from what specially concerned the future part and lot of the two chief apostles, Peter and John.—The phrase τοῦτο ἤδη τρίτον, *this is now the third time,* is singular; it conceals one of those subtleties of which we have remarked several in the course of this Gospel. It reminds us of the forms already explained, ii. 11 : ταύτην ἐποίησε τὴν ἀρχήν, and iv. 54 : τοῦτο πάλιν δεύτερον σημεῖον ἐποίησεν. We have

[1] B C omit δι.   [2] אּ B C D L X omit ουν.
[3] אּ G L X omit δι after τουτο.
[4] אּ A B C L, some Mnu. omit αυτου after μαθηταις.

seen in these two examples that the somewhat complicated phrases covered a rectification of the synoptical narrative. The same is the case here. It seemed, according to Matthew (and Mark?), that Jesus appeared *for the first time* to the disciples not in Judea, but in Galilee. By no means, says our author here; when He appeared to them in Galilee, *it was now the third time* that He showed Himself to them as the Risen One. The two previous appearances to which he alludes are evidently the last two of ch. xx. ver. 19 et seq. and ver. 26 et seq. He does not reckon that to Mary Magdalene, because, as he says expressly, he means to speak of appearances *to the disciples* only.

On the relation of these words of John to Luke's account and the enumeration of Paul, 1 Cor. xv. 5-7, two words only: The first two appeances in *Luke* (Emmaus and Peter) are not reckoned here by John, any more than that to Mary Magdalene, which is related by himself. The reason is in the *to the disciples*, ver. 14. The third (to the Twelve) comprehends the two, John xx. 19 and 26.—*Paul* sums up *the apostolic testimony*. He instances, 1st. Peter, the witness *par excellence;* 2d. The Twelve (comp. John xx. 19 and 26); 3d. The five hundred, at the head of whom were the Eleven (Matt. xxviii. 16-20); 4th. James, that personage who was so important as the *brother of Jesus;* 5th. The Twelve (ascension).—John xxi. is omitted as in Luke. Here, as elsewhere, John has repaired the omission of tradition.

Might it not be these last appearances indicated by Matthew and Paul of which our author gives a hint in the phrase: "*now the third time*," which leads us to suppose that there were others besides posterior to that which he relates here?—Thus all our narratives have their peculiarities in harmony with the object which inspires them, but they present no difference which it is not possible and even easy to reconcile.

A last question remains to us in regard to this verse: Why did John not include in his Gospel the appearance to the disciples which forms the subject of this appendix? The answer appears from what we have said above on occasion of the scene with Thomas. The two appearances to the disciples (ch. xx.) had for their aim to establish *faith* in the resurrection in the circle of the apostles, the *witnesses chosen* by Jesus. The present appearance no longer bore on the faith of the disciples; it was destined to assure them of their glorified Master's blessing and aid in the apostolic work which they were about to undertake. The Risen One, by the eloquent language of signs (fishing and eating), confirms not the fact of His resurrection, but the apostolic ministry which He had instituted during the days of His flesh. This appearance, therefore, did not enter into the framework of the fourth Gospel, as we have understood it. On the groundwork of this description relative to all the apostles, there now rises, in the second part of the narrative, a special revelation concerning the future of the two chief of them.

II. *Jesus with Peter and John.*—Vv. 15–23.

Jesus and Peter: vv. 15–19a.

As the preceding scene contained the confirmation of the apostolic ministry given by the Risen Jesus, so the following conversation is a reinstallation of Peter as director of the apostolate. No doubt Jesus had already pardoned his sin in the strictly private appearance which he had granted him (Luke xxiv. 34; 1 Cor. xv. 5). But he had not yet restored him to his position either as apostle or as chief of the apostolate. This is what He does in the first part of the following conversation (vv. 15–17).

Ver. 15. "*So, when they had dined, Jesus saith to Simon Peter, Simon, son of Jonas,*[1] *lovest thou me more than these? He saith unto Him, Yea, Lord; Thou knowest that I love Thee. He saith unto him, Feed my lambs.*"[2]—There is a remarkable resemblance between the present situation and that of the two scenes in the previous life of Peter with which it is related. He had been called to the ministry by Jesus after a miraculous draught of fishes; it is after a similar draught that the ministry is restored to him. He had lost his office by his denial beside a fire of coal; it is beside a fire of coal that he recovers it.— The form: "*Simon, son of Jonas,*" or rather, as it should probably read, according to the Alex.: "*Simon, son of John,*" is

[1] B C D L It^{plerique} read Ιωαννου instead of Ιωνα; ℵ omits this word.
[2] C D: προβατα instead of αρνια.

not contrasted unintentionally with the name *Simon Peter*, which is used by the evangelist in this very verse. It recalls to Peter his natural state, from which the call of Jesus had brought him, into which he had relapsed by his fall, and which now serves as the starting-point for his restoration. The allusion to the apostle's threefold denial in the three following questions cannot be doubted, whatever Hengstenberg may think to the contrary. The threefold profession of his love to Jesus is intended to efface, as it were, the triple blot which he himself caused. It is to furnish him with the opportunity of fulfilling this noble task that Jesus is now concerned. When he adds: "*more than these,*" Jesus certainly reminds him of the presumptuous superiority which he had claimed when he said, Matt. xxvi. 33, Mark xiv. 29: "*Though all shall be offended because of Thee, yet will I never be offended.*" No doubt John has not mentioned these words; but have we not found his narrative in constant relation to that of the Synoptics? Except for curiosity, it is unnecessary to quote the interpretation which refers *these* to the fishing implements or to the fish: "Lovest thou me more than thou lovest thine old profession?" Peter, with a humility inspired by the memory of his fall, first drops from his answer the last words: "*more than these;*" then for the term ἀγαπᾷν, *to love*, in the sense of veneration, complete, profound, eternal love, he substitutes the word φιλεῖν, *to love*, in the sense of cherishing friendship, simple personal attachment, devoted affection. He thinks he may claim this latter feeling, and yet he does so not without expressing a certain self-distrust, nor without seeking an authentication for the testimony of his own heart in the profound and infallible knowledge of the human heart which he ascribes to his Master. It is not omniscience in the absolute sense of the word which is in question here. Comp. ii. 24, 25. This appeal, as Luthardt says, softens the too decided tone which a simple *yea* would have had.

On this reply, Jesus assigns to him the care of His flock. "He confides those whom He loves to the man who loves Him," says Luthardt. The expression: "*the lambs,*" does not denote a special class of the members of the Church, the children and laity, for example, but the entire flock viewed in relation to the individual care and tender painstaking needed by all its members from him who is over them as the representative of the Chief Shepherd. The term *lamb* is a familiar one with the author of the Apocalypse. Of course its application is the more intense in proportion as those whom it designates have, moreover, the character of weakness. The term *feed*, βόσκειν, denotes the intimate sympathy which springs from love, tender direction, and strong aid.

Vv. 16, 17. "*He saith to him again the second time,*[1] *Simon, son of Jonas,*[2] *lovest thou me? He saith unto Him, Yea,*[3] *Lord; Thou knowest that I love Thee. He saith unto him, Lead my sheep.*[4] *He saith unto him the third time, Simon, son of Jonas,*[5] *lovest thou me? Peter was grieved because He said unto him the third time, Lovest thou me? And he said*[6] *unto Him, Lord, Thou knowest all things; Thou knowest that I love Thee. Jesus saith unto him, Feed my sheep.*"[7]—As the "*more than these*" had gained its object, Jesus now drops it; but He persists in using the most elevated term to denote love, ἀγαπᾷν. Peter, on his side, does not venture to appropriate such a term; but so much the more energetically does he affirm his love in the simple sense of the word φιλεῖν, and that while anew appealing to the searching glance of the Lord. On this condition Jesus again confides to him His flock, but with two characteristic differences. For the word βόσκειν, *feed*, which referred to the most personal care, He substitutes ποιμαίνειν, *lead*, like a shepherd. This term denotes the direction of the Church as a whole. According to the two manuscripts, the *Vatican* and *Ephrem*, He moreover uses the term προβάτια, here, strictly speaking, *little sheep*, instead of πρόβατα, *sheep*, which all the others read. And this reading is very possibly the true one; for, while expressing a feeling of tenderness, this word denotes a stronger and more advanced state than the word *lamb*, and forms the transition to the term *sheep*, πρόβατα.

Finally, the third question leaves Peter no longer in doubt

---

[1] ℵ omits δευτερον.
[2] Here again ℵ B C D It^{plerique} read Ιωαννου instead of Ιωνα.
[3] ℵ omits ναι.
[4] B C read προβατια instead of προβατα, the reading of all the others.
[5] ℵ B D It^{plerique}: Ιωαννου instead of Ιωνα.
[6] ℵ A D X: λεγει instead of ειπεν.
[7] A B C: προβατια instead of προβατα.

of the humiliating fact which the Lord wishes to recall to his mind; and he is the more painfully affected because Jesus now substitutes, as Peter himself had done from the beginning, the term φιλεῖν for ἀγαπᾶν, whereby He seems to call in question even that lower kind of attachment which the apostle had claimed. Peter feels the spear-point pierce even to the quick, and, gathering all his energy for a last affirmation, he appeals expressly to the Lord's most penetrating knowledge: "*Thou knowest all things,*" and under the eye of this omniscience he says: See if I do not love Thee! Three old manuscripts (A B C) here read (like two of them above) προβάτια; but is it not probable that the copyists, not apprehending the shades, have mistakenly repeated this diminutive, and that Jesus said this time πρόβατα, my *sheep*, which once again denotes the whole flock, but from the standpoint of its normal state. Jesus here resumes the term *feed*, whereby He gives Peter to understand that the general government of the Church should not hinder the pastor from occupying himself individually with each of the members of the flock. Acts xx. 31 shows that the apostles thus understood their commission. The passage, 1 Pet. v. 1–4, seems also to be an echo of these words of Jesus to the apostle.—It has been asked if Peter was simply restored by this second installation to the apostolate which he had in common with his colleagues, or if the words of Jesus include the idea of a primacy belonging to Peter in relation to the other apostles. Meyer seems to me to give the right answer to the question when he says that Peter is restored to his former position, and consequently that this restoration embraces the pre-eminence of Peter so far as it already belonged to his previous apostleship.

After restoring Peter to his apostleship in the first part of the conversation, Jesus announces to him in the second, vv. 18, 19a, what shall be the *end* of his ministry. The connection between this new idea and the previous dialogue is easy to understand. Peter, by his protestation of love to Jesus, had just effaced his denial; but the Lord promises him that he will one day accomplish this same task better than by words—that he will accomplish it in act by martyrdom. A similar connection of ideas may be seen, Acts ix. 15, 16.

Vv. 18, 19a. "*Verily, verily, I say unto thee, When thou*

wast younger, thou girdedst thyself, and walkedst whither thou wouldest: but when thou shalt be old, thou shalt stretch forth thy hands, and another shall gird[1] thee, and carry thee whither[2] thou wouldest not. This spake He, signifying by what death he should glorify God."—The form ἀμὴν, ἀμήν, Verily, verily, belongs exclusively to John. In the following saying there is a correspondence between the three members of the two propositions. To *"thou wast younger,"* corresponds : *"thou shalt be old."* Peter was married, and must have been of ripe age. He must then have been of intermediate age between youth and old age. The phrase *younger*, however, might also be applied to the present in contrast with the time of his old age, to which Jesus transfers Himself in thought. To the words: *"thou girdedst thyself,"* there correspond the following: *"thou shalt stretch forth thy hands, and another shall gird thee."* This correlation proves that the idea of *stretching out the hands* has no significance in itself, and is only the condition needed for the accomplishment of the act *of being girded by another.* One who is to be bound stretches out his hands either in token of complete resignation, and to give them over to be chained, or at least that the arms may not be pinioned with the body. It is therefore impossible to refer these words, as so many interpreters, including even Bäumlein, have done, to the act of crucifixion, in which the arms are extended on the instrument of punishment. This meaning is, besides, excluded by what follows : *"another shall carry thee whither thou wouldest not."* The idea of punishment occurs only in this last proposition ; the preceding words indicate merely the preparation for it. If the idea of extending the arms be applied to crucifixion, the word *gird*, which follows, must be applied to the act of binding the crucified one to the cross, or there must be seen in it an allusion to the *subligaculum* in this punishment, two meanings which are far from natural, and which are, besides, excluded by the antithesis: *"thou girdedst thyself,"* in the previous proposition ; then we must apply the words : *"another shall lead thee* (lit. *will carry thee) whither thou wouldest not,"* to the elevation of the crucified one to the height of the cross after having his hands nailed to the transverse beam on the ground.

---

[1] ℵ D Π : αλλοι ζωσουσιν.

[2] ℵ . ποιησουσι σοι οσα instead of οισει οπου.

But this meaning is forced, and does not well suit the antithesis: "*and walkedst whither thou wouldest.*" Some have seen in the words before us the contrast between self-will, which was the prominent feature of the apostle's natural character, and that submissive passiveness which was to become characteristic of his spiritual life. But then will this latter disposition not begin till the time of his old age ? Jesus is merely contrasting the *full liberty* of motion belonging to the man who has still the disposal of himself with the passiveness of the man who is led off bound. "*Whither thou wouldest not*," is spoken from the standpoint of natural feeling. By *another*, Bleek understands Jesus Himself. This explanation would only be admissible were there to be given to the thought the moral meaning which we have just set aside.—The phrase : "*by what death*," refers to the death of martyrdom in general, and not specially to the punishment of crucifixion, as we have just proved. This expression is simply opposed to the idea of natural death. The author speaks here of Peter's death as of a fact well known to his readers. This narrative was therefore drawn up after that event, which took place, according to most authors, in July 64, according to others one or two years later. The phrase : "to *glorify God*," to signify martyrdom, became a technical term in later ecclesiastical writings. Here we find it still in its original freshness. The phrase τοῦτο δὲ εἶπεν σημαίνων is peculiarly Johannine, as well as the ποίῳ θανάτῳ which follows ; compare xii. 33.

Jesus and John: vv. 19*b*–21.

This conversation refers to the future of John's ministry, as the preceding to the future of Peter's.

Vv. 19*b*-21. "*And when He had spoken this, He saith unto him, Follow me. Then Peter, turning about, seeth the disciple whom Jesus loved following ;*[1] *which also leaned on His breast at supper, and said,*[2] *Lord,*[3] *which is he that betrayeth thee ? Peter seeing*[4] *him saith to Jesus, Lord, and what shall become of this man ?* "—Very diverse meanings have been put on the com-

---

[1] ℵ omits ακολουθουντα ος.
[2] ℵ : λεγει instead of ειπεν ; ℵ C D add αυτω.
[3] ℵ C omit κυρις.
[4] ℵ B C D It^{plerique} Vg. Cop. Or. add ουν after τουτον.

mand: "*Follow me.*" Paulus understood it in the most literal sense: "Follow me in the place where I am going to bring thee to converse with thee alone." Chrysostom and Bäumlein: "Follow me in the active work of the apostolic ministry." Meyer: "Follow me in the way of martyrdom where my example leads thee." Luthardt: "Follow me to that invisible world into which I have already entered, and to which thou shalt be raised by martyrdom." We would not dispute the gravity and solemnity of this command; but it is absolutely impossible for us to believe that, when the text adds: "*Peter, turning about*," there is no indication of a motion made by Jesus, Peter *following Him* in the literal sense, a fact which speaks decidedly in favour of the meaning of Paulus. This meaning is confirmed by the following words: " He seeth the disciple *following* them " (ἀκολουθοῦντα); this identity of terms cannot be, as Meyer would have it, accidental. After announcing to Peter his martyrdom, Jesus began to move off, and commanded Peter to follow Him in the literal sense; and John followed them without any express invitation. Must we conclude from this that the meaning of the command: "*Follow me,*" is thus exhausted? By no means; for this step which Peter took in the following of Jesus was the first step in the way of obedience which was to guide him to the last, viz. martyrdom. Thus it is that the higher sense naturally links itself with the lower. It is vain for Meyer to scout this symbolism; it forms the basis of John's entire Gospel; it forced itself on our attention with the first word of the Gospel in the "*Follow me*" addressed by Jesus to Philip, i. 44 (follow me to Galilee on the way of faith), and we find it here again at the close in a manner equally evident.

What could be the object of the conversation which Jesus desired to have with Peter? Perhaps it was to give him the necessary instructions for convoking those hundreds of Galilean believers to whom Jesus wished to manifest Himself personally before wholly withdrawing His visible presence from the earth (1 Cor. xv. 6). We learn from Matt. xxviii. 16 that Jesus Himself, with this view, designated a certain mountain in Galilee. It was no doubt by Peter that He made His will known to His own on this point; perhaps He wished to communicate it to him at this time. This was therefore his first act us shepherd of the flock (ποιμαίνειν), the office which Jesus had just been committing to him. With the *turning about,* [ἐπιστραφείς] comp. xx. 14 and 16; it is an absolutely Johannine form. John followed Jesus and Peter; for the intimacy with Jesus, to which he had been admitted during His earthly life, authorized him to do so, and this is precisely what is expressed by the two epithets: "*the disciple whom Jesus loved,*" and: "*he who leant on Jesus' bosom, and said to Him* . . ." John was certain that nothing could pass between Jesus and Peter which should be kept a secret from him. Such is the true reason why that mark of supreme confidence which he had enjoyed at the last feast is here referred to (xiii. 25). It does not therefore contradict the Johannine origin of the narrative. The καί after ὅς, "who *also* (or in consequence)," indicates that this exceptional intimacy was precisely in connection with his character as the well-beloved disciple.

What is the true motive of Peter's question, ver. 21 ? It is not only the Tübingen school, but men like Olshausen, Lücke, Meyer, Bäumlein, who ascribe to this apostle a feeling of jealousy towards John. He is curious, they say, to know whether Jesus does not reserve for this privileged disciple a less painful future than that which He has just announced to himself. Such a feeling seems to us incompatible with the frame of mind into which the previous conversation must have brought Peter. Must not the love which he had just testified for Jesus, and the memory of his denial so vividly reawakened, have led him to regard martyrdom rather as a favour than as a misfortune ? Besides, Peter and John were closely bound to one another, and loved one another truly (ver. 7). The former, with his masculine nature, understood the tender and sensitive character of the latter; and it is his sympathy with a weaker nature which suggests to him the question, so full of interest: "*and this man, what shall become of him?*" If we think of the profound emotion which had just been produced on Peter's mind by the announcement of his tragical end, nothing will appear simpler than this question.

Vv. 22, 23. "*Jesus saith unto him, If I will that he tarry till I come, what is that to thee? follow thou me.*[1] *Then went this saying abroad among the brethren, that that disciple should*

[1] א A B C D It^plerique Vg. Or. place μοι before ἀκολουθεῖ.

not die: yet Jesus said[1] *not unto him, He shall not die; but, If I will that he tarry till I come.*"[2]—Peter's question, though dictated by a feeling of affection, was somewhat indiscreet; and the Lord makes him feel this by the words: " *what is that to thee ?* " The *coming of the Lord,* in the fourth Gospel (ch. xiv.- xvi.), denotes His coming *in the spirit* from Pentecost onwards. This meaning is not applicable here, for Peter was present at that event. The coming of Jesus in the passage xiv. 3 refers at the same time to the *death* of the apostles; and this meaning has been tried here. Jesus, it is held, predicts a natural death for John as the close of a long apostolical activity, in opposition to the martyrdom of Peter. This, or nearly this, is the meaning adopted by Grotius, Olshausen, Weitzel, Ewald. But it would follow from this that the Lord *comes* to seek only those of His own who die a natural death, and not those who perish by martyrdom; which would be absurd, and is contradicted by the account of Stephen's martyrdom. The coming of Jesus denotes also in some passages His invisible return to *judge Jerusalem,* and (for this correlative idea may be joined here) to establish His kingdom and make his cause triumphant in the Gentile world (Matt. x. 23, xvi. 28, comp. with Mark ix. 1 and Luke ix. 27; Matt. xxiv. 33, 34, etc.). This important epoch in the kingdom of God, from the year 70 to the end of the first century, was not witnessed by Peter; but John lived and took a preponderating part in it to the very end of his career. And it is to this difference between the two chief disciples that Baumgarten-Crusius, Luthardt, and others refer the promise of Jesus in this verse. This explanation is certainly preferable to the preceding; it is, I think, that which applies to Mark ix. 1 and parallels. It is therefore also possible here. Lastly, the Lord's coming denotes most frequently His glorious advent at the close of the present economy (comp. in John's First Epistle, ii. 28, iii. 2). Meyer and others apply this meaning here: " If I will that he tarry *till my Parousia.*" It appears, certainly, that this was how the contemporaries of John interpreted the words, since they had concluded from them that John would not die, but that, pre-

---

[1] א B C Or.: ουκ ειπιν δε instead of και ουκ ειπιν.

[2] We reject here the words τι προς σε (*what is that to thee?*), which are omitted by א, some Mnn. It^{alia}.

served till the Parousia, he would be changed with the then living believers (1 Thess. iv. 17; 1 Cor. xv. 51, 52). This meaning of the expression: "*till I come*," is certainly the most natural. But it raises the question: Did John really die, yea or nay? In the former case, what becomes of the promise implicitly contained in the words of Jesus? In the latter, how are we to conceive of a fact so extraordinary as that which would be revealed to us here: John remaining alive during all the present economy? Meyer thinks he can escape from the difficulty by means of the conditional form: "*If I will*," and laying special stress on the conjunction ἐάν, used here in preference to εἰ. The difference of meaning between ἐάν and εἰ proves nothing; for what matters it whether Jesus says: "*If I will* (εἰ)," or: "*If it happen that I should will* (ἐάν)"? As to the conditional form in itself, it does not remove the real difficulty. When He said: "*If I will*," Jesus must in any case have had before Him something precise, reasonable, and possible. The hypothetical form bore only on the realization or non-realization of the idea. But when He spoke thus, the Lord must have thought *something;* and it is this something which puzzles our understanding. For to hold that He threw out to Peter as possible a supposition which He regarded as impossible, is to reproach the seriousness of His character. In spite of the *if*, the problem therefore remains entire. The idea which I gave forth (1st ed.) may be called strange, as it is by Meyer,— the idea, viz., that the Lord here spoke of the possibility of preserving John, the last survivor of the apostolate, in constant connection with the progress of the Church to the very end, in a form mysterious and to us (who know at bottom the nature neither of life nor of death) impenetrable. Yet we shall be easily led, if we are resolved not to make play of this last word of the Lord in our Gospel, to give it this or some similar meaning. And a fact of this nature, inconceivable as it may appear, is not without biblical precedent. The primitive epoch of humanity had its Enoch, who knew not death; the theocratic epoch had its Elias, who was also exempted from its power; and may not the Christian epoch also have its representative set free from death? But I am aware that such a meaning will be denied to the saying of our Lord. In that case, it remains only to take refuge in the preceding explanation. For no one surely will bring his mind to accept either the explanation of Paulus: "If I will that he tarry *here,* to wait for us till I return with thee," or that of Bengel, Ebrard, Hengstenberg: "If I will that John remain in life till the day when he shall receive the apocalyptic revelation."[1]

Here the unity of the whole chapter opens up to us. As on the basis of the miraculous draught of fishes, which represents the future of all the apostles, there stands out the particular part assigned to the two chief of them, that of Peter, who suddenly leaves the boat to make his way across the waters to the very feet of Jesus, and that of John, who remains patiently in the boat to the end of the fishing, so in the future of the apostolic work in general there will stand out as two contrasted and prominent forms the ministry of Peter, the apostle who shall be removed from the Church by a speedy martyrdom, and the apostleship of John, who shall continue to be active within the Church till the establishment of the kingdom of God upon the earth. Here again we shall not let ourselves be staggered by the epithet *strange (wunderlich)*, whereby Meyer and Luthardt characterize this parallel. The question is not whether the correlation which we point out between the events of the fishing and the meaning of the conversation is or is not strange, but whether it is or is not in the mind of the author of the narrative. And so far as we are concerned, the answer is not doubtful. Thereafter we shall willingly accept Luthardt's idea, that in these two principal forms of apostleship there are represented the two permanent types of the Christian ministry, the testimony of blood by martyrdom, and that of speech by a Johannine and priestly activity.—After this saying relating to John, Jesus anew invites Peter to follow Him to receive His present commands, and so to return immediately to the active work of His apostleship, which had been for the moment interrupted (ver. 1). The σύ, *thou*, which Jesus here expressly isolates from the verbal idea (in opposition to the form, ver. 19), is related to the τί πρὸς σέ (" what is that to thee ? "): " *As to*

---

[1] The idea expressed by Holtzmann (art. "Johannes" in the *Bibel-lexicon* of Schenkel), that this saying of Jesus is only an application to John of the general promise (Matt. xvi. 28 ; Mark ix. 1 ; Luke ix. 27), is ingenious, but it does not correspond to the precisely-marked situation in which it is placed by our appendix.

thee, this is what concerns *thee.*"—The Alex. place the μοι, *me, to me,* before the verb: "It is *to me,* and no other, that thou must look; for it is in *my steps* that thou must walk."

The author does not give in ver. 23 the interpretation of the saying of Jesus. He contents himself with correcting the misunderstanding which eventually came to be attached to it, by reproducing its exact tenor. The last words: "*what is that to thee?*" not being necessary in this view, it is probable that the reading of the *Sinaiticus*, which omits them, is the true one. The present ἀποθνήσκει, *he dieth not*, is not the present of fact, but of idea. What is meant is not that John does not die at the time when the words are spoken, but that absolutely speaking he does not die. If we vividly imagine this λόγος, this common *saying*, we shall feel that the author reproduces it just as he hears it repeated in the Church at that very time. The interest of this rectification, besides, is not easily conceivable till that time, that is to say, immediately after or a little before the apostle's death, with the view of effacing or preventing the scandal caused by the contradiction between his death and the saying ascribed to Jesus; and it is probable that care was taken rather to prevent than to repair (see on ver. 24). Keim (i. p. 137) and Mangold (Bleek's *Einl.* 3d ed. p. 258), who place the composition of this appendix towards the end of the second century, are consequently obliged to seek a quite different object for this rectification. Its aim, according to them, is to reconcile the tendency of the Church of this epoch to establish itself comfortably here below with the declarations of Jesus about the nearness of His Parousia (comp. 2 Pet. iii. 4 et seq.). But on this understanding the remark of ver. 23 would harmonize nothing; but the contrary, since it appears from the exactly given tenor of the saying of Jesus, that John might *possibly* be present in life at the Parousia. And what purpose, besides, would it serve to exhume from oblivion, at the end of the second century, a lost saying in order to rectify it, while the Gospels contained so large a number of others perfectly well known, in regard to which the difficulty remained entire? It follows, therefore, from this passage, that, according to the view of Bleek, Meyer, Ewald, and Bäumlein, this appendix necessarily dates from the last years of the apostle's life, or from the time which immediately followed his death.—The καί adversative, *and yet*, before οὐκ εἶπεν, reminds us of one of the most uniform peculiarities of our evangelist's style (i. 8, v. 39, vi. 36, xv. 24, etc.).

Here is the end of the narrative contained in the appendix. What can be its *aim*? Here again the school of Baur supposes an ignoble manœuvre. The object, according to it, is to raise John, the apostle of Asia Minor, above Peter, the patron of the Roman church. Strange means to this end, the triple installation of Peter in his apostolic dignity (not without the idea of a primacy over his colleagues), and the promise made to this apostle of the most glorious death! Not to take into account that, according to Baur and his school, the whole Gospel was intended to make good the case of Rome against Asia Minor in the Easter controversy, which establishes a flagrant contradiction between the object of the appendix and that of the Gospel. Besides, Köstlin and Volkmar have come to suppose a wholly contrary intention. This appendix, according to the dictum of the former, is a flattery addressed to the bishop of Rome in favour of his supremacy; and, according to the second, an attempt to re-establish the authority of Peter, which the rest of the Gospel had undermined. We cite these vagaries; they need no refutation. Bleek, Meyer, and others more simply find the object of this narrative in the refutation of the false report circulating about John, vv. 22 and 23. But would this have required the reproduction of the entire fishing scene, of the repast, and of Peter's reinstallation? This intention, besides, seems to us inconsistent with the parenthesis of ver. 14, which divides the chapter into two, and thus gives a significance of its own to the first part of the narrative. The same objection holds also against the much too particular intention assumed by M. Reuss (*Gesch. der heil. Schrift. des N. T.* § 239), that of re-establishing the dignity of Peter, which had been compromised by his denial.—We have seen that the unity of the different pieces of which this appendix is composed only comes out clearly when it is regarded as intended to cast a survey over *the future of the apostolic ministry in general*—such is the meaning of the first picture, vv. 1–14, and over that of the *ministry of the two chief apostles* in particular—such is the object of the two conversations, vv. 15-23. It is likewise from this point of view that there opens up the relation between the appendix and the whole book. Lange, Schaff, and Hölemann have regarded this chapter as the counterpart of the prologue, and we have already seen that this idea is untenable. The matter in question here is not the celestial activity of Jesus as the counterpart of His divine activity anterior to His incarnation. It is not quite so far back in the Gospel we must go to find the counterpart of our appendix. The second part of ch. i. relates the first call of the apostles, in particular that of Peter and John. What Jesus did then provisionally at the beginning of the formation of faith, He definitively confirms on the foundation of faith acquired. The call to education for their mission is ratified by the call to the mission itself. This is what is described in the appendix. As not entering into the description of the development of the apostles' faith, this incident could not form an integral part of the Gospel. But as a glance thrown at the future of the apostolic ministry, it was its natural complement; for the consummation of their faith is their mission.

To *whom* are we to ascribe the composition of this narrative ? The Johannine type as to matter and style is so deeply and obviously imprinted on it, that only two suppositions are possible on this subject: either John himself composed this piece some time after having finished the Gospel, or we have here the work of that circle of friends and disciples who surrounded the apostle at Ephesus, who had often heard him relate the facts contained in it, and who have reproduced them in his own language. It is of small importance which of these two suppositions is chosen. Yet we must say that the first alternative, as it seems to us, deserves to be preferred. 1st. Would the disciples of John, in the enumeration of ver. 2, have placed their master in the last rank among the apostles properly so called ? 2d. Could they have preserved so delicately the slightest shades in the conversation between Jesus and Peter ? 3d. Who besides, more than John himself, would feel bound to correct the possible error arising from the saying uttered by Jesus in regard to him ? 4th. Finally, ver. 24, little as may be the value attached to the testimony it contains, settles the question in this way.

362   GOSPEL OF JOHN.

Conclusion of the Appendix.—Vv. 24, 25.

Vv. 24, 25. " *This is the disciple which testifieth of these things, and wrote these things :* [1] *and we know that his* [2] *testimony is true. There are also many other things which* [3] *Jesus did, the which, if they should be written every one, I suppose that even the world itself could not contain* [4] *the books* [5] *that should be written.*"
—From what pen do these two last verses proceed? On this point very different opinions prevail. Some (Hengstenberg, Lange, Weitzel, Hilgenfeld, Hölemann, etc.) regard them as both belonging to the author of the whole appendix. Others (such as Meyer, Tischendorf, etc.) ascribe ver. 24 to this author, and ver. 25 to a later interpolator. A third party, finally (Tholuck and Luthardt), regard them as both added to the appendix by one or more persons different from the author. Between these three views only a detailed study will enable us to decide. The author of these lines declares, in the first part of ver. 24, that he who has not only related (μαρτυρῶν, *which testifieth*), but also written (γράψας, *which wrote*) these things is the beloved disciple who has just been spoken of in vv. 20–23. First of all, *what things* (τούτων) are in question? Does such an attestation bear simply on the contents of the appendix? It is hard to believe this. The narrative had no such great importance as to call for this solemn declaration about its author. The editor of ver. 24 has therefore in view not only the appendix, but the entire Gospel. The conclusion, xx. 30, 31, had closed the Gospel. This new conclusion, imitating the preceding one, is intended to close at once both the Gospel and the appendix, while binding them into one whole. Can it proceed from the hand of the evangelist? No doubt we have heard John himself, xix. 35, declaring himself to be the witness on whose authority a particular fact is to be believed in the Church. But here the editor goes

---

[1] Instead of και γραψας, B D Cop. read και ο γραψας, and ℵ* and some Mnn.: ο και γραψας.
[2] B C D place αυτου before η μαρτυρια.
[3] Instead of οσα, which T. R. reads with 13 Mjj. (A D, etc.), ℵ B C X read α.
[4] ℵ B C Cop.: χωρησειν instead of χωρησαι.
[5] ℵ A B C D, some Mnn. It^plerique Vg. Syr. Cop. Sah. Or. omit αμην after βιβλια.—The whole of this 25th verse is wanting in ℵ (not in Cod. 63, as was long said erroneously after Mill, Wetstein, Griesbach ; see Tischendorf's 8th ed.).

further; he ascribes to John not only the authority of the testimony, but the fact of the writing. This declaration is therefore probably added by a person other than the apostle, whom special circumstances authorize to give forth such an attestation in the face of the Church. The οἴδαμεν, *we know*, which follows, confirms the idea that the writer of this note is by no means the author of the appendix and of the Gospel; for the latter never speaks of himself in the plural, and it is impossible to have recourse to the expedient of Chrysostom, who divided this verb into two words: οἶδα μέν, *now I know*. It is equally impossible to accept the explanation of Meyer, who ascribes these words to the author of the Gospel, and who thinks that he wrote them as an expression not only of his own feeling, but of the feeling of all the faithful who surrounded him. In this case, where the matter in question concerns the author personally, it is absolutely impossible to combine in one and the same "*we know*" the expression of the author's feeling and that of the persons surrounding him. The moral position of the former and of the latter in regard to this fact of consciousness is too widely different. This declaration, therefore, proceeds very obviously from a plurality of individuals. We cannot, it is true, name with certainty those who were parties to it. But the well-known passage of the Fragment of Muratori (Introd. i. p. 248) brings on the scene on this occasion the Apostle Andrew and other apostles (such as Philip) living in Asia at that time, as well as the bishops of Ephesus;[1] the famous passage of Papias[2] suggests also the thought of Aristion, of the presbyter John, and of Papias himself. In any case, we have certainly to do here with those in whose hands the apostle had deposited his writing, who had charged themselves with publishing it at time convenient, and who, when carrying out their commission, think themselves bound to accompany a work of such importance with this semi-official certificate.

Meyer justly brings out the contrast between the pres. partic. ὁ μαρτυρῶν, *he which testifieth*, and the past partic. γράψας, *he who wrote*. It follows thence that at the time

[1] "John the disciple, exhorted by his fellow-disciples and the bishops, said . . . ; that same night it was revealed to Andrew, one of the apostles . . ."
[2] Introd. vol. i. p. 49.

when this attestation was penned, John was still continuing, in addition to his now finished written testimony, that of his living word.—The term γράψας, *who wrote*, obviously does not exclude the process of dictation then generally employed. It may be said that Paul *wrote* the Epistle to the Romans, notwithstanding Rom. xvi. 22.—The information of this verse is, therefore, not only that John is the author of the Gospel, but that he was *still living* at the time when this declaration was made. But why is it necessary to add to a narrative which is the work of John himself an attestation like this: "*and we know that his testimony is true*"? If this declaration proceeds from John's colleagues in the apostleship, it simply certifies that their recollection of the facts accords with that of John, which assuredly implies nothing hurtful to his character. Is it not related in the Muratori Fragment that it was decided that John should write all in his own name, and that the others *should revise* his narrative (*recognoscentibus cunctis*)? If it emanates from the presbyters of Ephesus, it signifies that they, knowing the apostle personally, and having found him truthful and holy in all his conduct, are perfectly assured of the truth of his testimony in the Gospel narrative which he has left. There is nothing to prevent these two meanings from being applied here together. There is nothing, therefore, in this saying which is opposed, as M. Nicolas has alleged (*Revue germanique*, Ap. 1863), to the apostolic dignity of him who wrote the Gospel.

Does ver. 25 proceed from the same plurality of witnesses as ver. 24? There are three evidences which lead us to doubt this. First, the grammatical or syntactical form of the verse. Ver. 24 still bore the impress of Johannine simplicity. The construction of ver. 25 is more complicated. Then the verb in the sing. οἶμαι, *I suppose*, which contrasts with the plur. οἴδαμεν, *we know*, ver. 24. Finally, the too emphasized exaggeration which characterizes the verse. We feel ourselves carried somewhat beyond the simple gravity and sobriety of an apostle. But must we conclude hence that the verse has been interpolated at a date posterior to the publication, as is thought by Meyer and Tischendorf? It would be impossible in this case to understand how there were not spread throughout the Church a great many copies free from this addition. It is true the *Sinaïticus* omits it, but it is solitary in this respect, and there is no manuscript more chargeable than it is with omissions and inadvertencies. Besides, we have here to do probably with an intentional rejection, in consequence of the very proofs which we have been indicating. As this verse is wanting nowhere else, any more than ver. 24, it is probable that it accompanied the Gospel from the time of its publication, and that it proceeds consequently from the pen of some one of the members of that body from which the attestation of ver. 24 emanates. The tone of the verse is not without resemblance to that of the descriptions given by Papias in his well-known amplifications relative to the thousand years' reign; and as this Father is said to have been contemporary with Aristion, with the presbyter John, and even with the Apostle John (Introd. vol. i. pp. 49–54), it is not impossible that the subject of the verb *I think* may be Papias himself, a fact which would explain the strange notice discovered by Tischendorf in a manuscript of the Vatican, according to which Papias was the secretary to whom John dictated his Gospel.[1]

In any case, the meaning of the verse is, that if this narrative is *the truth* (ver. 24), it is not *all* the truth; for, says the author, the task of evangelic narration, if it were understood in the sense that it must furnish a complete history of the life of Jesus, could never be realized, not only because never could such a life be adequately contained in books, but also (οὐδέ, *not even*) because the whole universe would be too little to contain the books which would fulfil this condition. The meaning of this hyperbole, which taken literally would be ridiculous, even attenuated as it is by the word *I think*, is evidently this: the infinite cannot be completely contained within the compass of the finite; or: the category of *spirit* is and remains superior to that of *space*. Writings might be added to writings without end to describe the glory of the only-begotten Son, full of the grace and truth of God. . . . This indefinite series of writings would never exhaust such a subject.

From this detailed study we conclude: 1st. That the narrative, vv. 1–23, is from the hand of the evangelist. 2d.

[1] *Wann wurden unsere Evangelien verfasst?* p. 119.

That ver. 24 is a declaration emanating from the friends of John, who had called forth the composition of his Gospel, and to whom he had committed it after its completion (comp. what is said of Mark entrusting his Gospel to his friends in the Roman church who had asked it of him). 3d. That ver. 25 is written by one of them with whom the work was deposited, and who thought himself bound to close it thus, to the glory not of the author, but of the subject of the history. By these last words the entire work becomes one whole. Accordingly we are shut up to hold either that John is the author of our Gospel, or that the author is a forger who, 1st, palmed himself off on the world with all the characteristics of the apostle; who, 2d, carried his shamelessness so far that he got made out for him, by an accomplice of his fraud, a certificate of identity with the person of John; or who, more simply still, to save himself the trouble of finding a companion in falsehood, made out this certificate for himself in the name of another, or of several others. And he who had recourse to such ways was the author of a writing in which lying is blasted as the work of the devil (viii. 44), and truth glorified as one of the two essential features of the Divine character! If any one will believe such a story . . . let him believe it! (1 Cor. xiv. 38).

For my part, I rejoice to be able to say that the renewed study of this inimitable work has made the certainty of its authenticity shine before my view with evermore irresistible clearness. It is proved, as it seems to me, above all by the luminous transparency with which there is revealed in it the self-consciousness of Christ. A Divine life, humanly lived, Jesus offers Himself to the world as *the bread of life, come down from heaven*, that whosoever eats of it may realize through Him the sublime destination of our race: man in God, God in man. This conception bears within it the seal of its origin.

THE END.

www.ingramcontent.com/pod-product-compliance
Lightning Source LLC
Chambersburg PA
CBHW020306240426
43673CB00039B/717